Friar Thomas d'Aquino
His Life, Thought, and Works

FRIAR
THOMAS D'AQUINO
His Life, Thought, and Works

James A. Weisheipl, O.P.

Pontifical Institute of Mediaeval Studies Toronto

with
Corrigenda and *Addenda*

The Catholic University of America Press
Washington, D. C.

Library of Congress Cataloging in Publication Data

Weisheipl, James A.
  Friar Thomas D'Aquino : his life, thought, and work.

  Reprint. Originally published: Garden City, N.Y. :
Doubleday, 1974. With addenda and corrigenda.
  Bibliography: p.
  1. Thomas, Aquinas, Saint, 1225?-1274. 2. Philos-
ophers—Biography. 3. Theologians—Biography.
4. Christian saints—Biography. I. Title.
B765.T54W35   1983   189'.4 [B]   83-14326
ISBN O-8132-0590-5 (pbk.)

TO MY PARENTS
WHO GAVE ME MORE THAN
LIFE AND LOVE

CONTENTS

March 7, 1974, marks the seven hundredth anniversary of the death of St. Thomas Aquinas. Since March 7, 1274, is the only certain date we have in his life, it is fitting that the day and year be commemorated in various ways throughout the world. This book represents part of my contribution to the occasion. The last worldwide celebration was in 1923, the six hundredth anniversary of Thomas's canonization on July 18, 1323. So much new material has been discovered in the past fifty years that there is need of a summary and an evaluation of the facts unearthed by scholars who have given their best efforts toward understanding the life, thought, and works of Friar Thomas d'Aquino.

When I began writing this book, I thought of writing the kind of book that I should like to have read when I began my own Thomistic studies over thirty years ago. This goal was always foremost in my mind. However, as work progressed I had the suspicion that I was writing a book I should like to have on my reference shelf not only for consultation, but also for correction, for there are still many things that scholars do not know or understand about the life, thought, and works of Thomas d'Aquino. Perhaps some of our ignorance will never be dispelled. To say nothing of his doctrine, perhaps there will never be a "definitive" study of his life and works.

In general there are three kinds of source material for a study of Friar Thomas: early biographies, official documents, and the writings of Thomas embedded in the manuscript traditions. The early biographies of Thomas have been edited by Dominicus

Prümmer, O.P., and it is not likely that many more such biographies will be discovered. A better edition of these lives will, of course, shed a better light on Thomas's life. The official documents have been edited with great care by M.-H. Laurent, O.P., and it is not likely that many more documents will come to light in the years to come. The more fruitful source of further knowledge must come from the critical edition of Thomas's works and an appreciation of the complex manuscript traditions of these works. It is most likely that a deeper historical understanding of the texts and the manuscript traditions of his works will shed considerable light on the formation and development of Thomas's thought. For this kind of research specialists are needed, specialists who are hard to come by these days. Even though the thought of Thomas has a transcendent significance, it is wrong to read his works as though they were written in one sitting and devoid of all intellectual development. Thomas, like everyone else, developed intellectually and spiritually. The amazing fact is, however, that early in life Thomas grasped certain fundamental philosophical principles that never changed. Always there was development, deeper understanding, and even rejection of earlier views. But there was never a metamorphosis in his approach to reality. There was never a "conversion" or violent rejection of earlier thought, but only corrections and modifications that led to a fuller, more human, and more divine appreciation of the basic problems of life.

It is my sincere hope that this book will aid the pursuit of philosophical and theological truth. In the next few decades we can expect to see a revitalized interest in the study of Thomas d'Aquino. This revitalized interest may, perhaps, not come from Catholic centers of thought, but rather from secular campuses and interested individuals. With this in mind I have attempted to present a rather full picture of the life, thought, and works of Thomas.

The life of Friar Thomas d'Aquino spans the middle fifty years of the thirteenth century, 1224/5–74. His life and work reflect the vitality of thought and spirit that were typical of the age. It was a short life that fused the quiet of contemplation with the fever of activity. When one ponders the life's work of Thomas within

the designs of divine providence, one cannot help but apply the
words of Wisdom 4:13–14 to him:

In a short time he came to the perfection of a
full span of years. His soul was pleasing to
the Lord, who removed him early from a wicked world.

Even men who are not Thomists must pause and marvel at the
life of this saint who directed all his energies to the pursuit of
truth.

Particular gratitude is due to the Pontifical Institute of Mediaeval Studies for providing the opportunity, facilities, and encouragement needed to write a book such as this. I can think of
no place other than the Institute where this work could have been
written. And I can think of no more opportune time for its production. When one thinks of the violent opposition to Thomism
in the schools of today, one cannot help but feel that in the next
few decades the tide will turn toward a deeper and more realistic
appreciation of the "Common Doctor," the *Doctor Communis*, of
the Middle Ages. At the Pontifical Institute of Mediaeval Studies
the vital texts of the "Common Doctor" are studied not only for
their historical interest but, what is more important, for their
doctrinal significance in philosophy and theology today.

In the composition of this book the lecture notes of the late
I. T. Eschmann, O.P., have been utilized as far as possible. Points
of agreement and disagreement have been noted throughout. I
wish, therefore, to express my gratitude for his many years of
diligent study and for the lecture notes, which he himself made
available to me for *The New Catholic Encylopedia* and for the
writing of my own book.

I wish to express my special gratitude to Father Armand A.
Maurer, C.S.B., and especially to Mr. Paul Zomberg, who read
early drafts of my manuscript and made many valuable suggestions for improving the text. Gratitude is also due to Father
James B. Walker, O.P., and Father Timothy M. Sparks, O.P., for
supplying needed information when it was not available in Toronto. My gratitude is also due to Father Laurence K. Shook,
C.S.B., Dr. Donal P. Murnaghan, and Dr. Allan Walters for their

encouragement throughout the composition of this book. Finally I wish to thank many friends in Canada and the United States for the great interest they have taken in my writing over the past two years while this book was in progress.

James A. Weisheipl, O.P.

Toronto
Feast of St. Thomas Aquinas
January 28, 1973

Chapter I

SICILIAN BOYHOOD AND DOMINICAN YOUTH
(1224/5–52)

Encouraged by the revival of Thomism in the late nineteenth and early twentieth century, historians in Germany, Italy, and France have diligently collected and sifted every scrap of information to increase and broaden our knowledge of St. Thomas Aquinas and his times. Heinrich Denifle, Franz Ehrle, Clemens Baeumker, Martin Grabmann, Pierre Mandonnet, Pietro Castagnoli, Jacques Berthier, Angelus Walz readily come to mind, but there were many others who contributed to a fuller picture of Aquinas than can be gathered from a simple reading of the "Common Doctor" presented in the schools. The modern reader, influenced by the legitimate claims of historicism, knows that ideas as well as personalities must be understood in the full context of the times in which they developed.

There developed in the period of Neo-Thomism an unfortunate dichotomy between careful historians of St. Thomas and speculative "Thomists" that has led to the decline of Thomism in our day. The only satisfactory way to understand the sublime doctrine of Thomas Aquinas is to see it in a historical and speculative perspective. This is neither to say that his ideas do not transcend time, as historicists would have it, nor is this to say that history should replace ideas. What is needed is a unification of historical method and philosophical acumen. Strange as this may seem, unless the teaching of Aquinas is seen in its true historical perspective, there is not only the danger of misunderstanding his teaching, but also the danger of rendering Thomas irrelevant to our age. Therefore some attempt must be made to understand the historical perspective in which Thomas thought and wrote in order to appreciate the transcendental insights he contributed to man in every age. Just as historical biblical research of recent generations has not diminished the transcendent message of the Bible, so too a historical approach to St. Thomas and his writing cannot diminish the urgency of his message, but will make it all the more reasonable. Not only a saint, Thomas was above all a reasonable man, a man who makes sense: his teaching is not esoteric, but public and intelligible to all who would take the time to study it.

As a general background to his life, thought, and works, we should have an appreciation of the thirteenth century, especially of the many currents of thought, life-styles, and changes that took place. It is not easy to understand a century; we barely understand our own. What we must expect to find in the thirteenth century is constant change; changes produce movements, and movements occasion clashes, sometimes violent enough to change the whole course of history, but never enough to eliminate the past. Although a brief outline can never do justice to the dynamics of the thirteenth century, a number of movements must be singled out for a better understanding of Thomas. Among them must be noted the conflict between secular and papal powers, evangelism and the rise of mendicant Orders, spread of the mystical and prophetical doctrines of Abbot Joachim, and the growth of scholasticism in the schools of western Europe. The life of Thomas spans the mid-fifty years of that century, 1224/5–74. He lived and breathed the air of those changes; he himself changed, and he instigated new currents of thought destined both to be condemned and to be praised. The changes he effected are unintelligible without some understanding of what went before; nor is there any point in trying to read the bare facts of his life apart from the background of his life, thought, and works.

Thomas Aquinas was not only a genius, but he came at the propitious time in history when scholasticism itself blossomed forth in medieval thought. He was born just when the influential commentaries of Averroes came into the Latin West, and he was a contemporary of such great thinkers as St. Albert the Great and St. Bonaventure. He joined the Dominican Order in its infancy, when the Friars were full of zeal and love of the ideal proposed by St. Dominic. At first reading, the works of Thomas seem to be detached from contemporary events, but this is only a superficial impression. He was very much a man of his age and environment. A sound understanding of the man requires both an accurate grasp of his teaching and a thorough knowledge of the context in which he lived, moved, and had his being. Historical research during the past fifty years has shed much light on the views of his contemporaries; all have helped to illuminate the seemingly impersonal problems, arguments, and solutions offered by Thomas Aquinas.

Boyhood in the Kingdom of Sicily

(1224/5-44)

There is no documentary evidence on the day or year of Thomas's birth. The chroniclers and witnesses were themselves inconsistent, or at least vague, on this point. We know with certainty that he died on the morning of March 7, 1274, although Bernard Gui, who peculiarly gives the date as March 9, states that Thomas died in the "beginning of the fiftieth year of his age,"[1] which would place Thomas's birth date around 1224 or 1225. Both William of Tocco (c. 65) and Peter Calo (c. 28) give the date of death as March 7, 1274; and Tocco adds, "the saint being in his forty-ninth year," which would put the date of birth around 1226. Tolomeo of Lucca notes that "he died in the fiftieth year of his life, while others say forty-eight."[2] If Thomas died in his forty-eighth year, as some say, he would have been born in 1227. In the first canonization inquiry Nicholas of Piperno testified that Thomas "had seemed to the witness about fifty or sixty" years of age, thus placing the date of birth somewhere between 1214 and 1224.[3] At the same canonization inquiry in Naples, Octaviano of Babuco stated that Thomas "seemed to be about fifty or thereabouts" when he died.[4] At the same inquiry Friar James of Viterbo, a Dominican, testified that Thomas died, according to the usual view, in his forty-eighth year.[5] This would put the date of his birth in 1227. At the other end of the spectrum, the librarian of Monte Cassino, Mariano Armellino, writing in 1731, explicitly states that "Saint Thomas was born in 1220 on April 16 in the castle of Roccasecca, the father being Landulf Count of Aquino and the mother being Theodora Theatis, daughter of a Count."[6] Armellino's claim need not be taken seriously, for he gives no documentation or arguments, and he claims that Thomas was a fully professed Benedictine before becoming a Friar Preacher. This need not detain us at the moment.

William of Tocco, the earliest and one of the most reliable sources, states that Thomas "was in the forty-ninth year of his life,"[7] which means that he had passed his forty-eighth birthday, but not yet his forty-ninth, when he died. This means that Thomas was born in 1225/26, and died at the age of forty-eight. Bernard Gui, on the other hand, writing *after* he had read Tocco's *Life*, and who is in this case an independent witness, states that Thomas died "in the completion of his forty-ninth year and in the beginning of his fiftieth."[8] That is, Thomas was forty-nine years old when he died, but not yet fifty. According to this statement, Thomas must have been born in 1224/25, or more precisely between March 8, 1224, and March 7, 1225. After examining all the evidence, Pierre Mandonnet was content to say that "Consequently, he was born at the beginning of 1225 or at the earliest at the end of 1224." It is unlikely that we shall ever know the precise day or year. The Benedictine historian Mariano Armellino could be right in giving the day as April 16, but this is most unlikely, for Thomas would then be terminating his fiftieth year at the time of his death instead of "beginning" it.

At the turn of the twentieth century various places were claimed as the birthplace of Thomas. Some claimed Belcastro in the Abruzzi, others claimed the town of Aquino, and still others rightly insisted that Roccasecca is the place.[9] Today all historians admit without hesitation that Thomas was born in the Aquino castle of Roccasecca. It lies in the Terra di Lavoro, so called because of the fertility of the soil which is always ready to be cultivated. The Terra di Lavoro lies in what today is called the Roman Campagna, specifically in the Province of Caserta. In the thirteenth century this district was the farthest northwestern province of the *Regnum Siciliae*, the Kingdom of Sicily.

From Rome two main roads run southeast to Capua and then

jointly to Naples, the Via Appia and the Via Latina. Naples lies 143 miles southeast of Rome by the Via Latina, the inland route, and 147 miles from Rome by the Via Appia, the coastal route. The two modern railway lines, going south from Rome, follow roughly these two old roads. The Via Appia runs through the Pontinian marshes straight to Terracina on the Tyrrhenian Sea and then in a more easterly direction to Capua. The Via Latina, farther to the east and inland from the coast, passes through Anagni, Frosinone, and other towns between the Apennine and Volsci mountains. At Ceprano it crosses the river Liri and, following its valley dominated to the east by Monte Cairo (Cario) and farther south by Monte Cassino, it joins the Via Appia a few miles south of Teano. A spur of the Cairo Mountains is Monte Asprano, and on the western slope of this spur lies the Castello di Roccasecca. The ancient city of Aquino, Juvenal's birthplace, can be seen from the castle of Roccasecca; the ruins of Aquino and the castle of Roccasecca are still extant.

The castle of Roccasecca was built in 994 by Abbot Manson of Monte Cassino. But already in 996 it was attacked and occupied by Adenulf III, nicknamed Summucula, "great grandfather of those who are now [i.e., after 1100] known as the Counts of Aquino." In 999 Adenulf claimed both the title and rank of count.[10] With Lando IV, who died after 1137, the title of Count of Aquino disappears. Lando had two elder sons, Pandulf and Ronald I. Pandulf founded the second house of Aquino, which was later known as the Counts of Acerra. The younger son Ronald I became known as the "Lord of Roccasecca." By an exchange of territory with Pope Adrian IV, Ronald obtained possession of a second castle, Montesangiovanni, in the Papal States, besides owning one third of the county of Aquino. T. Leccisotti points out that "Thomas's father [Landulf] did not have the title of Count, but only that of *miles*, or knight, which title he bears also in the Necrologium" of Monte Cassino.[11]

Thomas was an offspring of the Roccasecca branch of the family. Thus Thomas's name "de Aquino" does not indicate the place of his birth in the city of Aquino, as some historians have thought, but the general family name. Tocco somewhat ambiguously says: "Thomas was born of the noble class of Counts of the house of Aquini in the Kingdom of Sicily."[12] This would be correct if the designation "noble class of Counts" refers to the family's past, distant more than one hundred years. Thomas was born in a family of lower nobility. Nevertheless the Signori de Roccasecca de Aquino were gentry and people of good taste and education.

Thomas's mother, Donna Theodora de Aquino, was a noblewoman from Naples (Theate) and of Norman origin. An opinion often expressed in older and even in some more recent biographies holds that she was the sister of the "queens of Sicily and Aragon." This is incorrect; Thomas was in no way related to the Emperor Frederick II. The story behind this fabrication is quite simple. In the other branch, namely that of Acerra, there was one Tommaso di Aquino, Count of Acerra, who was Landulf's cousin in the second degree. He was an eminent figure in the *regnum;* his name often occurs in the histories of Frederick II.[13] This Tommaso di Aquino, Count of Acerra, had a grandson or grandnephew, also called Tommaso di Aquino, Count of Acerra, who, in 1247, married one of Frederick's natural daughters, Marguerite von Schwaben. Thus Tommaso II di Aquino, Count of Acerra, son-in-law (if such he might be called) of Frederick II, was St. Thomas's "cousin" in the fourth or fifth degree. This is the full extent of a family relation between St. Thomas Aquinas and Frederick II of Hohenstaufen, and surely it is no bond of blood.[14] One of the great difficulties in sorting out anything like a family tree is that identical names for distinct persons keep cropping up in the documents.

Landulf had a large family. He must have been born during the 1160s or 1170s and took his first wife toward the end of the twelfth century. There are two documents relating to the election of Giacomo, son of Landulf, dated February 11, 1217, as abbot of the canons of the church of St. Peter Canneto.[15] Since Giacomo, or James, must have been in his twenties when the election took place (contrary to the rights of the Holy See), Landulf must have been in his mature forties at that time. There were at least two other sons from Landulf's first marriage to a woman of unknown name and origin, namely Filippo and Adenolfo; these three sons thus are St. Thomas's half brothers. Since practically nothing is known of these first sons of Landulf, it is sometimes denied or questioned by recent historians that they were members of the same household.[16]

Sometime in the second decade of the thirteenth century, Landulf took his second wife, Theodora of Naples. This second marriage resulted in the birth of at least four boys and five girls. The boys were Aimo, Rinaldo, Landolfo, and Tommaso.

Aimo, or Aimone, became a soldier and fought with the army of Frederick, accompanied him on the fifth crusade, was captured in 1232, was held for ransom on the island of Cyprus, and was eventually released through the intercession of Pope Gregory IX in 1233.[17] From 1233 onward Aimo supported the Pope's cause against Frederick. It is commonly said that Aimo died about 1269; at least he was still alive on March 23, 1254, when Marotta, confirmed as abbess of Capua, is mentioned as "sister of the noble man Aymo de Aquino, devoted to us and the Roman Church."[18]

Rinaldo, or Reginaldo, also served in the Emperor's forces until 1245. In 1240 he is mentioned as *valettus imperatoris*, i.e., the Emperor's page, a noble youth attending the sovereign's service and being trained—such at least was the custom at Frederick's court—for responsible office in the realm. In 1245, when Frederick II was deposed by Innocent IV at the Council of Lyons, Rinaldo changed allegiance and fought with the armies of the Pope against Frederick. Many historians, following the research of F. Scandone,[19] have identified this Reginaldo, or Rinaldo, with "master Reginald" who composed lyrical songs (*canzoni*) in the vernacular and who is known in the history of Italian lyrics and mentioned with honor by Dante.[20] According to Tolomeo of Lucca, it was Reginaldo who, with other soldiers from the fortress of Acquapendente, abducted Thomas on his way to the north with the Dominican master general, and returned him to Roccasecca on his mother's orders.[21] We shall discuss this more fully later. More important at the moment is that in 1246 Reginaldo was put to death by Frederick's orders after the conspiracy to assassinate him at Capaccio. This came one year after his deposition at the Council of Lyons. The Aquino family always considered Reginaldo a "martyr" to the faith and the Church. But certainly if Reginaldo was part of the conspiracy to assassinate the Emperor at Capaccio, Frederick had every reason to have the conspirators put to death. Because of the utter confusion at the time between what was of faith and what was of politics, it is difficult to think of Reginaldo as a "martyr." But the family certainly did so. Mandonnet[22] rightly warns us not to be too hasty in believing this sort of declaration. With these conspirators, he says, the intention to gain material advantages, by helping the Pope to triumph over Frederick, was perhaps stronger than their zeal to serve the interests of the Roman Church.

Landolfo, the third brother of St. Thomas, is practically unknown. Thomas, however, was convinced that Landolfo had to spend some time in purgatory.[23]

The political situation in which Thomas lived and where he was most directly involved through his family was one of the most confused experiences of the Catholic Church. This situation is reflected in the life and writings of Thomas, who has given us two answers to this unfortunate confusion into which the Christian world was plunged. One was doctrinal, the other personal. The doctrinal answer was to be given in one of his earliest works, the *Scriptum super Sententias* II, dist. 44, in which Thomas states that the Pope, in virtue of his canonical office, is the spiritual head of the Church and nothing else; every other political or worldly accretion to this essentially spiritual authority is a historical accident, which may or may not be there without in any way diminishing the Church's inner spiritual nature. Thomas's personal answer to this problem, the one which surely grew out of his experiences with his own family, was to refuse any position in the Church that would have involved him in temporal transactions, which the Popes and ecclesiastics of his time, especially Innocent IV, considered to be their ordinary and natural business. This is the most likely reason why Thomas refused the offer of the Pope to make him abbot of Monte Cassino, even when allowed to remain a Dominican Friar and wear his habit,[24] as well as the offer to promote him to archbishop of Naples with the addition of funds from the monastery of St. Peter ad Aram,[25] and finally his firm intention to remain a Friar even if he were to be offered a cardinal's hat.[26]

Thomas had four or five sisters, Marotta, Maria, Theodora, one unnamed, and possibly Adelasia. Marotta became a Benedictine nun and was confirmed as abbess of the convent of Santa Maria de Capua in 1254 by letter of Pope Innocent IV.[27] In this letter she is mentioned as the sister of Aimo of Aquino, who apparently was then head of the family. Marotta seems to have died around 1259, that is, before St. Thomas. Maria, a second sister, married Guglielmo of San Severino and died after 1286, that is, after St. Thomas. Their daughter, Catherine, was active at the time of the canonization process, and it was probably from her that William of Tocco obtained his knowledge of many of the family legends.[28] Theodora, a third sister, apparently younger than Thomas, married Count Roger of San Severino and Marisco.[29] She apparently died around 1310, having managed Roger's affairs after his death. One of her sons, another Thomas, became Count of San Severino and lived to take a prominent part in the canonization celebrations.[30] A fourth sister is unnamed; she was killed by lightning while still a baby at Roccasecca.[31] It is possible that Thomas had another, younger sister, Adelasia, wife of Roger of Aquila, Count of Traetto and Fondi.[32]

All biographers seem to be in agreement that Thomas was the youngest son by the second marriage of Landulf. Hence, according to the customs of the day, his parents were prepared to dedicate him to the Church. He seems to have had a nurse during his childhood, at least until the age of five.

Most of the legends of his early childhood narrated by William of Tocco and Bernard Gui have been considered as nothing more than basically ordinary family anecdotes. One of the stories told by both biographers is that when his nurse and mother took the infant to the public baths in Naples, Thomas seized a bit of parchment that lay unnoticed on the ground and put it into his mouth. When the nurse tried to take it away from him, the child began to cry loudly, "but when she let him keep it, he was quiet again." Such an episode is quite normal with children; they will pick up almost anything and put it into the mouth. When his mother finally got the scrap of parchment away from him, she noticed that the angelic salutation, *Ave Maria*, was written on it. This palliative happened to be of interest to hagiographers, who made capital on the prophetic implications of the incident.[33] Of greater significance is the incident of the terrifying storm that caused lightning to strike one of the castle towers

of Roccasecca. This lightning killed Thomas's little sister (unnamed) and some horses in the stable below the tower, but
Thomas and his nurse were found by Theodora to be unharmed.
All the biographers narrate the same story. For the hagiographer
it meant that Thomas was providentially preserved for a life of
sanctity and learning. From a psychological point of view this
event may explain why Thomas always had a fear of storms and
lightning.[34]

°   "After his fifth birthday," i.e., around 1230 or 1231, his parents
brought Thomas to the ancient Benedictine Abbey of Monte
Cassino.[35] As the youngest son in the family, he was brought as
an oblate (*oblatus*), that is to say, he was offered to God in the
Benedictine way of life for elementary training in the practice of
the rule and basic education. Landulf and Theodora had made
careful plans for the future of the family; Thomas, it was hoped,
would become abbot of Monte Cassino.[36] Such plans were not
idle, for this could have been managed quite easily. We already
mentioned that Thomas was later offered the abbacy of Monte
Cassino and that he refused it. The preliminary step to this position, or to any other Benedictine preferment, was presentation
of the child to the abbey as an oblate to learn the ways of piety.
There has always been some discussion as to whether or not
Thomas was truly a Benedictine monk. A necrologist of Monte
Cassino wrote in 1274: "he was made a Cassinese monk." One
thing is certain: the *oblatura* or *oblatio* of Thomas at the age of
five or six could not have constituted profession in the Order.
Oblatio and *professio* are two different acts. Even Mariano Armellino, whose attempt to prove that Thomas was a professed
Benedictine has been mentioned already, acknowledged the distinction of these two separate acts. He states that "in 1225, at the
age of five he was sent to the monastery of Monte Cassino by his
parents as an offering (*oblatus*) and dedication to God under the
rule of St. Benedict." And again "in 1235, at the age of fifteen, he
made his monastic profession in the same place."[37] In the *Summa
theologiae* II–II, q. 89, a. 5, Thomas was careful to distinguish a
dedication to religious life before the age of puberty, which can
be made by parents, and a profession of solemn vows at puberty,
requiring the full use of reason. During the early years following
the *oblatura* Thomas cannot be considered to have been a fully

professed Benedictine monk. If he ever became one, it would have been after he reached the age of puberty, and there is no evidence for this whatever. As a young oblate he would have been instructed not only in the ways of the spiritual life according to the Benedictine rule, but he would also have been given the rudiments of learning under the personal direction of a professed monk.

The *oblatura* of itself did not involve solemn vows, nor did it imply any irrevocable act on the part of the parents or the individual. Nevertheless we can say that he was at that time a "Benedictine" in the same sense that, when he became a novice in the Order of Preachers, he was a "Dominican" waiting to profess solemn vows.

The schooling at Monte Cassino was basically religious, but it also involved learning Latin and vernacular grammar, reading, writing, elementary mathematics, and harmony. For grammar Priscianus Minor was most probably used together with the *Barbarismus* of Donatus. Illustrations in grammar were to be found in the Latin of the "vulgate" Bible. The Psalms were undoubtedly learned by heart from the daily choral recitation of the Divine Office. Tolomeo of Lucca claims that Thomas became proficient in logic and the natural sciences at Monte Cassino.[38] But this can hardly be accepted at face value. Tolomeo is here confusing his studies in the abbey and his later studies at the University of Naples.

On the occasion of the *oblatura* of any candidate it was customary for the parents to make an offering to the abbey. A document dated May 3, 1231, records the donation by Landulf of Aquino of funds to repair two mills in the abbey estate, the profit from which was to pay for a yearly "grand banquet" for the monks. The same record mentions that Landulf had previously given twenty ounces of gold for the building and repair of the devastated monastery.[39] It is difficult to ascertain the value of twenty ounces of gold at that time. In 1914 Mandonnet estimated this as "une dizaine de mille francs." A comparative estimate might take into account the sum of twelve ounces of gold paid annually by the Emperor to a famous professor of law at the University of Naples, Master Peter de Isernia, who taught at the university in the 1220s.[40] Thus the gift of twenty ounces of gold was almost double the annual salary of a prominent professor of law.

Therefore it would seem that Thomas's entry into the monastery of Monte Cassino must have taken place late in 1230, after the peace of San Germano had brought hostilities to a close, or early in 1231 around the time his father Landulf made the offering to the monastery for rebuilding the abbey and for the monks.

Monte Cassino had been held by imperial troops from about 1225 onward. When Frederick II finally fulfilled his vow to go on a crusade to the Holy Land, a papal army under the command of a cardinal invaded the abbey and laid hands upon its valuable treasures to keep them from imperial forces. In 1229, after Frederick's return from the Holy Land, imperial troops with a contingent of Saracens among them invaded Cassinese territory and laid siege to the abbey. The following year, 1230, saw these campaigns ended by the peace of San Germano (present-day Cassino at the foot of the Cassino Mountain), concluded on July 23. Since it is most unlikely that Thomas would have been offered to the Benedictines of Monte Cassino during time of strife, it seems highly probable that Thomas was presented sometime between July 23, 1230, and May 3, 1231, having passed his fifth birthday and entered his sixth year.[41]

The treaty of San Germano, in spite of the real situation, gave every advantage to the Pope. For the time being it ended Frederick's first great fight with the curia, and for nearly ten years to come the strife was latent only. It was during these relatively peaceful years that Thomas lived as an oblate at the Abbey of Monte Cassino. But events finally caused Thomas to leave the abbey. In 1236 the abbot who had received him died; he was Landulfo Sinnibaldo, a distant relative of the Aquino family. It was not until February 1239 that the abbey obtained a new abbot. The excommunication of Frederick in March of that same year was the signal for another outbreak of hostilities between the Pope and Emperor. In April the abbey was occupied and fortified by imperial troops. Some of the monks were expelled. In June of 1239 an edict of Frederick's banished from the kingdom all religious born outside its territory. Only eight monks remained at Monte Cassino. It is obvious that in such circumstances there was no room for young oblates at the abbey. It was at this time that Thomas was supposed to have been solemnly professed as a Benedictine. Not only is there no record of this, but the political situation was in no way conducive to his permanent attachment to the Benedictine Order. He certainly was old enough to make religious profession as a Benedictine, for he was fourteen or fifteen years old, but there is no indication that he did so.

The earliest biographers say that Thomas returned to his father's house in the spring of 1239. William of Tocco states that the abbot "persuaded the boy's parents to send him to the University of Naples to study the liberal arts."[42] If Thomas had been a fully professed Benedictine there would have been no need to urge the parents to send him; the abbot himself would have undertaken this responsibility. In any case, "with the consent of both parents,"[43] Thomas was ready to enter the *studium generale* at Naples for the study of the liberal arts and philosophy. That same summer, while Thomas was most probably at home, his father, Landulf, was named one of the barons entrusted with guarding the Lombard prisoners captured at the battle of Cortenuova.[44] It seems that Thomas matriculated at the Naples studium in the fall of 1239, possibly still remaining a Benedictine oblate. For the next five years he devoted himself to serious study under the direction of university professors.

The studium at Naples was founded by Frederick II in 1224 to rival the papal studium at Bologna in particular. In the foundation charter of 1224 Frederick II explicitly stated that the first function of the studium was to train shrewd and intelligent men for the imperial service. As Ernst Kantorowicz points out,[45] Naples was the first utilitarian state university, distinguished from all existing colleges and Church institutions by the fact that teaching was to be carried out not for the sake of knowledge alone, but for the advantage of the state; it was, in fact, a nursery for imperial offices rather than for ecclesiastical preferment. It was predominantly a law school concerned with civil and canon law; and as a law school founded by a king, it had clearly two fighting fronts, one toward the Church, the other toward Bologna.[46]

Since the studium at Naples did not grow up spontaneously as had other studia of Europe, but was a creation of an Em-

peror, the studium suffered many vicissitudes. Walz notes that
lectures were suspended from 1229 to 1235 because pontifical
troops invaded the Puglia.[47] There was a temporary suspension
of lectures in 1239 in retaliation for Frederick's second excommunication, but the professors of the studium pleaded with him
not to close the studium altogether. When Frederick's anger
abated, classes resumed on November 14, 1239, when Thomas
entered the studium with other young nobles who were also
oblates. In 1252 King Conrad moved the studium to Salerno,
where there was already a school of medicine that dated back
for centuries. In 1258 King Manfred returned it to Naples. Yet
it was only under the influence of Charles I of Anjou in 1266
that the studium, now a university in name and in fact, revived
once more. It was in this revitalized university that Thomas was
invited to lecture in theology at a much later date.

It may be somewhat anachronistic to call this studium in
Naples a university, for the term had not yet come into common
usage. In the early days of the thirteenth century, it was better
known as a *studium generale,* just like other universities of this
period. The Neapolitan studium was called a "general studium"
because all branches of knowledge and culture were taught
there. While study of law was the predominant purpose of the
new imperial studium, it did have a fully developed arts faculty,
since all the seven liberal arts and philosophy were universally
accepted as the foundation for all higher studies. It also had a
small faculty of theology, probably one professor, and a token
medical faculty, perhaps again only one or two professors. Thomas
went to Naples in 1239 to study arts and philosophy; he did not
go to study theology, for he was not yet qualified.

Walz affirms, on the authority of Denifle[48] that the teaching
of theology at the Naples studium was "entrusted to the Dominicans" until their expulsion of 1239, though this expulsion was
probably only of those not born within the Kingdom of Sicily;
there was no particular expulsion of Dominicans as such. Rashdall,
quoting Origlia,[49] also states that the Dominicans left Naples
in consequence of the Emperor's dispute with the Pope in 1234.
But this can only mean that some of the Dominicians left, not
the entire community. Rashdall may also have had in mind the
general expulsion of 1239. In any case we know that Thomas

became acquainted with the Dominican Friars in Naples between 1239 and 1244.

It seems most probable that there was only one master in theology at the University of Naples at any one time. If so, then it would mean that the Dominican who left in 1239 was a foreigner who fell under the general edict. The only teacher of theology listed in Kantorowicz's list of professors at Naples is the well-known Benedictine Erasmus of Monte Cassino, who began lecturing in theology in 1240.[50]

The course in arts which Thomas took at Naples followed the usual pattern of medieval universities at the time with one important exception. Not only did he study the seven liberal arts with particular emphasis on logic, but he also studied the natural philosophy of Aristotle. At a time when Parisian students were forbidden to study Aristotle's natural philosophy and metaphysics,[51] Thomas was studying the *libri naturales* and most probably the *Metaphysics* as well. While in later days medieval universities classified the "three philosophies" as natural, moral, and first (metaphysics), early thirteenth-century classifications often grouped metaphysics with the *libri naturales*.

One important reason for the early, serious introduction of Aristotle's natural philosophy into the schools in southern universities was the culture prevailing in Frederick's court in Palermo. Charles Homer Haskins was one of the first to study the Aristotelian spirit in Frederick's court.[52] He showed that Latin, Moslem, and Jewish culture mingled freely in Sicily in a unique way that was peculiarly Sicilian. Translators of scientific and philosophical treatises were particularly encouraged by the Hohenstaufens. The most prolific and important of the Sicilian translators encouraged by Frederick was Michael Scot. He had previously translated works from the Arabic while still in Toledo in 1217—for example, Al-Bitrugi's *De sphera*, Aristotle's *De animalibus, De caelo, De anima,* and the influential commentaries of Averroes. The commentaries of Averroes were the most important single project of the early thirteenth-century translators. We do not know exactly who translated the rest of the Averroist corpus, but parts of it were in circulation by 1220 or by 1230, and these came from the pen of Michael Scot. The official position of Michael was that of court astrologer, but he made for the Emperor a Latin summary of Avicenna's *De animalibus* and busied himself with writings on astrology, meteorology, and physiognomy, all dedicated to Frederick. In other words, the whole breadth of Aristotelian science, Arabic astronomy, and Greek medicine flourished in Palermo, Salerno, and Naples prior to their assimilation in northern universities.

Practically nothing is known of the normal course of studies in the arts faculty at Naples. It is most probable that there was no "normal" procedure of studies, such as there was at Paris and Oxford in the later part of the century.[53] Naples undoubtedly followed the "common practice of the schools" in accepting boys around the age of fourteen or fifteen, registered them under a particular master, concentrated on the study of the text (*lectio*), and held disputations (*disputationes*) and repetitions (*repetitiones*) of the master's lectures. The basic text for the "old" and "new" logic was Aristotle's *Organon* and Boethius's commentaries. For grammar, Priscian's *Institutiones*, Donatus's two works, the *Ars minor* and *Ars maior*, as well as examples of classical Latin grammar and literature were available. For rhetoric, Cicero's *De inventione* and pseudo-Cicero's *Rhetorica ad Herennium* were used. For the quadrivium, the texts were most probably Boethius for arithmetic, the first six books of Euclid's *Elementa*, some abbreviated form of Ptolemy's *Almagest* for astronomy, and possibly the *Musica* of Boethius for music and harmonic theory. Theoretically, but never in practice, all of this was to be studied before taking up the extremely difficult books of Aristotle's natural philosophy. At a much later stage the period of time to be devoted to each subject was determined by statute; but for the early period we must presume that when the student had mastered all that he could from one master, he would or at least could be transferred to another master. This is the impression given by Peter Calo.[54] One of the basic rules accepted in early medieval scholasticism was that each student had to be enrolled under an individual master who was responsible not only for the intellectual development of the youth, but also for his morals and habits. Throughout the whole history of medieval scholasticism, masters had to testify on oath concerning a student's "knowledge and morals" (*de scientia et moribus*).

During his years at Naples Thomas grew to adolescence and

maturity. He seems to have been somewhat taller than most of his Italian contemporaries, and somewhat corpulent. The words in which Bernard Gui described Thomas's demeanor at Monte Cassino might be more appropriate to his adolescent years: "He was a quiet boy with an unusually mature bearing; saying little, but already thinking much; rather silent and serious and seemingly, much given to prayer."[55]

That Thomas studied logic and grammar and was introduced to the Aristotelian *libri naturales* there can be no doubt whatever. Many biographers imply that it was Albert the Great who introduced Thomas to Aristotelian learning, whereas in fact he was taught the natural philosophy of Aristotle at Naples. William of Tocco and Peter Calo preserved for us the names of two celebrated teachers under whom Thomas studied at Naples. "He was instructed in grammar and logic under Master Martin, and in natural sciences under Master Peter of Hibernia."[56] Bernard Gui also remarked that Thomas "made swift progress through grammar, logic and natural science."[57] Peter Calo was perhaps somewhat confused when he wrote that "when [Thomas] went beyond the teaching of grammar in a short time, he was given to Peter of Hibernia, who instructed him in logic and the natural sciences." Modern authorities are generally agreed that at Naples Master Martin taught grammar and logic, while Peter of Ireland taught natural philosophy.

In older biographies of Thomas these two names are usually mentioned, but no attempt was made to identify them or to study their possible influence on the intellectual development of the young Thomas. H. Denifle, for instance, in his erudite work on the rise of universities in the Middle Ages,[58] was unable to identify these two masters, and thought that Tocco might have invented their names. This situation changed with the discovery made by Clemens Baeumker in 1920 of a disputation held by Peter of Ireland in the court of King Manfred.[59] A short time later M. Grabmann discovered two more works of Peter in MS Vat. lat. 5989, where there is a commentary by him on the *Isagoge* of Porphyry and a commentary on the *Peri hermenias*; A. Pelzer discovered a commentary by Peter on *De longitudine et brevitate vitae* (commonly known in the Middle Ages as *De morte et vita*) in Vat. lat. 825.[60]

The conclusions of these discoveries of the 1920s can be summarized briefly. Frederick II's court was an important center not only of Aristotelian but especially of Averroistic studies. The translations made in this court were of Aristotelian Greek and Arabic authors, the most important of whom was Averroes, translated in part at Toledo and at the court in Palermo.[61] The works of Averroes slowly penetrated into Latin scholasticism after 1230, and their channels were the court in Palermo and the studium in Naples. C. H. Haskins rightly warns us not to exaggerate the extent of the translators' activity at Frederick's court; still the judgment seems hardly deniable that an important stream of Aristotelianism of the Greek and Arabic commentators, especially their more empirical views, originated in southern Italy. This is not to say that Thomas was taught directly or indirectly the Averroist view of natural philosophy in such a way that he absorbed its essential features. All that can be said is that Thomas was exposed to a more direct Aristotelianism than would have been possible under the influence of St. Albert alone, who frequently assimilated Neo-Platonic authors in his own version of Peripatetic philosophy. It would also seem that Thomas somehow came to prefer the Averroist literal commentary to the Avicennian paraphrase of the works of Aristotle. The main conclusion of the researches of the 1920s is that Aquinas was formed in the attitudes of Aristotelian thought through his teacher, Peter of Ireland, before he met Albert the Great. Nothing new has appeared in print concerning the Aristotelianism of Peter, except the suggestion that Peter's approach to problems discussed involved metaphysical views that are properly Aristotelian.[62]

Peter's disputation took place before King Manfred of Sicily. This means that it must have taken place between August 10, 1258, and February 26, 1266, while he was king. Peter's disputed question is a very interesting one, the subject of which is "Whether the parts of the body are made for the sake of their activities, or whether the activities are produced for the sake of these parts." In typical Aristotelian fashion he concluded that the organs are for the activities just as body exists for the sake of soul, and generally just as potency exists for act. However, this disputation took place around 1260, some twenty years after he had Thomas as his student. Nevertheless the suggestion of all the authorities is that Peter of Ireland was always an Aristotelian and became even more so as the years went by.

Grounds are much weaker for the identification of Master Martin. In 1952 Heinrich Roos claimed that this Martin was the well-known Martin of Dacia (of Denmark), who was a highly respected teacher of speculative grammar and logic in the thirteenth century. However, Roos later expressed doubts about this identification, since Martin of Dacia was still alive in 1340.[63] It would seem that Thomas's teacher Martin is still unknown and perhaps not overly influential on Thomas, although Thomas does use the name "Martinus" in two early works, in the *Sentences* I, dist. 36, q. 2, a. 3 ad 3, and in *De fallaciis*, c. 7, where there is no reason at all for suggesting the name "Martinus" in a context that would call for the standard "Socrates" or "Tullius."[64]

One further point ought to be made about Thomas's studies at Naples. He seems to have been taught a great deal about grammar and rhetoric. His sympathy with and expressions of poetry seem to have been implanted during his study of arts. Thomas never learned anything about calligraphy; he certainly never displays it in the extant autographs or holographs. In fact, in later centuries his typical handwriting was known as the *littera illegibilis*, sometimes called *littera inintelligibilis*. It is a very energetic and swift hand trailing behind the thought he was trying to express. One could almost say that when writing, Thomas was always in a hurry, without serious detriment to the thought he was about to express. Only a handful of scholars in the world today can read this handwriting. This being agreed upon, one must also point out the beautiful use of the *cursus* in his opusculum *Contra errores Graecorum* and his remarkable poetry, particularly in his liturgy for Corpus Christi. He may have developed his lyrical verse and prose later in life, but the essentials were already established before he left Naples in 1244 to join the Order of Friars Preachers, at the age of nineteen or twenty.

Thomas, it would seem, never incepted in arts or taught as regent master in arts at Naples. The length of time spent in the studium at Naples would have been sufficient, considering his conspicuous aptitude, for inception in arts. Regulations concerning inception in arts at Paris in 1215 state that a scholar must have completed his twentieth year before inception. We do not know what the customary procedure was at Naples in this early period, but it could not have been very different from the practice at Paris. We can only say that for Thomas, functioning as a master in arts at Naples was not as enticing as entering the Order of Friars Preachers. No doubt close association with the Friars at San Domenico played its part in attracting Thomas. But surely more important than that must have been the ideal of St. Dominic and the way of life shown by the mendicant friars. Consequently, he chose to enter the mendicant Order in the summer of 1244, thus frustrating his family's plan for him. Thomas's father had died the previous year, 1243, and the future of the family rested on Donna Theodora.

Young Manhood in the Order of Friars Preachers

(1244–52)

During his residence in Naples, studying at the imperial university, Thomas had ample opportunity to encounter and to observe the lives of the handful of Dominicans who had arrived in Naples in 1227.[65] Dressed in a white tunic, scapular, and capuce and a black outer cloak all made of wool, they lived conspicuously in the heart of the medieval city. Besides preaching in their own convent and wherever else possible, they wandered throughout the city begging for their food and other necessities. As Thomas passed through his adolescent years at the university, he could not have helped being impressed with their zeal for souls and evangelical poverty.

The Dominican Order, technically known as the Order of Friars Preachers, was founded by St. Dominic in 1215 in southern France. Dominic de Guzman was born in 1171 or 1172 at Caleruega, a village of old Castile in Spain, son of Felix of Guzman and Joan of Aza. He received his elementary training from a certain uncle, an archpriest. About the age of fourteen Dominic was sent to the nearby city of Palencia to study the liberal arts. Blessed Jordan of Saxony, writing on the early days of the Order, noted that at that time there flourished a studium of arts in that city.[66] After studying arts, Dominic enrolled in the cathedral school at Palencia, where he "spent four years in sacred studies."[67] Dominic had a great love for his books, and he annotated them carefully.[68] Nevertheless, during a particularly severe famine, Dominic sold his books to raise money for the needy.[69] His solicitude inspired fellow theologians and even secular masters of theology to follow his example. This was no easy decision for Dominic, for books are precious to any student, and Dominic had acquired a habit of study from a very early age. As a cleric Dominic belonged to the secular clergy and was a member of the cathedral chapter. In 1199 he was archdeacon of Osma and voted with the chapter to embrace a common rule of life. This entailed not only the acceptance of a common rule, namely, that of St. Augustine, but also the vows of poverty, chastity, and obedience, together with the choral recitation of the Divine Office, and a common way of life. He was, in fact, a Canon Regular of the Order of St. Augustine, and sub-prior of the cathedral chapter. In this way of life, Dominic devoted himself to ardent prayer and assiduous study.[70]

The turning point in Dominic's career came in the spring of 1203, when he was chosen by his bishop, Diego d'Acebes of Osma, to accompany him on a mission to Denmark.[71] In southern France, Bishop Diego and Dominic saw at first hand the devastation of society and the Church caused by the Albigensian heresy. "Dominic's zeal leaped into flame when he discovered that his innkeeper was a member of the sect."[72] He spent the whole night in debate with the innkeeper and succeeded in bringing him back to orthodoxy. Toward the end of the twelfth century and during the early part of the thirteenth, the Albigensians grew in number because of the zeal, evangelical poverty, and intellectual acumen of the leaders, the "Cathari." Numerous delegations of Cistercians and papal legates had been sent into the territory to convert the Albigensians; but these efforts met with little success. Bishop Diego and Dominic both soon realized that the heretics could be won over only by the practice of evangelical poverty, deep learning, and zeal for souls. "As poverty characterizes Francis, zeal for souls characterizes Dominic."[73] Although Dominic had achieved a certain success through his preaching, the heresy was not stifled until the secular arms of Simon de Montfort crushed it. There is no evidence whatever that Dominic took part in the military operations, but there is ample evidence that he ardently preached against the heresy throughout the territory of Toulouse and Languedoc.[74] In the calm of 1215, the learned Bishop Fulque of Toulouse appointed Dominic and his companions preachers for the diocese of Toulouse.[75] The first religious community of the Order was established there in April 1215, when Peter Seila, a citizen of considerable means, made profession in the hands of Dominic and deeded to the new community his three houses in Toulouse.

Episcopal authority to preach in the diocese of Toulouse was given to Dominic and his associates by Bishop Fulque in June 1215.[76] It was at this time, when Dominic was forty-five years old, that he and his six companions presented themselves to Alexander Stavensby, an English secular master in theology, then lecturing in the cathedral school in Toulouse. Stavensby, "genere, scientia et fama preclarus,"[77] was later professor at Bologna, member of the papal household, and eventually bishop of Coventry and Lichfield.[78] He was, therefore, the first teacher of the new band of preachers.

But Dominic wanted papal guidance and confirmation so that the mission of teaching and preaching might continue even after the death of Bishop Fulque and even in an expanded apostolate. The task of preaching was no longer limited to preaching against heresy, but expanded into the Catholic apostolate in its fullest extent. Evangelical preaching belongs by right to the episcopacy in the Roman Church. Never before had this task been taken on as the primary goal of any religious Order. Dominic visited Rome in November 1215 in the company of Bishop Fulque (who was going to the Lateran Council) to seek confirmation from Innocent III. Jordan of Saxony notes that Dominic sought confirmation on two points: "they petitioned the Lord Pope Innocent to confirm for Brother Dominic and his disciples an order that would be called and would be [in fact] an Order of Preachers; likewise that he would confirm the revenues that had been assigned to the brethren by the Count and by the Bishop."[79] No doubt Innocent wanted to await the outcome of the Council on the question of preaching and the founding of new Orders in the Church. Shortly thereafter, Innocent III confirmed the general task and name of the Order; and on December 22, 1216, Honorius III confirmed fully the purpose and authority of the Friars Preachers in his bull *Gratiarum omnium,* confirming the mission and the almost revolutionary character of the Order. Its mandate of preaching was intended to embrace every type of apostolic preaching—the communication of religious truth in the classroom, in writing, in pulpit and public sermons, and for the salvation of souls generally.

At the first dispersal of the Friars in August 1217, seven of the sixteen members were sent to Paris, and early the following year a foundation was made at Bologna.[80] In 1220 Dominic sent Friars to Palencia and Montpellier to establish houses, at the very time universities were being founded in those cities. One of Dominic's last official acts in 1221 was to send thirteen Friars to the university city of Oxford.[81] Since Dominic's Order was a clerical and canonical one, he sought to win clerics in the university centers. Students and even masters in arts entered in great numbers. Jordan of Saxony, the immediate successor of Dominic, was himself a bachelor in theology of the University of Paris.

Dominic sent his men to university centers, not to teach, for they were not academically qualified, but to learn, study, and become proficient in the sacred sciences. Learning for Dominic was an essential means for the apostolate he had in mind for the Church. As a Canon Regular of Osma, Dominic embraced the religious vows, choral recitation of the Divine Office, and a common life regulated by the *Rule* of St. Augustine. These same means he adopted for his new Order, adding the special means, "assiduous study of divine truth," required by the special goal of apostolic preaching. "Study," wrote Humbert of Romans, "is not the purpose of the Order, but it is of the greatest necessity for the aims we have mentioned, namely preaching and working for the salvation of souls, for without study we can achieve neither."[82] Just as no previous religious Order in the Church had ever embraced preaching as the goal, so none had adopted study as an essential means to the apostolate. For this reason the early

Preachers endeavored to recruit from university circles persons already dedicated to study.[83]

The importance attached to learning is evident in Dominican priories from the very beginning. The hub of every Dominican activity was the priory, which was spacious enough to hold large communities. W. A. Hinnebusch points out that the Order was "convinced that its purposes could best be achieved by large communities to preserve both the contemplative and apostolic sides of Dominican life."[84]

Every Dominican priory had to have a lector whose obligation was to give theological lectures on the Sacred Scriptures to all the brethren.[85] Not even the prior was exempt from attendance at these lectures. The degree of Lector in Sacred Theology (S.T.Lr.) was nothing more than the authorization of the Order to lecture within Dominican houses. It was not a university degree. Later, when priories were especially large, a number of lectors would be assigned to a house; one Friar, called the *lector primarius*, was entrusted with supervising all teaching and with deciding theological disputations. Thus even before the Order had any claim on the University of Paris, that is, before the Order obtained its first master in theology, every cleric in the Order was bound to the "assiduous study of sacred truth."

Canonically speaking, the Dominicans, like the Franciscans, were not monks or secular clerics. They were friars, a term derived from the English pronunciation of *frères,* the French word meaning "brothers." Friars did not take the vow of stability, therefore they could be transferred from one house to another or from one province to another by proper authority. The Friars Preachers were mendicants, that is, they lived on alms gathered from the faithful and from ecclesiastical subsidies. By 1221 the Order was sufficiently numerous to make the creation of distinct religious provinces desirable. These provinces were Spain, Toulouse, France, Lombardy, Province of Rome, Hungary, Germany, and England; over each province there was a prior provincial, who was subject only to the master general of the Order, who governed it under direction from the Holy See. The interesting thing is that, like the Canons Regular, the Preachers were all clerics, except for the *conversi,* whose task it was to assist the clerics. Although not every member of the Order preached (for this was a special prerogative), they were all called *Praedica-tores*, just as all Franciscans were called *Minores*. All Dominican Friars, whether actually engaged in preaching or not, were bound to the four means of achieving the goal, namely, the three vows, the obligation to choral recitation of Divine Office, community life according to the *Rule* of St. Augustine and the constitutions of the Order, and assiduous study of divine truth.

Many years later, when Thomas was writing his *Summa theologiae,* he had occasion to discuss types of religious life. He noted that there were three types of religious Orders in the Church: the strictly contemplative, such as the Benedictine and Cistercian; the active, such as those dedicated to caring for the sick or to ransoming captives; and the mixed, such as those whose life is contemplative but whose mission is active, as by preaching. He writes, "The highest place among religious orders is held by those which are ordained to teaching and preaching, which functions belong to and participate in the perfection of bishops."[86] He described the goal of the mixed form of religious life as *contemplare et contemplata aliis tradere*–to contemplate and to give to others the fruits of contemplation. By "contemplation" he meant not only the infused contemplation that comes from prayer, but also the acquired contemplation that comes from study. Such was the nature and goal of the Dominican Order. Young Thomas was quick to perceive that such was the life he wanted.

The church and convent of Santa Sabina in Rome were given to the Dominican Friars in 1221, while St. Dominic was still alive; this was the beginning of the Roman Province of the Order, the one to which Thomas belonged. The community in which he received the habit of the Order was established in Naples in 1227 as part of the Roman Province. This community acquired a new church and priory in 1231, which were dedicated to St. Dominic after his canonization on July 3, 1234. The Priory of San Domenico, which still exists, was the house in which Thomas was received into the Order, and the house to which he belonged.

St. Dominic died on August 6, 1221, and his successors were exceptional men who were able to direct the Order in the true spirit of its founder. Jordan of Saxony was master general from 1222 to 1237; he was succeeded by St. Raymond of Peñafort,

1238–40, and by John of Wildeshausen, commonly known as the Teuton, 1241–52. John was particularly gifted in knowing not only his native German and Latin, but also Italian and French. It was during the mastership of John of Wildeshausen that Thomas received his habit and made his profession.

I. T. Eschmann suggests that at some time during adolescence, Thomas ceased to be a Benedictine oblate and lived simply as a layman. Perhaps it was after the age of fourteen or sixteen that he ceased being an oblate, having still to make up his mind about the vocation he wished to pursue. During this period, too, he was closely associated with the Dominican Friar John of San Giuliano, who "encouraged him along the way."[87] Friar John, about whom we know little, probably acted as a counselor and friend to young Thomas during his adolescent years.

We do not know when Thomas received the Dominican habit. We have no documentary evidence, and the biographical sources are conflicting on this point. Bernard Gui states that he was "still below the age of puberty"; Tolomeo of Lucca explicitly states that he was "sixteen."[88] The Dominican constitutions in force under Jordan of Saxony state: "Let no one be received below the age of eighteen."[89] Even "eighteen" is an early age to receive the Dominican habit, since during the early days of the Order a very large number of Dominicans entered when they were mature men in their twenties and thirties. Tolomeo of Lucca and William of Tocco explicitly state that Thomas was received into the Dominican Order while Innocent IV was Pope.[90] But Innocent was elected at Anagni on June 25, 1243, and died at Naples on December 7, 1254. This fact alone disproves the earlier statements of Bernard Gui and Tolomeo of Lucca, for in this case Thomas could not have been younger than eighteen.

In view of the events that took place immediately after Thomas received the Dominican habit, there are two further pieces of circumstantial evidence. The first concerns the Emperor Frederick II. In August 1243 Frederick II came to Tuscany to make war on the papal cities. In April and May 1244 he was encamped in the vicinity of Acquapendente, and on May 7, 1244, Frederick himself was in Terni, a few hours' ride from camp. All the biographers of Thomas state that it was while

Frederick was in the area of Acquapendente, north of Rome outside papal territory, that Thomas was intercepted and returned to his home.[91] The most likely date of Thomas's capture, therefore, was in 1244, perhaps the early weeks of May 1244, thus placing his entry into the Dominican Order late in April 1244.

The second piece of circumstantial evidence is the presence of the master general John of Wildeshausen in and around the vicinity of Naples. Tolomeo states[92] that Thomas traveled from Naples in the company of the master general in the northward journey to Bologna where the general chapter was to meet on May 22. Mandonnet and Walz maintain that John the Teuton was not in Naples but in Rome, and that it was from there that Thomas continued his northward journey in the company of the master general. This is a minor point. The important point is that Thomas continued his northward journey in the company of the master general when he was captured. John had been at the general chapter of Paris in 1243, when Innocent IV had not yet been elected Pope. General chapters of the Order convened yearly on the feast of Pentecost. The 1244 chapter was held in Bologna on Pentecost, May 22. Therefore, Mandonnet's conclusion that Thomas received the Dominican habit toward the end of April 1244, was captured by Rinaldo and a company of soldiers from Frederick's army early in May 1244, and returned to his mother's house at Roccasecca seems convincing.[93]

If Thomas did receive the Dominican habit toward the end of April 1244, he was then nineteen years old. Apparently he did not finish his studies at the University of Naples, or at least he did not function there as a master in arts. The prior who received Thomas into the Order was Friar Thomas Agni da Lentini (Sicily), an eminent man who later became provincial of the Roman Province in 1252, bishop of Cosenza in 1267, and finally patriarch of Jerusalem in 1272.[94]

While the Dominicans of San Domenico were delighted that Thomas decided to be one of them, they did not know quite what to do with him. (Some years before in 1235, they had had considerable trouble with another novice who came from a noble family of the vicinity. This man's family broke into the cloister by night and took the novice away.) Normally Thomas would have spent his novitiate year at San Domenico praying, reading, and listening to the lector in theology. But that course was out of the question for an offspring of the powerful Aquino family. The Friars of San Domenico took counsel with the master general, John of Wildeshausen, who, according to the uncertain testimony of Tolomeo, was then staying in Naples. The suggestion that seemed most feasible was to send Thomas to Paris.[95] If the master general was in fact at Naples for the clothing of Thomas, then Thomas could have accompanied him at least as far as Bologna, where the next general chapter was to be held. What is certain is that Thomas left Rome early in May 1244 in the company of John of Wildeshausen, who was on his way to Bologna with some companions.

All the biographers note that Thomas was abducted while on the journey, but not all biographers are in agreement as to the motives behind the abduction. The earliest description is the sober account given by Gerard de Frachet in his collection of ancient memories called *Vitae Fratrum*. The account in this description simply states that while Thomas was on his way north to Paris in the company of the master general, he was waylaid by "his relatives," who took him to a distant castle where they hoped to change his mind about entering the Dominican Order.[96] Bernard Gui notes, however, that Donna Theodora was overwhelmed with joy to hear about Thomas's entry into the Dominican Order, and that she rushed to Naples "hoping to see Thomas there and encourage him in his purpose."[97] William of Tocco, embarrassed at the whole affair, seems to say that it was a misunderstanding that caused the Dominicans at Naples to send Thomas off to Paris. When Donna Theodora heard that Thomas had become a Dominican, she hurried off to Naples with her retinue. Not finding him there, she is said to have hastened on to Rome, where again Thomas was not to be found. Learning that Thomas was on his way to Bologna, she sent a messenger to her son Rinaldo (and possibly to a second son), then encamped near Acquapendente outside papal territory, to intercept Thomas and bring him back by force, if necessary. That a messenger was sent to Rinaldo by his mother is certain, but it is not certain from where the message was sent. It is more likely that Theodora did not need to go to Rome, but returned to Roccasecca.

Tolomeo of Lucca described the event as follows:

> Now serving under Frederick was one of Thomas's brothers, the lord Reginald, a man of no small worth and at that time of high standing in Frederick's court, though later the emperor had him put to death. No sooner had Reginald heard that his brother was in the neighborhood (Frederick meanwhile pretending not to know what was about to happen) than he took Peter of Vineis with him and some men at arms, and went and violently separated his brother from the master general, and forcing him to mount a horse, sent him off with a strong guard to one of the family castles in the Campagna called San Giovanni.[98]

Thomas of Cantimpré seems to be the source of the more virulent account of the abduction of Thomas by two of his brothers, described as *potentissimi ac feroci*. Thomas of Cantimpré's version is the best-known of the various accounts of Thomas's abduction and attempted seduction, printed in most stories about him.[99]

The truth of the matter is that Donna Theodora and her husband, Landulf, had made careful plans for the future of the family, and Thomas was to play an important part in its security. According to Mandonnet, Thomas's father died on December 24, 1243.[100] Mandonnet's evidence was a document recording the death of Landulf only by day and month, but not year. But it is quite possible that Landulf did die in 1243. Hence Donna Theodora felt it was her duty to see that the most advantageous plan was followed for the good of the family fortune. There can be no doubt that Donna Theodora wanted desperately to see Thomas and discuss the matter with him. She was not opposed to a religious vocation for him, but she was definitely opposed to his becoming a mendicant friar. It is natural that such a strongly motivated mother would want to discuss the good of her son and the future of the family. At this time Frederick had not yet been deposed by the Council of Lyons and the Aquino fortunes lay with him. After Frederick was deposed in June 1245, the whole situation of the Aquino family altered and new plans had to be made.

All of the early biographers mention "the brothers" of Thomas, in the plural. The only brother of whom we are certain was Rinaldo d'Aquino. Tolomeo of Lucca also mentions a companion, Peter of Vineis, who may have been the poet Pier delle Vigne mentioned by Dante.[101] In any case the brother (or brothers), with a military escort, galloped to the Aquino castle in papal territory called Montesangiovanni en route to Roccasecca, where Donna Theodora was waiting. Thomas of Cantimpré's description of Thomas lying in the family dungeon, suffering every kind of indignity, cannot be taken seriously, although it is the real source of the seduction story, repeated by so many biographers. According to William of Tocco's account,[102] Thomas was imprisoned in the family tower, and every inducement to make him change his mind and take off the Dominican habit was in vain. Finally one day the "brothers" induced a ravishing girl, seductively attired, into his cell to seduce him and thereby break his will. Indignant over this attempt, Thomas picked up a burning stick from the fire and drove the girl from his room. Having then made the sign of the cross on the wall with his charred stick, he fell into a deep sleep and two angels came to comfort him, girding him with a cord of angelic purity. The cord was bound so tightly that he awoke from his sleep. According to Tocco's account, Thomas never again had the hungry pangs of lust and remained a virgin throughout life. William of Tocco did not relate this incident at the canonization process, but he did claim to have heard that Thomas always remained a virgin. This last fact Tocco claims to have learned from Robert de Sezzé, "procurator of the Friars Preachers in Anagni, who preached at the funeral of Friar Thomas, at which time he said he heard Thomas's last general confession."[103] Here Tocco is completely confused, for, according to his own account in the Hystoria, it was Reginald of Piperno who heard Thomas's last confession and who preached the funeral oration.

Mandonnet has considered the evidence concerning this seduction episode very carefully and concluded that the story of this assault on young Thomas's virtue is not only believable but is a historical fact. All biographers repeat the story of the attempted seduction, at least for dramatic effect. However, J. A. Endres[104] and I. T. Eschmann reject the whole story outright.

They claim that the story originated from an interview which Tocco had with a Dominican *confrère* named Robert de Sezzé in December 1318; the story did not come from the family, not even from Donna Catherina de Morra, Thomas's grandniece. This Robert of Sezzé is supposed to have learned from his great-uncle that when Thomas was in the dungeon in Montesangio-vanni, his brothers "sent him a very beautiful girl seductively attired who would incite him to sin." Tocco's thirdhand story carried much weight with subsequent biographers. The biographers who mention the incident all seem to locate the temptation at the family castle of Montesangiovanni. This is a very important point. The escort would not have brought him there for any length of time unless his mother, Donna Theodora, was there in waiting. For it was Theodora's order that Thomas be brought to her. She wanted to see him, talk to him, and try to dissuade him from his Dominican vocation. There is every reason to believe that Theodora remained all this time in Roccasecca and that the period at Montesangiovanni was only a brief interlude. As one recent biographer concluded: "After his detention at Montesan-giovanni Thomas was escorted to Roccasecca, but it is not known when."[105] It is certain that Theodora would never have countenanced the introduction of a prostitute to beguile her favorite son. For this reason I. T. Eschmann denies the whole incident. However, Donna Theodora would never have known about it if the incident took place at Montesangiovanni and if she were at Roccasecca.

There is every reason to think that the prostitute episode is historical fact, as Mandonnet argues. However, the sequel involving the "angelic cord" need not be taken as more than an apt symbolization of Thomas's angelic chastity. The only possible witnesses were Thomas and the two angels. The two angels have not spoken, and Thomas seems never to have mentioned the incident. Bernard Gui, however, claims that "to the end of his life [Thomas] kept [the incident] in secret, except to brother Reginald [of Piperno], his socius and intimate, to whom he spoke of it humbly."[106] But there is no proof whatever that Reginald knew of the episode or that the biographers learned of it from him. Nor is there any mention of it in the sworn testimony of the canonization process. The angelic cord, therefore, can be taken as a magnificent symbol of Thomas's chastity, but no more. Mandonnet, who also argues for the purely symbolic character of the angelic cord,[107] agrees that the attempted seduction could not have taken place at the family castle at Roccasecca.

To sum up, then, shortly after reception of the Dominican habit at San Domenico in Naples, Thomas was sent north in the company of the master general, John of Wildeshausen, and his companions. This northward journey took place early in May 1244. Donna Theodora understood that Thomas's membership in a mendicant order altered family plans considerably. She sent a messenger to Rinaldo and perhaps to another son, asking them to intercept the traveling Dominicans. Rinaldo was then with Frederick's army at Acquapendente, north of Rome. The military escort was approved by Frederick, and permission was given for their interception and abduction of Thomas from his Dominican brothers. This probably took place during the second week in May. The escort tried to make Thomas remove the Dominican habit; when persuasion failed, the soldiers tried to take it off by force. Failing in this, they set him on a horse and forced him to travel to the family castle at Montesangiovanni. Apparently the "brothers" of Thomas became separated from the escort. The soldiers "shut him up pending the arrival of his brothers, who were expected to come soon."[108] It is most likely that Donna Theodora was waiting at Roccasecca, and was not at Montesangiovanni to greet Thomas. It would seem most plausible that the prostitute was sent to Thomas the very night of his arrival. The brothers may have been off in search of a likely woman to seduce Thomas. When they arrived, they induced the young girl to visit his room and see what could be done to break Thomas's will. By this time Thomas had already had a hard day and was in an indignant mood at being separated from his brethren. He was therefore short of patience and well disposed to seize a burning stick to force the girl out of the room and to pray ardently to be delivered from his adversities. It would seem natural that Thomas should fall to his knees with tears and prayers. After some time Thomas could be morally certain that he would never give up his virginity. Since there was no reason for

Thomas's abductors to remain in Montesangiovanni, the escort probably took Thomas to Roccasecca the very next day.

Donna Theodora was no doubt delighted to see her son. But all of her attempts to dissuade young Thomas from his decision—she even detained him for a year or more at Roccasecca—had no effect.

Meanwhile the Dominican Order, through John of Wildeshausen, protested the abduction and asked Pope Innocent IV to intercede with Frederick to punish those responsible for it. But this petition came to nothing. Not only was Frederick cognizant of the abduction by Rinaldo and his soldiers, but he had no friendly feeling for the Dominicans anyway, since they represented papal authority in his own realm.

Thomas arrived at Roccasecca with his brothers and companions in the second or third week of May 1244. Bernard Gui states that Thomas remained virtually a prisoner "for about two years."[109] Bartholomew of Capua testified at the canonization inquiry[110] that Thomas was held in confinement "for more than a year," while the sober statement of the *Vitae Fratrum* indicates that this period was "almost a year."[111] During this period the Aquino family did everything to persuade him to go along with family plans. Nothing could persuade him to abandon his Dominican vocation or to change his mind about ecclesiastical preferments. It is probable that out of the Aquino plans to have Thomas become abbot of Monte Cassino, there was the later offer to allow Thomas to remain a Dominican while being abbot. This would have been an anomalous combination, but no doubt the family clung to desperate hopes.

Thomas was virtually confined to the house. But it would be a mistake to think that he was treated like a prisoner. He had freedom to move about, to read, to write, and to talk to his sisters. One sister, Marotta, tried to argue with Thomas and convince him to obey his mother. After numerous discussions Thomas convinced *her* to give up the world and become a nun; she joined the Benedictines and eventually became prioress of Santa Maria in Capua in 1252.

Some biographers state that during his "captivity" Thomas was not allowed the comfort of seeing his Dominican brethren. This may have been true at the time of his original abduction and his one-night stay at Montesangiovanni, but it is not true of the Roccasecca period. Bernard Gui notes that Friar John of San Giuliano, who had been his friend during Thomas's studies at Naples, "was able to visit him frequently and bring him changes of clothing by the expedient of coming dressed in two habits, one of which, as soon as they were alone, he would take off and give to Thomas."[112] More important is the fact that Thomas had much time for private study, prayer, and conversation with his family. According to William of Tocco, Thomas spent this period of confinement reading the Bible and studying the text of Peter Lombard's *Sentences,* the official textbook of bachelors teaching sacred theology. A young man of nineteen or twenty would have a very difficult time comprehending Peter Lombard's work.[113]

On the explicit testimony of Tocco, Thomas compiled a treatise on Aristotle's *De fallaciis* dedicated "to certain nobles in arts." Walz denies that the known work with that title and printed in all the editions of Thomas's works is in fact the work mentioned by Tocco. For Walz the date 1244–45 "seems most unlikely."[114] Walz was under the impression that all of Thomas's writings on logic pertain to the last months of his life, simply because the letter sent by the arts faculty to the Order after Thomas's death mentions works on logic. Grabmann has also opted for a later date, placing it between 1268 and 1272.[115] A. Michelitsch, however, considers *De fallaciis* to be the first work compiled by Thomas and dates it 1244. Mandonnet writes that if the opusculum is authentic, then it could have been written in 1244–45, during Thomas's captivity at Roccasecca.[116] There seems to be no basis whatever for the suggestion that the published *De fallaciis* is not in fact the one mentioned by Tocco. If the *De fallaciis* was written in 1244–45, then we must postulate the same date for the very short work *De propositionibus modalibus,* which also is a youthful compilation.

The "nobles in arts" to whom *De fallaciis* is dedicated would undoubtedly be his former classmates at Naples, who by 1244–45 would have been young regent masters in arts. This short work is divided into eighteen chapters and discusses the fourteen types of syllogistic error that can occur in a sophistical argumentation, or disputation. It is a more compact presentation than Aristotle's own *Sophistici Elenchi* on which, in a general sense, *De fallaciis* is based. It would seem, however, that *De fallaciis* is more immediately based on some current manual of fallacies, such as the *Fallaciae maiores* of Peter of Spain, rather than on the text of Aristotle itself. A companion treatise of Thomas's early years is *De propositionibus modalibus*. This fragment of 114 lines gives every impression of being excerpted from a letter, written, perhaps, to one of his former classmates at Naples. It was published by I.-M. Bocheński with a lengthy commentary in 1940.[117] Bocheński regards the text he edited on the basis of four manuscripts as a superficial student exercise, perhaps unworthy of the genius of Thomas, but authentic nevertheless. Therefore both of these works on logic should be dated c. 1244, while Thomas was confined to his quarters at Roccasecca.

Thomas, it would seem, was confined to Roccasecca until the summer of 1245. Bernard Gui, following Tocco and Tolomeo,[118] depicts a dramatic escape for Thomas from the family household at Roccasecca. According to this story Donna Theodora "gave orders, cunningly, to relax the guard and so make it possible for him to escape." He made his escape by a rope let down from his window into the hands of certain brethren of the Order, who were advised of the plan. Thus, in a manner reminiscent of St. Paul, Thomas was again made in legend to look like a fugitive from his family. The older version of the *Vitae Fratrum* and the more substantial report of Bartholomew of Capua simply say that Thomas was "let go."[119] It is inconceivable that Donna Theodora, who was a strong, sensible woman, would connive at an escape by means of a rope let down from Thomas's window. When she could not convince Thomas to change his plans and when Frederick II was deposed on July 17, 1245, by the Council of Lyons, thus reversing the Aquino fortunes, she would naturally allow Thomas to leave the family household honorably with her blessing. There is no need to dramatize the incident by providing a Pauline escape from captivity. The most probable turn of events was that when the time seemed opportune—after the deposition of Frederick II—Theodora allowed Thomas to inform his brethren at San Domenico that he would depart; he probably left in the company of Friar John of San Giuliano and returned to Naples to await further orders from the prior. This was in the summer of 1245.

The Order's original plan for Thomas was not abandoned, but was to be implemented immediately. Thomas was to travel north to Paris for the next few years. Bernard Gui states that after Thomas was restored to the Order, he "was sent from Naples to Rome, whence the venerable father John the German [i.e., John of Wildeshausen] took him to Paris."[120] On this point all biographers are agreed. But on a related point there has been much controversy. Gui states that Thomas was "sent next to Cologne," as do Tolomeo of Lucca and William of Tocco.[121] Scholars such as H. Denifle, J. V. De Groot, F. Pelster, Walz-Novarina, and I. T. Eschmann maintain that Thomas was sent to Cologne immediately after arriving in Paris. Some French and English scholars insist that Thomas remained in Paris for the next three years of his life and was not sent to Cologne until Albert opened the *studium generale* there in 1248. The problem, therefore, is interpreting the phrase "deinde Coloniam." P. Mandonnet, M.-D. Chenu, P. Glorieux, M. Grabmann, V. Bourke, K. Foster, R.-A. Gauthier, and many other scholars maintain that Thomas spent the years 1245–48 studying in Paris.

All the original sources agree that it was to Albert that Thomas was sent. For example, Bernard Gui, following the statement of William of Tocco, writes: "where the great teacher the lord brother Albert the German directed a flourishing school of philosophy and theology." Tolomeo of Lucca likewise states unequivocally that Thomas "went to Cologne to Friar Albert." In other words, the implication is that Thomas went to Cologne only when Albert was there and when the general studium was established. It was not established until 1248, when the general chapter ordered four *studia generalia* be established in the Order: Paris, Bologna, Oxford, and Cologne. The most probable view is that Thomas spent the years 1245–48 at Paris and then went to Cologne, possibly with Albert. There is, of course, no intrinsic reason why Thomas could not have gone immediately to Cologne in 1245, for Cologne was a flourishing city, second only to Paris. The Dominican house there always had an outstanding lector in theology to teach the entire community—and in 1245 Thomas was not qualified to do more than listen to the community lector. Cologne was an important city. In fact the general chapter of the Order convened at the priory in Cologne in 1245 under the presidency of John of Wildeshausen; John himself could have brought Thomas to Cologne. However, the view that Thomas spent the years 1245–48 in Paris seems to agree better with the sources.

If Thomas spent three years in Paris before accompanying Albert to Cologne in 1248, the problem becomes not textual, but historical. What did Thomas do during those three years at Paris? Various theories have been proposed. The two most intriguing suggestions are that Thomas studied under Albert at Paris, and that he enrolled in the arts course at the university. Both suggestions involve great difficulties.

The first view, which is the generally accepted one, neglects the ordinary protocol of university teaching. Albert was a master of theology at the University of Paris, as was the French master in the other chair. His students would have been university clerics and Dominican bachelors assigned to him. Saint-Jacques in Paris was not yet a *studium generale* of the Order. As far as we know, his hearers would not have been the entire community living at Saint-Jacques. The two possible ways out of this difficulty are to say that Albert's lectures as master also served as community lectures, or that he was also lector for the whole priory, either of which seems most improbable and not at all documented. The function of Dominican masters with regard to the whole religious community has not yet been studied carefully. We know that one of the functions of a bachelor in theology in a Dominican house was to serve as student-master for all young students and to hear their repetitions of classes held that day. But we do not know how masters fitted into community life except that they were bound to the same means of perfection incumbent on all, such as attendance at community Mass and at certain hours of the choral office. My only point is that it cannot be assumed that Thomas studied under Albert at Paris.

The second view of Thomas's activities in Paris neglects the type of student enrolled in the arts faculty. Gauthier would have Thomas studying ethics under arts masters at Paris.[122] But in the thirteenth century no religious, be he monk or friar, could be enrolled in arts at a university or a secular studium. The ancient monastic law was that monks should not study books of classical authors and philosophers without dispensation.[123] This regulation was adopted by the Dominicans in their earliest constitutions.[124] It was taken to mean that no religious should devote himself to the study of philosophers and classical authors such as were taught in the medieval faculty of arts. "In libris gentilium non studeant" was taken over by all mendicant friars and was strictly observed until the Dominicans found it necessary to establish *studia artium* in various provinces of the Order to supply the great need of youngsters entering the Order without university experience and knowledge; already in Thomas's day boys of eighteen were entering the Friars Preachers without the necessary training in philosophy to study theology in the universities. In earlier days many men became Dominican Friars after they had studied the arts, and in some cases theology. Thomas had studied the arts at Naples, even though he did not take his masterate in arts. After becoming a Dominican he would not and could not have matriculated at Paris to finish arts. He would have spent his three years at Paris, before his going to Cologne, in prayer, in private study under the lector of the house, and in observing the Dominican way of life. If Thomas had been enrolled in arts at the University of Paris in 1246–47, as Gauthier insists, it is difficult to see how he would have been exposed to so many secular masters teaching ethics. He could have acquired the same knowledge by privately studying their books.

Nothing has been said by biographers about Thomas's novitiate year. V. Bourke says in passing that Thomas "spent most of his novitiate at home."[125] This is doubtful, for the canonical year of novitiate had to be spent in some priory of the Order. Hence it would seem that although Thomas received the Dominican habit in Naples in April 1244, it was not until the summer of 1245 that he was able to begin his novitiate at the Priory of Saint-Jacques. At the end of the canonical novitiate year, he would have made solemn profession of vows in the hands of the prior.

In summer of 1248 Albert was sent to Cologne to organize and preside over the first *studium generale* in Germany, which was authorized by the Dominican general chapter meeting in Paris at Pentecost, June 7. There is every reason to think that Albert took

Thomas with him to prepare for an eventual return to Paris after preliminary studies had been completed. It was a rare privilege for Thomas. We do not know what Albert thought of young Thomas at that time, but he certainly must have seen possibilities.

Albert was an extraordinary man in every way. In his own lifetime he was called "the Great" (*Albertus Magnus*). To his contemporaries he was known under the scholastic titles of *Doctor universalis* and *Doctor expertus*. To him more than to any other man, credit is due for having explained and presented Aristotelian thought "to the Latins." While Albert cannot be credited with introducing Thomas to Aristotle, he certainly augmented Thomas's knowledge and encouraged its growth. Albert's writings lack the clarity, brevity, and simplicity of Thomas's, but he had a breadth of scholarship and Germanic thoroughness that far surpassed his disciple's. Albert's knowledge is found to be the more remarkable when one considers that he came upon the new Aristotelian learning when he was already middle-aged.

Albert was the eldest son of a powerful and wealthy German lord of military rank. He was born in Lauingen on the Danube, near Ulm, c. 1200. The date of his birth has been contested by many historians. One group, following Quétif-Echard, F. Pelster, and H. Scheeben, gives the date as 1193. Another group, following Mandonnet, P. Glorieux, F. Van Steenberghen, and E. Gilson, insists that Albert was born in 1206 or 1207. The date c. 1200, however, seems to fit all the known facts more securely.[126]

Albert received his early arts training in Padua, at that time home of one of the leading schools in northern Italy, known for its interest in natural science. In the summer of 1223 Jordan of Saxony arrived in Padua to preach to young men of the city. At first he found a very cold reception, but soon ten young clerics sought admission into the Dominican Order. Among them were "two sons of two great German lords; one was a provost-marshall, loaded with many honors and possessed of great riches; the other resigned rich benefices and is truly noble in mind and body."[127] The latter has always been identified as Albert of Lauingen. Apparently Albert did not complete his academic training, but joined the Order before becoming a master in arts. He too was introduced to some of the new Aristotelian learning during his early training at Padua.

Since the Dominicans did not have a house of their own in Padua, Albert was sent back to Germany for his novitiate training in theology in one of the many houses of the province. Shortly after 1233 he was appointed lector of theology in the new priory at Hildesheim, then successively at Freiburg im Breisgau, at Regensburg for two years, at Strassburg, and at Cologne. During these years of teaching he wrote his treatise *De natura boni*, influenced largely by Hugh of Saint-Victor and William of Auxerre. In a way, this treatise is an anachronistic work, reflecting more of twelfth-century theology than that of the thirteenth.

The situation changed drastically when Albert was sent to Paris, "the city of philosophers,"[128] to prepare for the mastership in theology. He arrived in Paris, sometime in the early 1240s, just as the new Aristotelian learning was being felt, when the works of Jewish, Moslem, and Greek learning were flooding the academic market. He found the intellectual climate of Paris vastly different from that of his native Germany.

We cannot be sure of Albert's chronology at this time. He may have lectured cursorily on the Scriptures as a *baccalaureus biblicus*, and then on the *Sentences* of Peter Lombard for two years, c. 1243–45; on the other hand, he may have lectured on the *Sentences* for four years (to judge from the bulk of his written commentary), in which more probable case he would have been *baccalaureus Sententiarum* from 1241 to 1245. At that time Albert seems to have been more concerned about acquiring the new Aristotelian learning than in commenting on Peter Lombard. In 1245 he incepted in theology under Guéric of Saint-Quentin, and he continued to lecture as master in the Dominican chair "for foreigners" until the end of the academic year 1248. Albert was in fact the first German Dominican to become a master in theology at Paris.

Thomas arrived in Paris in May 1245, just about the time that Albert incepted and began his teaching career as master. If Thomas did "study" under Albert at that time, he would have attended the master's lectures on the Bible and his disputations in theology. Albert had just begun to compile his vast encyclopedia of Aristotelian learning. Apparently some of Albert's *con-*

frères asked him to write something that would make Aristotle's works on natural science "intelligible to the Latins." In response he undertook to explain, paraphrase, quote, and discuss all the branches of human knowledge, adding contributions from the Arabs, and even creating entirely "new sciences."[129] These sciences ranged through logic, natural science, rhetoric, mathematics, astronomy, ethics, economics, politics, and metaphysics. "Our intention," he said, "is to make all the aforesaid parts of knowledge intelligible to the Latins." This vast project took him about twenty years to complete and is one of the marvels of medieval scholarship.

In the summer of 1248 Albert was sent to Cologne to organize and preside over the first Dominican *studium generale* in Germany, commissioned by the general chapter in June. Before Albert gave up his mastership in Paris, which he had held for three years (1245–48), he was appointed first master of the studium in Cologne. The Dominicans had a very important community at Heilige Kreuz; the original priory there had to be enlarged to provide for a *studium generale* that would serve students from many countries, particularly from northern and eastern countries. In 1248 the Dominicans purchased a house near Heilige Kreuz on a street called the Stolkgasse for this purpose.[130] All other *studia generalia* commissioned by the general chapter were established in cities where there already existed a large house and a university of some standing. But in Cologne there was only the cathedral school. The Dominican studium under Albert can therefore be considered the forerunner of the University of Cologne.

If Thomas did indeed accompany Albert from Paris to Cologne, as seems probable, there is no suggestion among the early biographers that Albert had the least inkling of Thomas's gifts. There are too many stories about Thomas during the Cologne years that reveal Albert's interest and surprise. On his part, Thomas could not have found a more suitable teacher than Albert, who already had an enviable reputation. During the time Thomas was with him, Albert was a full-time teacher and writer with no official ecclesiastical positions to disturb his much desired leisure to study and continue with his commentaries on the writings of Aristotle.

Albert was basically an Aristotelian in philosophy. Not only had he accepted and incorporated the fundamental Aristotelian ideas into his own world view, but he expounded Peripatetic thought in a way that would be intelligible to his Latin contemporaries. However, there are two points that should be kept in mind when discussing the Aristotelianism of Albert.

First, Albert did not accept all the statements he himself made in his commentaries on Aristotle. It is true that Albert did not hesitate to correct Aristotle's views when these views contradicted his own observation, adding arguments of his own and evaluating the misinterpretations made by other Peripatetics. There are very few views in his commentaries that are not also expressed in his theological writings, the surest proof of Albert's Aristotelianism. Moreover, by the time he had arrived in Cologne as first regent master, he had already rejected Aristotle's teaching on the eternity of the world, motion, and time. He had already identified the insidious doctrine of Averroes and Alexander of Aphrodisias, which required only one human intellect for all humanity. And he had already rejected the "error of Plato" defended by his own contemporaries "who held that natural things are founded on mathematical and mathematical being founded on divine, just as the third cause is dependent on the second, and the second on the first; and so [Plato] said that the principles of natural being are mathematical, which is completely false."[131] In a relatively late work, the *Metaphysics*, Albert said that he had already rejected this view in the *Physics*: "This is the error which I rejected in the books of the physics, and which I will again reject in the following books of this science." Nevertheless, in a number of explicit statements, Albert disclaimed all credit for the Peripatetic views expounded. He maintained that they were simply Peripatetic doctrines that could be found by anyone if he searched diligently. In Albert's mind there seems to have been a distinction between a paraphrase of the Peripatetic view and what he himself thought: "nor can anyone discern in it what I myself think in natural philosophy."[132] Again in the *Metaphysics* he says, "In this work I have said nothing according to my own view, but all the views stated are according to the statements of the Peripatetics; and if anyone wishes to prove this, let him read their books, and let them praise or reprimand them, not me."[133] After a similar renunciation in his exposition of the

Politics, Albert adds: "I say this because of certain indolent people, who looking for comfort in their indolence, look at nothing in script except what they can criticize."[134] In all these passages Albert seems to be rebuking members of his own Order who opposed the introduction of Aristotelian views into Christian thought. In an interesting passage in his commentary on the *Letters* of Pseudo-Dionysius, Albert explicitly rebukes his own brethren: "There are some people who are ignorant in all ways and they wish to fight the use of philosophy; this is especially true among the Dominicans, where no one stands in opposition to them. They are like brute animals blaspheming against things they do not know."[135] Thus it is difficult to determine exactly what Albert's thoughts in philosophy really were.

The second point to remember about Albert's Aristotelianism is that in his theology Albert had no hesitation in accepting many Platonic views expressed in Augustine, Pseudo-Dionysius, Avicenna, and the *Liber de causis.* In particular it was the reputed antiquity of Pseudo-Dionysius that carried most weight. Throughout most of the Middle Ages, after John Scotus Erigena (800–85), Latin scholasticism accepted Pseudo-Dionysius as an apostolic witness to the faith, and as one to be respected almost on a par with biblical authors. Augustine too was respected by everyone and considered an authority in theological discussions. Later in the thirteenth century a crisis was brought about when "Augustinists" sought the authority of St. Augustine in all matters even of natural philosophy, astronomy, and medicine. At that stage, Albert declared his preference for the teaching of Aristotle in natural philosophy, Ptolemy in astronomy, and Galen in medicine, while Augustine's authority was to be restricted to theology.

It would seem that Albert's German disciples, Hugh of Strassburg, Ulrich of Strassburg, John of Freiburg, John of Lichtenberg, and Giles of Lessines, were more impressed with Albert's Platonism than with his solid Aristotelianism. Their attitudes were transmitted through Theodoric of Freiberg and Berthold of Mosburg to Meister Eckhart and other fourteenth-century mystics, specifically John Tauler, Henry Suso, and Jan van Ruysbroeck. In the fifteenth century small groups of scholastics at Paris and Cologne identified themselves as "Albertists" in opposition to Thomists. These groups were founded by Heymericus de Campo (Van de Velde) in the fifteenth century to oppose St. Thomas on such questions as the real distinction between *quod est* and *esse* as well as the psychological and epistemological question of universals. These were all later developments and have nothing to do with Thomas's years of study under Albert.[136]

William of Tocco reports that Thomas "had no sooner heard [Master Albert] expound every science with such wonderous depth of wisdom, than he rejoiced exceedingly at having so quickly found that which he had come to seek, one who offered him so unsparingly the fulfillment of his heart's desire."[137] Tocco goes on to say that in order to profit from this exceptional opportunity, Thomas "began to be more than ever silent, more than ever assiduous in study and devout in prayer." It may or may not be true that his Dominican brethren in Cologne called him the "Dumb Ox" (*bovem mutum*), as Tocco stated.[138] If so, the phrase sums up the two well-known features of Thomas, his large physique and the constant reserve he had cultivated since adolescence.

Two other reported incidents in Thomas's life at this period seem likely enough. The first occurred while Albert was lecturing on the *De divinis nominibus* of Pseudo-Dionysius. That Albert did comment on this work while Thomas was studying with him at Cologne is known from the best possible source: Thomas's own handwritten notes. According to William of Tocco, a certain *confrère*, unaware of Thomas's maturing ability, offered to help him with his studies through this difficult book. In all humility Thomas accepted this help with gratitude. But no sooner had the brother started his explanation when he lost the thread of the argument. To encourage the helper, Thomas proceeded with the argument step by step, and "even added a number of things that the master had not explained." Thereupon the student asked Thomas to coach him instead, which Thomas is supposed to have done with the usual caution to "tell no one."

The second incident is the story about the page of notes that Thomas dropped by accident in the corridor outside his room. One of his brethren noticed it, looked at it, and decided to show the notes to Albert, who was much impressed by the intelligence and speculative power that these notes betrayed. It was at that time that Albert planned to have a scholastic disputation on a difficult question treated in class. Albert decided to put Thomas in the *respondens* position of bachelor at the scholastic exercise, and to see for himself what the Dumb Ox would do. It is said that Albert was so impressed with Thomas's ability on that occasion that he said, "We call him the Dumb Ox, but the bellowing of that ox will resound throughout the whole world."[139] There is no need to accept that statement as historical fact. The important point of the story is that Albert had come to learn of Thomas's ability, and consequently he did everything he could to develop him. H. C. Scheeben[140] may be right when he states that from this time on, Thomas performed the functions of a bachelor—responding at disputations, reading the Scriptures cursorily, and in general serving as an apprentice to Albert.

One important function of a bachelor, or assistant, was to lecture cursorily on one or other book of the Bible. The Parisian term for this function was *cursor biblicus,* or *baccalarius biblicus.* A *cursor* is one who "runs lightly" over the text, that is, reading it, paraphrasing difficult passages, and rendering superficial glosses on the text. This procedure was radically different from that followed by a master, whose task was to explain every problem in the text, raise theological questions, and determine the truth of the matter. The *expositio ordinaria* or *magistralis* belonged to the master alone. The basic purpose of the *cursor* was to familiarize himself and the students with the text of Scripture. Among Thomas's writings there are three biblical commentaries singled out for their "sterility of doctrine" (*doctrinae sterilitas*): on the Prophet Jeremiah, on the Lamentations of Jeremiah, and in part on Isaiah. In the sixteenth century, Sixtus of Siena denied the attribution of the *postilla super Jeremiam* to Thomas because of its "sterility of doctrine," but it is certainly possible that the three commentaries were produced by Thomas in Cologne as a bachelor under Albert, as I. T. Eschmann suggests. Normally such biblical commentaries or glosses do not survive, for as a rule they are not worth preserving. If the three works are indeed the result of Thomas's cursory lectures on the Bible, then we have in them a rare opportunity to examine the type of work a *cursor biblicus* was likely to produce.

There were only two courses of lectures and disputations given by Albert during Thomas's apprenticeship that we know of from the early biographers of Thomas. William of Tocco mentions only the lectures on *De divinis nominibus* of Dionysius and the *Nicomachean Ethics* of Aristotle. The lectures on *De divinis nominibus* are a *reportatio* in the "illegible hand" of Thomas; they are preserved in Naples, Bibl. Naz. I. B. 54, consisting of 142 folios. If there existed a second *reportatio* of these same lectures, we would be in a better position to evaluate Thomas's intellectual growth at this time. As it is, we have only the manuscript version preserved in Thomas's hand and the printed version in final form found in the collections of Albert's writings. This is small basis for making a judgment on Thomas, but it is an invaluable aid to the study of Albert's genius.

The second of Albert's courses of lectures, on the *Ethics* of Aristotle "with questions," has also come down to us in the notes preserved by Thomas. William of Tocco states that when Albert lectured on the *Ethics*, "Friar Thomas studiously assembled the lecture and put it in writing."[141] The text of this course, although not preserved in the autograph of Thomas, has been carefully studied by A. Pelzer, G. G. Meersseman, O. Lottin, and others.[142] Now that the text has been published, scholars have an easier opportunity to study it.

It may come as a surprise that Albert, master in theology from Paris, would have lectured on moral philosophy, for no master in theology would have stooped to lecture in philosophy at Paris. But Albert was no ordinary theologian; he was regent in a new *studium generale* of the German Province, and he was convinced of the importance of a sound philosophical foundation for theology. Moreover, the *Ethics* had been translated only recently (1246–47) by Robert Grosseteste, and Albert could not resist such an opportunity.

We can be certain that during the three years when Thomas was with him, Albert lectured on the Bible, the official text for theologians. Following Van Steenberghen, Bourke notes[143] that Albert's published lectures on the Psalms, Jeremiah, Daniel, the Gospels, and the Apocalypse date from these years; but there is good reason to doubt that the Gospel commentaries date from this time, and perhaps the commentary on the Apocalypse also should be dated later. What needs to be remembered when discussing Albert's lectures at this period is that he was continually at work on his Aristotle paraphrase; we also know that he finished the final version of his commentary on Book IV of the *Sentences* at Cologne in 1249.

One year after Thomas left for Paris, Albert was elected provincial of the German Province and served in this capacity for three years (1253–56). This administrative burden involved making decisions for the good of the whole province, visitating Dominican houses as well as convents of Dominican nuns, and undertaking long journeys on foot. Nevertheless, he continued his prolific writing and scientific research. In 1256 Albert was in the papal curia at Anagni with St. Bonaventure to defend the cause of mendicant Orders against the attacks of William of Saint-Amour and his colleagues. While at the curia at Anagni, he is said to have lectured on the whole of St. John's Gospel and on some of the Epistles. Whatever must be said concerning these "lectures in the curia," we are certain that he held a public disputation at the request of Pope Alexander IV against the Averroist doctrine of the unicity of the human intellect for all mankind.

Resigning his office of provincial, he resumed teaching in Cologne, 1257–60. But by the end of 1260 he was appointed to succeed a removed bishop of Regensburg. His own reluctance had the support of Humbert of Romans, general of the Dominican Order, but to no avail. On January 5, 1260, Pope Alexander IV ordered that Albert be installed as bishop of Regensburg. Subsequently, with conditions settled in the diocese of Regensburg and with the election of a new Pope, Albert was allowed to resign his see in 1262; but in February of the following year he was ordered by Urban IV to preach the seventh crusade throughout Germany and Bohemia (1263–64). It was not until 1269 that he was free to return to teaching and writing in Cologne. The interesting thing is that Albert, though burdened with many non-academic assignments, continued to write, lecture, and hold disputations. The four years during which Thomas studied under Albert (1248–52) were the most propitious years both in Albert's life and in the life of young Thomas.

Although Thomas severed relations with his family in the pur-

suit of learning and Dominican formation, we must not forget
that Emperor Frederick II was deposed from rulership by the
Council of Lyons on January 17, 1245. From the point of view of
the Holy See, the subjects of Frederick were no longer obliged to
recognize his authority as ruler; in fact, they were forbidden
to do so, and any assassination plot to remove the deposed Emperor would have been justified. There was such a plot to assassinate Frederick at Capaccio in 1246, when Thomas was in Paris
as a novice (or in Cologne, as the case may be), but it failed.
Involved in the conspiracy was Thomas's brother Reginaldo, who
had abducted him near Acquapendente, and the powerful Morra
family, related to Thomas by marriage. When the plot failed,
Frederick ordered Reginaldo's execution. The Aquino family
considered Reginaldo a "martyr" in the cause of the Pope, as we
have already mentioned. We have no idea how the assassination
attempt affected Thomas or whether he thought of his brother as
a "martyr." No doubt Thomas received the news of Reginaldo's
death with sorrow and a willingness to forgive all past injuries.

The position of the Aquino family was not secure. Others who
had taken part in the plot to assassinate Frederick were exiled
from the kingdom. Undoubtedly relatives of the Aquino family,
such as Roger de Morra, took refuge in Montesangiovanni in
papal territory, but with incomes severely reduced. According
to Thomas of Cantimpré and Tolomeo of Lucca, it was while
Thomas was a student in Cologne that Pope Innocent IV offered
him the dignity of the abbacy of Monte Cassino while allowing
him to remain a Dominican.[144] Such a benefice would have
been very profitable to the Aquino family. If such an offer was
indeed made sometime near the death of Abbot Stephen II in
January 1248, it was clearly instigated by the Aquino family.
But Thomas refused the benefice, just as he always refused ecclesiastical honors. The position of the Aquino family did not rest
secure until the death of Frederick II (December 13, 1250),
while Thomas was studying in Cologne.

One other point needs to be mentioned here: Thomas's ordination to the priesthood. The bull of canonization simply states that
after his profession "he made such progress both in science and
in the things of the spirit that he was raised to the priesthood
while he was still young."[145] The minimum canonical age for

ordination to the priesthood in the thirteenth century was twenty-five. Thomas became twenty-five years old in 1250. Therefore it would seem that Thomas was ordained in Cologne sometime in 1250 or 1251. The mendicant Orders of friars generally ordained their men at the earliest possible date, for reasons that were not always spiritual, just as they tended to produce as many masters in sacred theology from Paris as quickly as possible, contrary to the practice among the secular clergy. The secular clergy were wont to remain in their professorial chairs until something more lucrative came along; consequently they rarely promoted their bachelors to the rank of regent master.

In 1252, the master general John of Wildeshausen asked Albert to recommend some student who could be sent to Paris to prepare for the mastership in theology. Albert, according to William of Tocco, replied by letter, strongly recommending Thomas, "describing his proficiency in learning and religious life."[146] However, the master general hesitated to follow this recommendation, no doubt because of Thomas's age. Compared to all other students the Dominicans had ever had preparing for the mastership, Thomas was too young. Eschmann correctly states that the statutory age for clerics beginning to lecture on the *Sentences* at Paris was twenty-nine.[147] Thomas was only twenty-seven at the time Albert recommended him. Normally there might not have been any problem, for Dominicans easily obtained dispensations from the chancellor as well as from the Holy See. But the situation of the Friars was tense at that moment. The secular masters very bitterly objected to the Friars' presence because the latter had on several occasions shown their unwillingness to conform to university decisions (see the following chapter). Therefore it was inopportune to challenge university authorities just then through the nomination of a *Sententiarius* who needed a dispensation to begin lectures on the *Sentences* of Peter Lombard. But Albert knew how to apply pressure. He urged the Dominican cardinal Hugh of Saint-Cher, a former master of Paris, to support his candidate. The cardinal was, in 1252, a papal legate in Germany, and he met with John the Teuton in Soest in Westphalia to discuss Thomas's qualifications. Later Hugh of Saint-Cher wrote to John, urging him to send Thomas to Paris to prepare himself "ad legendum *Sententias*."[148] In Tocco's words, "At the instance of the Lord Cardinal Hugh, the master [general] accepted him [Thomas] as bachelor in the aforesaid studium [of Paris], writing to him and ordering him to proceed at once to Paris and to prepare himself to read the *Sentences*."

Besides the fact that it was Albert's idea to send Thomas immediately to Paris, and the fact that it was the insistence of Hugh of Saint-Cher that accomplished this, there are two small points to be noted. First, it was the prerogative of the master general, not of the university or the general chapter, to appoint men to the Dominican *studium generale* at Paris to prepare for the mastership in theology. Later it became the prerogative of the Dominican general chapter to appoint two men yearly to Paris "ad legendum *Sententias*." The second point is that the chosen Dominican began by lecturing on the *Sentences*, not cursorily on the Bible. The normal course for a secular cleric at Paris was this: on becoming a bachelor, he was a *cursor biblicus* for one or two years before going on to the *Sentences*. Mandonnet assumed that this "normal" course was followed also by Dominicans; hence he maintained that Thomas lectured cursorily on the Bible for two years first, and then on the *Sentences* for two years before incepting as a master. Even from what little we know now, we can say that no Dominican ever lectured cursorily on the Bible when he came to Paris. A dispensation from this first lectureship was readily granted to Dominicans because they had already lectured for several years on the Bible and were already familiar with it. The purpose of the *cursor biblicus* was to familiarize himself and his students with the text of Scripture. But every Dominican priory had a lector whose purpose it was to lecture on the Scriptures. It is clear from the master general's letter that Thomas was to proceed to Paris and prepare himself to lecture on the *Sentences* immediately; that is, he was appointed *baccalarius Sententiarum*, and not *cursor biblicus*. This must have been the case also with Albert himself, as we have intimated, although there is no documentary evidence to confirm it.

Thus in the fall of 1252 Thomas went to the Priory of Saint-Jacques in Paris to prepare himself to begin teaching the *Sentences*. These were troubled times in Paris. The amicable relations that existed earlier between the Dominicans and the secular masters of the university had turned to bitter hatred and strong opposition. It was into this milieu that Thomas was sent, too young in years and too reluctant in heart to engage in controversy. The antimendicant controversy was to overshadow all of Thomas's days in Paris. The Paris that Thomas entered was a Paris far different from the one Albert had known ten years earlier. Perhaps Albert did not realize this; or if he did, he had great confidence in the Thomas he "discovered."

Chapter II

"SENTENTIARIUS" IN THE CITY OF
PHILOSOPHERS

(1252–56)

In late summer of 1252 Thomas Aquinas and at least one companion arrived in Paris for the beginning of the academic year. Thomas was commanded by the master general, John of Wildeshausen, to prepare himself to lecture on the *Sentences* of Peter Lombard as a bachelor in theology, a *baccalarius Sententiarum*, or *Sententiarius*. There can be little doubt, judging from Bernard Gui's account of Thomas's reactions four years later,[1] that Thomas was fearful and overawed by the assignment, fully convinced of his own insufficiency. Not only was he canonically too young to undertake the assignment, but he was also considerably younger than all of his Dominican predecessors at the university. Most of his predecessors were in their forties when they lectured on the *Sentences*; Thomas was only twenty-seven years old. Most of his predecessors were better prepared than he, having degrees in arts and many years of experience lecturing on the Bible in various houses of the Order; Thomas was *cursor biblicus* under Albert for only a few years. He had reason to be apprehensive.

Thomas was assigned to Paris thirty-five years after the first Dominicans arrived "to study, preach, and establish a priory."[2] It was twenty-four years after the first Dominican, Roland of Cremona, lectured on the *Sentences* for one year before becoming a master. Thomas arrived at Saint-Jacques at a time when tension was mounting against mendicants at the university. In the early days of the Order, the University of Paris welcomed the new Preachers with open arms; it provided a secular master of theology to be their teacher and protector; it even provided a house and chapel, which would become the famous Priory of Saint-Jacques.

Grounds for dissension were supplied almost from the very beginning of Dominican participation in the university, when the Order acquired a second chair of theology during the dispersal of the masters between March 1229 and April 1231. During the thirties and forties the Order showed itself more interested in producing a great number of masters in theology for the whole Church than in contributing to the closed solidarity of masters loyal to the faculty of theology as such. By the early 1250s, animosity between some secular masters of the university and mendicant friars grew in intensity, dividing the city of philosophers into two opposing groups: secular masters under William of Saint-Amour, claiming papal privileges, ancient tradition, and the oath taken by all to protect the rights of the university; and mendicant friars, who also claimed papal protection, privileges, and dispensations. Thomas's first active years in Paris, from 1252 to 1259, were most crucial for the mendicants and for the teaching career of Thomas himself.

Saint-Jacques and the University

In 1217, perhaps on Pentecost, May 14,[3] St. Dominic assembled his sixteen followers and announced his intention to send them throughout the world. He announced that seven would go to Paris and four to Spain, leaving himself and five brethren at Saint-Romain in Toulouse. The result of this announcement was not only consternation, but also strong opposition from the small band of followers, from bishops, and from Simon de Montfort. The Order had been fully approved by Honorius III only a few months previous, on December 22, 1216. But Dominic would not be dissuaded. On August 15, 1217, the appointed seven set out for Paris in two groups, having elected one of their number, Matthew of Paris, to be their superior with the extraordinary title of abbot. The title was never again used in the Dominican Order, but at the time it signified that Matthew would be Dominic's representative in Paris and successor in the Order should Dominic die before other provisions could be made. The second general chapter of the Order, held in Bologna in 1221 under the direction of Dominic, established the permanent title of local superior as "prior" for a canonically established priory, and "provincial" over a whole province of priories. The Parisian group was the first to establish a priory beyond Toulouse, that of Saint-Jacques, and Matthew became its first prior.[4]

The first group to set out for Paris consisted of Dominic's brother, Mannes, the lector Michael of Fabra, and a lay brother, Odier of Normandy. They arrived in Paris on September 12, 1217. The second group, arriving three weeks later, consisted of Matthew of Paris, Bertrand of Garrigues, John of Navarre, and Lawrence of England. Of these the two most important Friars were Matthew of Paris, who was superior of the community, and Michael of Fabra, who was to be its first lector in theology. Dominic thus established the rule expressed later in the primitive constitutions: "A priory without a prior and teacher shall not be allowed."[5] The Friars presented themselves to Peter of Nemours, bishop of Paris, and showed him the papal bull establishing the Order and recommending it to the hierarchy. The bishop allowed the Friars to rent the hospice of Notre Dame, opposite the bishop's residence, and opened the doors of the theological school of the cathedral chapter. The Friars rented this unsatisfactory hospice for less than a year. Even the Pope's personal letter of recommendation of February 1218 brought no favor or help from Bishop Peter of Nemours, who was leaving Paris on a crusade to the east with the king.[6] The situation did not change until Pope Honorius III requested the university to intervene.

Apparently, a letter of Pope Honorius III, dispatched from Rome about the month of April 1218, asked the university in general and perhaps master John of St. Albans, dean of the chapter of Saint-Quentin, in particular to provide suitable lodging for the Preachers, to protect the new Order, and to instruct the Friars in theology.[7] This letter is no longer extant, but in the letter of May 4, 1221, Honorius refers to the fact that master John, dean of Saint-Quentin, was teaching the Preachers "by our command."[8]

This master John of St. Albans, as W. A. Hinnebusch points out, has been generally known to historians since 1633 as "John of Barastre."[9] This designation of master John is completely unknown in the sources, which refer to him solely as John of St. Albans or John, dean of Saint-Quentin. The anonymous compiler of the *Monumenta Conventus Sanjacobei* states that he was an Englishman who came to Paris to study medicine, but who, after obtaining his degree and practicing for a short time, renounced this to study theology. The place name of master John as of "St. Albans," an almost exclusively English place name, would indicate that he was an Englishman.[10] He seems to have lectured in the theological faculty at Paris for thirteen or fourteen years before relinquishing his chair to John of St. Giles, another Englishman who first studied and practiced medicine before turning to theology. It was not at all uncommon for an English student to seek an English master. Both of these English masters played an important and indispensable role in the relation between Saint-Jacques and the university. At the time the Friars arrived in Paris in 1217, master John of St. Albans was also chaplain to the king, Philip Augustus, whose confidence he fully had.[11]

On receipt of the letter from Honorius, master John and the university provisionally gave the Dominicans a hospice with a chapel at the far end of the Grand rue Saint-Benoît, adjacent to the Porte d'Orléans. It was at the far end of the left-bank area that would later be called the Latin Quarter. The hospice was originally built in 1209 by master John and his friend Simon de Poissy and his wife Agnes, as a hostel for students at the university, but as time went on it became rather a hostel for pilgrims traveling to or from the shrine of Saint James at Compostella in Spain. The hostel and chapel were naturally dedicated to St. James; eventually it was given to the custody of the university for its original purpose.[12] The donation made by John and the university to the Friars Preachers was made on a temporary basis sometime in the summer of 1218.[13] On behalf of the Preachers, Matthew of Paris accepted this donation; and on August 6, 1218, he and his six companions moved to Saint-Jacques.[14] This is the official date for the founding of the Dominican Priory of Saint-Jacques in Paris. The Dominicans were given full possession of the building and land on May 3, 1221.[15] In this donation, master John and the university claimed only the usual privileges of founders and patrons, which included special place of honor in gatherings, prayers, Masses, and a share in all the good works of the brethren.

But there was a special problem about this arrangement. The chapel of Saint-Jacques was in the parish of Saint-Benoît, which, together with two other churches in the area, belonged to the cathedral chapter of Notre Dame. Therefore the Dominicans were prohibited from chanting Divine Office or holding any public service in the chapel lest revenues be taken from Saint-Benoît. It was not until the summer of 1220 that a settlement was made at the insistence of Honorius III. But even this was not fully satisfactory, for besides having to pay an annual indemnity to compensate Saint-Benoît and the canons of Notre Dame for any diminution of revenues from offerings, burial fees, and gifts, the Friars were allowed to hold public services only on certain major feast days.[16]

When St. Dominic arrived in Paris toward the end of June 1219, he found a community of thirty Friars.[17] Despite the restrictions on preaching and holding public services at Saint-Jacques, a surprising number of young men entered the Order, some of them clerics with a degree in arts. Because of the restriction on preaching, Dominic, anxious to recruit members of the university, gave colloquia, or informal discussions, that persuaded "many excellent clerics" to join the Preachers.[18] Among the students who listened to Dominic's informal talks at Paris was Jordan of Saxony, master in arts and bachelor in sacred theology, who heard him tell of the vocation and miraculous cure of Reginald of Orléans.[19] Although Jordan was moved by Dominic and opened his heart to him, he did not enter the Order until almost a year later, for Dominic simply suggested that he become a deacon.[20]

Reginald of Orléans was a most extraordinary man. He had been dean of Saint-Anian in Orléans, had studied canon law at Paris, and had taught there for five years.[21] Moreover he had a dynamic personality that appealed to young men, and he was a persuasive preacher. He wanted to devote his life and ability as a preacher in an apostolate of evangelical poverty but was uncertain how to go about it. During Lent of 1218 Reginald passed through Rome on a pilgrimage to Palestine with his bishop, Manasses of Seignelay, but he fell seriously ill, and doctors de-

spaired of his life. However, he was miraculously cured through
the intervention of the Blessed Virgin, who anointed his feet and
showed him a habit of the Dominican Order.[22] Reginald immediately made his profession in the hands of St. Dominic, who
was prepared to send him directly to Bologna, where the small
group was sadly in need of leadership and a new priory. But
Bishop Manasses insisted that Reginald accompany him to Palestine as planned. On his return from the Holy Land, Reginald
went directly to Bologna, where he arrived on December 21,
1218, and received the Dominican habit. Reginald was so much
like Dominic that Dominic made him his vicar in Bologna,[23]
just as he had made Matthew his vicar in Paris. Reginald worked
an astounding change in the community at Bologna by his sanctity, eloquence, dedication, and personal magnetism.[24] Within
a short time, he brought many university students and professors
into the Order and secured the church and domicile of St. Nicholas of the Vineyards, which was more satisfactory than the one
they were living in.[25] During this time Reginald received Roland
of Cremona into the Order, who was to become the first Dominican master in theology at Paris.[26] Since Paris was more important than Bologna at the time, Dominic decided to send Reginald to Paris, much to the dismay of the Bolognese, to appeal to
professors rather than only to undergraduates, and to work out
some legal settlement between Saint-Jacques and the canons of
Notre Dame. Reginald thus succeeded Matthew as prior and
vicar in Paris.

Master Reginald of Orléans arrived at Saint-Jacques toward
the end of October 1219.[27] Although Reginald's preaching drew
great crowds and moved many, only two made profession into
his hands before he died: Jordan of Saxony, the second master
general of the Order, and his intimate companion Henry, canon
of Utrecht, who later became prior at Cologne. Jordan himself
tells us, "I know that at Paris Master Reginald received the profession of only two persons; of these I was the first; the other was
Friar Henry."[28] However, as Jordan relates, he and Henry delayed until Ash Wednesday, February 12, 1220, after the death
of Reginald, when Jordan, Henry, and a companion Leo received
the Dominican habit and began their novitiate (*tirocinium*).[29]
Jordan, Henry, and Leo were among the first German clerics

received into the Order; German laymen had been received
into the Order a few years earlier. Reginald died probably in
January 1220, and was buried in the church of St. Mary of the
Fields, since the Dominicans had not yet acquired their own
cemetery.[80]

The construction of the new Priory of Saint-Jacques, completed in "two years," began early, probably in 1219 or 1220,
made possible by the munificence of King Louis IX of France.[81]
Not only did the Dominicans live almost exclusively on alms
provided by the king, but the new priory itself owed to him its
dormitory and its great refectory ("large enough to accommodate 300 friars").[82] The average number of Friars at Saint-
Jacques in the 1220s and 1230s was 100, and there is record of
more than 120 Friars in 1223.[83] The new structure was sufficiently complete for the Order to hold its third general chapter
there in 1222. At this general chapter Jordan of Saxony was
elected to succeed Dominic, who had died on August 6, 1221.
Between 1222 and 1245, the general chapter of the Order, meeting annually at Pentecost, alternated between Paris and Bologna.

More important for our purpose is the fact that the Holy See
and the University of Paris looked upon the Dominicans at
Saint-Jacques as students of theology, not as mendicants or even
as religious. The papal bull of March 4, 1220, explicitly refers to
our "beloved sons, the friars of the Order of Preachers, studying
the sacred page at Paris."[84] The university gave them a house
intended for students and a respected master as protector and
teacher. Master John of St. Albans, a secular master, began lecturing within the priory itself sometime in 1220. Master John, in
other words, established his professorial chair within the walls
of Saint-Jacques and instructed not only the secular clerics enrolled under him, but also the whole Dominican community. His
ordinary lectures would have been exclusively on the text of
Sacred Scripture. If he had a bachelor studying under him, this
bachelor would have given cursory lectures on the text of Scripture and possibly given ordinary lectures on the Sentences of
Peter Lombard. But it is not certain that in the 1220s master
John would have had a bachelor, for the term and clarification
of the bachelor's function were not introduced until 1231.[85] It
would seem that at least in the beginning the lectures of the

secular master replaced the function of the Order's lector in the priory. According to Glorieux, John of St. Albans continued to lecture in his chair of theology until 1226, when a secular student, John of St. Giles, became master and succeeded John of St. Albans and continued lecturing to the Dominicans. Unfortunately none of the writings or lectures of John of St. Albans are known today.[36]

Thus the Priory of Saint-Jacques became the foremost studium in the Order, but it was not until 1248 that it became a *studium generale* together with Bologna, Oxford, and Cologne. From the very beginning of Dominican participation in the university, Dominican Houses of Study in Paris and elsewhere were "public studia." That is, non-Dominican religious and the secular clergy were free to attend lectures in the priory and share in the riches of knowledge. This was the common legislation in the Dominican constitutions until recent years.[37] The "public" character of Dominican studia was necessitated by the relations between Saint-Jacques and the University of Paris, since John of St. Albans, John of St. Giles, and all Dominican masters were members of the university. The same situation obtained in Bologna and later in Oxford.

The colloquia of Friar Matthew of Paris and Reginald of Orléans moved many clerics to enter the Order. Among the more outstanding novices received by Matthew were Vincent of Beauvais, future author of the *Speculum maius* and tutor of royalty; Gérard of Frachet, future provincial and author of the *Vitae Fratrum;* André de Longjumeau, future companion of Louis IX during the crusades and ambassador to the Moslems of Egypt and Palestine; Clement and Simon Taylor, the two founders of the English Province; and a certain "Geoffroy de Blévex, one of the more renowned masters in theology of the University of Paris."[38]

The preaching of Bl. Jordan of Saxony recruited an astonishing number of clerics. During the first four weeks of his preaching in Paris after he became master general in 1222, twenty-one clerics entered, six of them being masters in arts; in 1228 he received forty; and in 1236, his last appeal, he brought seventy-two into the Order.[39]

Between 1223 and 1263 the Dominicans at Saint-Jacques ac-

quired considerable property either by purchase or donation.[40]
A spacious new church was completed about 1259. The complex
of the priory and church of Saint-Jacques became one of the
larger establishments on the left bank; the fronting street itself
was renamed, from the Grand rue Saint-Benoît to the rue Saint-
Jacques, extending from Petit Pont to the Porte d'Orléans, later
called Porte Saint-Jacques. The entire structure, however, was
destroyed during the French Revolution in the eighteenth century.

The reception of Roland of Cremona (d. 1259) into the Order
by Reginald of Orléans, while the latter was prior of San Niccolò
in Bologna in 1219, caused an extraordinary furor, for Roland
was a renowned master in arts, "the glory of the University of
Bologna."[41] He was immediately sent to Paris as lector in the
Priory of Saint-Jacques, but he was relieved of this obligation
by the general chapter of May 17, 1220; no doubt master John
was at that time beginning his lectures within the priory. There
is no record of Roland's whereabouts between 1220 and 1228,
when he was sent to the general chapter meeting in Paris on
Pentecost under the generalship of Jordan of Saxony. But it was
in Paris that arrangements were made for Roland to enroll under
master John of St. Giles as *Sententiarius* for one year, 1228–29,
before incepting as master—the first Dominican to do so. Most
likely Roland spent the years 1220 to 1228 teaching theology in
various Dominican priories, so that when he arrived, his degree
in arts from Bologna and his teaching experience in theology
could have been and were accepted by the University of Paris as
equivalent to studies done in Paris. His *Summa super Sententias*
in the form of disputed questions has been published only in
part.[42] It seems that after his inception as master, Roland continued to lecture on the *Sentences,* as did many others, as we
shall see.

In May 1229,[43] Roland of Cremona obtained from the chancellor the license to incept as a master in theology, just when the
masters of the university had voted to go on strike on March 27,
1229. Master John of St. Giles and the community of Dominicans
saw no reason to join the strikers as they left Paris, for the
studium of Saint-Jacques was intact and could carry on the ordinary teaching as usual. At that time the masters of theology at

Paris had twelve chairs of theology; Roland apparently succeeded in the chair held by Bl. Boniface from 1222 to 1229.[44]
This was the first chair obtained by the Dominicans. Boniface
went to Cologne during the dispersion of the masters and was
there named bishop of Lausanne on March 11, 1231, before the
return of Parisian masters in April 1231.[45]

Usually when masters of a university wished to redress a
grievance against the town or ecclesiastical authority, they
would suspend all academic acts, that is, they would vote to
go on strike. In serious situations, they would even leave the
city with their students and teach elsewhere. This is what happened in Paris during the "great dispersal of scholars" from
March 1229 to April 1231; masters and students simply left
Paris for other centers of learning. This was an effective way of
putting economic pressure on the town, for this meant a considerable financial loss to the town.

Considering the fact that the Dominicans did not join in the
university protest, it is very puzzling how Roland could have
been accepted so readily by the community of masters when it
returned in April 1231. It is even more difficult to imagine how
Roland could have been accepted as *Sententiarius* for only one
year, and function as master for only one additional year, contrary to all previous custom. In any case, Roland was a bachelor
for one year (1228–29) and regent master for one year (1229–
30).

While Roland was regent master in the Dominican priory together with the secular master John of St. Giles, he had as his
bachelor, or assistant, Hugh of Saint-Cher (d. March 19, 1263).
Hugh was undoubtedly much better qualified academically than
Roland, for he was a doctor of law from Paris and was already a
bachelor in theology when he entered the Order of Preachers on
February 22, 1226.[46] Hugh of Saint-Cher likewise lectured on
the *Sentences* for only one year, 1229–30, succeeding Roland as
master from 1230 to 1235.[47] From facts such as these we know
that bachelors did lecture on the *Sentences* before the term
"bachelor" and the bachelor's proper functions came into statutory use from 1231 on. But both Roland and Hugh continued to
lecture on the *Sentences* even after they became masters. It was

only later that lecturing on the *Sentences* was reserved to bachelors, the *Sententiarii*.

During the "great dispersion" of masters and students, master John of St. Giles himself entered the Order of Preachers. On September 22, 1230, John preached a moving sermon in Saint-Jacques on the virtues of evangelical poverty; at mid-point he descended from the pulpit to receive the Dominican habit and then returned to the pulpit to finish his convincing sermon.[48] It is a significant point that John of St. Giles kept his professorial chair in the university, retaining it for three years after joining the Order. The procedure was the same when, in 1236 or early in 1237, the English master Alexander of Hales became a Franciscan and continued in that chair for at least another two years, before John of Rochelle, a Franciscan, succeeded him. Thus it was that, during the "great dispersion" of the academic community, the Dominicans obtained two chairs in theology: one from Roland's inception as a Dominican and one from John of St. Giles's conversion—both of them established within the Priory of Saint-Jacques. The Franciscans obtained their one chair later, after the return of masters and students.

Since September 14, 1207, the university was allowed only eight chairs of theology by the letter of Pope Innocent III.[49] But by 1218 the university was allowed to have twelve chairs, three of which were reserved for the canons of Notre Dame, including the chancellor.[50] The two Dominican chairs and the one Franciscan chair did not effect any change in the number of chairs of theology in the university: Roland of Cremona succeeded Boniface, and John of St. Giles retained his legitimate chair; and when Alexander of Hales became a Franciscan around 1236, he likewise retained his former chair. In 1258 three more chairs were authorized to accommodate the Cistercians, the Benedictines, and the monks of Val-des-Ecoliers.

It is interesting that Roland of Cremona could legitimately incept in theology during the dispersion of the masters, and that John of St. Giles became a Dominican during this same period. These events were readily accepted when the secular masters returned to Paris and resumed teaching in April 1231, but nevertheless they were the source of the hostility turned toward the mendicant friars twenty years later.

The Franciscans, who received full confirmation from Pope Honorius III on November 29, 1223, arrived in Paris in 1219, just two years after the Dominicans. It would seem that when they arrived in the intellectual center of Christendom, they had no idea of becoming attached to the university, but rather sought to save souls through their example of evangelical poverty and exhortative preaching. Under Friar Pacificus, who became their first provincial, they at first lived near the Abbey of Saint-Denise outside the city. In 1228 there were thirty Franciscans living in that house. In 1231 the friars moved into the city and began to build on land belonging to the Abbey of Sainte-Germain des Près, near the university quarter. Three years later the Franciscans received this property from the abbey through the kind bequest of King Louis IX.[51] The site was enlarged in 1240, and the Grand Couvent des Cordeliers was built; in 1263 the church was consecrated, and it became one of the officially recognized churches for the preaching of university sermons. By this time the Franciscans were fully incorporated into the university. By 1298 there were 140 Franciscans living in the Great Convent of the Cordeliers.[52] Eventually the street in which the Franciscans lived was renamed rue des Cordeliers, which intersected the rue Saint-Jacques at the Dominican priory, and hence not far from the Priory of Saint-Jacques.

It is not certain whether there was any kind of theological instruction given to the Franciscan friars before Alexander of Hales became a Franciscan in 1236 (or early 1237).[53] Naturally he brought his professorial chair with him, much as master John of St. Giles had done for the Dominicans. It is possible that Alexander of Hales performed the same office for the Franciscans as did John of St. Albans for the Dominicans, namely lecturing to the whole community, but there is no evidence of this. Alexander of Hales was a wealthy young Englishman who caused "a sensation in the academic world" when he became a mendicant at the age of forty or more, just thirty years after the death of St. Francis of Assisi (October 3, 1226), and seven years after the first Dominican lectured in the University of Paris.

Alexander lectured to the Franciscan community and some seculars for only two years before surrendering the chair to his student and successor, John of Rochelle. John lectured as master in the Franciscan chair for six years until his death early in 1245; Alexander died a few months later (August 15, 1245). However, the succession of Franciscans was established:

Franciscan Chair[54]

Alexander of Hales	1236–38
John of Rochelle	1238–44
Odo Rigaldi	1244–47 (later bishop of Rouen)
William of Melitona	1247–54
St. Bonaventure	1254–57 (later minister general and cardinal)

It is impossible to say what would have happened if Alexander of Hales had not become a Friar Minor. There might not have been an intellectual tradition in the Franciscan Order. "If we put together the few statements St. Francis made on the matter of studies," wrote Gilson, "it is clear that he never condemned learning for itself, but that he had no desire to see it developed in his Order. In his eyes it was not in itself an evil, but its pursuit appeared to him unnecessary and dangerous. Unnecessary, since a man may save his soul and win others to save theirs without it; dangerous because it is an endless source of pride."[55] Once the Franciscan chair was recognized by the *consortium magistrorum* of Paris, there was never any attempt to suppress it from the university, but there was a widespread antimendicant sentiment, which felt that mendicants had no right to be in the university at all.

Once the Dominicans obtained two chairs of theology in the university, there was need for some orderly procedure in filling them with a succession of Dominican masters. The Dominican general chapter decided that one of the two chairs was to be filled by members of the Province of France; this was the chair originally filled by Roland of Cremona, who was succeeded by Hugh of Saint-Cher. The other chair was reserved for "foreigners," that is, Dominicans from all the other provinces put together; this chair, brought into the Order by the Englishman John of St. Giles, was the one filled by Thomas d'Aquino when he incepted as master.

A schema will help to make clear the succession of masters up to the time Thomas became regent master in theology:[56]

Chair for Externs		Chair for Parisians	
John of St. Giles	1230–33	Roland of Cremona	1229–30
Guéric of Saint-		Hugh of Saint-Cher	1230–35
Quentin	1233–42	Godefroid of Bléneau	1235–42
Albert the Great	1245–48	Stephen of Venizy	1242–43
Elias Brunet	1248–56	Lawrence of Fougères	1243–44
Thomas Aquinas	1256–59	William of Etampes	1244–48
		Bonhomme	1248–55
		Florent of Hesdin	1255–57
		Hugh of Metz	1257–58
		Bartholomew of Tours	1258–59

Each of these masters was previously enrolled on the university *matricula* of his predecessor as a bachelor. Although the writings and lectures of the majority of these men are now lost or unknown, it may be safe to suggest that each bachelor lectured on the *Sentences* for one year or more before incepting, as well as responding in public disputations. By the time of Thomas d'Aquino, the function of the bachelor was fairly well established in the curriculum of the university. Normally the bachelor had to lecture on the Bible *cursorie*, that is, he was a *biblicus* for one year unless the equivalent had been exercised in some recognized *studium* or priory. Then he became a lecturer on the *Sentences* for at least one, more often two years, and in some cases four years. Besides lecturing on the *Sentences* under the direction of the master, the *Sententiarius* had also to respond in "ordinary disputations" and in the Lenten and Advent quodlibets. It would seem that at Paris few if any Dominican bachelors in the thirteenth century had to lecture *cursorie* on the Bible, for they had already functioned in this capacity elsewhere. However, provision for bachelors lecturing *cursorie* was made in later statutes of the university.[57] At least it is certain, Mandonnet and others notwithstanding, that when Thomas Aquinas arrived in Paris in 1252, he was to lecture on the *Sentences* as *Sententiarius* and not on the Bible as *biblicus*. By this time, lecturing on the four books of the *Sentences* was restricted to bachelors, and masters were ordered to lecture exclusively on the Bible and dispute as they would.

"Sententiarius" in Paris

(1252–56)

Thomas's four years of lecturing on the *Sentences* were turbulent years beset with many vicissitudes arising from the antimendicant controversy and from legislation brought on by this controversy. The scene was hostile from the very day Thomas arrived in Paris. The history of this controversy and Thomas's role in it will be considered later. Here we are interested in Thomas the bachelor lecturing in Saint-Jacques to fulfill the requirements for inception as master.

When settled at Saint-Jacques, Thomas would have to be enrolled on the *matricula* of a master. That is, he would have to have a master under whom to work. This was an old requirement, long antedating the statutes of Robert Curçon in 1215: "There is to be no student at Paris who does not have a definite master."[58] Thomas had only one choice, since he was preparing to occupy the Dominican chair for "foreigners." Elias Brunet from the Province of Provence was regent master in theology in the Dominican chair for "foreigners" from 1248 to 1256, that is, from the time Albertus Magnus relinquished his chair until the time Thomas incepted. Unfortunately no writings of Brunet are known to exist.

The "sentences" were a systematic collection of patristic texts intended to probe more deeply into the mysteries of faith. Such collections were the logical development of biblical glosses. These biblical glosses followed the order of the Bible. But the "sentences" were a rearrangement of patristic views (*sententiae Patrum*), touching on all major Christian teaching following the order of the Creed: the Trinity, creation and creatures, Christ and the virtues, and finally the sacraments and the four last things. There were many such collections of "sentences" in the early twelfth century, originating largely from the school of

Laon under Anselm and Ralph. The most extensive and success-
ful collection was that compiled in four books by Peter Lombard
in Paris about the middle of the twelfth century. The success of
this collection owed little to the fact that Peter Lombard was
bishop of Paris (1159–60), but rather followed from the character of the work itself. It traced a moderate course between the
excessive rationalism urged by the school of Peter Abelard and
the extreme positivism followed by the more traditional theolo-
gies of the monks. It was, in fact, a happy combination of patristic and biblical authorities (later called "positive" theology)
with speculative rationalism sponsored by the new breed of
scholastic theologians. In the prologue, Peter Lombard stated
that his purpose was to present sacred doctrine "in a small
volume consisting of patristic views (*Patrum sententias*) together with their testimony, so that the inquirer would not have
to search through numerous tomes, for the synthesized brevity
which he seeks is offered here without much labor." He goes on
to say that he wishes to have "not only the favorable reader, but
also the generous critic, especially where it is a profound question of truth, which would have as many proponents as it has
dissenters."

Peter not only presented long passages from the writings of
the Church Fathers and other early authorities, but also posed
new problems for speculation. Sometimes he would offer a solution, but oftentimes he abstained, leaving further speculation to
others.

Despite the fact that Peter made generous use of "positive"
patristic and biblical sources, he was severely attacked by Walter
of Saint-Victor (d. after 1180) as one of the "four monsters of
France," the others being Peter Abelard, Gilbert of Poitiers, and
Peter of Poitiers.[59] Theologians opposed to the scholasticism of
the schoolmen feared the growth of rationalism in matters of
faith and the attempt to put "God into a syllogism." Peter of
Poitiers (d. 1196) produced the earliest gloss on Peter Lombard's *Sentences* and produced his own *Sententiarum libri* V
before 1175 (PL 211).

If we are to believe Roger Bacon, the English master Alexander of Hales was the first to lecture publicly on the *Sentences*
while a master of theology.[60] According to Bacon this was the

fourth fault, or "sin," in the teaching of theology, for it led theologians to prefer the subtleties of the *Sentences* over the simplicity of the Bible. Nevertheless, thus it was that "Alexander, still a secular master of theology, began the practice among theologians at the University of Paris of using the *Sentences* of Peter Lombard as the ordinary text for his lectures in theology."[61] The Franciscan editors of Alexander's *Glossa in quatuor libros Sententiarum Petri Lombardi* place the date of its composition between 1223 and 1227. We have already seen that the two earliest Dominican masters, Roland of Cremona and Hugh of Saint-Cher, lectured on the *Sentences* both while they were undergraduates and while they were fully qualified masters from 1229 to 1235. The first to lecture on the *Sentences* at Oxford, at a later date, was the Dominican master Richard Fishacre, while he was a master (c. 1241–48); we know that his doing so evoked a strong rebuke from Robert Grosseteste, bishop of Lincoln, in 1245, so that the Pope had to intervene in order to allow Fishacre to continue in this practice.[62] At Paris the definitive role of bachelor was established after 1231, and the task of giving ordinary lectures on the *Sentences* was restricted to the bachelor. We do not know when this clarification came about at Paris; it must have been sometime around 1235–40 that the status of bachelor was canonically established. In any case, by the time Thomas arrived in Paris in 1252, it was the role of the bachelor to be an apprentice under a determined master, to lecture *ordinarie* on the *Sentences* from two to four years, and to respond to objections in certain theological disputations. Apart from the short interval when the practice of Alexander of Hales was followed, the basic text for all masters in theology was the Bible, the *sacra pagina*.[63]

The brevity, clarity, and veracity of Thomas's lectures as master, noted by his early biographers, were already evident in his lectures on the *Sentences*. Although Thomas relied heavily on the lectures of his former teacher, Albert the Great, his own style of teaching shows clarity of thought, brevity of expression, and directness of approach.[64] This is not to say that Thomas's *Scriptum super Sententias* is without subtlety or complexity. It is in fact a work of much labor and thought, representing the very best he was capable of at the time. According to Bernard Gui,

"God graced his teaching so abundantly that it began to make a wonderful impression on the students. For it all seemed so novel —new arrangements of subject-matter, new methods of proof, new arguments adduced for the conclusions; in short, no one who heard him could doubt that his mind was full of a new light from God."[65] Roughly the *Scriptum* on the *Sentences* can be compared with the modern Ph.D. thesis. Although the *Scriptum* is a work of genius, it does not represent the final and definitive thought of Thomas, such as we find in his later works, particularly the *Summa contra gentiles*, the *Summa theologiae*, and his *Quaestiones disputatae*.

In his lectures, Thomas followed the normal procedure of the age: he (or another) read a passage of the text of Peter Lombard aloud, which was then analyzed through a *divisio textus*; he explained cursorily the meaning of each point made, and then a question or series of questions arising from the text was analyzed. The basic unit of discussion was the *quaestio*, which was divided into articles and even *quaestiunculae*. The analysis of the question reveals the scholastic method at its best.[66] The proposal to discuss certain questions, broken down into articles, was the prerogative of the bachelor of the *Sentences*. In his choice of questions and articles, the bachelor followed not only scientific necessity, but also current interest among theologians. It is most probable that the bachelor was under the direct guidance of his master when choosing questions to be discussed. In the *Sentence* commentaries of Albert the Great, Bonaventure, and Thomas, there is some semblance of relevance to the text expounded in the questions that are raised; in later commentaries, especially in the fourteenth century, there is little or no relevance between the text of Peter Lombard and the questions discussed.

Peter Lombard divided his four books into two groups, following a statement made by St. Augustine, for whom "all doctrine is either of things or of signs."[67] Thus the first three books form a kind of unity in their discussion of the Trinity, creation, Christ, and the virtues. The fourth and last book of the *Sentences* discusses the seven sacraments, which are signs, or symbols. Thomas, however, following a suggestion of Alexander of Hales,[68] divided the four books into two groups of two each:

the first two deal with the *exitus* of all things from God, while the last two deal with the *reditus* of all things to God. This dual aspect of the flow of all things from God and the return of all things to God was to remain a basic framework for Thomas. His *Summa theologiae* would also be organized in the same way; it is the great Dionysian and Plotinian cycle of emanation and return.

Bachelors were obliged by a late statute to present an *introitus* or *principium* to each book of the *Sentences* to be lectured upon. This inaugural lecture was to be delivered between the feast of the Exaltation of the Holy Cross, September 14, and the feast of St. Dionysius, October 10. In the case of Thomas, who lectured for four years on the *Sentences*, it would seem that at the beginning of each academic year he would have to present his inaugural between September 14 and October 10, at which time the masters began their ordinary lectures. Later, when it was customary for bachelors to lecture on two books a year, the second and fourth would begin with an *introitus* at the beginning of the Hilary, or spring term. When, at a much later date, bachelors covered the whole of the *Sentences* in one academic year, it was specified that the *principium* should be held in October, the beginning of January, the first of March, and the first of May.[69] If Thomas was indeed obliged to present a *principium* prior to his ordinary lectures on the *Sentences*—and it would seem that he was—then this inaugural lecture is either lost to posterity or it is the "prologue" that appears in all printed editions.

In 1912 F. Salvatore published two *sermones* of Thomas which were intimately connected with academic procedures.[70] The first one is the well-known *principium* beginning "Rigans montes de superioribus suis." It is now acknowledged to have been his first inaugural lecture, given when Thomas incepted in theology in 1256. The second *sermo* begins "Hic est liber mandatorum Dei," and it is disputed as to the occasion on which it was delivered. Mandonnet, thinking that Thomas was *cursor biblicus* at Paris from 1252 to 1254, considered this second *sermo* to be the *principium* of Thomas for his cursory lectures on the Bible, when he was *baccalarius biblicus* at Paris. It seems to me more

likely that the second *sermo* is also connected with the inauguration of a new master at inception, as I shall explain later when
we come to talk about inception. Hence, according to our hypothesis that Thomas was never *cursor biblicus* at Paris, this
secundus sermo could not have been his *principium* in 1252.
First, such a *principium* was not required of the *cursor biblicus*
at that time. Second, Thomas came to Paris in 1252 to lecture on
the *Sentences* ("ad legendum sententias") and not to lecture
cursorily on the Bible.[71] Third, there is not one shred of documentary evidence to indicate that he was a *cursor biblicus* at
Paris. The important point to note is that Thomas began lecturing on the *Sentences* in the fall of 1252 and may have had to
present an inaugural lecture to fulfill university requirements.
But this inaugural lecture, or *principium,* is not known to us—
unless it consisted of the prologue and first question in the
printed editions.

The first question that Thomas raised concerning Peter Lombard's prologue was the nature and method of theology, a strictly
introductory lecture not treated by Peter himself. The ordering
of this question is a brilliant example of an introduction to theology, that is, to *sacra doctrina.* The question has five articles
dealing with (1) the existence of such a doctrine, (2) whether
its nature is one or many sciences, (3) whether it is speculative
or practical, and if it is speculative, whether it is to be called
wisdom, knowledge (science), or understanding, (4) the subject of such a doctrine, and (5) its intrinsic method. This same
framework was utilized by Thomas in the first question of his
Summa theologiae, but with greater clarity and precision. Even
in this first question Thomas clearly shows a difference between
his own teaching and that of St. Bonaventure and others who
preceded him.[72] In his third question of the *Summa,* concerning man's knowledge of God, he laid the foundation for all
subsequent questions concerning the nature of God known both
by reason and by faith, that is, *De deo uno.* Peter's *Sentences* begins with the discussion of the Trinity, leaving little opportunity
to discuss the nature of "the one God" as He can be known by
reason. In the *Summa,* the question is given separate consideration, but in the *Scriptum super Sententias* Thomas simply de-

voted distinction 8 to discussing the more important problems in this area. In the very opening question of distinction 8, Thomas immediately established his whole approach to God and the world on the real distinction between *esse* and nature in creatures and their identity in God. For him, the most proper name of God is "to be" (*esse*), or "He who is" (*qui est*). In the *Summa*, Thomas would continue to hold that from the viewpoint of *id a quo imponitur* and the signification of that designation, the term *qui est* is more proper than the term "God"; but from the viewpoint of *id ad quod imponitur* and the uniqueness of the divine nature, then the Tetragrammaton, or Yahweh, is the most proper, for it designates the hiddenness, the mysteriousness, and the silence of God.[73]

In the text of Peter's *Sentences*, it was not always easy to determine whether a statement expressed was a direct quotation from the Fathers or a personal statement made by Peter himself. An interesting example of this occurs in the discussion of temptations of the flesh in *Sentences* II, dist. 24, cc. 6–13. Peter followed closely the discussion of St. Augustine's *De trinitate*, XII, where the progressive character of temptation in man is compared with the progressive nature of the first sin. In the Garden of Eden the serpent, representing sensual movements, entices Eve, representing lower reason, to eat of the forbidden fruit which she then offers to Adam, representing higher reason. When higher reason consents to the temptation, the sin is clearly mortal; when lower reason, Eve, alone eats of the forbidden fruit, the sin is venial. But what about the case when Eve does not consent, and the movements of the flesh are confined to the senses? Are these first movements (*primi motus*) also venial sins? Peter Lombard concluded his quotation from Augustine with the stark statement: "If therefore the enticement to sin is held fast in the sensual motion alone, the sin is venial and the lightest of all."[74] Early commentators did not refer this statement to Augustine. But Alexander of Hales, Bonaventure, and Albert the Great attributed this sentence to St. Augustine, and maintained on his authority that first movements of the flesh are venial sins even when lower reason is not conscious of them. T. Deman showed that the erroneous attribution of this statement to St. Augustine was common among thirteenth-century theologians.[75] Thomas also maintained (with Albert, Bonaventure, and Alexander) that first movements (*primi motus*) of the sense appetite toward an illicit moral object, such as toward any of the seven capital sins, are venially sinful, even though they are the lightest of all sins (*peccata levissima*). He accepted the teaching of Hugh of Saint-Victor, also quoted by Peter Lombard, that "a temptation of the flesh cannot arise without sin."[76]

However, when Albert discovered that the text upon which he relied was not St. Augustine's, but Peter Lombard's, he changed his position completely and taught (with Simon of Tournai, Alan of Lille, and the first two Dominican masters at Paris) that such movements of the sense appetite (*motus primi*) arise spontaneously and are in no way under the dominion of free will; and therefore are not sinful, not even venially.[77] Thomas, on the other hand, maintained his original position taken in the *Scriptum super Sententias* that all such initial movements of the sense appetite toward an illicit object are sufficiently under the domain of free will to constitute them venially sinful, but the lightest of all. There was no change whatever in the teaching of Thomas on the sinfulness of *secundo primi* movements of the sense appetite (initial emotions, or temptations of the flesh) even antecedent to conscious awareness.[78] For Thomas these movements of emotion prior to deliberation or even awareness could each have been prevented if the mind had been thinking of something else, and this possibility indicates sufficient freedom to constitute sin.[79]

The purpose of this excursion into doctrinal subtleties was to show the importance of determining what scholastic authors thought to be of patristic authority in the work of Peter Lombard. Modern critical editions carefully point out by quotation marks the actual text of the source quoted, but such was not the case in the Middle Ages. It is therefore interesting to note that Albert the Great completely changed his view and rejected the authority of Peter Lombard once he discovered that the text in question was not Augustine's. In the Middle Ages, masters did not hesitate to reject the authority of Peter Lombard when they had sufficient reason for doing so.

Around 1250, according to H. Denifle,[80] the masters of Paris had rejected eight propositions of Peter Lombard; they were commonly held to be untrue:

1. that charity, which is the love of God and neighbor, is not something created, but the uncreated Holy Spirit itself (*Sent.* I, dist. 17).
2. that the terms *trinus* and *trinitas* do not bespeak something positive, but only privative (*Sent.* I, dist. 24).
3. that the good angels had the reward of heaven before they merited it subsequently (*Sent.* II, dist. 5 and 11).
4. that no ingredient in food is transformed into human nature, neither by generation nor by nutrition (*Sent.* II, dist. 30).
5. that the soul divested of the body is a person (*Sent.* III, dist. 5).
6. that during the three days Christ was in the tomb, He was man (*homo*) (*Sent.* III, dist. 22).
7. that John's baptism by the imposition of hands was equivalent to the baptism of Christ, so that a person baptized by John in the name of the Trinity need not be baptized again (*Sent.* IV, dist. 2).
8. that the power of baptizing interiorly (*interius*) can be given to others, and that the power of creating can be communicated to creatures as ministers (*Sent.* IV, dist. 5).

Bonaventure, who listed these propositions to reject them,[81] also mentions other propositions as not generally held by the masters or rejected as less probable; but the eight principal theses listed by him, Bonaventure claims, were universally rejected by the masters of Paris. In company with his peers, Thomas rejected only four and a half out of eight propositions, namely 1, 4, 5, 7, 8 (second part). He agreed unreservedly with the "Master of the Sentences" on the second proposition, against the "common opinion" of the Parisian masters. On the remaining three propositions, 3, 6, 8 (first half), Aquinas held that the Parisian masters were right to dissent from Peter Lombard, but he does not agree with them that those three were totally untenable, given the right qualifications and distinctions. "The impression is inescapable that the very real respect Aquinas felt for the Master and for Masters in no way limited his own freedom of manoeuvre."[82]

Thomas's commentary on the *Sentences* was always known as the *Scriptum super Sententias,* to indicate that it was a work completely written by him and revised for publication, and not a simple *reportatio* recounted by a student during the process of delivery. An autograph copy of part of the Third Book exists in Vatican MS Vat. lat. 9851, fol. 11ra–99vb. Whether the existence of this autograph will prove an asset or a detriment in the reconstruction of the exemplar remains to be seen; the autograph could turn out to be a first draft written by Thomas but not submitted to the stationers of Paris as the final copy.

In this earliest major work by Thomas, all of his principal conclusions are established: the real distinction between *esse* and essence in creatures and their real identity in God; rejection of the hylomorphic composition in separated substances, or angels; the pure potentiality of first matter; the unicity of substantial form in corporeal creatures; consideration of the agent and possible intellects in man as powers of the individual soul; insistence that matter designated by quantity is the sole principle of natural individuation; insistence that nature is not the "efficient cause" but only the active principle in the free fall of natural bodies; and defense of the possibility of natural motion in a void. In theology also his basic principles stand out clearly: e.g., the hypostatic union of human nature in Christ; transubstantiation of bread and wine into the Body and Blood of Christ; the infinite difference and distinction between what is of nature and what is of grace.

Nevertheless, Thomas did not reach full maturity of his speculative thought in the *Sentences.* There are many points on which Thomas later abandoned earlier opinions, resulting in some discrepancy between the teaching of the *Sentences* and the teaching of the *Summa theologiae.* After Thomas's death there were not only numerous summaries and condensations of his works, but also concordances to harmonize or bring out more clearly the development of doctrine.[83] Among the many extant concordances in manuscript form, Grabmann and Mandonnet note Paris MS lat. 14550 (s. xv), fol. 273^v, where the rubric reads: "Articles and points follow in which Friar Thomas [speaks] better in the *Summa* than in the *Scriptum.*"[84] Grabmann notes that in Klosterneuburg MS 322 there is another entitled: "Articles in which Friar Thomas speaks better in the *Summa* than in the *Scriptum*."[85] Among the best-known concordances are the short concordance beginning "Pertransibunt plurimi" by an English Thomist of the early fourteenth century, Thomas Sutton, printed among the works of St. Thomas,[86] and the concordance compiled by Peter of Bergamo, which also has been printed.[87] While some of the contradictions are only apparent and can be reconciled, the great majority show a development in Thomas's thought between the *Scriptum* and the *Summa*.

The ordinary time for masters to lecture was always the canonical hour of prime, which, depending upon the time of year, was about six o'clock in the morning; this was considered the best time of day. On days when the master ordinarily lectured, the bachelor followed the master and began at nine o'clock, when the bell of Saint-Jacques rang for the canonical hour of tierce. On days when the master did not lecture, the *Sententiarius* could begin at six. On days when the master was scheduled to hold a disputation, he alone lectured in the faculty and no one else, neither other masters, nor *Sententiarii*, nor *biblici*. According to the fully mature statutes of Paris, bachelors began reading the *Sentences* on the day after the feast of St. Dionysius, October 9, and finished the year's work by the feast of SS. Peter and Paul, June 29.[88] It would seem that an academic period normally lasted two or three hours.

Besides lecturing on the *Sentences*, Thomas had to take part in the ordinary disputation of the masters. This meant that he had to respond to objections during a disputation both of his own master and also of other masters. In this way other masters could evaluate the competence of young *Sententiarii*. According to a late statute, before a license to incept was given by the chancellor, the bachelor had to respond at least five times in public disputations; that is, he had to respond in the bishop's *aula* when a new master incepted in theology, in the *vesperies* of a new master, once in the Sorbonne at a time when masters did not lecture (i.e., between June 29 and September 14), once in the Lenten or Advent quodlibet, and finally once in the general disputations.[89] This was the minimum requirement. No doubt Thomas and other bachelors of his day responded much more often, for there always had to be a *respondens* in all disputations conducted by a master. The task of the *respondens* was to reply to objections raised by those in the audience. His task was not to give the final solution, or "determination," of the question disputed, but only to maintain the other side of the question. Thomas had experience in responding to objections when he was bachelor under Albert the Great in Cologne. Bernard Gui tells of an incident under Albert, in which Thomas repeated the objection and gave a distinction that not only answered the objection, but seemed to dissolve the whole opposition. Albert is supposed to have replied, "Thomas, you seem to hold the position not of one responding, but rather of one determining."[90] More will be said of the technique of the disputed question in the next chapter, when we discuss Thomas the master.

Before Thomas began lecturing as master, he composed two very significant treatises for his brethren. Tolomeo of Lucca notes that he wrote these before he became master ("infra magisterium"), i.e., before he was thirty-one years old.[91] Tolomeo entitles these works *De quidditate et esse* and *De principiis naturae.* Nicholas Trevet, depending on the archives of Saint-Jacques, gives their titles more precisely. The first is *De ente et essentia ad fratres et socios suos;* the second is *De principiis naturae ad fratrem Sylvestrum.*[92] It is therefore clear that both of these early treatises were written in response to requests by his *confrères.* Many, if not most, of Thomas's writings were similarly evoked by fraternal charity and apostolic zeal for the good of others.

The widely popular treatise *De ente et essentia,* extant in more than 179 manuscripts, is an expository work in metaphysics wherein most of Thomas's fundamental ideas in philosophy are expressed clearly, even at this early stage of his career. Rather than presenting arguments for a particular point of view, it explains common terms in metaphysics, such as *ens, natura, essentia, genus, species,* and *differentia.* It is a short treatise of six chapters, explaining the various meanings of the terms "being" and "essence," and how the word "essence" is verified analogically in composite substances, separated substances, and in accidents. It is an unequivocal expression of (1) a real distinction between created essence and existence, (2) the pure potentiality of primary matter, (3) denial of materiality in separated substances, (4) participation of all created reality, material and immaterial, in the divine being, and (5) the Aristotelian dependence of logical predicables and abstracted forms on existing individual realities. This work is highly original, even though it is heavily indebted to Avicenna's *Metaphysics*.

The short treatise *De ente et essentia* was the first work of Thomas to be commented upon by later Thomists. Its earliest known commentator is Armand of Bellovisu (fl. 1313–40), whose commentary (c. 1319) exists in many manuscripts and was published once.[93] The eminent Cardinal Cajetan also commented upon this work in his youth, in 1494–95, at the age of twenty-five.

Thomas's *De principiis naturae* was dedicated to an otherwise unknown Dominican, Friar Sylvester, of the Priory of Saint-Jacques. It too consists of six expository chapters, which rather than serving to prove by demonstration the existence of the Aristotelian principles of matter, form, and privation, takes these as proved and discusses the nature and interrelation of these natural principles, the nature of the four causes, the coincidence and priority of causes, the different ways in which each of the causes and principles is to be understood by analogy. This treatise is derived from the first and second books of Aristotle's *Physics*, but it is remarkable that Thomas immediately expands his conception of matter to include prime matter, a pure potentiality for *esse substantiale*.

There is no way of determining the precise dates of these two treatises, but it is clear that they were written in Paris before 1256. Mandonnet and Walz arbitrarily assign *De principiis naturae* to the year 1255; Pauson dates it 1252–54; Roland-Gosselin, thinking that *De principiis naturae* is prior to *De ente et essentia*, places its date near 1254; and Perrier places it "between 1254–56." At present there seems to be no hope of ever determining the exact date. It is enough to know that these two non-polemical, strictly expository works were written shortly before 1256, when Thomas was still a *Sententiarius*.

The only polemical work written by Thomas before he was accepted by the other masters of Paris was *Contra impugnantes Dei cultum et religionem*, written in 1256, opposing the attack by William of Saint-Amour against mendicants in the University of Paris.

° *Antimendicant Controversy in the University of Paris*[94]

(1252-57)

When the secular masters and students returned to Paris after the strike in 1231, they were no doubt surprised to see not only one Dominican lecturing in the university, but two. Possibly eyebrows were lifted, comments made, and perhaps there was a certain resentment against the chancellor for condoning this development during their absence. In due time, however, the presence of Dominicans in the university was accepted by the *consortium magistrorum,* and the two Dominicans had equal voice in the decisions of the masters. Master John of St. Giles undoubtedly should have gone on strike with the other masters on March 27, 1229, but he did not. Not only did Roland incept as a master under him, but Roland's successor, Hugh of Saint-Cher, was in the professorial chair, and John of St. Giles himself had become a Dominican seven months before the strike was over, on September 22, 1230, bringing his chair into possession of the Dominicans. While the existence of this second chair later provided grounds for bitter complaint, at that time nothing was said or done to suppress one of the Dominican chairs. Not until February 1252, twenty-one years later, was anything done about it.[95] By that time master William of Saint-Amour had been regent master for two years and was most determined that the mendicants be removed from the university and even suppressed entirely.

In the 1230s and '40s, resentment grew among the secular masters in the university against the mendicants, the two Dominicans and the one Franciscan. No doubt, as Thomas of Cantimpré would have it,[96] the seculars' teaching had been overshadowed, if not eclipsed, by the mendicants' greater dedication and especially by the outstanding excellence of their teaching. Literary production by the seculars during those years was relatively small; their influence with the students and their reputation for learning were feeble. Proof of this can be seen in their own manifesto of February 4, 1254,[97] and in such critics as Roger Bacon and Humbert of Romans. Roger Bacon remarked, perhaps with his usual exaggeration: "For the past forty years the seculars have neglected the study of theology and philosophy."[98] Humbert of Romans, the fifth master general of the Order of Preachers, wrote, "Many masters of theology at Paris, envying the number of our own doctors, the multitude of scholars, and the grace of doctrine, once drew up a statute in clandestine meetings . . . against all religious orders."[99] There is enough evidence to show that there was a certain amount of envy and jealousy that gave rise to their growing resentment. But there was much more to the controversy than ordinary human weakness.

I. T. Eschmann and Louis Halphen[100] state that there was an ecclesial reason for the growing animosity. The secular masters at the university and a great many French bishops looked upon the Friars as exponents and instruments of papal policy with regard to university affairs and ecclesial renewal of the Church under Rome. Although the University of Paris was a "pontifical" institution in virtue of the papal charter of 1215 and its innumerable privileges before and after, the masters were not anxious to have what Coulton called a "papal militia" dictating policies contrary to current legislation and legitimate customs in the name of papal privileges. The mendicant friars maintained that by papal mandate they had the right to preach in any diocese and to hear confessions independently of the local ordinary, because their authorization came from the bishop of Rome, who had jurisdiction over the whole of Christendom. Because of this supradiocesan privilege given by the Popes, the French hierarchy wanted nothing more than the elimination of the friars or their complete subjection under themselves. Even as early as the first phase of the controversy (that is, 1252–57), the French hierarchy found in William of Saint-Armour a learned spokesman for their grievances and a representative of their narrow, parochial concept of the Church. As the antimendicant controversy widened beyond the mere question of mendicants teaching in the university, the more did the French bishops resent the interference of the Holy See. It was the beginning of what Eschmann called a certain "Gallicanism *ante litteram*."

When Thomas arrived in Paris in the summer of 1252, he found that in the preceding February the seculars of the university had issued a statute restricting each religious Order to one chair each. "The aforesaid masters [in theology] ordain that each college of religious be content with one master actually teaching for each [community] and only one for the future."[101] This was a direct attack on the second Dominican chair, which Thomas was to occupy. The two Dominican masters, Elias Brunet and Bonhomme, as well as the Franciscan master, William of Meliton, refused to recognize the statute, since it was contrary to the mind of the Holy See and the hoped-for reform of the Church through learning.

The secular masters at the university were sincerely concerned about their own future and their control of the university. In 1252 there were only twelve chairs allowed in the faculty of theology. The canons of Notre Dame, including the chancellor, always had three chairs, and the mendicants had three chairs, thus leaving only six for the secular masters. The chancellor and the canons could be counted upon to support the three mendicants, thus creating a stalemate. By 1258 three more chairs had been given to religious Orders—Cistercian, Benedictine, and Premonstratensian. Two more would be added with the coming of the Carmelites and Augustinians. This eventuality, which the secular masters perhaps feared, would mean that the secular clergy, who started the university, would always be in the minority even with the expansion of the university. This eventuality actually did come about, particularly when the two-thirds majority rule came into effect with the bull *Quasi lignum* of Alexander IV on April 14, 1255.[102]

As far as the mendicant Orders were concerned, they were not interested in the University of Paris as an end in itself, but rather as a means of obtaining learned men for the vast apostolate of the Church. Their apostolate was supranational and supradiocesan; they were founded by the Holy See in order that they might reform and renew every aspect of the Church. The Dominicans in particular, whose mission was preaching, clearly needed the competence that came with study and learning.

It must be admitted that the *studium generale* of Saint-Jacques and the Cordeliers amounted to three universities within a university, with their own appointments of bachelors to become masters, their own standards of voting on students and their promotion, and indeed their own inceptions. As for the masters incepted by the Dominicans, it could be said that the almost yearly production of masters in the chair of France was perhaps reckless and imprudent, but the Province of France was thinking of the great need for such men in France and in the Church; it was not thinking of the good of the University of Paris. The secular masters objected as much to the proliferation of masters in the Dominican chair of France as they did to the second chair of the Order.[103]

John of Wildeshausen, master general of the Preachers, died on November 4, 1252. It was under him that Thomas had spent his early Dominican days. A new general would have been elected at the next general chapter, scheduled to be held in Buda, now Budapest, on Pentecost in 1253. For some reason the chapter was not held that year, so that a new general was not elected until the following year in Buda at Pentecost, 1254.[104] The new general was Humbert of Romans, provincial of Provence. But between the death of John and the election of Humbert, the Order was without direction and leadership for almost two years when the Order was most in need of someone to plead its case to the Holy See.

In April 1253 the secular masters drew up a document[105] announcing that they had been on strike for more than a month because four scholars and one companion were beaten up, imprisoned, and left half dead by the night watchmen of the city, and no satisfaction was forthcoming from city officials. The document also claimed that the delay in obtaining satisfaction was caused by the fact that the two Dominican masters, Elias Brunet and Bonhomme, and one Franciscan master, William of Meliton, refused to suspend teaching. Therefore they were excommunicated and expelled from the "consortium of masters" until they swore to uphold the statutes of the university, particularly the statute of 1252, limiting religious Orders to one chair each. There was a further prohibition forbidding each master from permitting the *principium* of a bachelor or himself attending it (unless he previously agreed to live by the oath to follow university statutes) or to permit him to lecture in the meantime. This prohibition directly affected Thomas Aquinas, but, as far as we know, he did not suspend his lectures on the *Sentences*. The mendicants, despite the absence of a general, appealed to Innocent IV. On July 1, 1253, the Pope lifted the ban of excommunication and ordered the seculars to readmit the mendicants to the "college of masters" and the "consortium of the university."[106] This order went unheeded, and the masters promulgated the April statutes on September 2, 1253. Thus from March until the end of the academic year the seculars suspended classes for a second time, and the mendicants refused to stop teaching.

In reply to the papal injunctions of July and August, the secular masters issued a long letter on February 4, 1254, listing their grievances, including the existence of two Dominican chairs, the failure of mendicants to comply with university oaths and statues, and the great threat of declining prestige of secular masters.[107] Thus by February 4, 1254, the two Dominicans had not yet come to terms with the university; therefore they were still effectively expelled. The Franciscans, however, were reconciled sometime between September 2, 1253, and February 4, 1254, through their minister general, John of Parma, who accepted the one-chair statute; Bonaventure was accordingly allowed to lecture as master in the Franciscan school during the academic year 1253-54,[108] but he was still not accepted by the consortium of masters.

Early in 1254 new wood was added to the fire by the untimely publication of *Introductorius in Evangelium Aeternum* by a Franciscan enthusiast of Abbot Joachim of Flora, Gerard de Borgo San Donnino, proclaiming that the third stage of the world had begun around 1200.[109] Gerard had collected scattered prophecies into a coherent and repetitious whole, dividing human history into the three ages of the Old Testament, of the New, and of the Eternal Gospel, these corresponding to the Father, the Son, and the Holy Spirit. The age of the Eternal Gospel would see the withering away of the Church of Christ and the rise of a new spiritual destiny heralded by new prophets, the war with antichrist, and the triumph of the free spirit of love. No longer would men be held in bondage by the law of Christ, the Church of Christ, and its sacraments. Antichrist and his ministers were all those who refuse to submit to the New Gospel of the Spirit.

Among the Joachimites of the day, the way was prepared by the evangelical preaching of the mendicants, whose founders were "Christ like" and whose rapidly growing numbers astonished the world. The initial date for the new age at that time was the year 1260; Gerard de Borgo San Donnino felt it his duty to introduce readers to the new age and the *Evangelium Aeternum.*

The *Introductorius* of Gerard was attacked immediately, but without name or exposition of contents, by master William of Saint-Amour in his *Liber de Antichristo et eius ministris.*[110] William's treatise is a very scholarly work presenting all the biblical and patristic sources that describe antichrist and his ministers; only the views of Abbot Joachim are refuted. But it is not difficult to see that the "pseudo-preachers" and the "pseudo-prophets" refer to the Dominicans and Franciscans, respectively. At the same time a list of thirty-one heresies were excerpted from the *Introductorius* and from Joachim's own *Concordia veteris et novi testamenti.*[111] H. Denifle has shown that the list of errors was compiled by the same Parisian masters who opposed the mendicants. This list of errors and a copy of the *Introductorius* were sent to Pope Innocent IV by the bishop of Paris, in the care of William of Saint-Amour, who was on his way to the papal curia as procurator of the university, together with Odo of Douai and Christian of Beauvais, two colleagues. William and his companions arrived at the curia in July 1254 with his case against the mendicants and his proof of heresy against the Franciscan Gerard de Borgo San Donnino. Innocent IV handed the book over to a commission of three cardinals for examination, Odo of Tusculano, Stephen of Praenestino, and Hugh of Saint-Cher. The commission of cardinals did not finish their examination until next October 1255, during the pontificate of Alexander IV.

William of Saint-Amour and his companions were able to convince Innocent IV that great harm might befall the Church from the begging friars. Therefore, Innocent IV, who had done so much to promote the mendicants in their evangelical work, issued a bull *Etsi animarum* on November 21, 1254,[112] rescinding all Dominican and Franciscan privileges of preaching and hearing confessions without authorization from the local ordinary. Other privileges granted by himself and his predecessors were also rescinded. The mendicants, both Dominican and Franciscan, were left desolate; they could only obey.

Two weeks later, Innocent IV was dead (December 7, 1254). Eight days later, on December 15, Rainaldo de' Conti di Segni, former cardinal protector of the Franciscans, was elected Pope with the name Alexander IV. He was consecrated at Naples on December 20. Two days later Alexander rescinded his predecessor's bull *Etsi animarum* with his own bull *Nec insolitum*, restoring the mendicants' privileges of preaching, hearing confessions, holding burials, and solemnly singing their own liturgy, with due precautions.[113]

On April 14, 1255, Alexander IV issued the most important bull of his career, *Quasi lignum vitae*.[114] In this long letter Alexander again confirmed the privileges given to the friars by his predecessors, clarifying more sharply than before the limits of these privileges. Moreover, he ordered that the two Dominican masters, Bonhomme and Elias Brunet, be received as members of their consortium. This letter served as a norm for future policy and practice. That same day, Alexander wrote a short letter to the university demanding that the Dominicans be accepted in the consortium of masters within fifteen days under pain of suspension from office.[115]

William of Saint-Amour was furious. In Paris he carried on his own campaign against the mendicants, particularly against the Dominicans, who were still excluded from the consortium of masters. During 1255 and the early months of 1256, William held public disputations and preached many sermons on such delicate questions as legitimate begging, the nature of true poverty, and the need of monks to work with their hands instead of teaching in a university. These questions were taken up and refuted by Bonaventure in his disputations between October 1255 and January 1256.[116]

The end of 1255 and the beginning of 1256 were most critical for the Dominicans, more so than for the Franciscans, who had come to some partial agreement, at least as far as the university was concerned. At that time William of Saint-Amour and his closest followers aroused the clerical students so much that the Dominicans were afraid to go outside the priory to beg. In September 1255, when the Dominican master Florent of Hesdin gave his inaugural lecture for the year's work, King Louis IX had to send the royal archers to protect Saint-Jacques and its Friars from harm.[117] For this outburst of demonstrations and riots in the rue Saint-Jacques, the Pope rebuked the bishop of Paris, and demanded that justice be done.[118] Near the beginning of April 1256, the master general of the Dominican Order, Humbert of Romans, wrote a long letter to the Friars at Orléans about the ordeal the Parisian brethren had to endure.[119] William of Saint-Amour did all he could to arouse the young clerics against the mendicants, and against the Dominicans in particular.

In October 1255 the commission of cardinals delegated to examine the *Introductorius* of Gerard de Borgo San Donnino finished its work and declared the work heretical. On October 23, 1255, Alexander IV ordered Reginald, bishop of Paris, to collect all copies and fascicules of the work and to burn them in public, but he cautioned that no undue aspersions were to be cast on the Franciscans. Those who refused to comply within the time determined by the bishop were to be excommunicated.[120]

It was just at this time that Thomas Aquinas received his license to incept in theology. The papal letter of March 3, 1256, expressed gratitude to the chancellor for having granted the license to Thomas even before he received the Pope's previous letter.[121] The bull *Quasi lignum vitae* of April 14, 1255, stipulated that the chancellor was to grant the license on worthy candidates even before he was asked to do so.[122] Thomas incepted in theology under Elias Brunet sometime in April 1256, but he may not have begun teaching until the following academic year. In any case, he was not immediately accepted by the consortium of masters or the "collegium of the university." But from April on, Thomas was at least a functioning master, although not formally recognized as such by the consortium of masters, that is, the faculty of theology.

In March of 1256, about a month before Friar Thomas incepted, William of Saint-Amour published the first version of his most devasting attack on the mendicants, *De periculis novissimorum temporum*. William himself claimed to have produced five versions of this "brief treatise."[123] By August 1256 the final version was in circulation.[124] The treatise was circulated by William and his followers among French bishops in order to arouse drastic action. In June or July, King Louis IX sent a copy to the Holy See. Alexander IV submitted the treatise *De periculis* to a commission of four cardinals, Odo of Castro (Tusculano), John of Tolleto, Hugh of Saint-Cher, and John of Gaietano.[125]

In the summer of 1256, Bonaventure replied to William's treatise with his own *De perfectione evangelica*.[126] Between July and September, Thomas of York, a Franciscan, published another reply considerably inferior to Bonaventure's, known from its opening words as *Manus quae contra omnipotentem*.[127] Between September and the end of October 1256, Thomas produced his closely reasoned reply to *De periculis*, entitled *Contra impugnantes Dei cultum et religionem*.[128]

By the end of September the commission of cardinals finished its work, and William's treatise *De periculis* was condemned by Alexander IV in the bull *Romanus Pontifex* issued at Anagni on October 5, 1256. Thomas made no reference to this condemnation in his *Contra impugnantes;* therefore, the Leonine editors argue, Thomas's work must have been composed between September and November. But word of the condemnation of October 5 could hardly have taken two months to reach Paris, the center of the controversy. On October 21, Alexander wrote a short letter informing three bishops, including the bishop of Paris, of the condemnation of *De periculis* and ordering that all copies of this work be burned; those who failed to comply with these wishes within eight days would be excommunicated.[129] In other words, it would seem that Thomas did not know of the condemnation when he wrote his reply. The presumption is that if he had known of it, he would somehow have mentioned it; but it would not have taken him two months to hear about it. Therefore one could infer that Thomas's treatise was written between September and the end of October 1256, when he was a functioning but unrecognized master.

Conditions at Paris, however, did not improve until William of Saint-Amour was exiled from Paris to his native village of Saint-Amour by the king early in 1257.

Eschmann calls William's *De periculis* "a bitter harangue."[130] It is divided into fourteen chapters according to the fourteen points he made in the prologue. But it is often repetitious, rambling, and disorganized. He protests in the prologue that he is not writing against anyone nor attacking any religious state approved by the Church; but he feels that the present generation must be warned of the imminent dangers of antichrist and his ministers. For him, fifty-five years have already passed since the ministers of antichrist began roaming the world, and 1260, when the rule of antichrist is to come, is only a few years away. The *De periculis* is very similar in argument to his *De antichristo*, but in it he implicitly accepts the prophetic vision of Abbot Joachim and Gerard de Borgo San Donnino, and utilizes it to his own advantage. William attacked primarily the office of teaching and preaching, hearing confessions, and mendicancy. In general, he argued that if religious claim to be perfect, or more perfect than the secular clergy, then they should eschew teaching, for their claim is contrary to the will of God, contrary to religious life, and contrary to humility, which virtue they are supposed to practice. The office of preaching was given to bishops and the parochial clergy, and to no one else (c. 2, 9–13). Since the religious life is the lowest state in the terrestrial hierarchy, the office of preaching cannot be communicated to religious (c. 2, 13). Hearing confessions is the proper work of a pastor, who must hear the confessions of his parishioners if he is to understand the needs of his people. Finally, their mendicancy is illegitimate, for no one has a right to alms who can support himself by other means, namely, manual labor (c. 12). Mendicants pretend to be holy, but in fact they are parasites living off the work of others; and they are living contrary to the will of Christ, who said, "If you wish to be perfect, sell what you have and give it to the poor, and come follow me." They should live not by begging, which is forbidden by St. Paul, but by work: "by working well, but not by begging" (c. 12, 31). William suggested that the best way to stop the mendicant friars was to proscribe their begging and thus force them to seek the necessities of life elsewhere: "For it is evident that by taking away begging or looking for the necessities of life, the usurpation of preaching would also be denied the pseudo-preachers" (c. 12).

Thomas's reply is careful to present all of William's arguments; indeed he presents them more clearly than William had himself. After listing the arguments, Thomas proposes the possible counterarguments and then gives a lengthy determination to the question, much after the manner of a master deciding on a disputed question. Thomas argues that not only are teaching and religious life not incompatible, but if an Order is founded expressly to combat error by truth, its members have an obligation to study and to teach others the fruits of their labor. Even a multiplicity of teachers is permitted and required because what one man does not know, another may. Finally, only religious who have given up involvements in commercial affairs have the leisure to study and teach. As for preaching, Thomas admits and even insists that monks do not have the right to preach without the explicit permission of the bishop. The like holds true for the hearing of confessions. But, Thomas insists, "religious, when authorized by the pope or by a bishop, may lawfully hear confessions," and by the same token may lawfully preach. As for mendicancy, religious do not refuse work, but work for the good of souls by their apostolic labors. They not only have a right to beg, but they have an obligation to fulfill the Gospels lest they meddle in secular affairs and prevent their own spiritual development.

Thomas's arguments in reply to William of Saint-Amour are more profound and extensive than can be summarized here. The center of the conflict, it would seem, was the fact that William and his followers never grasped the significance of the new religious Orders established by the Holy See to renovate the Church. For William, the friars were to be equated with monks, and just as monks are forbidden to teach, preach, and hear confessions without the local authority of the bishop, so too should the friars be forbidden. He did not see that a friar is not a monk; that he is a cleric bound to sacred doctrine, its purity, development, and diffusion by teaching, preaching, writing, and other apostolic activity; that a monk, on the other hand, is not a cleric (except under special circumstances, and then only to supply the needs of a monastery), his task being to work with his hands, chant the Divine Office, and seek personal sanctification. William's inability to understand the needs of the Church and the role of the new religious Orders made the conflict inevitable, even apart from personal animosities. In particular, he failed to understand the Order of Preachers, its preaching mission, its dedication to study, and its mandate from the Pope.

It used to be said on the authority of William of Tocco[131] that Thomas, Bonaventure, Albert the Great, and the master general John of Vercelli debated the antimendicant issue with William of Saint-Amour at the papal court in Anagni. It used also to be said that Thomas composed his *Contra impugnantes Dei cultum et religionem* at Anagni, at the command of the Pope ("de mandato Summi Pontificis") during the general chapter at Anagni in 1256. Although this legend is accepted by Quétif-Echard and H. Denifle, there is no evidence for it. Not only was there no general chapter at Anagni (where the Pope resided) during the thirteenth century, but the master general at the time was not John of Vercelli, but Humbert of Romans. There is no evidence that Thomas was at the papal court, although Albert the Great and Bonaventure seem to have been there. The Leonine editors reject the legend and insist that the *Contra impugnantes* was written in Paris.[132]

Furthermore, there is no evidence that Thomas's *Contra impugnantes* in any way influenced the decision of the Holy See in its condemnation of October 5, 1256. His treatise came too late to be of any use in this decision, for he was still in the process of composing it when the condemnation was issued from Anagni. It is possible, however, that Bonaventure's treatise *De perfectione evangelica*, of the summer of 1256, had some influence.

One minor point should be considered here. Tolomeo of Lucca states that this work "against William of Saint-Amour" was written before Thomas became a master: "infra autem magisterium."[133] Yet all historians today agree that *Contra impugnantes* was written in September–October (or November) 1256, after he obtained the *licentia docendi* from the chancellor and after he incepted in theology—that is, after April 1256. The problem is easily resolved, for clearly Tolomeo considered the "magisterium" to mean acceptance into the *consortium magistrorum*, which occurred on September 12, 1257. Therefore, Thomas must have been a master of theology when he wrote *Contra impugnantes*, but was not accepted as such by the masters of the University of Paris until a year later.

The exile of William of Saint-Amour did not bring the conflict between seculars and regulars to an end. William kept up a flow of correspondence with his two closest followers, Gérard d'Abbeville and Nicholas of Lisieux; it was they who revived the controversy ten years later.

Chapter III

REGENT MASTER IN THEOLOGY AT PARIS
(1256–59)

At the height of animosity against the Dominicans at Saint-Jacques, during the academic year 1255–56, Thomas Aquinas was directed to proceed to the degree of master in theology. The papal bull *Quasi lignum vitae* had been promulgated the previous spring. Throughout the academic year the infuriated William of Saint-Amour preached vitriolic sermons against the mendicants, held public disputations against their right to exist, and prepared the first version of his *De periculis novissimorum temporum,* aimed at proving that mendicants are the ministers of antichrist. The winter of 1255–56 was the severest the Dominicans at Paris had to endure. William and his colleagues, Chrétien of Beauvais and Odo of Douai, had aroused not only the secular students of the university, but a section of the laity as well, to physical violence. No sooner was a friar caught sight of, wrote Humbert of Romans in April 1256,[1] than he was surrounded by the human swarms that poured forth from every house and hostel in the narrow street, hurrying as if to a spectacle. Instantly the air was full of the "tumult of shoutings, the barking of dogs, the roaring of bears, the hissing of serpents," and every sort of insulting exclamation. Filthy rushes and straw off the floors of the dwellings were poured upon the cowled head from above; mud, stones, and sometimes blows greeted him from below. Arrows had been shot against the priory, which had henceforth to be guarded day and night by royal troops.

The general chapter of the Dominican Order met in Paris at Pentecost. There the members learned at first hand the hostility directed against the Friars. In their *Acts* they directed that "until further orders every priory shall recite weekly the seven penitential psalms, the litany and prayer to Our Lady, the prayer to St. Dominic, and the prayer *Ineffabilem* with versicle, for the safety of the Order."[2]

Such were the circumstances under which Thomas obtained his license, made his inception, and took up, in the fall of 1256, the regentship in the *schola extraneorum*. The troubles he had at his inception are mentioned in a letter of Pope Alexander IV, June 17, 1256: "The aforesaid masters and students have had no care, as we well know, to preserve that concord which was established [by the bull *Quasi lignum vitae*]; they challenged it with their urge to continue the fight. In the most unworthy manner, they have opposed those who desired to attend the lectures, disputations, and sermons of the friars, in particular those who wished to be present at the inception of our beloved son fr. Thomas d'Aquino."[3] By June, as we know from the letter of Humbert, the hostility was "somewhat tempered."[4]

Toward the end of February 1256, Aimeric of Veire, chancellor of the university, wrote to the prior of Saint-Jacques ordering him to command on his part "the aforesaid Friar Thomas to receive the magisterium in theology, notwithstanding any custom whereby others might be preferred to him, and to prepare himself accordingly without any contradiction."[5] Five years earlier, in May 1250, Innocent IV had ordered the chancellor to give the license in theology to those religious qualified to receive it, even though they themselves had not petitioned for it.[6] This order was repeated in *Quasi lignum vitae* of April 1255. We do not know what prompted the chancellor to choose this particular time to confer the license; the early biographers say, however, that Thomas had "zealously and fruitfully completed his course of study."[7] Although March or April would have been the proper time to petition for the license, Thomas could hardly have completed his lectures on the fourth book of the *Sentences*. He did not have a complete text to present to the stationer's until sometime in 1257. William of Tocco expressly says that Thomas wrote on the *Sentences* during his years as bachelor and "in the beginning of his mastership."[8] Therefore it is possible that the last few distinctions were not delivered in class or given by

Thomas while he was in fact a master completing the academic year 1255–56.

Be that as it may, Thomas was ordered to prepare for his inception, and for the grave responsibilities of a regent master in theology at the University of Paris. The initiative had come from the chancellor of the university, Aimeric of Veire, who granted the *licentia in theologiae facultate docendi.* In a special letter from the Lateran on March 3, 1256, Alexander IV commended Aimeric for having granted this license before his own letter on the subject had reached him.[9] The implication is that had Aimeric not granted this license when he did, he would have been required to do so by the Pope's previous letter, which is now lost.[10] Alexander again referred to the troubled situation in the university and urged that Thomas proceed with his *principium* in the theological faculty as soon as possible.

That same day Alexander wrote another of his strong letters to Reginald Mignon of Corbeil, bishop of Paris (1250–68), to excommunicate all masters who were preventing students and auditors from attending the lectures and disputations in the schools of the Dominicans: "Indeed it has come to our attention that the aforesaid masters, scholars, and auditors miserably presume to prevent people from giving alms to our beloved prior and friars of the Order of Preachers at Paris, or prevent them from attending sermons and lectures in their house, or let them confess their sins to them, even though they have faculties to hear confessions from the local ordinary or from the authorized priest." The bishop is instructed to excommunicate such perpetrators publicly and solemnly, notwithstanding any indulgence whereby the Pope's orders would be impeded or delayed.[11] Presumably Alexander wished to forestall any demonstrations or riots at Thomas's inception in the second Dominican chair of theology.

The Dominicans were ready to give up their claim to the second chair in order to establish peace, but the Pope expressly forbade them to take such a course.[12] Therefore the Dominicans were hard pressed, caught between the Pope and his clearly stated policies on the one hand, and the hostility of university masters on the other. There was nothing for Thomas to do but to proceed as commanded.

Thomas was terribly upset.[13] He tried to excuse himself on the ground of insufficient age and learning, but without effect. Since obedience left him no escape, he had recourse as usual to prayer. What followed is "one of the most popular stories about St. Thomas," says Foster, "and very well attested."[14] Bernard Gui's account is the most straightforward:

> In the spirit of truth he prayed to the supreme Teacher, using those words of the Psalmist, "Save me, O Lord, for there is now no saint: truths are decayed from among the children of men" (Ps. 11:1). With tears he begged for that understanding of divine things which had become so rare among men, and also for inspiration as to the theme he should choose for his inaugural lecture. Then he fell asleep and dreamed. He seemed to see an old man, white haired and clothed in the Dominican habit, who came and said to him: "Brother Thomas, why are you praying and weeping?" "Because," answered Thomas, "they are making me take the degree of master, and I do not think I am fully competent. Moreover, I cannot think what theme to take for my inaugural lecture." To this the old man replied: "Do not fear: God will help you to bear the burden of being a master. And as for the lecture, take this text, 'Thou waterest the hills from thy upper rooms: the earth shall be filled with the fruit of thy works'" (Ps. 103:13). Then he vanished, and Thomas awoke and thanked God for having so quickly come to his aid.

Bernard Gui presents this anecdote as a dream and not a vision; however, a Florence MS, intending to correct this impression, explicitly states that it was a vision.[15] In any case, Thomas took as the text of his *principium* the verse "Rigans montes de superioribus," etc. (Ps. 103:13). This fact was well established before the actual manuscript of the *principium* was discovered by Francesco Salvatore and published in 1912; today it is listed among the authentic works of Aquinas.

Inception in Theology

(Spring 1256)

Thomas's solemn inception in theology took place between March 3 and June 17, 1256; most of his biographers place the date sometime in April or May. It took place at Saint-Jacques under circumstances already described.

We do not know when the ceremony of inception was instituted, nor do we have a history of its ceremonial development. No doubt its complexity in the fourteenth century grew out of a modest ceremony originating, most probably, in the second half of the twelfth century. It signified the launching of a new master on his academic career, and consequently his acceptance by the consortium of masters. The first prerequisite was the *licentia docendi* granted by the chancellor after the deposition of the masters. In the early twelfth century, the chancellor of the cathedral school granted the license to those he deemed worthy without any control by the masters; as this involved a payment of a fee, simoniac licenses were not infrequent. With the emergence of the masters' guild, or *consortium magistrorum*, the masters succeeded in requiring the chancellor to grant the license following some kind of deposition as to the worthiness of the candidate, as well as granting an explicit acceptance of the new master into its consortium. Already in 1213 the chancellor could not refuse the *licentia docendi* to anyone deemed worthy by "the greater part of the theologians actually teaching." However, he could still grant the license to a candidate not supported "by some masters or by any one master."[16] The chancellor could never refuse the license to anyone approved by the masters, but he could always grant the license on one not unanimously approved. In *Parens scientiarum* of April 1231, often called the "Magna Carta" of the University of Paris, Gregory IX required that within three months after the petition for the license the chancellor had to convoke all masters in theology living in the city to determine the "life, learning, fluency, as well as the intention and hope of progress" of the candidate so that the license could be granted in fair conscience.[17] Nevertheless, as I have said, the chancellor could always grant the license to those he deemed worthy, provided he had the testimony of two or three masters that all requirements had been fulfilled.[18] Once the *licentia* had been granted, the candidate could proceed with his inception in theology. Acceptance into the guild of masters was another matter; even in *Quasi lignum vitae* this question is discussed separately.[19]

The earliest detailed account of inception "secundum usum Parisienem" is contained in a Bologna MS first published by Denifle.[20] Although this description was composed "after 1362," it sheds light on what might have been the custom at Paris in the mid-thirteenth century. It will be helpful and illuminating to present here a paraphrase of this detailed account.

Inception was a solemn ceremony whereby a new master was inaugurated into a faculty of the university and began his duties of lecturing and determining disputed questions as his "ordinary" right. This ceremony took place on two days. The first part, called *vesperies*, took place in the evening (around "nineteen hours"), whence its name. The second took place in late morning in the middle of tierce, and was called inception proper, or *aula* in Paris, because it took place in the bishop's hall. Eight days before the day of his *vesperies*, the *vesperiandus* brought copies of four questions to be disputed to the home of all the masters and formed bachelors. The day selected had to be a *dies legibilis et disputabilis*, all other lectures and disputations in the faculty being suspended. All members of the faculty were bound to attend.

There was a clearly specified order of procedure. The first phase was the *expectiva magistrorum*, in which the first question was briefly disputed between the inceptor and the *respondens*, who was a bachelor; this took place under the presidency of the presiding master, who was normally the former master of the young inceptor. After this, all the other bachelors disputed, raising objections, to which there were no responses. When all were finished, the responding bachelor summarized the first argument and responded to it. Then one of the senior masters present proposed the second question to be disputed, arguing both for and against it. The inceptor then restated the question and argued his position, reverently forming "his beautiful, subtle, useful, somewhat prolix but strictly theological view." To this the senior master, remaining seated, objected with three or four arguments, and the inceptor responded reverently to the first three objections and rebuttals, or "subsumption." After this all the senior masters present proposed objections to what had been said for or against the view of the inceptor in two or three arguments, to which the inceptor could reply only twice. The first two questions having been disputed, the presiding master brought the proceeding to its climax with his commendation of Sacred Scripture and the outstanding character of the inceptor, who was normally one of his former students. Since he knew the inceptor so well, he often brought humor into his commendation through allusions, puns, and other connotations suggested by the name or physique of the individual. Finally, the presiding master announced the day of inception, the *aula* (or *aulica*), as well as the book the young master would lecture on during the year and the location of his school.

In the second phase, usually the following day, all the masters and students of the theological faculty gathered about the middle of tierce, that is, between ten and eleven o'clock in the morning, at the usual place of inception, all other lectures and disputations being suspended. The inceptor sat in the middle of the podium with the chancellor or his representative on his right hand, followed by all the senior masters; on his left sat the presiding master under whom the inception was taking place, followed by all the junior masters. First the inceptor received the sworn testimony of formed bachelors who would soon incept themselves. The presiding master, having placed on his head the master's biretta, placed one on the head of the inceptor, saying, "I place on you the magisterial biretta in the name of the Father, and of the Son, and of the Holy Spirit. Amen." The bedell then distributed birettas to the other masters to place on their heads. The biretta, or doctor's cap, was at that time the only symbol of authority; later the ring, originally a signet ring, was added. Then the chancellor gave the *licentia incipiendi* to the inceptor, who thereupon delivered his inaugural lecture (the *principium*), commending Sacred Scripture. Although this lecture was one of the high points in inception, it was supposed to be "brief" and "quickly terminated." Then one of the students proposed the third and most important question to be disputed. The respondent was a pre-appointed formed bachelor, who restated the question and reverently presented in response "a scientific and strictly theological position" with three conclusions dutifully proved and three corollaries. To this the inceptor objected with three arguments and rebutted the response twice. The fourth question to be disputed was argued among the junior and senior masters themselves. First, the oldest master proposed the question and argued for and against it, addressing his remarks to the youngest master, who, remaining standing throughout the discussion, replied "magisterially with a succinct position." The oldest master then stood up and presented two or three arguments against this position, and the youngest repeated the arguments and replied. For a third time the oldest master rose and rebutted the arguments, to which the youngest again replied and sat down. Then the second oldest master rose, posed the same question, and argued for and against it with different arguments from those already used; the second youngest master, standing, argued a position "altogether different" from that of his junior. Then the new master, the inceptor, "determined" the third question briefly with one conclusion and no proof, for he would take up this question on a later day with all the arguments and determine it *magistraliter*. With the inception ceremony over, the newly created master was led out of the hall by his colleagues, *confrères*, and friends preceded by the bedells, and brought to his own residence for a day of rejoicing. Whatever festivities were held in his honor, the new master was not allowed to leave the city until he had delivered his first lecture, which complemented his inaugural, and given his definitive response to the third question proposed at inception.

When the ceremony of inception was over, the inceptor was a full-fledged master, but he was obliged to complement his inception by certain functions proper to his state as master; this complement was called a *resumptio,* or *reassumptio.* On the first *dies legibilis* following inception, he had to give a lecture "in which he brought to completion his incomplete *principium in aula.*" This, in fact, was another *commendatio sacrae Scripturae* complementing what he had said at inception. After this initial "lecture" he discussed what remained to be said concerning the second question disputed *in aula.* It will be remembered that at the time of inception the young inceptor took a definite position on the question, and that all masters were expected to oppose it. Whatever remained to be said could be brought up at this time. No doubt, it was a summary of the fundamental arguments for and against the question, and a brief presentation of the young master's original view. The most important act of this day, however, was the determination of the third question. At inception the young master simply stated his conclusion without proof. There was, in fact, no proper determination, and one of the important functions of a master was to give a determination, or solution, to questions disputed. On the first day after inception a summary disputation was held on this question, the *respondens* for this disputation being his own bachelor. The young master posed the objections, repeating the arguments of the masters presented at inception; the responding bachelor, no doubt, repeated the responses as best he could. Then the young master "determined" the question *magistraliter*, that is, "completely."

Since this procedure called *resumptio* took all morning, no bachelor lectured on the *Sentences* in that school, but *cursores* could read the Bible in the afternoon. It is explicitly stated that all formed bachelors were supposed to be present at this determination. But it is not clear whether other masters likewise suspended their lectures on that day; they certainly were not obliged to be present, and they already knew what the determination would be from the conclusion stated at inception.

The foregoing description of inception and its completion is taken, as was said, from a fourteenth-century MS dated by Denifle "after 1362." We cannot be certain how much of it pertains to the middle of the thirteenth century, or how much would be applicable to the procedure at Saint-Jacques in 1256. We know that the Dominicans "even held their own inceptions," which means that the entire ceremony was held in Saint-Jacques and no part of it in the bishop's *aula*. We can also be certain that the two fundamental aspects, namely, the lecture and the disputations, were an essential part of the ceremony, perhaps somewhat elaborated by 1362. On the whole, however, the procedure just described can be taken as reflecting more or less the common practice in the schools of thirteenth-century Paris.

Thomas was only thirty-one years old when he incepted in theology, having been dispensed from the ancient statute requiring that a master be not less than thirty-five years of age. The presiding master under whom he incepted was Elias Brunet of Bergerac, regent master of theology in the Dominican chair for foreigners. Thomas's inaugural lecture, or *principium*, as we know, was based on the text "Rigans montes de superioribus suis;

de fructu operum tuorum satisabitur terra."[21] It was delivered at his inception on the second day of the ceremony, in the morning, sometime in April or May 1256, and not in the summer months, as some have argued.[22] Inception in theology could never be held during the long vacation.[23] Neither was this *principium* held on the opening day of the academic year 1256–57, as some have contended. Nor was it a sermon preached at Sainte-Geneviève, as others have imagined.

The theme of Thomas's inaugural address was the Dionysian principle that divine providence has ordained all higher gifts, both spiritual and corporeal, to descend from the highest even to the lowest through intermediaries. Just as the rains from above water mountains and form rivers that flow to the earth and fecundate the soil, so spiritual wisdom flows from God to the minds of listeners through the mediation of teachers. In this law of divine wisdom there are four points to be considered: the sublimity of spiritual doctrine, the dignity of its teachers, the status of its listeners, and the order of instruction.

As to the first point, Thomas held that the sublimity of sacred doctrine can be seen from its origin, its subtlety of content, and its sublimity of end. The origin of sacred doctrine is divine wisdom, which dwells on high. Its content is divine wisdom, some truths of which are inserted in the hearts of all men, even though imperfectly; there are other higher truths that are grasped only by the ingenuity of wise men trained in the use of reasoning; and there are the sublimest truths, which surpass all human reason. These latter are handed down by sacred teachers, learned in the text of Sacred Scripture, for it is on this level that Wisdom itself is said to dwell. The sublimity of sacred doctrine can be seen from its end, for it has the highest goal of all, namely, eternal life.

Because of this sublimity of doctrine, its teachers hold an eminent position comparable to the mountains watered from above. These teachers are comparable to mountains for three reasons: their elevation from the earth, their splendor in illumination, and their protective shelter against harm. Thus just as mountains are high above the earth, so teachers contemn earthly matters and aspire to heavenly things alone; mountains are the first to be illuminated by the rays of the sun, so teachers of

Sacred Scripture are the first to receive mental splendor by participating in divine wisdom; and just as mountains protect the valleys, so teachers defend the faith against errors. Therefore teachers should be elevated in their lives so as to illumine the faithful by their preaching, enlighten students by their teaching, and defend the faith by their disputations against error. It is to these three functions, preaching, teaching, and disputing, that the text of Titus 1:9 refers: "able both to exhort in sound teaching and to confute opponents."

The status of listeners is comparable to the earth made fruitful by the streams in three ways: its lowliness, firmness, and fecundity. Thus the listener should be humble in receiving sacred doctrine, firm in discriminating between right and wrong, and fruitful so that the good listener may promulgate many words of wisdom from the few that are heard.

Finally, the order of communication is touched upon from three points of view. First, just as the teacher himself cannot grasp the whole of divine wisdom, so he should not try to communicate to the listeners all that he knows. Second, only God has this wisdom by his nature; teachers share in this abundantly, though not completely; and listeners share in it sufficiently to fructify. Therefore, the wisdom that is communicated is not attributed to the teacher, no more than the first fruits of the earth are attributed to the mountains, but to God who is above. Third, the power of communication belongs properly to God and only secondarily to teachers, who are only ministers and servants of divine wisdom. But for them to be apt ministers of wisdom, God requires four qualities: innocence, learning, zeal, and obedience. Although no one by himself and of himself is adequate to such a ministry, he may hope that sufficiency will come from God: "our sufficiency is from God" (2 Cor. 3:5). Therefore the teacher ought to beg this from God: "If anyone needs wisdom, let him seek it from God, who gives to all abundantly and does not reproach, and it will be given to him" (Jas. 1:5). Let us pray that Christ grant it to us. Amen.

The Florentine MS G. 4. 36 (Conventi soppressi, S. Maria Novella), containing this *principium*, contains also a second *principium*, a *sermo secundus fratris Thomae*, a commendation of Sacred Scripture more in the traditional and proper sense of the word; it divides all the books of Scripture, and is based on the text of Baruch 4:1, "Hic est liber mandatorum Dei, et lex quae est in aeternum; omnes qui tenent eam pervenient ad vitam."

P. Mandonnet, assuming that Thomas was *cursor biblicus* for two years at Paris before lecturing on the *Sentences*, always insisted that this "second lecture" served as Thomas's *principium* in 1252, when he began lecturing cursorily on the Bible. This view is followed unanimously today by all editors and biographers of Thomas,[24] but, as I have said, there is no evidence whatever to support it. Not only was Thomas never a *cursor biblicus* at Paris, but there is no evidence that such a *principium* would have been required of the *cursor*, for the task of a *cursor biblicus* was academically and intellectually insignificant. It is clear that Thomas's task in 1252 was to begin his lectures on the *Sentences*.

From the position of the *sermo secundus* in the MS, it would seem to be of later date than the preceding *principium* and of the same nature as the first *sermo*. But it is more reasonable to hold that the second lecture represents the lecture given in the *resumptio* on the first *dies legibilis* following inception; that is, the more plausible hypothesis is that the commendation of Sacred Scripture was the complementary lecture given by the young master at his *resumptio*. This second lecture was supposed to complement what had been said by him in the *aulica* following *vesperies:* "in which lecture he brought to completion his incomplete inaugural lecture given *in aula*."[25] There is, in fact, a recognizable continuity between these two addresses. The first discusses the sublimity of sacred doctrine given by divine wisdom to the teacher to hand on to the faithful so that their lives may be nourished; the second discusses the authority, immutability, and utility of divine wisdom as found in the Old and New Testaments, given to man in the *liber mandatorum*. Therefore, these two addresses should be read in conjunction with one another and as an integral part of the inception ceremony.

Similarly, historians have, for the most part, failed to investigate or discuss the questions disputed at inception. These questions, of course, could never be constructed a priori. But there are strong indications that two of the four questions disputed by Thomas at his inception do in fact exist and are preserved in his authentic writings. Quite by chance, as it seems, half of the MSS containing *Quodlibet 7* also contain two appended disputed questions. In the printed editions these are question 6 with three articles (or if one follows the consecutive numeration, questions 14, 15, 16), which discusses the senses of Sacred Scripture, and question 7 (or 17 and 18), which discusses in great detail the role of manual labor in the over-all polemic with William of Saint-Amour. All authorities agree on two important points. First, these two unrelated disputed questions in no way belong to or are related to *Quodlibet 7;* they are not quodlibets at all, but two distinct *quaestiones disputatae.* For some unknown reason they have been appended to *Quodlibet 7* in half the MSS. Second, *Quodlibet 7* contains in essence a summary of the quodlibet Thomas held at Paris during Advent in 1256, that is, during Thomas's first academic year as regent master. It was his first quodlibet. Authorities discussing these two *quaestiones* seem to place them among the "extra-serial" disputations arising from his classwork in 1255–56 or 1257.[26] But that is hard to believe, especially because during his first academic year, Thomas conducted a regular series of disputed questions *De veritate,* as we shall see, and the only occasion available for free questions would have been the Advent quodlibet, which, as it happens, in no way touches the antimendicant controversy then raging in Paris. But some might argue that it was precisely because of the raging antimendicant controversy and William of Saint-Amour's argument concerning the need for mendicants to perform manual labor, instead of teaching and preaching, a special occasion arose despite the fact that William's *De periculis* was condemned on October 5 of that year. But on this hypothesis, there is no way to account for the extra-serial disputation on the senses of Sacred Scripture with which it is always associated.

A more satisfactory theory would seem to be that these two *quaestiones* appended to *Quodlibet 7* are two of the four questions discussed in the ceremony of inception. The question of the senses of Sacred Scripture could very well be "question two" discussed at that time. The question on manual labor could very well be "question three" discussed at inception. As we know, the "third question" was the most significant of the four questions; it was not only the longest question disputed at inception, but the one the inceptor was bound to "determine" in the *resumptio* on the first *dies legibilis et disputabilis* following inception. It is hard to imagine that such a burning question would have been neglected by Thomas on the very occasion of his laying claim to the second Dominican chair in the university. In any case, I am sufficiently convinced that the two questions appended to *Quodlibet* 7 constitute questions two and three debated at Thomas's inception.

The second question raised for discussion, as we have seen, was posed by a senior master who argued both for and against it. The inceptor then argued his position reverently, expressing "his beautiful, subtle, useful, somewhat prolix but strictly theological view." Against this the senior master posed three or four objections, and afterward all senior masters raised objections to what had been said by the inceptor or the senior master. There was no final resolution to this question at inception, except in the sense that the inceptor had already stated his theological conclusion.

Concerning the disputed question on the senses of Sacred Scripture, three points are raised: first, whether the words of Sacred Scripture contain more than only the literal sense; second, whether there are four senses as Augustine and Bede testify; and third, whether any other writings contain these senses. Thomas's position on this subject in no way differs from the one later proposed in *Summa theologiae* I, q. 1, a. 10, eleven years later. For him, there are two basic senses in Scripture: the literal, indicated by the words used to express the truth intended by the author; and the spiritual, indicated by things, persons, and events narrated to signify other things, persons, and events. The literal, or historical, sense is at the foundation of the spiritual sense and is the only sense valid for theological argumentation. Moreover, the spiritual sense is not a personal or private interpretation (sometimes called an "accommodated" sense). Rather it is a true sense explicitly indicated as such in other parts of Scripture. In other words, the spiritual sense is a true, objective sense intended by the Holy Spirit—for example, the idea of Christ as the new Adam, the brazen serpent elevated by Moses in the desert, the paschal lamb, and so forth. But there are three kinds of spiritual sense, all directed toward believing correctly and acting correctly. For acting correctly in order to reach eternal beatitude, there is the *moral*, or *tropological*, sense. For believing correctly, the spiritual sense includes both the OT figures signifying Christ and His Church, the *allegorical*, or *typical*, sense, and the NT figures signifying the Church triumphant both in its head and in its members; this latter is generally called the *anagogical* sense.

While the terms used by Thomas and other authors are not always consistent, the meaning intended by the four traditional senses of Scripture is always clear. The historical, or literal, sense is exactly what the human and divine authors intended by the narration. The spiritual sense, founded on the literal and explicitly claimed as such by a sacred author or tradition, refers to events, statements, and figures of a later age; it is a distinct truth. Sometimes, according to Thomas, the passage of Scripture contains all four senses. Thus Christ's life and the figure of Christ can be interpreted in all four senses: the historical Jesus is the literal sense; beyond this there is the allegorical, as when His historical body "refers to" the mystical body that is the Church, the moral, as when His life is taken as an example for our own actions in imitating Him, and the anagogical sense, as when the life of Christ demonstrates to us the way to eternal glory.

The disputed question *De opere manuali religiosorum* would seem to be the all-important "question three" discussed on the second day of inception. If so, it was disputed in April or May 1256, at the height of the antimendicant controversy with William of Saint-Amour. Most authorities on this point consider the *quaestio* to be an extra-serial disputation arising from classwork in 1255-56 or 1256-57. Bourke seems to think that it arose from classes held in the academic year 1255-56;[27] Chenu[28] suggests the date 1257, during Thomas's first academic year as master; and Walz-Novarina[29] dates it 1255-56. Bourke seems surprised that this *quaestio disputata* should be attributed to Thomas the bachelor, when such disputes are generally attributed to the determining master! But there can be no doubt that Thomas was in fact a master when he determined this question, and not a bachelor. Moreover, it is most probable that it was disputed and written before, not after, the condemnation of William's *De periculis* on October 5, 1256. Therefore, it is not probable that it was disputed and written during the academic year 1256–57. The most plausible theory is that *De opere manuali* was one of the questions disputed by Thomas at his inception. This view is also held by P. Castagnoli,[30] who places this question together with the one on the senses of Sacred Scripture within the context of inception.

P. Synave[31] has shown that this same question was discussed by Thomas in *Summa theologiae* II–II, q. 187, a. 3, "Whether religious are bound to work with their hands." In this work Thomas followed the stronger arguments already presented in the polemic *Contra impugnantes Dei cultum et religionem,* and not those presented in the disputed question *De opere manuali.* On this basis Synave argues that the *Contra impugnantes* is posterior to the less satisfactory arguments in the question *De opere manuali.* The only public occasion on which this question could have been debated is his inception in theology in April or May 1256.

Briefly, the question deals with two points: whether manual labor is a matter of moral obligation, and whether those who are engaged in spiritual works are excused from manual labor. Thomas argues that there are three purposes achieved by manual labor: combating idleness, controlling sensuality, and providing for the necessities of life. But these goals may be achieved by means other than manual labor. Thus idleness and sensuality may be overcome by a great variety of spiritual practices. As for the necessities of life, no one man can provide for all his needs; a mechanic should not be expected to grow his own food, nor should a lawyer or teacher be expected to weave his own clothes. The precept to work is a command not only of positive law read in the Scriptures, but also a command of natural law. But a precept either of natural or positive law binds in two ways: the first obliges every single person in order to guarantee his personal integrity; the second obliges the human species as a whole in order to guarantee the integrity of the whole human race, e.g., the precept to "increase and multiply and fill the earth" (Gen. 1:28). When the natural law dictates that one combat idleness and control sensuality, it does not specify the means for doing so. Thus individuals have an option on the means chosen for attaining the goal established by nature for the whole human race. Since no man can provide for all of his needs, but needs the help of others, the natural law requires that all men help each other and provide for one another according to their professional and natural abilities. Thus the precept to work with one's hands obliges the human race, but not every individual in it.

Thomas then discusses whether one who is devoted to spiritual work, such as preaching and teaching, must work also with his hands. His answer follows from the previous determination, namely, that "those who are engaged in spiritual work and who can live licitly without manual labor, are not obliged to work with their hands." Thomas then lists four kinds of spiritual offices which benefit the community, and are therefore licit means of acquiring a livelihood: ecclesiastical judges, preachers, those who sing Divine Office, and teachers of Sacred Scripture. The work of these men immediately effects the common good of man, while the work of those engaged in private prayers, fasting, and the like does not. These latter may or may not be obliged to work with their hands, depending on the needs of the community. Religious who engage in spiritual activities devoted to the common good are not bound to do manual labor, but are worthy of being supported by society; hence the licitness of begging, and the legitimacy of mendicant friars.

The whole of this question is important for a theology of work —a question that needs to be studied and taught in every generation, including our own. Some misguided priests today demean the importance of their spiritual message and service when they insist that their livelihood must come from manual labor. Dominicans in particular, ordained to preach the word of God, chant the canonical hours, and teach sacred doctrine, have a right to live by alms of the faithful, as Thomas explains. But they must not think that preaching, chanting, and teaching are works of supererogation to be performed "on the side." They must see their service to the people of God as a dedication of their whole life, sealed by solemn vows and the oath to live by the constitutions of the Order.

After Thomas held his *resumptio* in April or May 1256, he continued to write. It is not likely that he began a new course as master or continued his baccalaureate teaching for the remainder of the academic year to June 29. It would seem rather that Elias Brunet concluded the academic year in his own chair at the university, and that Thomas did not begin his teaching as master until September of the academic year 1256–57. Not only did he have to complete his *scriptum* on the fourth book of the *Sentences,* but he also had to devote much time to composing his *Contra impugnantes,* discussed in the preceding chapter. The *Contra impugnantes* was completed in Paris sometime in September or October, prior to his having heard of the papal condemnation of *De periculis* on October 5, 1256.

"Magister in Sacra Pagina"

The personal title *Magister in sacra pagina* designates the medieval teacher in his formal task of lecturing on the Scriptures, the "sacred page." It was the most ancient designation of a medieval theologian. Toward the end of the thirteenth century and thereafter, the title "Doctor in Sacred Theology" took precedence, no doubt because the Bolognese canonists preferred to be called "doctor" rather than "master" and because "theology" came to be looked upon more and more as a science, primarily speculative and secondarily practical.[32]

Throughout the entire Middle Ages the basic text of the masters' classes was the Bible—always the Bible. The extraordinary abundance of *Sentence*-commentaries that have survived would seem to give the impression that masters preferred the Lombard to the sacred text. But nothing could be further from the truth. The *Sentences* received more attention than the biblical text only in the brief period between Alexander of Hales's gloss, 1223–27, and approximately 1235, when the function of a bachelor was clearly defined. Denifle not only considers these commentaries on the *Sentences* as something secondary, but he even says that "the commentaries on the *Sentences* are the most imperfect products of the theological literature of the Middle Ages."[33] The masters had ample opportunity to display their speculative brilliance in the *quaestiones disputatae,* which they were bound to hold a number of times (*pluries*) within an academic year. But even in these theological disputations, the authority of the sacred text was primary; the testimony of patristic and ecclesiastical sources ranked next; and the use of philosophical reasoning ranked last.[34] Nevertheless it must be admitted that scholastic theologians not only indulged in rational argumentation, but excelled in it.

At one time in the Order of Preachers it was customary to supply a "socius" for the master in theology. The function of socius is best illustrated by Reginald of Piperno, who was socius to Thomas from 1259 onward. He was a lector in theology, a priest, and a very competent secretary from the Roman Province of the Order. In other words, most authorities now agree that Reginald was assigned by the Roman Province to assist Thomas in all his needs after Thomas returned to Italy from Paris. Reginald's functions as socius were to hear the master's confession, to serve him at Mass, to say Mass himself and allow Thomas to serve or at least attend if he were ill, to accompany him on journeys, to take dictation, and even to copy Thomas's *littera inintelligibilis* into legible script. He was more than a mere secretary who copied and took dictation; he was a personal companion, looking after all Thomas's needs. Reginald of Piperno, an Italian slightly younger than Thomas, served in this capacity from 1259 until Thomas's death. He served the needs of Thomas in much the same way as Godfrey of Duisburg did for Albert the Great in Germany.[35]

Many authorities claim that Friar Raymond Severi served in this capacity when Thomas first arrived in Paris in 1252, and for seven years after. Severi was a very young priest, from the Province of Provence, who could not speak Italian but who claimed to have heard Thomas's confession, to have served his Mass, and to have had Thomas as server for "seven years."[36] Friar Raymond Severi, according to Tocco, swore many times to the fact that in all seven years when he was with Thomas in Paris, hearing his confessions, he never heard Thomas accuse himself of once having given in to temptations of carnal desire and only most rarely of ever having "first movements of the flesh."[37] The "seven years" alluded to here are taken by Walz-Novarina to mean the years from 1252 to 1259. It is by no means certain, but still possible, that Raymond Severi was Thomas's socius in the technical sense of the term.[38]

Friar Thomas began lecturing on the Bible as master at the beginning of the academic year 1256–57; lectures began on the day following the feast of the exaltation of the Holy Cross, September 14.[39] In virtue of the license granted by the chancellor and the ceremony of inception, Thomas was a fully fledged master in theology who occupied the Dominican chair for foreigners at Saint-Jacques. However, he had not been accepted into the *consortium magistrorum*. William of Saint-Amour said that he would prefer to call a strike and leave the city rather than associate with the Dominicans. In fact Thomas lectured a whole year and worked through two long summer vacations—a total of sixteen months—before he was accepted by the university masters.

The turning point came on Sunday preceding the feast of the Assumption, August 12, 1257, when Thomas and Bonaventure were grudgingly acknowledged as suitable for membership. This acknowledgment and subsequent admission were effected only as the result of the condemnation of William of Saint-Amour's *De periculis*, the sworn repudiation of it by his followers, and numerous ordinations, exhortations, and commands issued by Pope Alexander IV.

On October 5, 1256, William of Saint-Amour's *De periculis novissimorum temporum* was condemned in Rome, following the examination of the book by a commission of bishops.[40] Almost two weeks later the Pope sent a letter to King Louis IX of France informing him of the condemnation, for it was he who had sent the book to Rome for examination; the Pope also commended the Preachers and Minors to his care.[41] Two days later, the Pope wrote again to Louis to enlist the help of Peter de Lamballe, archbishop of Tours, Odo, archbishop of Rouen, and Reginald Mignon of Corbeil, bishop of Paris, to have the Dominicans and Franciscans accepted by the Paris academic community.[42] Two days later he communicated with the two archbishops and Reginald to condemn William's *De periculis*; and that same day, October 21, he wrote to the entire French hierarchy to come to the support of the Dominicans and Franciscans. Two days later, October 23, he received the sworn testimony of two of William's colleagues, Odo of Douai and Chrétien of Beauvais, to follow fully the papal bull *Quasi lignum vitae*, to reject the errors contained in *De periculis*, and to receive into the academic community at Paris the Dominican and Franciscan friars, specifically Thomas and Bonaventure.[43]

In reply to a petition from the cathedral chapter of Rheims to Alexander to relax the punishment imposed on William of Saint-Amour, Odo of Douai, Nicholas dean of Barro supra Albam, and Chrétien canon of Beauvais, Alexander IV wrote a long letter on November 10, 1256, defending the rights and virtue of the Dominicans and Franciscans, and ordering that William's book be solemnly condemned within eight days under pain of excommunication.[44] Throughout the winter, spring, and summer of 1257, Alexander wrote in this strong vein to everyone concerned; and he ordered that the chancellor of Paris grant no license to anyone who would not swear to uphold the statutes of *Quasi lignum vitae*. On May 12, 1257, he rejected the pleas of certain unnamed Paris masters as frivolous, and insisted that *Quasi lignum vitae* be inviolably observed.[45] On July 14, 1257, Alexander wrote again to Reginald Mignon, bishop of Paris, to procure the admission of Thomas d'Aquino and Bonaventure into the consortium of masters at Paris.[46] On August 9, 1257, Alexander wrote directly to William of Saint-Amour, depriving him of all benefices, excommunicating him, and placing all his teaching and preaching under interdict forever.[47] Two days later he wrote to King Louis of France requesting that he forbid William's re-entry into the Kingdom of France—thus implying that William was known to be outside of France at that time.

It was not until the fall of 1257 that the Dominican and Franciscan masters were admitted into the consortium of Paris masters. Although Thomas incepted as master in April or May 1256, Bonaventure had incepted in the Franciscan chair in April 1253, three years earlier. The Paris masters had refused to recognize both, even though both of them had been lecturing in their respective chairs as masters. According to J. G. Bougerol,[48] Bonaventure obtained license to incept toward the end of the academic year 1252–53, having completed his thirty-fifth year as required by university statute. Recognition by the consortium was of little importance to Bonaventure personally, for he had been elected minister general of the Franciscan Order on February 2, 1257, when he was forty years old. Thus none of Bonaventure's lectures as master were recognized by the consortium of regent masters. But this recognition was of importance to Thomas personally, for he had two more years of lecturing ahead of him at Paris, and without this recognition his students could not be considered members of the University of Paris. By this recognition, however, both students and masters were reinstated.

The turning point came on Sunday, August 12, 1257, when Chrétien of Beauvais made a public statement of submission in the Franciscan church of the Cordeliers before the assembled Franciscans and Dominicans, including Bonaventure and Thomas. Although Reginald, bishop of Paris, subsequently wrote a public letter describing the entire affair, he himself did not preside but sent a representative instead.[49] On that occasion Chrétien first protested his innocence in face of the charges brought against him by the mendicants. He insisted that his actions had been misinterpreted and misrepresented by the mendicants to the Pope, that he was not and never had been a rebel to papal commands, nor disobedient, and that he had never refused to associate with mendicants, as was reported. In fact, he said, "after they [the Friars] were excluded from the university, I was with them in the school of Master James of Guérande, Canon of Tours, and I took their side." Desiring to show himself obedient in all matters, he promised the Pope that he would obey in all matters and even took an oath to this effect.

Chrétien had come to the Cordeliers to make a public profession of his loyalty on five counts. First, he professed acceptance of the bull *Quasi lignum vitae* with all of its ordinances, and promised that he would not knowingly act against it, nor give help or counsel, in public or in private, to opponents of this papal document. Second, henceforth insofar as was within his power, he would "accept into the academic community and into the University of Paris the Friars Preachers and Minors residing in Paris as masters, together with their students, and especially and expressly Friars Thomas d'Aquino, of the Order of Preachers, and Bonaventure, of the Order of Minors, doctors of theology." Chrétien went on to say, "I expressly accept the aforementioned doctors as masters; and in keeping with the aforementioned command, I shall see to it that these men are received in good faith by the university, that is, by the masters and students dwelling in Paris, and against the foregoing I shall never offer counsel or consent."[50] Third, he stated that he would exact no statutes, obligations, or oaths contrary to *Quasi lignum vitae*. Fourth, he further promised that he would permit no more trouble, strikes, or threats of removal of the university from the city of Paris. Finally, he repudiated the book *De periculis* and condemned all the errors it contained, specifically the identification of "pseudo-apostles and pseudo-prophets as well as ministers of Antichrist" with friars of the Order of Preachers and Order of Minors.

No doubt it was shortly after Chrétien's public statement that Thomas d'Aquino and Bonaventure were fully incorporated into the consortium of the University of Paris. We have no document declaring that the friars were incorporated on any specific date, but it was probably during the month of August that incorporation occurred. Possibly it was not even a public announcement, but only a verbal understanding. Bourke's account of master Chrétien's public statement makes it a humiliating occasion for Chrétien, whose words were "terse and bitter." He believes Reginald, bishop of Paris, wanted "to have as little to do with the proceedings as possible," and for this reason sent a delegate in his place.[51] Bourke also understands the public statement of Chrétien to be the full incorporation of Thomas and Bonaventure into the university. But on that occasion Chrétien spoke only in his own name and not in the name of the consortium; he merely said that he personally accepted them and that he would "see to it (*procurabo*) that these men are received in good faith by the university."

Thus the first phase of the antimendicant controversy came to a quiet end. William was exiled to his native town of Saint-Amour by order of Louis IX, King of France. William's immediate followers, Chrétien canon of Beauvais, Odo of Douai, Nicholas dean of Barro supra Albam, all submitted and repudiated the errors in William's *De periculis novissimorum temporum*. With the incorporation of the Dominican and Franciscan masters into the consortium of theologians, there was temporary peace. But this peace was not to last long. Hostility flared up again eleven years later at the instigation of Gérard d'Abbeville, who continued a steady correspondence with William of Saint-Amour

(d. September 13, 1272) after his exile. This later renewal of hostility was one of the reasons why Thomas was ordered to Paris for a second regency. But for the moment peace was restored, the mendicants could grow and prosper, and Thomas could turn his mind to other matters of greater importance in the university. Thomas was to lecture for two more years at the university in the Dominican chair for foreigners.

In his three years as master at the University of Paris, Thomas lectured, disputed, and preached, fulfilling all the requirements of his office. Already in the twelfth century the function of a regent master in theology was threefold: to lecture (*legere*) on a suitable authority universally recognized as such, to dispute (*disputare*) and determine questions brought up for discussion by himself, other masters, or students, and to preach (*praedicare*) university sermons, as well as others when the occasion presented itself. Peter Cantor (d. 1197) in the twelfth century had summed up the role of these three functions of a theologian:

> The exercise of Sacred Scripture consists therefore in three things: the lecture, the disputation, and the sermon. The lecture is, as it were, the foundation and underpinning of the rest. . . . The disputation is like walls for the building, because nothing is fully understood and faithfully preached unless it is first chewed by the teeth of disputing. But preaching, which is served by the other functions, is, as it were, the roof and covering for the faithful from the heat and unrest of vices. (*Verbum abbreviatum*, c. 1, PL 205, 25.)

The basis of the whole scholastic method was the text. A portion of the text, the sacred page, was read aloud in class. Not all students in the mid-thirteenth century had a personal copy of the Bible, and even if they had, a section of the text was read to refresh the memory. After the reading of the text, the master divided the section into parts. This division was most important, for by division, it was held, the mind comes to understand the whole. Then a line-by-line and word-for-word explanation was given, with reference to other texts of Scripture, the Fathers of the Church, and rational argument. Whenever conflicting statements appeared, either because of some apparent contradiction in the text of Scripture or in the comment of some ecclesiastical authority, the arguments from both sides would be debated briefly and a solution found. Without a basic respect for "authority," there could have been no scholastic method.[52] Arguments pro and con fundamentally involved respect for authority. When the argument in the *Glossa*—itself a collection of patristic explanatory notes—contradicted another authority or even reason, the task of the master was to explain the different senses in which the statement could be true. In other words, in the scriptural passage being discussed, there often arose "little disputations" within the commentary. By explaining the senses in which each authority could be understood correctly, the master expanded the depth of meaning contained in the scriptural passage.

In the scriptural commentaries of Friar Thomas that have come down to us, we distinguish between a *reportatio* and an *ordinatio*. A *reportatio* is a report of the live lecture taken down by a student or scribe. It does not purport to be an official redaction. This is the case with Thomas's lectures on Paul's first letter to the Corinthians, chapter 11 to the end of Hebrews, the lecture on Matthew, the lecture on the first four nocturns of the Psalter, and a number of others.[53] The commentary on John is in a slightly different category, for it was taken down during the lectures by Reginald of Piperno and later "corrected by Friar Thomas." On the other hand, an *ordinatio* is a finished product written or dictated by the author himself. Such is the case with all the commentaries on Aristotle, the *Quaestiones Disputatae*, the rest of the scriptural commentaries, the two *summae*, as well as all replies to queries sent to him. In the MS tradition of some early catalogues, the *ordinatio* is referred to as an *expositio*, while the *reportatio* is generally called a *lectura*, as we find in the so-called "official catalogue," presented by Bartholomew of Capua in the process of Thomas's canonization.[54]

If we exclude the *Catena aurea*, a special kind of work that can be dated with relative certainty, and the possibility that some of the extant commentaries were cursory lectures given in Cologne (see chapter 2), there are ten distinct works that must be ascribed to Thomas as the fruit of his mature years as master: the commentary on Job, that on the prophecies and lamentations of Jeremiah, that on the Psalms, that on the Canticle of Canticles, and those on Matthew, John, and the letters of Paul respectively.

In addition, there is the commentary on Isaiah, of debated date, which some seem to think is the work of a cursor; others, following Mandonnet, date it 1256–57, making it the fruit of Thomas's first year of teaching as master in Paris. The fact is that these biblical commentaries are extremely difficult to date in relation to the life of Thomas. I. T. Eschmann insists that it is too difficult and unprofitable to assign specific dates to the commentaries on Scripture.[55] Eschmann's position is a strong reaction to Mandonnet's "scholastic determinism," which would, he remarks, deprive Thomas of "the liberty to write what he pleases, when he pleases." Perhaps Eschmann's reluctance is a bit too hasty and sweeping. In any case, Mandonnet's position leaves much to be desired in the way of proof, even though it is accepted by many other scholars today.

Mandonnet's "concordism" by which Thomas's Scripture commentaries are linked to specific academic years must be used with great caution, for it is one thing to date the live lecture, and quite another to date the written product of those lectures or disputations. However, since Mandonnet's chronology is the basis for subsequent authors and scholars, it should be kept in mind. He has assigned the Scripture commentaries as follows:

1. first Parisian regency (1256–59):
   Isaiah, 1256–57
   Matthew, 1257–59

2. teaching in the papal states (1259–68):
   Canticle of Canticles
   Lamentations (*In thronos Jeremiae*)
   Jeremiah
   Paul (*reportatio*)

3. second Parisian regency (1269–72):
   Job, 1269–70
   John, 1270–72

4. teaching in Naples (1272–73):
   Psalms
   Paul, Romans–1 Corinthians 10 (*expositio*)

It will be noted that Mandonnet assigns none of the Scripture commentaries to Thomas's period of cursory teaching, whether in

Cologne or Paris. Further, he insists that according to Parisian custom, Thomas alternated between one book of the Old Testament and one of the New.[56] As for the commentary on St. Paul, Mandonnet assigns the lecture or *reportatio* to 1259–68, and the *expositio* to 1272–73. But Bernard Gui explicitly refers to Thomas as lecturing on St. Paul at Paris: "Once in Paris, when he was writing on Paul's epistles, he came to a passage which baffled him until, dismissing his secretaries, he fell to the ground and prayed with tears; then what he desired was given to him and it became clear."[57]

According to Mandonnet's assignments, Thomas commented on the prophecy of Isaiah during his first year of teaching as master in Paris, that is, 1256–57. It does not have the theological depth found in the exposition on Job or in the lectures on Matthew, John, and Paul. Neither does it contain the myriad citations of the Church Fathers, nor the discussion of the intricacies of the text that are found in his commentaries on Job, Matthew, John, and Paul. Rather it is a running commentary on each of the sixty-six chapters of the text.

The story is told by William of Tocco and other biographers[58] that on one occasion, while Thomas was composing his commentary on Isaiah, he came to a passage that baffled him because of the obscurity of the text. He fasted and prayed assiduously, begging for understanding of the text. One night, when he stayed up to pray, his socius Reginald overheard him speaking, as it seemed, with other persons in the room; though what was being said the socius could not make out, nor did he recognize the other voices. Then shortly afterward, Thomas called out, "Reginald, my son, get up and bring a light and the commentary on Isaiah; I want you to write for me." After an hour of continuous dictation, as though he were reading from a book, he dismissed Reginald and bade him sleep in the short time left till morning. But Reginald refused to leave until Thomas told him to whom he had been speaking. After much begging and abjuration Thomas admitted that the apostles Peter and Paul had been talking to him, explaining all that he wanted to know. Then Thomas dismissed Reginald with his customary remark, "Never tell anyone else of this as long as I live." This story was repeated by Tocco under oath during the canonization process at Naples, at which time he mentioned his sources. Tocco states that he learned of the incident from Francis de Amore of Alatri, vicar of the bishop of Nola, who had knowledge of it from Reginald of Piperno.[59]

A section of the commentary on Isaiah, chapters 34:1 to 50:1, is to be found in a holograph copy in MS Vat. lat. 9850, together with the holographs of the *Contra gentiles* (I, c. 13, to III, c. 120) and *Super Boethium De trinitate* (q. 3, a. 2, to q. 6, a. 4).[60] A. Dondaine, assuming the commentary on Isaiah to be early, argues that Reginald of Piperno must have been Thomas's secretary even during the first Parisian regency.[61] This view, however, is contrary to the wide belief that Reginald became Thomas's secretary and socius only after Thomas returned to Italy. One could also argue that if Reginald became socius to Thomas only after 1259, then the commentary on Isaiah must be of late composition.

Some authorities argue that Thomas wrote in his unintelligible hand (*littera inintelligibilis*) only early in his career, and that later in life he had only to dictate to secretaries. But we know that even during his first Parisian regency he had such secretaries as Friar Raymond Severi, Friar Nicholas de Marsillac, Friar Peter d'Andria, Ligier de Besançon, and others. At the same time it is to these years that the autographs are assigned! Moreover, the testimony of William of Tocco shows that Thomas's whole adult life was occupied with holy activity, so that "he would always pray and meditate or read, preach, write or dictate" (*scriberet vel dictaret*); elsewhere also Tocco refers to Thomas's "writing or dictating" (*scribendis aut dictandis quaestionibus expendebat*); and he notes that Thomas wrote what he taught and dictated (*scribere vel dictare*).[62] It would seem from this testimony that Thomas himself both wrote and dictated throughout his academic life; and consequently it would be dangerous to assume that Thomas wrote his own works in his own hands when he was young but only dictated later when he returned to Italy. Therefore no argument as to date of composition can be based on the existence of an autograph passage; that is, from the fact that Thomas's commentary on Isaiah survives in an autograph fragment, we cannot argue that it is an early work.

In other words, Thomas's commentary on Isaiah could just as well have been written later than 1256–57 with the help of Friar Reginald of Piperno.[63] It could have been delivered during one of the ten years of residence in the papal states. If Thomas lectured on a second book of Scripture, either of the Old or New Testament, we are not yet in a position to argue the point.

The *Lectura super Matthaeum* is clearly a work written while Thomas was in Paris, and dates most likely from his first years there as master. There are several internal references to Paris and to France, which would indicate a Paris origin. It is a *reportatio* taken down in the classroom, partly by Friar Peter d'Andria, and partly by a secular cleric named Ligier de Besançon (Leodegarius Bisuntius).[64] Mandonnet suggests that it took Thomas two years to deliver the *lectura* because it is twice the length of the exposition on Isaiah. Walz-Novarina[65] suggest that the first fourteen chapters were reported by Peter d'Andria, while chapters 15 to 28 were taken down by Ligier de Besançon. This hypothesis may, however, involve an oversimplification of the question.

The story is told by William of Tocco, copied by Bernard Gui, and reported by Bartholomew of Capua and Antonio of Brescia in their sworn deposition in the canonization process at Naples[66] that one day, Thomas and some students, returning from a visit to the relics of Saint-Denis, were struck by the beauty of Paris in the distance, with its city walls and the splendid towers of Notre Dame. As they drew near to the city, one of the students said to Thomas, "Look, Master, what a fine city Paris is! Wouldn't you like to be the lord of it?" Thomas answered, "What would I do with it?" Hoping to receive an edifying answer, the student said, "You could sell it to the king of France and use all the money to build all the places for the Dominican Friars." "I would rather," replied Thomas, "have the homilies of Chrysostom on the Gospel of Saint Matthew." Undoubtedly Thomas had seen or heard reference made to John Chrysostom's commentary; but apparently, if the anecdote is true, he had not yet found a copy to read. By the time Thomas lectured on Matthew, he certainly had found a copy and read it very carefully, for he refers to Chrysostom at the very beginning of his commentary. Altogether in this *lectura* Chrysostom is quoted 215 times, a number just slightly less than the references to Augustine and slightly more than those to St. Jerome. Chrysostom's homilies on Matthew had been translated in part from the Greek by Anien de Celeda in the early fifth century; but a new complete translation was made by Burgundio of Pisa (d. 1194) in the twelfth century. G. Mercati[67] has shown that Thomas used the homilies of Chrysostom on Matthew in the version of Burgundio.[68] The same Latin version was used by Thomas for his *lectura* on Matthew and for his *Catena aurea* on Matthew compiled a few years later.

The two earliest catalogues of Thomas's works refer to the lectures on Matthew as "defective" and "incomplete."[69] These references are undoubtedly to the two lacunae in the three Italian MSS known. One lacuna is long and conspicuous; it extends from Matthew 5:11 to 6:8. The other is shorter, 6:14–19. In other words, in the current Marietti edition, nn. 444–582 (the old Lectio 13–17) and nn. 603–10 (the old Lectio 19) are spurious, as was noted by R. Guindon,[70] who has shown that the spurious passages are influenced by the *Summa Alexandri* and the *Postilla* of Hugh of Saint-Cher. Soon after, H.-V. Shooner showed that the spurious section is taken from Peter de Scala, a Dominican who died in 1295, and who also wrote a commentary on Matthew.[71] Bartholomew of Spina, the first editor of the text in 1527, noticed the lacunae and supplied the deficiency by using the commentary of Peter de Scala without any indication of his substitution.[72] Shooner also discovered the authentic text of Thomas in the library of the University of Basel (B. V. 12). It is ironic that when the Dominican feast, the Patronage of Saint Thomas, was first introduced in the Dominican calendar in the 1920s, the homily for third lessons was taken from the unsuspected spurious part of the *lectura* commenting on "Vos estis sal terrae." This feast was established on the thirteenth of November to allow festivities outside of Lent, since the original feast of Thomas, which had always been celebrated on March 7, the date of his death, invariably fell in Lent. The November 13 feast has since been abolished, and Thomas's feast has now been transferred to January 28.

Thomas, as we have seen, lectured for three years as master in Paris, 1256–59. During that time he lectured on Matthew for one or two years. It is not likely that he commented on Isaiah at that time, but it is not clear what other book he lectured on as well. While Thomas lectured in Paris he had a number of secretaries to write down his classroom lectures on Matthew and to jot down the arguments in public disputations.

As a "Master in the Sacred Page," Thomas had to hold public disputations "a number of times" (*pluries*) throughout the academic year. The primitive catalogue submitted by Bartholomew of Capua as part of the process of Thomas's canonization gives the basic chronology of these *quaestiones disputatae:* "in three parts: one part disputed at Paris, namely *De veritate;* the second in Italy, namely *De potentia Dei,* and the rest; the third at the second time in Paris, namely *De virtutibus* and the rest."[73] The intriguing question is how much is included in the phrase "and the rest" (*et ultra*). At least the designation of the first Parisian disputations, *De veritate,* over a period of three years, is clear. Strictly speaking the title of this work designates only the first question in the total collection of 29 questions; in the catalogue of Nicholas Trevet, the work is titled *De veritate et ultra.* In the current Marietti edition, *De veritate* contains 29 questions and 253 articles.

Mandonnet was convinced that the basic unit of the disputation was the article within a question. He therefore devised a scheme to accommodate each article to a day in the academic year (see Table). Since there were forty-two weeks in an academic year, if one knows how many articles exist for disputation, one should be able to calculate the number of times Thomas disputed during each academic year. As the Table indicates, Mandonnet frequently had to separate articles within a question by a whole summer vacation, as when in analyzing Thomas's second year of lecturing, 1257–58, he had to separate question 20, article 4, from question 20, article 5, by a whole summer! Such a conclusion is surely unreasonable, for article 4 and article 5 belong to the same question being disputed. P. Glorieux, trying to revise Mandonnet's tables, has at least the merit of keeping all questions intact with their articles.

A. Dondaine has clearly shown the anomaly of Mandonnet's theory.[74] If each article is supposed to represent a single solemn disputation, there would have been a serious disrupture of the faculty of theology. We would have to suppose that Thomas held 253 disputations in his three years at Paris, two every week; and since each disputation was made up of two parts, the debate and the determination, Thomas would have presided over four sessions a week—thus leaving no time for the other eleven masters to dispute or teach at all. Clearly Mandonnet's assumption is not reasonable.

Dondaine reasonably claims that the basic unit of the disputation is the entire question, no matter how many articles each question has. It seems certain that each master personally designated the number of points, or articles, each question would have, depending on the nature of the question. While Dondaine's view is more reasonable than Mandonnet's, it does not solve all our doubts. It does not, for example, explain how a question of twenty articles compares with a question of two articles in an afternoon session.

The technique of a *quaestio disputata* is not altogether clear. It would seem that on the first day, the day of the actual dispute, the respondent was a bachelor. In Thomas's case, the senior bachelor was William of Alton, an English Dominican who succeeded Thomas in 1259–60. Or the respondent could have been his junior bachelor, a fellow Roman, Annibaldo d'Annibaldi, who succeeded to the chair, 1260–62, and later became cardinal in 1262 and died at Orvieto in 1272. The official task of the bachelor at all disputations was to respond to objections that came from the audience, in the order in which they were presented on the point (or article) proposed by the master. Possibly his task was also to provide arguments "sed contra," but of this we cannot be certain. As each objection was raised and refuted by the bachelor, a scribe would write down the arguments and replies. The disputation would thus continue throughout all the points (or articles) indicated by the master. Some sessions were long and intricate; others were relatively short (three hours were probably allowed for the debate). On the following day, after considering each argument pro and con, the master gave his *determinatio*, or resolution, to the entire question; this resolution naturally followed the order of the previous day, namely the order of the articles (if there were any). Very often the master followed the "responses" given by his bachelor. The version of the disputa-

CHRONOLOGY OF THE QQ. DISP. OF THOMAS

P. MANDONNET

(Introd. to Paris ed., Lethielleux, 1925)

Paris	1256–57	De veritate	aa. 1–84	=	qq. 1–8
—	1257–58	—	aa. 85–166	=	q. 9–q. 20, a. 4
—	1258–59	—	aa. 167–253	=	q. 20, a. 5–q. 29
Anagni	1259–60	De potentia	aa. 1–21	=	q. 1–q. 3, a. 8
—	1260–61	—	aa. 22–42	=	q. 3, a. 9–q. 5, a. 8
Orvieto	1261–62	—	aa. 43–63	=	q. 5, a. 9–q. 7, a. 9
—	1262–63	—	aa. 64–83	=	q. 7, a. 10–q. 10
—	1263–64	De malo	aa. 1–20	=	q. 1–q. 3, a. 3
—	1264–65	—	aa. 21–40	=	q. 3, a. 4–q. 4
Rome	1265–66	—	aa. 41–60	=	q. 5–q. 8, a. 2
—	1266–67	—	aa. 61–80	=	q. 8, a. 3–q. 13, a. 3
Viterbo	1267–68	—	aa. 81–101	=	q. 13, a. 4–q. 16
—	Sept.–Nov. 1268	De unione	aa. 1–5		
Paris	Jan. 25–June 1269	De spirit. cr.	aa. 1–11		
—	1269–70	De anima	aa. 1–21		
—	1270–71	De virtutibus	aa. 1–20	=	to De carit, a. 7
—	1271–Easter 1272	—	aa. 21–36	=	from De carit. a. 8

P. GLORIEUX

("Les Q. Disp. de s. Thomas," RTAM 4 [1932] 22)

Paris	1256–57	De veritate	aa. 1–84	=	qq. 1–8
—	1257–58	—	aa. 85–168	=	qq. 9–20
—	1258–59	—	aa. 169–253	=	qq. 21–29
Anagni	1259–61				
Orvieto	1261–65				
Rome	1265–67	De potentia	aa. 1–54	=	qq. 1–6
Viterbo	1267–68	—	aa. 55–83	=	qq. 7–10
—	Sept.–Nov. 1268	De spirit. cr.	aa. 1–11		
Paris	Jan. 25–June 1269	De anima	aa. 1–21		
—	1269–70	De virtutibus	aa. 1–36		
—	1270–71	De malo	aa. 1–5	=	q. 1
—	1271–72	—	aa. 6–101	=	qq. 2–16
—	May 1272	De unione verbi	aa. 1–5		

tion given to the stationer of the university should not be confused with the oral debate, for the final version was completely edited and documented by the master often at a much later date.

In the case of the questions *De veritate*, the procedure and text are quite clear. The questions were disputed over a period of three years. In the first year of teaching (1256–57) Thomas disputed the first seven questions, which have something of a unity: (1) on truth, (2) God's knowledge, (3) divine ideas, (4) the "verbum," (5) divine providence, (6) predestination, and (7) the "book of life." Possibly some of these discussions were carried over an extra day, but there is no evidence of that. Hence, Thomas held a public, or solemn, disputation only eight times, or possibly nine times, throughout the whole academic year of forty-two weeks. In the second year (1257–58) he disputed thirteen times (qq. 8–20), again on questions having a kind of unity: (8) angelic knowledge, (9) angelic communication, (10) the mind as an image of the Trinity, (11) on teaching, (12) prophecy as knowledge, (13) ecstasy, (14) faith, (15) higher and lower reason, (16) synderesis, (17) conscience, (18) Adam's knowledge in paradise, (19) the soul's knowledge after death, and (20) Christ's human knowledge in this life. In his third year of teaching (1258–59) Thomas disputed only nine times: (21) on goodness, (22) desire for good and the will, (23) the will of God, (24) free will, (25) sense desire, or "sensuality," (26) human emotions, (27) grace, (28) justification of the sinner, and (29) grace as it is in the soul of Christ.

It seems infinitely more reasonable to say that Thomas disputed 8 or 9 times in 1256–57, 13 times in 1257–58, and 9 times in 1258–59 than it is to say that he disputed 253 times throughout the first three years of teaching, or 84 times each year, or 2 full disputations each week. I. T. Eschmann accordingly referred to Mandonnet's concordism as "academic determinism," wherein Thomas was not allowed to be sick a single day, and wherein Thomas was seen as a disputing machine.

Quodlibet questions were a special kind of disputation that masters could hold, if they wished, during Advent and Lent. By definition a quodlibet was a public disputation about any subject whatever: "de quolibet ad voluntatem cuiuslibet."[75] For this kind of disputation there was also a bachelor to respond and a master to give his determination, just as in the ordinary disputations throughout the year. The main difference is that in a quodlibet, masters could not propose the subject to be discussed; this came from any student or master in the audience: "de quodlibet." The proposal of a question for discussion could come from anyone permitted in the room: "ad voluntatem cuiuslibet." Often such questions were an embarrassment to the master, who was bound to determine them in that session. At one time Mandonnet believed that Thomas himself originated quodlibetal questions,[76] but when quodlibets of earlier masters were discovered it became clear that Thomas was merely using a tool that others had created. One might almost say that only masters of some daring would expose themselves to "any kind of question" raised from the floor.

According to Mandonnet's chronology, about which there has been little discussion, Thomas allowed himself to be asked about any question during his first three years of teaching in Paris. It should be noted that quodlibet discussions were held only in the University of Paris at that time, and not outside that academic community. Moreover, quodlibet discussions were held only during Advent and Lent, and were frequently called the Christmas or Easter quodlibet. According to Mandonnet,[77] Thomas's *Quodlibets VII* to *XI* date from his first regency in Paris:

Advent, or Christmas Quodlibet	1256—*Quodl. VII*
Lent, or Easter Quodlibet	1257—missing
Advent, or Christmas Quodlibet	1257—*Quodl. VIII*
Lent, or Easter Quodlibet	1258—*Quodl. IX*
Advent, or Christmas Quodlibet	1258—*Quodl. X*
Lent, or Easter Quodlibet	1259—*Quodl. XI*

By the very nature of a quodlibet, there is no inner connection among the questions raised from the floor; the only unity each has arises from the time of year in which the questions are raised. Thus in Thomas's *Quodlibet VII*, there are five "questions" discussed, each divided into "articles," having no relation to one another; they range from the possibility of seeing God face to face, to the question whether punishment in hell involves physical worms and physical tears. We have already mentioned that two *quaestiones disputatae* were later attached to *Quodlibet VII*, Thomas's first quodlibet; these are the question on the senses of Scripture and the one on manual labor.

According to the Parisian bookseller's list of 1304,[78] both the *De veritate* and all the quodlibets were then available. *De veritate* consisted of forty-six pecias (or fascicules) and could be rented for copying for four soldi; the quodlibets consisted of twenty-four pecias, and rented for eighteen denarii.

The importance of Thomas's disputed questions cannot be overestimated, for in his questions he reveals the genius of an outstanding master who allowed himself full rein to delve into the profundities of theological truth. While the later *Summa theologiae* was written for beginners, the commentaries on Scripture and the *quaestiones disputatae* were written for the proficient.

Little can be said at this time about Thomas's preaching career during his first Parisian regency. One of the serious obligations of masters was to preach sacred doctrine. University sermons were always in Latin, and they were listed in the university calendar. Even bachelors had to preach a specified number of times before they could incept in theology. There were, of course, other types of sermons. Some were preached in the vernacular for the faithful, such as during Lent or other times when a series of vernacular sermons was called for. Very often a vernacular sermon or series was organized first in Latin, with the particular points to be preached and the biblical examples to be used in illustration included. Many of these sermon notes have survived in Latin, but the vernacular texts seem to be lost.

It is certain that Thomas never preached in French, for he never learned that language, even though he lived more than ten years in Paris. But when he was in the papal states in Italy and in Naples, we know that he did preach in the Italian vernacular.

During his last few months in Paris, he preached many sermons in Latin. When Thomas was preaching on Palm Sunday, April 6, 1259, a bedell of the Picard nation, Guillot, interrupted Thomas and began reading "a certain famous pamphlet" attacking the mendicant friars. We do not know what happened next; most likely he was stopped by the faithful in the congregation.

This incident came to the attention of Pope Alexander IV, who wrote to Reginald, bishop of Paris, from Anagni on June 26, 1259. In the Pope's eyes this pamphlet was William's *De periculis*, already condemned publicly.[79] However, Denifle[80] says that it is not easy to say what pamphlet this could have been. We know that pamphlets shorter than William's *De periculis* had been written and had circulated "afresh both in Latin and in the vernacular with the addition of popular ditties and unseemly songs."[81] The bedell Guillot was deprived of his office and income in perpetuity and excommunicated. Anyone else who kept, copied, or sold such pamphlets was to be *ipso facto* excommunicated. It was the duty of Reginald, bishop of Paris, to see that all papal decrees were carried out.

In the spring of 1259 Thomas presided over the inception of his successor in the Dominican chair for foreigners. This successor was the Englishman William of Alton, who was Thomas's senior bachelor. William incepted sometime in spring and became regent master in the Dominican chair for foreigners for only one academic year, 1259-60. Annibaldo d'Annibaldi, Thomas's junior bachelor, succeeded William for two academic years, 1260-62.[82] Annibaldo, nephew of Cardinal Richard Annibaldi, belonged to the Roman Province, as did Thomas; therefore they had a common ground for conversation in the Italian vernacular. In December 1262, Annibaldo himself was created cardinal by Urban IV with title to the church of Dodici Apostoli. In his commentary on the *Sentences*, written probably in 1258-60, Annibaldo adhered so closely to the doctrine of Thomas that for a long time it was thought that Thomas himself revised his own commentary or wrote another one and dedicated it to Annibaldo. This text is published in the *Opera Omnia* of Thomas's works, and entitled *Scriptum in IV Sententiarum ad Hannibaldum*. This was printed many times as Thomas's own. Thomas did, however, dedicate part of his *Catena aurea* of the four Gospels to Annibaldo after the death of Urban IV on October 2, 1264, as we shall see.

Before discussing the ten years Thomas spent in Italy prior to his return to Paris, we should consider briefly the influential *Summa contra gentiles*, a work begun in Paris and finished in Italy.

Extracurricular Activities

By extracurricular activities is meant all those writings and commitments of Thomas that did not originate from strictly academic obligations. One of the most important of these is the *Summa contra gentiles*. Like the more famous *Summa theologiae*, the *Summa contra gentiles* was not taught in the classroom, nor did it originate in the classroom. According to tradition, it was a work requested by Raymond of Peñafort, who after serving as master general of the Dominican Order for only two years, 1238–40, resigned to work in Barcelona, and died on January 6, 1275. The basis for this ancient tradition in the Dominican Order is the *Chronicle of the King of Aragon, James II*, written by Friar Peter Marsilio in the Dominican Priory at Barcelona, and completed on April 2, 1313.[83] In it Friar Peter states:

> Ardently desiring the conversion of infidels, he [Raymond of Peñafort] asked the illustrious doctor of the sacred page, master in theology, Friar Thomas d'Aquino of the same Order, who, next to Albert, is considered the greatest philosopher among all clerics in this world, to write a work against the errors of the infidels that would both take away the thick atmosphere of darkness, and unfold the doctrine of true light to those willing to believe. That master did what the humble petition of such a father required, and he produced a work called the *Summa contra gentiles*, which is thought to have no equal in its field.

It would seem that in about the middle of the thirteenth century a *studium arabicum* was established at Barcelona for the training of Dominican missionaries to work among the Moslems and Jews. Thomas's work was not intended for beginners, but for missionaries who were more or less familiar with the errors they had to combat. Dom Peter Marc suggests that the original petition for such a work came from Ramón Martí, the well-known Catalan missionary in Spain and the author of *Pugio fidei*, who visited Paris toward the end of 1269. If the idea originally came from Ramón Martí, it was still apparently the influence of Raymond of Peñafort, at a much earlier date, that made Thomas realize the importance of the missionary efforts in Spain and North Africa. Since learned Moslems and Jews had thoroughly assimilated Aristotelian teaching, the task of Thomas was to attack specific errors by name and doctrine with a barrage of arguments so that if some arguments failed to convince, other arguments might. Not all Thomas's arguments in this work have equal logical force, for many are dialectical in nature and not demonstrative. Some are appeals to authority; others are closely reasoned passages, developed at great length.

From the testimony of Antonio of Brescia given during the canonization process in Naples, we know that part of the *Summa contra gentiles* was written in Paris. Antonio states that he heard from Friar Nicholas of Marsillac, who was a disciple of Aquinas's and conversant with him for "a long time in Paris," that among other things Thomas was a lover especially of poverty, so that when he was writing the *Summa contra gentiles,* he did not have regular sheets of paper (i.e., parchment) to write on, but used small scraps.[84]

The traditional view is that Thomas began work on the *Summa contra gentiles* during the third year of his first Parisian regency, 1258–59, and finished it at Orvieto in 1264.[85] This traditional view holds that the particular time referred to by Nicholas of Marsillac is the first Parisian regency. Dom Peter Marc, however, interprets the testimony of Nicholas as referring to the second Parisian regency, that is, 1269–72. This proposal, if accepted, would require complete restudy of the chronology of Thomas's works, and presents us with an impossible situation.[86]

The incomplete autograph of Thomas's *Summa contra gentiles,* extending from Book I, c. 13, to Book III, c. 120, is contained in Vatican MS Vat. lat. 9850, fol. 2ra-89vb. That is, a major portion of this important work exists with all its cancellations, revisions, and corrections, and it can be examined critically; this has been done by the editors of the Leonine edition of Thomas's works, v. 13–14. Thomas's own handwriting, illegible as it is except to a few scholars, has all the marks of a man writing swiftly, but generally carefully; there are many corrections, deletions, additions, and changes.[87]

It is difficult to determine how much of this text was composed at Paris. Some scholars, including Chenu[88] and A. Dondaine,[89] maintain that Thomas completed the text up to III, c. 45 (because some of the manuscripts end there); but the autograph copy continues to III, c. 120, without break. Other scholars contend that Thomas had not written more than the first fifty-three chapters of Book I in Paris.[90] In any case, the entire *Summa*, which is entitled in some MSS as *Liber de veritate catholicae fidei contra errores*, but mentioned in all the early catalogues as *Liber* or *Summa contra gentiles*, was finished at Orvieto in 1264. Tolomeo of Lucca is careful to indicate that it was written during the pontificate of Urban IV (1261–64): "Also during the pontificate of the same pope [Urban IV], he wrote a book against the gentiles and questions De anima."[91] This statement should be taken to mean that the work was completed under the pontificate of Urban IV, but begun during the pontificate of Alexander IV. Dom Marc has argued that, since Tolomeo of Lucca is in error on some points, he could be in error about the dating of the *Summa contra gentiles;* but as I. T. Eschmann notes, "Not infrequently Tolomeo's chronologies are defective, but in this case he seems to be right."[92]

Although the *Summa contra gentiles* is written in four books, it is divided into two basic parts: Books I–III dealing with truths about God that can be known by human reason, and Book IV, truths about God and divine things that can be known only by revelation. The first three books develop the basic Dionysian theme of God and all that man can know of Him by reason with the aid of philosophy (Book I), the emanation of all things from God (Book II), and the return of all things to God (Book III). Book IV discusses those truths which are completely beyond what unaided human reason can determine; it discusses four major issues that must be believed to attain salvation: the Trinity (cc. 1–26), the Incarnation (cc. 27–55), the sacraments as effects of the Incarnation (cc. 56–78), and the resurrection of the body and final judgment (cc. 79–97).

Since the infidels, against whom the missionaries would debate, were familiar with the philosophy of Aristotle and the writings of Avicenna, the first three books rely heavily on Aristotle and Avicenna. Although Thomas occasionally mentions Avicenna only to reject his errors, elsewhere Thomas's exposition of Avicenna's doctrine may be taken as implicit acceptance of it.

Avicenna's influence is particularly evident in chapters 22, 25, and 26 of Book I, where Thomas discusses the absolute simplicity of God, who is *necesse esse*. The metaphysical apogee of Thomas's natural theology is found in chapter 22, where he argues that *esse* and essence are identical in God. This chapter adheres almost verbatim to Avicenna's *Metaphysics* VIII, 4, but Avicenna's name is never mentioned in it.

In Book II, which treats of the emanation of all things from God, Thomas adheres strictly to the needs of the Moslem mission. That is, he selects for discussion only the major differences between the teachings of Christian and Moslem philosophy: the power of God (cc. 6–14), free creation *ex nihilo* (cc. 15–38), the distinction between creatures (39–45), spiritual substances (46–55), the union of soul and body in man (56–72), the possible and agent intellect of man (73–78), the human soul (79–90), and finally in a brief discussion, separate substances (91–101).

Book III deals with the return of all things to God; in it Thomas argues against both Moslem and Jewish philosophies. He shows that God is the ultimate end of all men, for He is the First Principle of all. In his lengthy discussion of divine providence and governance, he shows in great detail the return of all things, even individual men, to their ultimate goal, for God has care of all things from the lowest to the highest. From chapters 111 to 163 he argues that both Mosaic law and grace are aids whereby man can attain this goal.

Much of the same field is covered more systematically in his *Summa theologiae*. The difference is that in the later work Thomas was developing an over-all view of the whole of theology for beginners; therefore only the most direct and simple arguments were used to establish an organic whole of what beginners ought to know before progressing onward. In the *Summa contra gentiles* Thomas was primarily an apologist selecting the most important issues separating Christians from Moslems, Jews, and heretical Christians. While beginners can be satisfied with one or two salient arguments that often demonstrate the truth, missionaries in Spain and North Africa needed a great number of arguments, even dialectical arguments, to show the errors in gentile philosophy and convince infidels of the truth of the Christian religion.

Although Thomas's *Summa contra gentiles* was not a university text, it was sold by the University of Paris's stationer as late as February 1304; it was listed as containing fifty-seven pecias, and sold for forty-four denarii, the same as for the third part of his *Summa theologiae* in fifty-five pecias.[93] In the fourteenth and fifteenth centuries it was translated into various Near Eastern languages.

Before Thomas left Paris, he wrote an exposition on Boethius's *De trinitate* and *De hebdomadibus*, two anomalous and almost anachronistic works. These two treatises by Boethius are the second and third of his five theological tractates. In the twelfth century they were the subject of numerous commentaries by the early schoolmen. But Thomas seems to have been the only outstanding figure in the thirteenth century who commented on them. Strictly speaking, his commentary on Boethius's *De trinitate* is not complete, for his analysis extends only to the first few lines of chapter 1; it consists of a scholastic commentary on the prooemium and the opening lines of chapter 1 together with six illuminating questions on the text. These questions deal with man's knowledge of divine things (q. 1), manifestation or discussion of divine truth (q. 2), the relation of faith to man (q. 3), the cause of diversity (q. 4), the division of the speculative sciences (q. 5), and the methodology of the speculative sciences (q. 6). Although this is a theological tractate, philosophers of recent times have devoted much thought to questions 5 and 6, dealing with the classification and methods of the speculative sciences. Scholars since Uccelli had known that half of the commentary, question 3, article 2, to the end, exists in autograph in MS Vat. lat. 9850, fol. 90ra–103vb. But it was only recently that a textual analysis was made of this work by P. Wyser, B. Decker, L.-B. Geiger, P. Gils, and a few others. The pioneer doctrinal analysis made by Geiger is well known to all Thomistic scholars.[94]

Questions 5 and 6 are of special interest because they contain the only extensive discussion of the sciences and scientific method written by Thomas. In question 5, article 1, Thomas examines the traditional classification of the speculative sciences into natural science, mathematics, and divine science (or metaphysics) in general; in the following three articles he discusses each in particular.

For all the ancients, including Boethius, there are only three generically distinct speculative sciences worth talking about: natural science, mathematics, and metaphysics, each hierarchically distinct from the other by a certain abstraction from matter in such a way that mathematics is more abstract than natural science, and metaphysics more abstract than mathematics. Frequently these are implicitly or explicitly viewed as distinct "grades of abstraction." While each science abstracts from a certain kind of matter, both natural science and mathematics consider their formal object enmeshed in some kind of matter. Thus, for Thomas, following Boethius and Aristotle, the natural scientist prescinds from making statements about individual instances as such, and examines the entire universe that is enmeshed in matter and motion, i.e., all scientific statements in natural science are about tangible bodies in motion, their principles, definitions, and laws. If this is to be called "abstraction," then natural science abstracts the whole nature of a species from its individual instances. This is called "total abstraction," for it leaves out of consideration only the individual instances of the nature, which could be called its "parts." In reality this kind of abstraction is common to all the sciences; they do not make laws about the individual as such, but only about universal facts or cases in general.

On the other hand, all branches of mathematics are concerned with extensive and numerical quantities; they leave out of their calculations the actual matter in which these quantities are found. This is called "formal abstraction," for it discusses quantities as though there were no "matter" in which these "forms" exist. Strictly speaking, for Thomas the mathematical sciences alone really "abstract," for the mathematician patently leaves out of consideration sensible matter in which quantities really exist; they are not interested in wooden triangles or copper triangles, but only in "triangles." The only kind of "matter" left in mathematical abstraction is "intelligible matter," i.e., the mental existence of a given quantity under discussion.

Thomas's unique contribution to the discussion of the sciences concerns metaphysics. Both Aristotle and Boethius say that metaphysics "abstracts" from all matter. In the first redaction of his commentary Thomas himself used the expression, but in the process of revising the text, he changed the word *abstractio* to *separatio*, thus indicating clearly his personal view of metaphysics. The metaphysician, according to the corrected text of the commentary, does not really abstract at all, for he is concerned with all beings precisely as they are being. That is to say, if a negative judgment can be made that "not all beings are material," then there is a new subject to be studied. Thus, if it can be shown that there is something in the universe that is *not* material, but "separated" from matter, it cannot be studied by the natural scientist or the mathematician, but must be studied by the metaphysician. This "separation" from matter means two things: first, that there exists something which is completely immaterial (God, separated substances, the human soul), and second, that not all common terms, such as "substance," "act," "potentiality," and "causality," are necessarily restricted to material things, but they are conceived and used analogously of both material and immaterial reality. Thus to the objection that even matter and motion are beings, and therefore they should be studied in metaphysics, Thomas replies that metaphysics does consider matter and motion and even individuals, but only insofar as they are beings, not insofar as their individual and specific nature makes them distinct from other things (q. 5, a. 4 ad 6).

One other point ought to be made here. Thomas admits that there are forms of mathematical knowledge that study matter and motion, such as astronomy, mechanics, optics, and even musicology. These sciences he calls *mediae,* for they depend on pure mathematics for the principles they use, and on natural science for data. It would seem that Thomas was the only philosopher in the Middle Ages who used the expression *scientiae mediae* in this sense (cf. q. 5, a. 3 ad 6 and ad 7). Thomas understood well the nature of applied mathematics, at least in its philosophical structure.

The date of Thomas's commentary on Boethius' *De trinitate* has been partially settled by M.-D. Chenu, who discovered that Annibaldo d'Annibaldi used this work in his brief commentary on the *Sentences*, which he taught under master Thomas. Annibaldo lectured on the *Sentences* probably in 1258–60, and finished writing his commentary shortly thereafter. Eschmann and Chenu date this commentary 1260–61. Therefore Thomas's exposition of Boethius's *De trinitate* was completed by 1258 or 1260 at the latest.[95]

All the early biographers of Thomas note that he *dictated* this commentary on Boethius: "dictaret super tractatum boetii de trinitate."[96] Nevertheless a large portion of that commentary exists in autograph. Therefore we should be cautious about making generalizations on Thomas's writing and dictating; he could have dictated what he himself had already written in his *littera inintelligibilis*. If so, the suggestion that Thomas wrote and dictated all his life can be understood in that sense. We know for a fact that some of his secretaries, such as Reginald of Piperno and certain others, could read Thomas's handwriting so as to transcribe the text into more legible script—but this was at a much later date.

Thomas's memory and powers of concentration were extraordinary. According to Bernard Gui, his memory was extremely rich and retentive: "Whatever he had once read and grasped, he never forgot."[97] Gui goes on to say: "Still stronger is the testimony of Reginald, his socius, and of his pupils and those who wrote to his dictation, who all declare that he used to dictate in his cell to three secretaries, and even occasionally to four, on different subjects at the same time."[98] Gui further mentions that one of Thomas's secretaries, a Breton named Evan from the diocese of Tréguier, relates that Thomas, after dictating to him and two other secretaries, would sometimes sit down to rest from the work and, falling asleep, would go on dictating in his sleep, with Evan meanwhile continuing his transcription.

The full title of the third theological tractate written by Boethius is "How substances insofar as they exist are good." In the Middle Ages it was commonly known as *De hebdomadibus*, a term taken from the opening sentence of the work. Thomas's commentary on this short tractate by Boethius is divided into five *lectiones*. The central question is whether beings are good by their own essential nature (*per essentiam*) or by reason of participation (*per participationem*). This treatise, among others, helped Thomas to establish his philosophy on a real distinction between *esse* and *quod est*. Although Boethius's distinction is not identical with what Thomas made of it, Thomas frequently appeals to Boethius and Avicenna as his source for the real distinction between *esse* and *quod est*, as he understood it. The central theme of the tractate is that although there are many kinds of "good," nevertheless "all things are good insofar as they are derived from the first good," who has goodness by his very nature. This work is essential for our understanding of the Thomistic development of the doctrine of participation and for the study of the real distinction between *esse* and *quod est*.

The date of *In librum Boethii De hebdomadibus* is uncertain. In the catalogues it is listed with *In Boethium De trinitate*, and many scholars accept the association, dating both around 1256–59.

There is no indication why Thomas chose to write commentaries on these two Boethian tractates. Possibly they were private lectures given at Saint-Jacques, but that does not seem likely. It is also possible that someone asked for clarification of these two tractates, and that Thomas obliged him with a short commentary. In any case, these two commentaries show the development of Thomas's thought during this early period at Paris.

Before returning to Italy at the end of the academic year 1258–59, Thomas was summoned to take part in the Dominican general chapter meeting at Valenciennes early in June. Thomas was not present as a member of the chapter, for it was a "Provincials' chapter," meaning that only acting provincials in the Order were expected to attend it.[99] But Thomas was invited to be a member of a special commission established by the master general Humbert of Romans to discuss studies in the Order and to suggest what might be done to promote them. Assigned to this commission were Bonhomme, Florent of Hesdin, Albert the Great, Thomas d'Aquino, and Peter of Tarentaise—all masters in theology of Paris.[100]

In a sense, the collected statutes of the commission formed a kind of *ratio studiorum*, the first of its kind in the history of the Dominican Order. Besides detailing the rules governing the behavior of lectors and students, its most significant item seems to be that students needing further training in the arts, i.e., philosophy, should be sent to provinces having such studia with well-qualified lectors. It would seem that by 1259 many young men sought entrance into the Dominican Order but had no proper training in the arts and philosophy. Early in the history of the Order, many youngsters entered the Order after they had some training in the liberal arts and the three philosophies, namely, natural, moral, and first philosophy, or metaphysics. The commission warned that good teachers should not be given tasks to perform that interfere with their primary task of teaching. Lectors teaching in a "solemn studium" are to have a bachelor to teach under their supervision. Lectors are to remain teaching as long as possible; lectors on sabbaticals should go to school, especially for the disputations held therein. Everything should be done to promote the teaching of the lectors and the learning of the brethren. If no lector is available to teach "publicly," someone should be provided to teach "privately" either Bible history or *summa de casibus*, or something of this sort, "lest the brethren become lazy."

The significance of this commission, which was established "to promote study" in the Order, is that the master general and the provincials were intent on promoting the ideal of study intended by St. Dominic. The early constitutional statute that required even priors to attend class when possible was reiterated in the decisions of the commission. Had more details been spelled out by this commission, we would have a better insight into the workings of an ordinary priory, one not blessed, as was Saint-Jacques, with its two masters, four bachelors, and many willing students.

When Thomas left Paris in the spring of 1259, he left many intimate friends behind. Little did he know that he would return to a much different Paris ten years later. His life for those ten years was one of personal development in his service to the Church, the papacy, and the Order.

Chapter IV

MASTER THEOLOGIAN IN THE ROMAN PROVINCE

(1259–65)

The next ten years of Thomas's life are difficult to document historically. The early biographers, except for Tolomeo of Lucca, delineate the chronology carefully until he became a master at Paris, and then, suddenly, they turn full attention to miracles, visions, and other external marks of his sanctity; for their legenda were written with an eye to Thomas's canonization. Further, the aids to reconstructing those ten years are frugal compared to those related to the theological curriculum in Paris and the anti-mendicant controversy, and to the abundance of papal letters published in the *Chartularium* of the University of Paris. Even the testimony of Tolomeo of Lucca cannot be relied upon completely to give an accurate account of events. In most cases, Tolomeo's account must be carefully weighed and checked against other known facts. Thomas's writing and teaching during his sojourn in Italy are particularly difficult to ascertain because the evidence available leaves much room for speculation. Nevertheless, some historical facts can be unearthed from the testimony of witnesses given in the canonization process, from contemporary documents, and even from the early biographers themselves.

In short, we are on less secure ground for this period of Thomas's life and works than we were in earlier chapters. If, as Mandonnet observes, Thomas was present at all provincial chapters, we can say with certainty where he was for the few days of the chapter, but little else; the acts of both provincial chapters and general chapters tell us almost nothing about Thomas or his activities. Thomas's writings themselves fare somewhat better; they can be examined for intrinsic dependencies, changes of thought, the occasion of writing, and other details that can help us to determine more precisely when the particular work was written. Most of Thomas's writings were a direct response to the needs and requests of others. All of his writings should probably be seen as an act of apostolic service to the intellectual needs of the Church and the needs of men seeking the truth. This aspect of his work is most clearly seen in the literary apostolate undertaken during his ten years in the Roman Province.

Tolomeo of Lucca explicitly states that Thomas, "after three years of lecturing as master [in Paris], . . . returned to Italy at the time of Urban IV, under whose pontificate he wrote many useful works."[1] Later, "for certain reasons (*ex certis causis*) he returned from Paris, and at the request of Urban he did many things and wrote much."[2] But there is an intrinsic contradiction in saying that after three years of teaching in Paris Thomas returned to Italy at the time of Urban IV. Urban was elected on August 29 and crowned Pope on September 4, 1261, at Viterbo. His pontificate extended from August 1261 to October 1264; by 1261 Thomas had been in Italy for almost two years, and was already attending provincial chapters as a preacher general. He finished his three years of teaching in Paris in the spring of 1259.[3] Today most historians, following Mandonnet, agree that Thomas left for Italy after his three years of teaching as master, 1256–59, during the pontificate of Alexander IV, who died at Viterbo on May 27, 1261. However, it is clear that Thomas was never assigned to Anagni during the pontificate of Alexander, as Mandonnet believed.

Tolomeo's statement that Thomas returned to Italy from Paris "for certain reasons" has aroused the curiosity of many historians who would like to know why Thomas left Paris. Six possible causes have been suggested, some of them simply outlandish.[4] The simple explanation is that he had finished his assignment in Paris, and William of Alton, an English Dominican, was ready to succeed Thomas in the chair for foreigners. No doubt, Thomas's own province of Rome also wanted him back as soon as possible; for some extraordinary reason, superiors always want their students to return "as soon as possible."

As mentioned in the previous chapter, Thomas was present at the general chapter of Valenciennes early in June 1259, although he was not a member of the chapter. Since Valenciennes is a considerable distance north of Paris, Thomas must then have returned to Paris, if not to complete the academic year on June 29, at least to gather his books and other belongings for the long trip south. He could have traveled to Italy in the company of other Dominicans from the chapter, perhaps in the company of the master general, Humbert of Romans, and his own provincial. On the other hand, Thomas may have remained in Paris a few more months, until fall, reaching his destination in Italy toward the end of 1259 or early 1260. Denifle,[5] Walz,[6] and Dondaine[7] seem to favor the latter hypothesis or some adaptation of it. Thomas undoubtedly did not arrive in the Roman Province before the provincial chapter of Rome in September 1259, at which the provincial presided. Indeed it would seem that in that month neither the provincial nor the capitular fathers knew when to expect him; if they had, the chapter would undoubtedly have appointed him preacher general; they did so the following year when he "had returned from Paris as a master in theology."[8]

The logical place for Thomas to go was to his home Priory of San Domenico in Naples, where he had received the Dominican habit. It was now twenty-five years since Thomas had seen this Priory, and he barely knew it when he received the Dominican habit; it thus would be a new experience for him.

The commonly accepted view today (following Mandonnet) is that Thomas went immediately to the curia of Pope Alexander IV, who had done so much for him—but this view lacks foundation in any document. If Thomas had gone to Anagni, where Alexander made his residence, it seems that Tolomeo of Lucca would certainly have recorded this fact, especially if Alexander had requested that he come, as some historians claim. Tolomeo's history is based entirely on the chronology of the Popes. As it was, Tolomeo associated Thomas's return with Urban's pontificate, not with Alexander's. Mandonnet claimed not only that Thomas went to Anagni, but that he lectured on Isaiah and disputed the questions De potentia during the "academic" years 1259–61.[9] The truth is, rather, that Thomas probably spent that time in Naples: there is no documentary record that he was in Anagni at any time during the pontificate of Alexander IV; none of the early biographers even hint at it; and the hypothesis suggested by Mandonnet and repeated by subsequent authors is without support of any kind.

During the first canonization inquiry, July 12 to September 18, 1319, at Naples, Friar Conrad of Sessa, a friar seventy-seven years of age, testified that he had known Thomas for many years and talked freely with him at Naples, Rome, and Viterbo.[10] This chronology (omitting Orvieto, where Conrad apparently did not live) is surprisingly accurate. Thomas first went to Naples where he lived until assigned to Orvieto in 1261. Afterward he was assigned to Rome, and then to Viterbo. The testimony of Friar Conrad thus confirms our suspicion that Thomas, upon leaving Paris, first went to Naples.

There is, indeed, every indication that Thomas spent the first year and a half after his return to the Roman Province at San Domenico in Naples, engaged in writing his *Summa contra gentiles,* which he had barely begun in Paris. During these years at Naples he may have replaced the lector of the Priory, but of this possibility there is no evidence. No doubt, it is likely that he did take over the teaching responsibilities of the lector; but whether he did or no, Thomas seems to have had ample opportunity to write one major work, or a part of it, undisturbed by the great multiplicity of tasks that usually engaged him. Never again would he have such leisure to write. Even so, the autograph of the *Summa contra gentiles* gives every indication of haste, as usual; and Thomas seems to have written only the first book during his residence there.

The *Summa contra gentiles* was completed during the pontificate of Urban IV, as Tolomeo testifies,[11] and after his *Contra errores Graecorum* (summer 1263). Book II could not have been written before 1261, for in it Thomas quotes Aristotle's work on animals in the new Greek-Latin translation of Moerbeke. The Aristotelian work on animals existed at first in an Arabic-Latin translation comprising nineteen books and bearing one general title, *De animalibus.* This was the version Albert used for his long commentary, or paraphrase. William of Moerbeke, however, made a new, complete Greek-Latin translation distinguishing the five sections of the original work, giving them their original titles: *De historiis animalium, De progressu animalium, De motu animalium, De partibus animalium,* and *De generatione animalium.* The new translation of *De partibus animalium* was finished at Thebes on December 23, 1260. When, therefore, Thomas cites *De generatione animalium* in chapters 21, 88, 89, and *De motu animalium* in chapter 72 of Book II, the quotations incontrovertibly point to 1261 as the earliest date of composition for this book.[12] As we shall see, Book IV must have been completed sometime during the year 1264, the last year of Urban's pontificate.

When the *Summa contra gentiles* was finished, it was copied at least twice, and one was sent off immediately to Raymond of Peñafort in Barcelona. However, in order to accomplish this task, even in the unlikely case that Thomas had written Books I–III, c. 45, in Paris (as Mandonnet, Chenu, and A. Dondaine claim), he would have needed at least one secretary to transcribe the *littera illegibilis* of the autograph into legible script for Raymond. Fortunately, from the moment Thomas arrived in the Roman Province, he was assigned Reginald of Piperno as a *socius continuus.* Reginald was to spend the greater part of his life in the service of Thomas, going wherever he did, taking dictation, transcribing, serving Mass, hearing confession, and assisting in every way.[13] Obviously Reginald would not have been able to read Thomas's script during the first year or two of their association. So Thomas would have been obliged to dictate the text to Reginald; while dictating, Thomas could have made corrections and alterations. In any case, there was a period of time between completion of the autograph and sending the *Summa contra gentiles* to Raymond of Peñafort.

Thomas was the first member of the Roman Province to become a master in sacred theology of Paris, just as Albert was the first member of the German Province to do so. Thomas was, in the words of Masetti, the "splendor of the Roman province."[14] One way of showing him esteem was the assignment of Reginald of Piperno to be Thomas's permanent socius. Another mark of esteem was his appointment as preacher general (*praedicator generalis*) for Naples: in 1260 the provincial chapter met in Naples on September 29, and "in this chapter many preachers general were appointed; among them was Friar Thomas d'Aquino who had returned from Paris as a master in theology."[15] Another document states that "Thomas was made preacher general for Naples in the chapter of 1260; and only four of them were made."[16]

In the thirteenth and fourteenth centuries only the preachers general had a personal and permanent right to vote in the provincial chapters. That is, they had voice as a permanent right in all provincial chapters by reason of being preachers general and not by reason of being provincial, prior, or socius, which carried their own right of active voice. Thus the members of the chapter governing the province were, besides the preachers general, the acting provincial, the priors during their term of office, and one socius from each priory, elected by the community for a particular chapter. From the early days of the Order the province was governed by elected superiors and the preachers general; they met in chapter once a year following the general chapter of the Order. A preacher general was a capable preacher who preached and made all arrangements for preaching in a specified area, namely, the area of the priory; as such, he was exempt from the jurisdiction of the prior in certain matters. Then, as now, there could be only as many preachers general as there were fully established priories. It was not until 1407 that masters in sacred theology obtained the same rights and legislative duties as were held by the preachers.[17] In other words, if the Roman Province wanted Thomas to have direct voice in the yearly chapter of the province, they had to appoint him preacher general, and this they did for the Priory of Naples from 1260 until his death.

Thomas attended all the provincial chapters until he returned to Paris in the fall of 1268. The following list of chapters[18] which Thomas attended as preacher general will give some idea of the traveling Thomas had to do during his stay in the Roman Province:

> 1261, September 14, at Orvieto
> 1262, July 6, at Perugia
> 1263, September (?), at Rome
> 1264, September 29, at Viterbo

1265, September 8, at Anagni
1266, August 5, at Todi
1267, July (?), at Lucca
1268, May 27, at Viterbo (also place
    of general chapter)

The provincial chapter at Orvieto, September 14, 1261, assigned
Thomas to be lector "at the priory of Orvieto for the remission of
his sins."[19] Urban IV was crowned Pope at Viterbo on September 4, ten days before the chapter; a year later he made his residence in the new papal apartments in Orvieto and lived there
during most of his four years as pontiff. Urban certainly did not
ask the chapter to assign Thomas to Orvieto. Nevertheless, this
assignment set the pattern that was later to be legislated in the
general chapter of Bologna in 1267: "The prior provincial of the
Roman province should diligently see to it that the priory where
the [papal] curia resides, should be provided with suitable friars
for the needs of the curia, particularly the prior and the lector."[20]

Orvieto with Urban IV

(1261-65)

During the four years Thomas spent at Orvieto, a warm friendship developed between Urban IV and himself. When Urban arrived with his curia in 1262, Orvieto became a center of much activity; scholars, diplomats, bishops, and missionaries from all
Christendom came to his court at one time or another, some of
them remaining for a considerable time. Although Urban was engaged in a losing war with Manfred, son of Frederick II, he
"was a great friend and promoter of philosophical studies,"[21]
and he was deeply concerned with reconciling the schismatic
Greek Churches with Rome. It was in this atmosphere that
Thomas discovered new horizons in accurate translations of
Greek texts and in the value of Greek theology.

The poet Master Heinrich of Würzburg wrote an encomium of
the court at Orvieto in 1263-64, entitled *De statu curiae Romanae*. In a few lines he describes the illustrious court and the

presence of a great philosopher of considerable eloquence who had become the wonder of the scholarly world:

> Whoever comes will find whatever he thirsts for;
> That house is equipped with all the arts.
> There is someone there, O Philosophy, who, if the
> House burned to the ground, would design a new one.
> The new builder would erect it in finer fashion and,
> By his art, would prove superior to men of old. (vv. 877–82)

The editor of the poem, Hermann von Grauert,[22] considered this philosopher to be Thomas d'Aquino. However, as Martin Grabmann has pointed out, the philosopher alluded to can be none other than Heinrich's countryman, Albert the Great.[23] Citing numerous contemporary sources, mainly German, that referred to Albert as "a great philosopher" and "the wonder of the world," Grabmann showed that Albert was better known to his contemporaries as a philosopher than as a theologian, even though he was a master in theology of Paris and bishop of Regensburg. In fact, he was far more famous than Thomas ever was during his short lifetime.

Albert, as provincial of Germany (1245–57), traveled to the court of Alexander IV at Anagni to defend the mendicant Orders in the controversy with William of Saint-Amour in 1256; he came again to the Roman curia in 1261, this time to petition for release from his bishopric. Passing by way of Vienna, Albert arrived at the curia of Alexander IV at Viterbo in July 1261, but he found that Alexander had died in May. Urban IV, who was elected on August 29, heard his plea and absolved him from the episcopal office he had reluctantly accepted in the first place, allowing him to draw up a will to be kept in the curia. Urban also allowed Albert to remain at the curia, which he did until February 1263, when Urban designated him to preach the crusade in Germany and Bohemia.[24] When Urban IV moved his curia to Orvieto in the fall of 1262, Albert came with him, making his residence, no doubt, at the Dominican Priory of San Domenico from the fall of 1262 until February 1263. It is not surprising that Master Heinrich the poet should allude to the great philosopher who made all parts of philosophy "intelligible to the Latins."[25] At that time, discovering the Aristotelian treatise *De motu animalium* in the Moerbeke translation, Albert published it with a commentary in the same style as he had in his earlier works.

While Albert accompanied the curia at Viterbo and Orvieto, it is possible but most unlikely that he lectured and disputed. However, when Albert was at the court of Alexander IV at Anagni in 1256, not only is he said to have lectured on the whole of St. John's Gospel and part of St. Paul, but, as he himself tells us, he held a disputation at the request of the pontiff against the Averroist doctrine of the unicity of the possible intellect for all men. This disputation, according to Albert, was later made into a treatise called *Contra Averroem* (or *De unitate intellectus*).[26] Because of these lectures and this disputation, Albert is often described as one of the "Masters of the Sacred Palace," about whom more will be said later.

Also at the court of Urban IV was Giovanni Campano of Novara, one of the most important mathematicians of the thirteenth century; of special importance are his detailed commentary on the *Elements* of Euclid and the *Theorica planetarum* composed at the request of Urban. Principally known today as an outstanding geometrician, extolled in all histories of science, he was at the court as chaplain and physician to Urban and later to all succeeding Popes until the end of the pontificate of Boniface VIII. He died on June 28, 1298.[27]

All historians of the subject insistently claim that the Flemish Dominican William of Moerbeke (c. 1215–86) must also have been at the court of Urban IV at Orvieto, thus making possible the grand edifice of Christian thought that was to emerge from the collaboration of Thomas d'Aquino and Moerbeke under the patronage of Urban. A great part of William's laborious task of translating, according to Grabmann, "was in the service of the Christian Aristotelianism created by the Angelic Doctor."[28] Vernon Bourke baldly states that "William of Moerbeke, O.P., already a well-known translator of philosophic and scientific works from the Greek, was recalled from the missions and stationed at Orvieto"[29]—a claim for which there is no evidence whatever. Even Grabmann, on whose authority Bourke relies, is able to do no more than quote extensively from older historians who assume and eulogize the collaboration, such as A. Jourdain (1853),

F. Margott (1864), S. Talamo (1881), H. Rashdall (1895), J. V. De Groot (1907), P. Mandonnet (1911), A. Walz (1927), M. de Corte (1932), M. de Wulf (1936), A. Pelzer (1936), and F. van Steenbeeghen (1942). For example, in 1895 Rashdall wrote:

> Thomas Aquinas endeavoured to procure better translations from the original Greek, and his efforts were seconded by Pope Urban IV. Special translations or special revisions of the existing Graeco-Latin translations were prepared for his use by a Dominican William of Moerbeke, Archbishop of Corinth.[30]

Perhaps the view of those historians was best expressed by P. Mandonnet when he said in 1911:

> Thomas Aquinas, disciple of Albert, undertook on a new level the work of his master. The Roman Church, which was ever facing this inevitable problem of the diffusion of Aristotle's writings, was no stranger to the enterprise. If she did not first conceive the project, she fully encouraged it. Indeed, it could not have been by chance that William of Moerbeke, the new translator of Aristotle, and Thomas Aquinas, the new commentator, were found simultaneously at the papal court, at the moment of carrying out their double task. Urban IV, who had brought them together at the very time he was renewing the old prohibition against teaching the books of the Stagirite [1263], had obviously committed this work to them.[31]

There is no historical documentation to show that William of Moerbeke was at the papal court during the reign of Urban IV. But the source of the problem lies with the testimony of Tolomeo of Lucca, who wrote concerning Thomas and the pontificate of Urban IV:

> At this time, Thomas—directing the studium at Rome—also wrote commentaries covering almost the whole field of philosophy, both moral and natural, but with particular attention to ethics and metaphysics, which he treated in a very striking and original way.[32]

As we shall see, it was not until 1265, after the death of Urban, that Thomas was assigned to direct a Dominican studium at

Santa Sabina in Rome. Therefore, it was not during the pontificate of Urban IV. All historians are aware of this, but they insist that the groundwork for these commentaries was laid at Urban's court when Thomas asked Moerbeke for more accurate translations of Aristotle. The basis for this insistence is found in the catalogue of Stams (c. 1320), where the following notice is given of William of Moerbeke:

> Friar William of Brabant, [Archbishop] of Corinth, translated all the books of natural and moral philosophy from the Greek into Latin at the instigation of Friar Thomas (*ad instantiam fratris Thomae*).[33]

The legend that William translated or revised all the books of Aristotle *ad instantiam fratris Thomae* has been perpetuated in almost all the sources available, both ancient and modern. Grabmann even feels that books translated by Moerbeke before meeting Thomas, such as the work on animals, and books of other authors, such as Proclus, Themistius, and Simplicius, should be interpreted as done *ad instantiam fratris Thomae* by "extension."[34]

The point we wish to make here is that William of Moerbeke was not at the court of Urban IV with Thomas d'Aquino, and that there could not have been any collaboration sponsored or seconded by Urban. This is not to say that William was never at the papal curia or that he did not know Thomas. On the contrary, Moerbeke was "chaplain and penitentiary" of the Pope at the court of Clement IV (1265–68) at Viterbo. He continued in this capacity during the long vacancy in the Holy See and during the pontificates of Gregory X (d. January 10, 1276), Innocent V (d. June 22, 1276), Hadrian V (d. August 18, 1276), John XXI (d. May 20, 1277), and Nicholas III (d. August 22, 1280). As Grabmann has shown, William of Moerbeke was not appointed archbishop of Corinth until April 9, 1278.[35] The See of Corinth was made vacant by the transfer of Robert of Conflans, O.P., to the See of Cosenza.

Moerbeke also knew Thomas d'Aquino well. They were together for more than a year in Viterbo at the court of Clement IV between the summer of 1267 and the fall of 1268, when Thomas journeyed for a second time to Paris. Moreover, William and Thomas could have met any number of times while Thomas was regent of studies in Rome, for the distance between Rome and Viterbo is negligible. But we do not know of any occasion that brought them together.

Thomas was certainly anxious to procure translations "which contain the truth of Aristotle's views more clearly."[36] He quickly utilized Moerbeke's translations of Aristotle's writings on animals, as we have seen. And he was the first to use the numerous translations and revisions made by Moerbeke at Viterbo, such as the *De anima* (1268), Simplicius on the *Praedicamenta* (1266) and his *De caelo* (1271), Themistius on the *De anima* (before 1270), and especially Proclus's *Elementatio theologica* (1268). But this is not the same as saying that William made these translations *ad instantiam fratris Thomae* or that there was "collaboration" between these two scholars. It would seem that William of Moerbeke turned simply and spontaneously to translating before he met Thomas and continued long afterward. Thomas, no doubt, encouraged William at Viterbo and even asked that copies be sent to him as quickly as possible—otherwise it would be difficult to explain how Thomas could be the first to utilize them so soon after their completion. While Thomas eventually commented on the revised versions of Moerbeke, he was not all that meticulous in his quotations from Aristotle in his major works. Often he would lapse back to the older translation from Greek or Arabic, even in the same work, as Gauthier has shown.[37] Indeed, when commenting on such an important work as Aristotle's *Metaphysics*, Thomas apparently did not wait for Moerbeke's revision, but started with the current *Metaphysica media.*

Although Thomas made a careful study of Aristotle's text, it would seem that while Thomas was in Italy he had no intention of commenting on the works of Aristotle. Not only are there no commentaries dating from this period,[38] but there was no obvious need for him to do the work. He was a master in theology, deeply engaged in theological questions, especially after he conceived the idea of a *Summa theologiae* while teaching in Rome. To speak of "collaboration" or "frequent consultation" during the Italian period is gratuitous and incongruous; it does not fit the temper of the known facts. It was not until Thomas was in Paris for a second time (1269-72), met the Averroist threat head on, and realized the plight of young masters in arts, that he saw the urgency of such an apostolate. All of this will be developed as we progress with our story. Here we wish only to dismiss the fabrication expressed by Mandonnet and others of a grand plan devised by Urban IV to bring Thomas and William together to lay the foundations of a Christian Aristotelianism to be developed by Thomas d'Aquino. William of Moerbeke simply was not at the court of Urban IV at Orvieto. He was still in Greece. Thomas arrived in Orvieto with his belongings in September or October 1261, after the provincial chapter. Albert the Great arrived with the Roman curia a year later in the fall of 1262. For the next four or five months Albert and Thomas could discuss their mutual interests and renew their deep friendship. But there was no William.

Thomas, as we have seen, was assigned to the cathedral city of Orvieto as lector of the Dominican Priory of San Domenico, founded in the period 1230-34.[39] That was his formal function. As such, his duties were clear and well established in the Dominican Order. His task was to lecture to the whole Dominican community on a book of Sacred Scripture, any book. The Priory was not a studium, although it may have had young novices. During his period as lector, according to Tolemeo of Lucca, he "expounded the book of Job."[40] Tolemeo mentioned it, because at that time Thomas committed to writing a detailed *Expositio in Job "ad litteram."* While this commentary, one of the most important of Thomas's Scripture glosses, abounds with quotations from Aristotle, it deals with the profound mystery of divine providence, a subject Thomas was much concerned with in his *Summa contra gentiles*, Bk. III, written about the same time. No doubt, Thomas first lectured on Job to the community and later committed his thoughts to writing, adding an abundance of source material and quotations. Many modern authors, instead of mentioning Job, state that Thomas commented on Jeremiah, Lamentations, and on some of the letters of St. Paul at this time.

Tolemeo did not say that Thomas lectured at the papal curia or that he was a Master of the Sacred Palace. This raises a number of important questions. Was Thomas at this time or any other time "lector at the Roman curia," as Mandonnet claimed? Was Thomas, by reason of being lector of the Dominican Priory or by any other reason, Master of the Sacred Palace, as most authors claim?

Before these questions can be answered, we must carefully understand the meaning of certain technical terms in documentary use during the thirteenth and fourteenth centuries. Further, we must outline briefly the development of studia in the Roman curia and in religious Orders during the same period, considering only those surrounding the Apostolic See. Finally we must consider the situation as it existed at the time of Thomas, particularly when he was in the Roman Province, assigned to Orvieto and Viterbo.[41]

There is a Dominican tradition dating to the early fourteenth century, specifically to 1342–45, claiming that St. Dominic was the first Master of the Sacred Palace, and that thereafter only Dominicans occupied this position, as is the case today.[42] A Master of the Sacred Palace today is the Pope's personal theologian, and he performs numerous functions, though considerably curtailed from those he had in earlier centuries. While it is a position of great honor, it is not an honorary or titular position; rather, it is one of considerable responsibility and labor. The Dominican list of such masters has always contained the names of Albert the Great and Thomas d'Aquino.[43] Our question is whether we are justified in calling Thomas a master in theology at the papal school, that is, a Master of the Sacred Palace.

The growth of medieval education must be seen in the light of the third and fourth Councils of the Lateran. The reform decrees of the third Lateran Council in 1179 under Alexander III declared that each cathedral church was to have a school attached and a master to teach theology and grammar to the secular clergy and poor scholars; he was to have an adequate benefice to support his needs. The fourth Lateran Council in 1215, under Innocent III, noting that in many dioceses nothing had been done to implement the earlier decree, strongly emphasized the need for teaching theology to the secular clergy. It decreed in no uncertain terms that not only every cathedral church, but every collegiate church, where possible, was to have a competent master appointed by the bishop to teach theology (and grammar) without charge, for which he was to have a benefice.[44]

The notion of cathedral schools goes back to patristic times;

some of them developed into full-fledged universities, such as Paris and Bologna. The Councils simply reminded bishops of their grave obligation to educate their clergy for the *cura animarum*. For education in theology, often elemental, a teacher had to be provided by the bishop, if he himself did not teach his clergy. Young boys too had to be taught Latin grammar if they were to learn theology and serve the needs of the local diocese. Teaching was done within the confines of the cathedral chapter, and often the teacher (*lector*, or *magister*) was a canon of that cathedral; but according to the decree of Lateran IV, this was not necessary. The Pope himself, as bishop of Rome, had the obligation to provide for the education of the diocesan clergy. In keeping with tradition and the decrees of the Councils, he established a school at the Lateran, the Cathedral of Rome, and provided teachers of theology, one of whom was Stephen Langton, the famous English master from Paris, who taught theology "at the Roman church, where he had a prebend."[45] In order to encourage clerics to attend these cathedral schools, Honorius III, by his apostolic constitution *Super specula* of November 16, 1219,[46] allowed professors and students to be absent from their benefice for a period of five years and continue to receive revenues, even though canon law required residence of beneficed clergy. In the case of Rome, the Lateran school clearly had nothing to do with the Roman curia; it was simply a local school for the training of the local clergy.

After the coronation of Frederick II in 1220, the Popes were unable or unwilling to reside for any great length of time in Rome at the Lateran palace, partly because of military hostilities of the time. Therefore papal palaces were built in various cities of the papal states to serve as residence for the Pope, his curia, and his entire household. Honorius III, Gregory IX, Innocent IV, Alexander IV, Urban IV, and Clement IV moved their residence frequently, mainly between Rome, Anagni, Orvieto, Viterbo, and Perugia. Later Popes also moved about, but not out of necessity; hostilities ended with the battle of Tagliacozzo on August 23, 1268, when Charles of Anjou, brother of Louis IX of France, defeated Conradin, grandson of Frederick II. In a certain sense, it was not until 1309, when the Popes resided at Avignon, that stability was restored to the Roman curia.

While Innocent IV resided in Lyons during the "second year" of his pontificate, he conceived the unique idea of establishing a school of theology and law, attached to the curia and open to clerics of the universal Church. By a bull of 1245, he established such a school for the many clerics who "flock from different parts of the world to the Apostolic See as to a mother."[47] Henceforth there was to be a studium where ordinary lectures were to be given in theology and law, both canon and civil. Rashdall is correct when he says that it was primarily a school "for civil and canon law, but there was also a theological faculty."[48] In view of this, students attending such a studium were to have the same privileges, freedom, and immunity "enjoyed by students in schools where there is a *studium generale.*" That is to say, besides the ordinary clerical privileges, they were to enjoy the freedom granted by *Super specula* of 1219, namely, absence from benefice for five years, and personal use of revenues. This freedom was inevitable in a studium providing for the needs of clerics "from different parts of the world."

The school established by Innocent IV in 1245 was not conceived of as competing with the local cathedral school of Lyons, which served diocesan needs. Rather it belonged to the Roman curia (*studium Romanae curiae*) envisaged as the administrative organism of the universal Church; in this lay its unique character; it was *sui generis.*[49] The school of the papal palace was not part of the curia, but was attached to it (*studium curiae, studium sacri palatii*). Its teachers (*lectores curiae Romanae, magistri sacri palatii,* etc.) were not officials of the curia; they were not paid by the curia, but had their own prebends. Before 1309, masters, or lectors, in the apostolic school were not even "masters" in the technical sense of being graduates of a university; they were teachers who explained the Bible to young clerics, much as a master did in the cathedral schools. They did not lecture to the curial staff, nor did they dispute questions before the consistory of cardinals. They were teachers largely without degrees who taught law or theology in a school sponsored by the Pope for clerics from any part of the world.

Contemporary documents also speak of "illiterate" habitués and simple "pilgrims" (*pelegrini*) who attach themselves to the Holy See. For these, the apostolic school of the curia provided classes in grammar. Hence it is commonly said that grammar was taught "in the curia."

When Innocent IV left Lyons for Perugia in 1252, the entire curia and the palace school, both teachers and most of the students, went with him, just as the papal infirmary for the sick and poor who came to the Holy See as to a mother also went with him.[50] The diplomatic corps attached to the Holy See and officials of religious orders also went with him at their own expense and convenience. Thus the papal school became essentially a mobile studium. Many authors see this mobility as one of its strange and unique features, unlike any studium of the Middle Ages since the days of Charlemagne.

When using the word "studium," one must be careful to distinguish the various meanings it had in the Middle Ages, especially when talking about a *studium generale*. Although *studium* originally meant "the application of one's self" to something, or "zeal," it was used in medieval Latin to mean a stable "teaching situation" or a "place" or "school" where such teaching was held. The one who taught was said "to conduct a school" (*regere studium*) or "to hold school" (*studium tenere*). Thus an actual teacher was called a "regent" (*regens*) as distinct from a teacher who did not actually teach (*non-regens*). In the context of the medieval university, a "regent master" was one who not only obtained the degree of master, but also conducted classes in a *studium generale*.

The phrase "general studium" in the context of medieval university Latin, on which all other uses of the phrase depended, had at least three distinct meanings, or applications. Basically, the word "general" meant the opposite of "particular," but it could be understood in various ways. Above all, a *studium generale* is not to be equated with a university such as Bologna or Paris; nor is it to be equated with a university such as Oxford or Cambridge. On this point many historians of medieval learning and many biographers of Thomas err in their understanding of the phrase. They have missed the fundamental meaning of *studium generale*. This meaning was clearly expressed by the famous jurist Henry of Segusia (Hostiensis, d. 1271) when he stated: "a studium is called 'general' when the trivium and quadrivium, theology and the sacred canons are taught there."[51]

In other words, a *studium generale* was a place where "general knowledge" was taught, which to the medieval mind meant philosophy (arts), theology, and law (both canon and civil). To this, one must add another note of generality, namely, that a *studium generale* was "open" to all dioceses or provinces. Thus a province of a religious Order could have a *studium generale*, meaning not only that all faculties were represented, but also that it was open to members of other provinces and even to outsiders. A province having a studium just for its own members was said, at a later date, to have a *studium particulare* or *provinciale*, as in the case of most cathedral schools. In the general and particular studia in this sense, there was no question of degrees being granted in any faculty, such as the "master's degree." The ability to grant degrees (*licentia docendi*) was characteristic of a university, e.g., Oxford, Cambridge, and a host of other studia (universities) which sprang up in the thirteenth and fourteenth centuries under papal or imperial auspices.[52] But even in this sense of a "university," *studium generale* is not to be equated with a university in the strictest sense, as used by Denifle, Rashdall, Creytens, and many others. For them, a university is one that granted degrees which had general or universal rights from time immemorial, namely the *ius ubique docendi*. Strangely enough, despite the constant efforts of English kings, Oxford and Cambridge never obtained this right from the Holy See.

Therefore, the papal studium founded by Innocent IV in 1245 as belonging to the curia, or sacred palace, was a *studium generale* in the sense that it had the faculties of theology, law, and grammar, and that it was open to clerics "from different parts of the world." But it was not a "university" in the medieval sense of the term, for it did not grant degrees. This status did not come until Clement V (1305–14) declared the *studium Romanae curiae* to be a university with a right to grant the degree of "master."[53] Then, and only then, were fully qualified masters required for the teaching of arts, theology, and law; only then were there *cursores, baccalarii,* and *magistri,* such as any medieval university had. When Clement V declared the papal studium in the curia to be a "university," teachers of theology had to be *magistri in theologia* in the technical sense of being graduates from a university. The first regent master in theology in the new papal university "of the Roman curia" was the French Dominican Guillaume de Pierre Godin, a graduate of Paris.[54] Creytens seems to suggest that the strict sense of *magister sacri palatii* required him to be an official of the papal curia, such as happened under Clement V. But this is an unwarranted restriction of the title.

Mendicant Orders quickly established *studia generalia* for their members shortly after they were founded. As early as 1246 the Dominicans required four provinces, namely, Provence, Lombardy, Germany, and England, to establish "solemn and general studia" in some suitable house of the province, to which each provincial of the Order could send two students.[55] These studia were erected in Paris, Bologna, Cologne, and Oxford. The Franciscans, Augustinians, and Carmelites soon followed this example. During the second half of the thirteenth century a strange terminology came into use that can be misleading and is easily misunderstood. However, the abundant official acts of the Austin Friars from the late thirteenth century onward leave no doubt as to what was meant; later capitular acts of the mendicant Orders confirm the universality of this terminology

Since the term "curia" meant not only the administrative organism of the Church, but also the locality of the curia, religious Orders extended the term to apply to their own houses in that locality. Thus the religious house, prior, lector, and studium came to be called *conventus curiae Romanae, prior curiae, lector curiae Romanae,* and *studium Romanae curiae.* The earliest documentary use of this terminology dates from 1276, when the provincial chapter of the Augustinian Friars assigned Friar Leonardo of Viterbo, a lector, to teach "in the curia at Viterbo."[56] At the general chapter of the Austin Friars meeting at Florence in 1287, four general studia at least were to be established in Italy, namely, "in the Roman curia, Bologna, Padua, and Naples."[57] The expressions "lector in the curia," "studium of the Roman curia," and, for the first time, "master of the curia" are used by the Augustinians freely in their official acts of 1295.[58] The fourteenth-century documents of the Carmelites employ the same terminology. The earliest references to a Dominican studium "of the curia" are to be found in the provincial chapter of Anagni in 1285, referring to "students of the curia," who apparently were studying both theology and the arts (philosophy).[59] Official acts of the other mendicant Orders date from the fourteenth century, but they too employ the same terminology. The official acts of the Franciscans, which are extremely sparse, reveal nothing.[60] However, the chronicles and other unofficial documents of the Franciscan Order reveal a clear distinction between their own general studium "in the curia," whose teachers are called "masters," "regents," or "lectors of the Roman curia" on the one hand, and "lectors of the sacred palace" on the other. The Chronicle of the twenty-four ministers general lists a number of outstanding theologians, beginning with John Pecham in 1277, who were "lectors of the palace in the curia," or simply "lectors," or "masters of the sacred palace." There can be absolutely no doubt that between 1277 and about 1300 there were at least seven Franciscan theologians who were teachers of theology in the papal palace school; they were "masters of the sacred palace" as distinct from masters or lectors of the studium belonging to the Order located in the friary "of the Roman curia." In other words, documentary evidence from the four major mendicant Orders requires that a distinction be made between the papal studium founded by Innocent IV in the papal palace and the *studium generale* of a particular religious Order located in its own house. Thus the lector of a particular religious house, even if it be a *studium generale* and he be a *magister regens*, cannot be identified with a lector of the papal palace. The clearest proof of this is that the lector or *magister* of the palace school was never appointed by a religious Order; that authority always belonged solely to the Pope.

When the Pope decided to move his curia and his palace school to another city, there was naturally great confusion among religious Orders that had their own *studium generale Romanae curiae*. Officials of the religious Orders and the entire studium of the Order would be transported to the new locality. This practice provided some bizarre situations, as when the Pope decided to move to a city where the religious Order already had a general studium and a regent master. This situation happened to the Augustinians in 1385, when Urban VI moved his court to Naples, where the Friars already had a general studium.[61] Before settling in Avignon in 1309, Clement V transferred his residence so many times in France that the Austin Friars decided to situate their *studium curiae* in Perugia, the residence of Clement's predecessor, until the superiors could decide what to do.[62]

When the Popes finally returned to Rome in the course of the fifteenth century, the studium of the papal palace lost its reason for being, since there was already in Rome a *studium Urbis* founded by Boniface VIII in 1303. The mobile studium of the sacred palace was therefore suppressed in the sixteenth century, probably by Leo X (1513–21), and its students were transferred to the existing Roman University.[63] No doubt it was at this time that religious Orders suppressed their own *studia Romanae curiae* in favor of stable studia in the city of Rome.

Now what about Thomas when he was lecturing in the Dominican Priory of San Domenico in Orvieto? Was he "lector of the Roman curia"? Was he Master of the Sacred Palace?

First of all, at that time such terminology was not in use, at least not in official use. It can be admitted, however, that a few decades later Thomas's function could have been designated as *lector in curia Romana* in the sense that the priory would have been called a *conventus curiae Romanae*. But there was no *studium generale* of the Dominican Order at Orvieto, certainly not at that time. Thomas was sent by the provincial chapter from Orvieto to Rome in order to establish a studium, but even this Roman studium was not a *studium generale*. Only a general chapter could establish a *studium curiae*, a general studium, like those established by the Dominican general chapter of 1246. But Thomas was assigned by the provincial chapter of 1265 to establish a studium in Rome. This kind of studium, as we shall see, was a "general studium" only in the sense that it taught theology to all students of the province; such a studium would eventually be called a "provincial studium." But the term *lector curiae Romanae* was always used in the context of a general studium, established by a religious Order to accompany the papal court and its studium. Therefore, Thomas could not have been, in any technical sense of the phrase, a *magister* or *lector curiae Romanae*.

We have shown a distinction, despite the confusing terminology, between the *studium curiae* of a religious Order and the *studium sacri palatii* that accompanied the papal curia. It is only in the latter context that the office of Master of the Sacred Palace developed; its development from the Avignon period onward is easily documented. This position has always been held by a Dominican appointed by the Pope. It is the development of this position in the period between 1245 and 1276 that is difficult to reconstruct. The earliest reference to a teacher in the palace school is to the Dominican Bartholomew de Bregantiis, who was referred to by Innocent IV on February 9, 1252, simply as "regent in the theology faculty in our curia."[64] Franciscan and Dominican chronicles of the late thirteenth and the early fourteenth century as well as all official acts of the mendicant Orders of the fourteenth and fifteenth centuries clearly distinguish between members of the palace school and the Order school. No Order ever appointed a Master of the Sacred Palace, that is, a lector of theology teaching in the palace school; this authority, as I have said, belonged solely to the Pope. When Thomas was assigned to Orvieto in 1261, he certainly was not assigned to teach in the palace school. One might say that the assignment to Orvieto was made at the Pope's request. But, as close as we can determine today, Urban IV did not take up residence at Orvieto until the fall of 1262. Therefore, Urban IV was unlikely to have asked the Roman Province to assign Thomas to Orvieto in 1261. But one might say that after Urban took up residence, he could have asked Thomas to teach in his palace school. But why should Urban bother to do that? He undoubtedly already had a lector accompanying his studium, and Thomas already had a job. There is no evidence of any such appointment by Urban or of any substitute lector provided for San Domenico. Even at that time it was impossible for one man to occupy both positions. Therefore, we must conclude, Thomas was not a Master of the Sacred Palace.

Following Mandonnet, modern biographers have assumed that an appointment to the palace school would have been a promotion, and only a promotion would have been befitting a master of Paris. But quite the contrary is true. Without doubt the University of Paris was the center of the intellectual life in Christendom, while teaching in a papal school, even by appointment of the Pope, was no promotion. Neither was teaching at San Domenico in Orvieto a promotion! But that is not to the point. There is no need to look for promotions or situations befitting a master of

Paris when talking about a Friar outside the Parisian context. Thomas, like every Friar, returned to his own province to do what was required for the good of the Church and the Order. Moreover, teaching in a papal school, such as existed at that time, could in no way be considered any special honor. He would have been addressing not the whole curia of cardinals and other dignitaries, but only simple clerics from various parts of the world who happened to be at the curia at that time. To do this kind of teaching there was no need for the lector to be a graduate of any university. We must not think of the position as it later became, but as it existed during the reign of Urban IV. Mendicants were frequently appointed to the palace school because they needed no salary or benefice, and furthermore they were generally better educated in their schools than the secular clergy were in theirs. Considering the kind of education imparted in the papal school, we must conclude that an appointment to teach theology in the papal palace would not have been a "promotion" for Thomas, but a distraction.

Urban IV found in Thomas's companionship much more than a possible teacher for his curial school. He found a learned theologian who could give sound theological advice, as well as supply writings of universal and perennial value. Tolomeo of Lucca clearly states that "at the request of Urban he [Thomas] did many things and wrote much." It was at Urban's request that Thomas began his continuous commentary on the four Gospels (*Catena aurea*) and wrote his *Contra errores Graecorum*. From both of these undertakings Thomas learned much from the Greek Fathers of the Church.

Influence of Greek Theology

I presume it goes without saying that Thomas knew practically no Greek, except for a few technical words and phrases. R. A. Gauthier has shown, beyond measure, that Thomas was ignorant of Greek.[65] Therefore Thomas had to depend on the available Latin translations. Nevertheless, Thomas had an uncanny ability to grasp the *intentio auctoris*, the sense intended by a Greek author. His grasp of the intention of an author far surpasses that of schoolmen like Roger Bacon, whose caustic remarks about William of Moerbeke's translations imply that Roger alone knew Greek! A glance at the multiplicity of translations of the Scriptures today shows how vastly different translations can be. Therefore it is imperative to know the translation Thomas used at the various stages of his intellectual development. In theology Thomas was not at all concerned about procuring a better translation of the Bible than the Vulgate he owned, but he was deeply concerned about understanding the precise meaning of the councils of the Church and of the Greek Fathers. Therefore he went out of his way to procure better and more accurate translations of their documents and writings. In philosophy, too, he was concerned about better translations of Aristotle that could be provided by William of Moerbeke. But in no way did Thomas parade his academic solicitude in this matter; whenever he recalled a different translation, he would simply say "in the other translation" the reading is such and such, and proceed with his interpretation. Neither did Albert know Greek, but that ignorance in no way prevented him from making Aristotle intelligible to the Latins. Albert, too, had an extraordinary ability to get at the heart of the matter, even though the translations he had at hand were often faulty and hopelessly obscure. It would seem that among the contemporaries of Thomas and Albert, those who knew Greek had little speculative ability, while people like Thomas and Albert, who knew no Greek, had most to contribute to speculative philosophy and theology.

The Quaracchi editors of the *Summa* of Alexander of Hales note that Thomas d'Aquino was the first Latin scholastic writer to utilize verbatim the acts of the first five ecumenical councils of the Church, namely in the *Catena aurea* (1262–67) and in the *Summa theologiae* (1266–73).[66] Sometime between 1260 and 1263, Thomas discovered the acts (*acta*) and proceedings (*gesta*) of the early councils. While he was still in Naples, Thomas could have studied and copied out passages from Monte Cassino Library MS 2, a twelfth-century manuscript, which contains the acts of Ephesus and Chalcedon in the Latin translation of Rusticus. Or he could have found a fuller copy in the papal archives after the curia moved to Orvieto in the fall of 1262. His earliest use of conciliar documents is found in his *Summa contra gentiles*

IV, 25, written in 1263, where the debated question of the procession of the Holy Spirit is discussed. This question involves the addition of *filioque* to the Latin Creed of Nicaea confirmed by the first Council of Constantinople. In the Greek version of the Nicaean Creed, the Holy Spirit is said to proceed from the Father. Instinctively the Latins expressed their belief that the Holy Spirit proceeds from the Father "and from the Son"; this phrase is not found in the Greek, and it was to become one of the hotly debated points in every question of union between the eastern and western Churches. While the *filioque* problem emerged as a crucial point in later centuries, it was not even discussed at Nicaea or Constantinople I. The problem at that time was the "consubstantiality" of the Son with the Father, for Arius taught that the substance of the Son is different from and less than that of the Father, and semi-Arians argued that the Son's substance (hypostasis) is "similar" to the Father's, but not identical.

Thomas's teaching on the processions within the Holy Trinity is clear and simple: the only words we have with which to discuss the mystery are to be found in Sacred Scripture. The words "son" and "generation" are applied only to the Second Person of the Trinity; the word "father" is applied only to the First Person in his eternal act of generating the Son. Therefore, the term "son" cannot be applied to the Third Person, nor can the Father be said to "generate" or "beget" the Holy Spirit. If one talked about the Father as "generating" or "begetting" the Holy Spirit, there would be no way to acknowledge the personal distinction between Son and Spirit; the Son would be the Spirit, and the Spirit would be the Son, without distinction of Persons, which would be contrary to the faith professed by the Greek Fathers of the Church. Therefore, the Holy Spirit must proceed from the Father in a way that is distinct from the procession, or generation, of the Son. This distinction can lie only (1) in the principle *from which* the Spirit proceeds, and (2) in the name of the procession. As to the principle, the only possibility is for the Spirit to proceed "from the Father and from the Son," both as co-principles of the eternal procession of the Holy Spirit. As to the name of the procession, we can give it the name "spiration" or the name "procession" itself. Thus, the Spirit would *belong to* the Father and to the Son, while remaining distinct from them. The councils of the

Church thus declared the "consubstantiality" of the Persons in the Trinity, as well as the distinction of Persons in their relationship of one to the other.

As important as conciliar documents were to Thomas's teaching on the Trinity, it was in his Christology that new light was shed by the decrees of Ephesus and Chalcedon.[67] Before discovering the Latin texts of these councils, Thomas knew, as did all his contemporaries, something about the teaching of Nestorius and Eutyches from Boethius's tractate *De persona et duabus naturis contra Eutychen et Nestorium*. The commonly accepted definitions of "person" and "nature" were excerpted from this tractate. But Boethius applied these definitions to the mystery of the Incarnation only at the end of his work, and even then in an imprecise manner.

Nestorius, patriarch of Constantinople (428–31), condemned the teaching of some monks concerning the divine maternity of Mary. These monks even went so far as to call Mary the "Mother of God," *Theodokos* (*deipara*, or *Dei genetrix*). For Nestorius, God could have no mother, for He existed from all eternity; Nestorius therefore insisted that Mary could only be called *Christodokos*, the mother of Jesus Christ, thus teaching that the hypostasis or person of Christ, born of Mary, was other than the divine person begotten of the Father. Later Nestorians were willing to admit a unity of "person" in Christ, but they insisted that the hypostasis (*substantia*) of Christ the man is other than the divine hypostasis of the Trinity. Thus, while emphasizing the infinite gap between the human nature of Christ and His divine nature as God, Nestorius and his many followers, schooled in the theologate in Antioch, also taught that an infinite gap exists between the hypostasis begotten of Mary and the Second Person of the Holy Trinity. In other words, Nestorius taught not only a duality of nature (*physis*) in Christ, but also a duality of substances (*hypostasis*).

To the Latins, the Greek terminology of the councils was confusing, for *hypostasis* literally means *substantia* or *subsistentia*. Yet, it would seem, one could not say that there are three subsistences in the Trinity, for in Latin this would be equivalent to saying that there are three distinct substances in the Godhead. The Latins preferred to translate *hypostasis* as "person," but the etymology of *per-sonare* is identical with the Greek *prosopon*, meaning a "mask," or "face," through which performers uttered their lines in a play. This was the term used by Sabellius and his followers to deny the trinity of hypostases in the Godhead; for him the various names of "Father," "Son," and "Holy Spirit" are so many masks through which the divine essence speaks and acts. This early heresy was condemned in the third century. With the development of Latin terminology during the long Trinitarian and Christological controversies, *hypostasis* was better translated as "person."[68] Thus Nestorius taught that there are two persons in Christ as well as two natures.

The Council of Ephesus was convoked in 431 by Theodosius II at the instigation of St. Cyril, patriarch of Alexandria and representative of Pope Leo I in the Council. Much to the surprise of Nestorius, his views were condemned and the Council declared that the human nature of Christ is united to the divine, not by a fusion of natures (*secundum naturam*) but by an identity of person (*secundum hypostasim*). In other words, the Council of Ephesus declared as a matter of revealed doctrine that there is only one person in Christ—the Divine Word—and a duality of natures that always remain distinct, except by reason of the Divine Person.

One of the monks denounced by Nestorius in his sermons was the archimandrite Eutyches, who taught that in Christ there is an intimate fusion of natures, so that after the Incarnation there was in Him only one person and one nature. The Council of Chalcedon was convoked in 541 by the Emperor Marcion under the presidency of St. Flavian to consider the orthodoxy of the extreme view proposed by Eutyches. The Monophysite (one-nature) position held by Eutyches was condemned outright as contrary to orthodox belief, and the Council declared that Christ has two distinct natures, in no way fused or changed into one. A fusion or union of natures would imply that the new nature was less than divine and more than human; there would result a *tertium quid* that was neither divine nor human. Therefore the unique union between the Divine Person and the concrete, individual human nature in Christ can only be called "hypostatic," for the union takes place *in* the hypostasis (person), or *secundum hypostasim* as the Council of Chalcedon declared.

Later writings of Thomas, such as the *QQ. de potentia, Catena aurea*, the commentaries on John and the first letter of Paul to the Corinthians, as well as *De rationibus fidei* and other works that discuss the Incarnation, utilize verbatim the texts of the early councils. Geenen claims to have located about thirty passages throughout twenty-two works of Aquinas that explicitly use the text of Chalcedon in discussing the error of Eutyches.[69] The profoundest impact of the conciliar texts, however, is to be found in the third part of the *Summa theologiae*, where Thomas discusses the Incarnation; one might say that the intricate problems of fifth-century theology are relived in the objections, replies, and "sed contra" of the *Summa*.

One cannot say with Baches that information concerning the early councils belonged to "a tradition in the schools." Nor can one say that such information circulated in a kind of florilegium. Certainly in the case of Thomas, conciliar texts are carefully cited and explicitly located in their *acta, gesta*, session, or canon, as the case may be. After the careful work of Geenen, one is forced to say that Thomas had access to the full texts of the early councils. These texts Thomas discovered either at Monte Cassino in 1260 or at Orvieto in 1262–63.

Throughout his pontificate, Urban IV was deeply concerned with a union of the Greek and Latin Churches, which were initially split in the ninth century under Photius and definitively split in the eleventh under Michael Cerularius. As early as August 1261 the Greek Emperor Michael VIII Paleologus wrote to Urban asking him to send legates to Constantinople to discuss union. The timing seemed right; and overtures were made on both sides that culminated in the Council of Lyons in 1274. But it was not until the Council of Florence in 1439 that a partial union was achieved. One of the intermediaries in the early period was Nicholas of Durazzo, bishop of Cotrone (modern Crotone) in Calabria, southern Italy.[70] We know that Michael VIII Paleologus wrote directly to Nicholas in 1261 inviting him to come to Constantinople in an unofficial capacity, if nothing else. Nicholas was a Greek by birth and culture, but Latin in education. Innocent IV referred to him as "a beloved master, clerk in our household, and learned in both Latin and Greek."

It would seem that Nicholas compiled a *Libellus de pro-*

cessione Spiritus Sancti et de fide trinitatis contra errores Grae-corum, purporting to show that the Greek Fathers taught the Latin doctrine of *filioque*. This *Libellus*, discovered by P. A. Uccelli in 1869, was originally written in Greek and addressed to the Emperor; it was an amalgam of Greek texts attributed to Athanasius, Basil, Gregory Nazianzenus, Gregory of Nyssa, John Chrysostom, and Cyril. A Latin copy of the alleged authorities was sent to Urban IV around 1262 for his consideration.[71] For some unexplained reason, a large part of the *Libellus* consists of falsifications, fabrications, and false attributions; without the aid of something like the Leonine edition, it would be almost impossible to determine where an authentic quotation ends and where the fabrication begins. How anyone could have expected the *Libellus* to serve as a basis for union of the Greek and Latin Churches is a mystery defying all imagination. Any good Greek theologian could have detected its forgeries, just as did Latin scholars in later centuries. Of its 205 quotations, only 5 were previously known to Latin theologians of the thirteenth century.[72] By far the longest section of the *Libellus* is devoted to the procession of the Holy Spirit, while short notice is given to the problems of papal primacy, consecration of unleavened bread, and purgatory.

While Thomas was hard at work on the final part of his *Summa contra gentiles* and on the continuous patristic gloss on Matthew, he was given the *Libellus* to examine theologically. Although Thomas did not question the authenticity of the various texts quoted, but repeated the falsifications of the original, he was clearly disturbed and "ill at ease" with the text,[73] as can be seen on two counts. First, he was unhappy about the use of certain technical expressions, such as *hypostasis* meaning "substance" or "essential person," *logos* translated as *sermo mentalis*, and "*coessential*" meaning "consubstantial," and so forth, which, if understood in a Latin context, could be heretical. In a magnificent prologue Thomas explains the role of a good translator: he is one who always has his eye on what was intended by the author, and not simply on a word-for-word rendition. He shows a fine historical sense when he explains that before a critical problem is worked out by the Church, authors tend to speak with less circumspection; thus before the Arian heresy, early writers were not always careful in their statements concerning the divine essence; similarly, Augustine spoke without sufficient precision concerning free will before the Pelagian heresy. Therefore authoritative statements of the Fathers must be seen in their historical context, and their "meaning" (the *intentio auctoris*) must be carefully understood. Second, Thomas divides his reply to Urban into two distinct parts: first, he considers doubtful statements made by the Fathers in the *Libellus*, that is, expressions that cannot be accepted at face value, and, second, he shows how other statements of the authorities can be used to teach and defend the true faith. Thus the first part of his *Contra errores Graecorum* consists of thirty-two chapters that express caution in the use of the authorities cited, while the second part consists of thirty-one chapters that expound the Catholic teaching concerning the procession of the Holy Spirit in the Trinity. Seven short chapters are added to defend the primacy of the Roman pontiff, and one chapter each on the consecration of unleavened bread in the Eucharist, and the existence of purgatory.

Within a very short time the existence of the *Libellus* was forgotten, and the treatise *Contra errores Graecorum* was considered a veritable arsenal of arguments that could be used against the Greeks. Pope Gregory X asked Thomas to bring his treatise with him to the Council of Lyons in 1274. Before Uccelli discovered the *Libellus* in the Vatican Library in 1869, the true nature of Thomas's treatise was completely misunderstood. The falsification of authorities was blamed on Thomas, and the treatise received nothing but scorn from scholars. The seven chapters dealing with papal primacy came under special fire at the time of Vatican Council I (1870), when papal infallibility was defined as a doctrine of faith. Thomas merely reproduced the authorities found in the *Libellus*. It is indeed surprising that Thomas did not supplement the *Libellus* with his own acquaintance with some of the Fathers or at least with his own knowledge of the decrees of Chalcedon. As it was, Thomas only criticized some of the biblical texts alleged by Nicholas to prove the procession of the Holy Spirit from the Father and from the Son.

The treatise *Contra errores Graecorum* was completed before

Book IV, c. 69, of the *Summa contra gentiles* was written, since in that chapter Thomas summarizes the same arguments advanced in the treatise II, 39, concerning the consecration of unleavened bread. Therefore it is clear that Thomas labored simultaneously on *Summa contra gentiles, Contra errores Graecorum,* and on the *Catena aurea* on Matthew, a contemporary work.

The turning point in the development of Aquinas's theology was his labor on the continuous gloss on the four Gospels.[74] Eschmann even calls it a turning point in "the history of Catholic dogma." From the dedicatory letter of Thomas to Urban IV, it is clear that the pontiff requested Thomas to write a continuous gloss of this kind. Despite the fact that there were many glosses in existence, Thomas produced a most extraordinary compilation of the best quotations of all the Fathers known to him, some of which were especially procured by him for this work.

The original title of this work was simply *Glossa* (or *Expositio*) *continua in Matthaeum, Marcum, Lucam, Johannem.* Thomas himself referred to it simply as "a continuous exposition of the aforesaid Gospels." Nicholas Trevet lists the work when he says, "[Thomas] glossed the four Gospels with a continuous explanation taken from sayings of the saints."[75] In the fifteenth and sixteenth centuries this gloss was widely known, highly esteemed, and affectionately called the *Catena aurea,* the golden chain. It numbers among the most widely diffused works of Aquinas, both in manuscript and in print. Editors and biographers are loud in their praise of it. In the nineteenth century a number of Oxford scholars, among them John Henry Newman and others of the Oxford movement, produced a magnificent English translation of the *Catena* on all four Gospels. One of them, M. Pattison, Fellow of Lincoln College, Oxford, wrote the following appraisal:

> [All former glosses had been] partial and capricious, dilating on one passage, and passing unnoticed another of equal or greater difficulty. But it is impossible to read the Catena of St. Thomas, without being struck with the masterly and architectonic skill with which it is put together. A learning of the highest kind, not mere literary book-knowledge, . . . [but] a thorough acquaintance with the whole range of ecclesiastical antiquity; . . . a

familiarity with the style of each writer, so as to compress into a few words the pith of a whole page, and a power of clear and orderly arrangement in this mass of knowledge, are qualities which make this Catena perhaps nearly perfect as a conspectus of Patristic interpretation. Other compilations exhibit research, industry, learning; but this, though a mere compilation evinces a masterly command over the whole subject of theology.[76]

Pope Urban IV commissioned Thomas to produce such a gloss in the earliest years of their friendship, that is, in the last months of 1262 or early in 1263. Urban was still alive when the *Catena* on Matthew was completed, for it was dedicated to him in 1263. Eschmann refers to a Parma MS, Bibl. Palat. 1, containing this part of the *Catena* and dated 1263. This date means that the *Catena* on Matthew took less than a year to complete; the other parts of the *Catena,* namely, the gloss on Mark, Luke, and John, were not completed by the time of Urban's death in October 1264, and so were dedicated to Annibaldo d'Annibaldi, O.P., a former student of Thomas's at Paris, who had been created cardinal by Urban in December 1262. Therefore it would seem that Thomas had not yet completed the gloss on Mark when Urban died in October. "Lest the work begun under obedience be left imperfect through negligence," Thomas wrote in his dedication to Annibaldo, "I have summoned with much labor diligent zeal so to complete the exposition of the four Gospels, observing the same format in quoting authoritative statements of the saints and in mentioning their names at the outset."

In his dedication of the *Catena* on Matthew to Urban, Thomas notes that when a passage or statement is taken from the standard *Glossa ordinaria,* he will simply state the fact without further precision, but when the statement is taken from one of the Fathers he will state, for example, "Jerome," meaning Jerome's commentary on Matthew. However, in the case of John Chrysostom, the specific passage will be listed with the title "Super Matthaeum" to distinguish it from his "homilies." Thomas noted the special problem with passages from Chrysostom because the text available was faulty (*translatio vitiosa*); consequently he had to summarize the sense intended without adhering to the actual words.

In his dedication Thomas stated also the goal he hoped to achieve by his continuous gloss:

> My intention in this work is not only to pursue the literal sense [of the passage], but also to set out the mystical; sometimes to demolish errors, as well as to confirm the Catholic truth. This would seem to be called for, because from the Gospel especially we receive the norm of Catholic faith and the rule of the whole Christian life.

In his dedication to Annibaldo, Thomas noted, "In order that the aforesaid exposition of the saints be whole and continuous, I have seen to it that certain passages from the Greek doctors were translated into Latin" (*in Latinum feci transferri*).[77] Beginning with the gloss on Mark, Thomas's research into Greek patristic sources became more and more intense. Because of this research into Greek theological sources, the *Catena* marks a turning point in the development of Aquinas's own theology, as well as in the history of Catholic thought and dogma. According to Geenen,[78] Thomas quoted twenty-two Latin Fathers and fifty-seven Greek Fathers throughout the *Catena aurea*. We do not know who aided Thomas in procuring more and better translations from the Greek Fathers. It could have been William of Moerbeke, who, in 1265, was in Viterbo at the court of Clement IV, as we have said above. On the other hand, the translator could have been an unknown linguist in the court of Urban in 1263–64, when Thomas was working on his *Catena* on Mark. In any case, Eschmann is right when he says:

> It seems that in the first part of his Italian sojourn, in the years of Urban IV, Thomas, in a way, discovered Greek theology, the part it played in theology, and the consequences which would ensue, if it were neglected, as indeed it was neglected, in a theology that was nourished merely by Latin thought.

Of all the Greek theologians, the one who most influenced Thomas and indeed all of his contemporaries was Pseudo-Dionysius the Areopagite, a man purporting to be the disciple of St. Paul mentioned in the Acts of the Apostles 17:34. The *Corpus Areopageticum* was introduced into the Latin West in 827, when the Greek Emperor Michael Balbus sent a Greek copy, consisting of four treatises and ten letters, to Louis the Pious as a token of friendship. The *Corpus* contained *De divinis nominibus, De theologia mystica, De hierarchia caelestia, De hierarchia ecclesiastica,* and letters addressed to such apostolic contemporaries as Theraputa, Caius, Polycarp, Titus, and John the Evangelist. This codex is still extant in Paris, Bibl. Nat. gr. 437. Desiring a translation of the text, Louis gave the copy to Hilduin, abbot of Saint-Denys, who knew very little Greek. It was not until about 860–62 that John Scotus Erigena translated the text anew from the same codex at the request of Charles II, the Bald; henceforth Pseudo-Dionysius was made available to the Latins in all its richness of Platonic thought. Hilduin also wrote a life of Dionysius, the mystical author of the *Corpus,* claiming not only that Dionysius was the disciple of St. Paul and author of the *Corpus,* but also the patron of Paris and founder of the Abbey of Saint-Denys. Thus were three distinct persons amalgamated into one, whose feast day was widely celebrated on October 9, especially in the schools of theology. The author of the *Corpus* is still unknown; he seems to have been an early sixth-century author, who was perhaps a Monophysite, trying to pass his works off as contemporary with St. Paul. The alleged antiquity of the *Corpus* gave it an authority second only to the canonical books of Scripture.

Thomas commented on only one book of the *Corpus Areopageticum,* namely, *De divinis nominibus,* sometime during the first part of his Italian sojourn. It was certainly written before 1268, when William of Moerbeke translated the *Elementatio theologica* of Proclus, for in the Dionysian commentary Thomas was unaware of the influence of Proclus. Mandonnet dates the commentary "after 1260," and Walz dates it as early as 1261. We do not know the occasion of its composition, nor do we know whether the commentary originally consisted of oral lectures or whether it was written simply to be read. We have already seen that when Thomas was in Cologne, Albert commented on this work in class. Thomas's own work could very well have been based on lectures given to the Dominican community in Orvieto or more probably in the studium in Rome.

At the outset, Thomas acknowledges the obscurity of the text, and he gives three reasons for it: first, because the style and manner of speaking are identical with that of the Platonists, which style is uncustomary among moderns; second, because whole arguments are often couched in a few words or even in only one word; and third, because a point is often made in a prolixity of apparently unnecessary words needing to be sorted out by the careful reader.

The burden of *De divinis nominibus* is to show that only a few names can be applied to the Godhead, for God is, in fact, above all conceptions of "being," "goodness," and the rest. It is thoroughly Neo-Platonist in conception and terminology, but Thomas accepted the Dionysian treatise as of near apostolic antiquity and, therefore, of considerable authority in theology.

One other treatise should be mentioned here because it was undoubtedly written in 1264, shortly after the completion of the *Summa contra gentiles,* and pertains to the over-all effort to convert the Saracens, Greeks, and Armenians to the Church of Rome. It is called *De rationibus fidei contra Saracenos, Graecos et Armenos ad Cantorem Antiochiae.* The unknown cantor of Antioch wrote to Thomas, perhaps at the suggestion of his bishop, the Dominican Christian Elias,[79] concerning the attacks on the true faith by Saracens, Greeks, and Armenians. The precise points that these groups made were listed by the cantor and repeated in Thomas's reply. Briefly, they were five in number, and had previously been explained by Thomas "elsewhere," namely in the *Summa contra gentiles:* (1) the Saracens say that Christ cannot be the Son of God, for God has no wife; (2) they also say that the crucifixion of Christ could not be for the salvation of the human race, for if Christ were divinely omnipotent, he could have saved the human race by other ways and prevent men from sinning; (3) Christians claim to eat their God in the Eucharist, but if their God were as big as a mountain, he would have been entirely eaten up by this time; (4) the Greeks and Armenians say that between death and the final judgment, the souls of men are neither punished nor rewarded; (5) the Saracens, Greeks, and Armenians say that if God knows all things and wills them, man's death and sin are necessarily willed by God.

The cantor of Antioch requested a summary of moral and philosophical arguments that could be used against those who attack the true religion. Thomas obliged the cantor with the long letter known today as *De rationibus fidei*. However, at the very outset Thomas admonished the cantor not to try to demonstrate truths that are beyond reason, for that would derogate from the true faith, which exceeds not only our understanding, but also that of the angels. The goal of the missionary should not be to demonstrate the faith, which would bring ridicule on the faith, but to defend it against arguments, none of which can demonstrate the contrary. Hence St. Peter (1 Pet. 3:15) does not say that one should be prepared to prove the faith that is within him, but to give satisfaction for that faith (*rationem fidei*). That is, the Christian disputant should be prepared to show that what the Catholic faith professes cannot be rationally disproved. As the title of the treatise indicates and the reference to 1 Peter 3:15 suggests, the reply to the cantor of Antioch is a summary of the main problems faced in the *Summa* against the Moslems, Greeks, and Armenians, all of them embraced in the title of "Gentiles." Twice in his letter Thomas refers to a fuller treatment "elsewhere"; these can refer only to the *Summa contra gentiles*. Thus we can infer that the reply to the cantor of Antioch was written shortly after the major *Summa* was completed; the date of its composition is thus placed in 1264, a very busy and productive year for Thomas.

The Feast of Corpus Christi

Liturgical compositions rarely circulate under the name of their author or compiler, but rather as a "practice" of some Church, diocese, religious Order, or locality. Nevertheless from the fourteenth century onward, there has been a strong indication that Thomas composed the whole liturgy for the feast of Corpus Christi and its octave at the request of Urban IV. It should not come as a surprise that the earliest witness of this claim is from the early fourteenth century. Even today the original author, or at least the one who composes the first draft, of papal encyclicals is not known until long after the event; even then one can only calculate a guess. If it is difficult to determine the author of the first draft of an encyclical, it is much more difficult to determine the author of new liturgies. Nevertheless, for the feast of Corpus Christi, the claim has been made repeatedly since the early fourteenth century that Thomas composed this liturgy at the request of Urban IV.

As Foster points out, "Tolomeo's is the only strictly contemporary witness to St. Thomas's authorship of the Corpus Christi office."[80] Tolomeo in his history, published between 1312 and 1317, is very explicit and detailed in his statement:

> By order of the same pope, Friar Thomas also composed the Office for Corpus Christi—the second commission from the pope to which I referred above.[81] This Corpus Christi Office Thomas composed in full, including the lessons and all the parts to be recited by day or night; the Mass, too, and whatever has to be sung on that day. An attentive reader will see that it comprises nearly all the symbolic figures from the Old Testament, clearly and appropriately relating them to the sacrament of the Eucharist.[82]

William of Tocco, possibly dependent on Tolomeo, also lists the liturgy of Corpus Christi among the works of Thomas: "He wrote the Office of Corpus Christi at the request of Pope Urban, in which he set forth all the Old [Testament] symbols relating to this sacrament, and assembled the truths that pertain to the New."[83] On the other hand, there is no mention of it in the so-called "official catalogue," i.e., the original list supposedly compiled by Reginald of Piperno, copied by Bartholomew of Capua for the canonization inquiry, and repeated in Prague MS Metrop. Kapit. A. XVII. 2. Presumably Reginald would have known whether Thomas wrote the liturgy for Corpus Christi or not. Its absence in the "official" list seems to suggest that Thomas did not write the liturgy that was later attributed to him.

There are two basic questions to be discussed: the precise text in question, and Thomas's authorship. Certainly the text as it now stands in the current Roman rite or Dominican rite did not come from Thomas. The text in the current liturgical books of the Church is that of the fifteenth-century Roman liturgy, which was introduced in the collections of Thomas's writings by Antonio Pizzamano only in 1497. The revised text of the fifteenth century was reformed by Pope Pius V in the sixteenth century, and again by Piux X in the twentieth.[84]

First, however, we must be clear as to what is meant by "composing" a liturgy. It does not mean creating *de novo*. Rather it means selecting and combining older elements from the Scriptures, the Fathers, and existing liturgies, only rarely venturing to write anew the hymns and prayers in order to express the theological and devotional views of the Church more appropriately. It must be admitted that before Urban IV issued the bull of 1264 extending the feast of Corpus Christi to the universal Church, there were Corpus Christi liturgies already in existence; but that fact does not eliminate the compilation of the new liturgy proposed to the entire Latin Church, the so-called Roman liturgy. Clearly someone had to compile it. Was that someone Thomas?

The evangelical movements among the laity of southern France and northern Italy frequently embraced heretical ideas and attitudes. While the Albigenses of southern France denied that the Eucharist is a sacrament, popular movements in the northern countries, particularly in Belgium, led to an intense devotion toward the sacred host.[85] The Eucharistic movement was popularized and extended by the Beguines, pious women who attached themselves to churches, monasteries, and priories. Such names as Marie of Oignies, St. Julienne of Mont-Cornillon, Christine of Saint-Trond, Ida of Nivelles, Isabel of Huy, and notably Eva, the recluse of Saint-Martin's, are known to us. The center of this Eucharistic movement was the diocese of Liège. The central focus of this devotion was the consecrated host itself. It became customary to reserve the Blessed Sacrament in the tabernacle; to display the host in an ostensorium left exposed on the altar, sometimes even during Mass; to ring bells at the time of elevation so all present could behold the Eucharist; and to conduct the Benediction of the Most Blessed Sacrament. Devotion to the "Body of the Lord" became so intense that in the summer of 1246, urged on by St. Julienne, Robert of Torote, bishop of Liège, authorized and stabilized the devotion on a special feast day, which was to be the first Thursday after Trinity Sunday.[86] Thursday was chosen as an extension of Holy Thursday, when the Lord instituted the Sacrament. The solemnities of Holy Week curtailed the expressions of love due to the Body of Christ. Therefore a special day was set aside outside of Lent to celebrate the feast more solemnly. For this occasion a certain John, a religious of Mont-Cornillon, composed a liturgy that was accepted throughout the diocese of Liège.[87]

In 1252 the cardinal legate of Germany, the Dominican Hugh of Saint-Cher, was so impressed by the Eucharistic solemnities he saw in Liège that he extended this feast throughout the territories of his legation by an ordinance of December 29, 1952.[88]   °
This ordinance was confirmed in the following year by Hugh's successor, Cardinal Pietro Capocci.[89] Jacques Pantaléon, the future Urban IV, himself witnessed the solemnities in Liège. Before his election as Pope, he spent some time in Liège as archdeacon and knew that version of the feast. He knew not only Robert, bishop of Liège, but also St. Julienne of Mont-Cornillon and Eva, the recluse of Saint-Martin's. It would seem that many petitions came to the Holy See to make this feast universal for the Church. Pope Urban IV and his predecessors were well aware of the Eucharistic movement in Belgium, but did nothing until the Italian populace was roused by a miracle of their own, the celebrated "miracle of Bolsena."

The earliest record we have of this miracle is in the *Chronica* (III, tit. 19, c. 13) of St. Antoninus of Florence (d. 1459). According to this chronicle, a German priest on pilgrimage to Rome was once celebrating Mass in the church of St. Cristina in the little Umbrian town of Bolsena; he was seriously disturbed by doubts about the transubstantiation of the bread and wine, which were suddenly resolved when he saw Blood issue from the consecrated elements and drench the corporal.[90] Rumor of this miracle spread quickly throughout the village of Bolsena, and a procession was soon formed to bring the bloodstained corporal to Urban IV, who was then in Orvieto, a very short distance from Bolsena. It is generally considered that at that time Urban determined to extend the feast of Corpus Christi throughout the world.

There is no date given, other than 1264, for the miracle depicted by one of Raphael's paintings that now hangs in the Vatican. On August 11, 1264, Urban promulgated the bull *Transiturus,* stating that the feast was to be instituted throughout the universal Church and that the new liturgy was to be used.[91] Certainly by August 11 the new "Roman liturgy" of the feast was ready for distribution. There can be no doubt that Urban wanted the new solemnities to be obligatory throughout the Christian world. That same day Urban sent another bull, similar to the one he had just signed, to the patriarch of Jerusalem, together with the liturgical text containing "nine lessons, with responses, versicles, antiphons, psalms, hymns, and prayers especially suitable for this feast."[92]

On September 8, 1264, Urban sent a personal letter to Eva, the recluse of Saint-Martin's, in Liège, relating the inauguration of this feast in the papal court. Together with this letter Urban sent a "quaternum" containing the text of the Roman feast.[93] This extraordinary document indicates the type of relationship Urban had with his friends in Liège. The Roman celebration of this new feast must have taken place between August 11, when the new liturgy was promulgated, and September 8, when Urban described the solemnities to Eva of Saint-Martin's. Hence the first Roman celebration of this feast did not take place on the day specified for Corpus Christi, namely, the first Thursday after the octave of Pentecost, which in 1264 would have been June 19; rather it took place in Orvieto between August 11 and September 8. But the important point is that the liturgy for the Mass and office on the feast and during the octave was completed by August 11, when copies were distributed. The new liturgy was called "Roman" to distinguish it from previous liturgies that were diocesan, national (as in Germany), and Cistercian. It is this Roman liturgy of Corpus Christi that is attributed to Thomas.

The Roman liturgy contained both the Mass and the office for the feast and for the entire octave. The Mass (*Cibavit eos*) seems to have remained more or less intact throughout the liturgical reforms of Pius V and Pius X. The antiphons, prayers, and sequence are undoubtedly from the original Roman liturgy for the feast. The sequence for the Mass is particularly striking. While there were precedents for this sequence and the hymns of the office, there are none identical with it. The sequence *Lauda Sion* in the Mass is remarkable not only for its poetry, but also for its theological content; the individual stanzas can easily be aligned with the Eucharistic teaching of Thomas as found in the third part of his *Summa theologiae*. Traces of this sequence can be found earlier, but none with its beauty or profundity.

The part that suffered most during the liturgical reforms was the night office, Matins, when the nine lessons of the original were replaced. For example, the readings for the second nocturn today are taken from a spurious sermon, attributed to Thomas, on the Eucharist.[94]

The three magnificent hymns of the office are not identical with any hymns known to have been previously written. The hymn for first and second Vespers is the *Pange lingua*, sung for processions on Holy Thursday, which concludes with the well-known *Tantum ergo*, sung for centuries during Benediction of the Blessed Sacrament. The hymn for Matins, *Sacris solemnis*, has many similarities with older Ambrosian hymns; it concludes with the well-known *Panis angelicus*, made popular in this century by many singers on the concert stage. The hymn for Lauds, *Verbum supernum prodiens*, has many similarities with a hymn in the Cistercian liturgy of Corpus Christi, but is by no means identical to it.[95] It concludes with another couplet formerly sung at Benediction, the *O salutaris hostia*. In brief, it can be said that all of these hymns have their antecedents in older liturgies, but none of them can be found complete before the Roman office of Corpus Christi. Therefore whoever compiled the Roman liturgy for this feast also reworked the hymns.

The oration used in the office and the Mass in the primitive Roman liturgy is particularly beautiful, both in its poetic organization and in its theological profundity:

> O God, who under this wonderful Sacrament has left us a memorial of your passion, grant we pray, that we may venerate the sacred mysteries of your Body and Blood so as to feel constantly the fruits of your redemption within us, who lives and reigns . . .

This prayer for Corpus Christi involves the simultaneity of three aspects as it looks to the past, present, and future of the Eucharistic gift. It is a memorial of the past sufferings and death of

Christ, a veneration of the present Body and Blood of Christ in the Eucharist, as well as a prelude to the fruits received now and forever. The separation of bread and wine is a sacramental separation of Body and Blood; this is symbolized in the very nature of "sacrament" as sign. However, from the moment of consecration each species contains the whole Christ, Body and Blood, soul and divinity; this reality signified by the species is the true God we now venerate and adore. But this reality is also a symbol of the grace and glory we receive; this grace and glory are the "fruits" of Christ's redemption. These three aspects were fully developed by twelfth-century theologians, who had a precise terminology for discussing the sacraments: *sacramentum tantum, res et sacramentum,* and *res tantum.* The nature of a sacrament is to be a symbol, a sign of something interior to the sacrament. In Baptism the *sacramentum tantum* is the actual pouring of the water and the significance of the words used; it signifies the interior cleansing of the soul through the sacramental character of Baptism, the *res et sacramentum;* the ultimate reality (*res tantum*) is the life of God, the grace given to the soul. So in the Eucharist. The *sacramentum tantum* is the visible species signifying through the words of consecration the separation of Body and Blood; after consecration the species of bread and wine signify Body separated from Blood, and Blood separated from Body. This sacramental separation is the dying Christ of Calvary, and thus a memorial of the past. However, the living Christ, whole and entire in each species, is the God we adore here and now; it is the *res et sacramentum* that are not only signified by the sacrament (*res*) but also signify something else in its role as symbol (*et sacramentum*). It is the grace and glory we obtain from the author of all grace that is the *res tantum.* Thus the past, present, and future are all contained in the Eucharistic sacrifice. These three aspects are carefully kept in mind throughout Thomas's discussion of the Eucharist in the third part of the *Summa theologiae.*

Cyrille Lambot and L. M. J. Delaissé, the two leading authorities on this question, while recognizing the existence of the Roman liturgy for the feast of Corpus Christi, are reluctant to attribute it to Thomas d'Aquino, their basic reason being the procrastination of the Dominicans. The argument, in effect, goes thus: if Thomas had written the liturgy, the Dominican Order would have adopted it immediately instead of waiting fifty-four years. In fact, the Order did nothing until new measures were taken by the Holy See in 1317. Therefore, Thomas could not have been the author of the Roman liturgy of Corpus Christi. This procrastination and indifference on the part of the Order must be admitted, but I do not think that this argument against Thomas's authorship is conclusive.

The bull *Transiturus* was promulgated on September 11, 1264, and the solemnities of the feast were held at Orvieto between August 11 and September 8. But Urban IV died on October 2 of that same year, and nothing more was heard of the bull. The Council of Vienne was held from October 16, 1311, to May 6, 1312, under Clement V. Clement was determined to have all the laws of the Church that had been enacted since Gregory IX, but that had not yet been codified, collected into a single *Constitution*, henceforth known as the "Clementines." At the Council, Pope Clement V introduced the bull *Transiturus* of Urban IV, which was barely recognized by any Order or diocese represented.[96] Since Clement V died before his project was completed, the *Constitution* was promulgated by John XXII in 1317. From this moment on, the universal Church was to institute the feast of Corpus Christi.

Not until the meeting of the general chapter of the Dominican Order at Lyons in 1318 was it ordained that "throughout the whole Order the office of Corpus Christi is to be held on Thursday within the octave of Trinity, as laid down in the constitutions of the Council of Vienne; the master of the Order should try to provide [the text of] the office."[97] In the general chapter of 1322, held at Vienne, the Order formally adopted the feast:

Since our Order ought to conform in the divine office to the Holy Roman Church, in so far as possible, and particularly in an office which is a product of our Order by apostolic command, we now wish that the office of Corpus Christi, composed, as it is said (*ut asseritur*), by the venerable doctor Thomas d'Aquino, be observed throughout the entire Order on the Thursday after the feast of the Trinity and throughout its octave inclusive, and that the aforesaid office be inscribed in the *Ordinarium* in the appropriate places.[98]

Certainly by 1322 the capitular fathers were willing to admit three things: (1) that an office of Corpus Christi was composed by a member of the Dominican Order ("a product of our Order") at the request of Urban IV, (2) that the Order had been remiss in not incorporating this feast in the Dominican *Ordinarium*, and (3) that the author of the "Roman office" was Thomas d'Aquino. The expression "as it is said" (*ut asseritur*) does not imply hearsay or rumor, as some claim, but must be interpreted in the light of the previous phrase "a product of our Order," namely Friar Thomas d'Aquino. By 1322 the process of Thomas's canonization was already well advanced, so far advanced, in fact, that John XXII was ready to canonize him in the following year. The statements of Tolomeo of Lucca and William of Tocco could have been known to the capitular fathers, at least to some of them. The capitular ordinance of 1322, as I understand it, is an implied apology for neglecting the bull *Transiturus* of 1264. The general chapter of 1265 should have conformed to the wishes of Urban IV and adopted the feast and its octave into its own calendar, regardless of who composed the liturgy. One might wonder what Thomas thought about this negligence. The only excuse possible is that so many other orders, as well as dioceses and countries, also neglected the bull.

Urban IV died at Perugia on October 2, 1264, and was buried there in the cathedral church. Six days later Guy Foulques of Saint-Giles, another Frenchman, was elected Pope and took the name of Clement IV; he was consecrated on February 15, 1265, at Perugia. Cardinal Hugh of Saint-Cher had died at Orvieto on March 19, 1263, and was buried there.[99] Humbert of Romans, the master general who governed the Order for ten years, died on July 14 of the same year. The general chapter meeting in Paris in 1264 elected John of Vercelli as Humbert's successor. The new master general ruled the Order for nineteen years, including the ten remaining years of Thomas's life. After the death of Urban IV, Thomas continued as lector in the Dominican Priory of San Domenico in Orvieto until 1265, when the provincial chapter of Anagni assigned him to open a studium in Rome. Between the death of Urban in October and the new assignment to Rome in September of the following year, Thomas not only lectured to the Dominican community at Orvieto, as he had previously done, but he assembled glosses for his *Catena* on Mark. It was a quiet year of lecturing, research, and writing.

Chapter V

REGENT MASTER IN ROME AND LECTOR AT VITERBO

(1265–68)

Thomas was forty years old when he was assigned to Rome to open a studium for the province in 1265. That date happened to be a turning point in the history of Italy and the papacy; the tyranny of the Hohenstaufens was exchanged for the tyranny of the Angevin kings of Naples.[1]

When Frederick II died in 1250, the succession was carried on by his eldest son, Conrad IV, who had been king of Rome since 1237, and who was crowned Emperor on December 13, 1250. But Conrad reigned only four years, leaving at his death only an infant son to succeed him. Manfred, Frederick's older, bastard son, seized power and carried warfare to the very door of the papacy. On July 8, 1264, Urban IV wrote to Aimo of Aquino to resist the troops of Manfred and to prevent him from taking possession of Montesangiovanni.[2] On that same day, Urban wrote also to Thomas II of Aquino, Count of Acerra, asking him not to allow enemy troops to enter the territory around Montesangiovanni.[3] But papal forces were powerless against the large armies of the Hohenstaufens, who had Ghibelline support in and around Rome. In desperation, rather than come to terms with Manfred, Urban invited Conradin, grandson of Frederick II, to come to Italy, contrary to the advice of Louis IX of France and Baldwin II, ex-Emperor of Constantinople, both of whom were then present at the papal court. As a Frenchman, Urban IV appealed to Louis IX of France to come to his assistance. Apparently Louis thought that he could not bring his own forces to Italy, for he was preparing to lead the seventh crusade to the Holy Land; but he did ask his brother, Prince Charles of Anjou, to come to the assistance of the Pope. By September 1264, Ghibelline forces had moved to the environs of Orvieto; revolts broke out in Orvieto, where Urban IV and Thomas Aquinas were living. On September 9, Urban "fled" north from Orvieto to Perugia, where he died on October 2.

Charles of Anjou arrived in Rome with his troops in May 1265, a few months before Thomas himself arrived there to open the studium. Charles, Prince of Anjou, was welcomed by Cardinal Annibaldo and a number of other cardinals, as well as by the people of Rome. The new Pope, Clement IV (1265–68), also a Frenchman, ordered Cardinal Annibaldo and three other cardinals to invest Charles with the crown of Sicily. With the title of kingship secure, Charles left Rome on January 20, 1266, accompanied by the cardinal legate, Richard Annibaldi. In February, Charles met up with Manfred and his main army northeast of Naples; on February 26 the two armies clashed in a bloody battle at Benevento. Manfred, refusing to surrender or be taken alive, pitched himself into the height of the battle until he was mortally wounded. Roger of Sanseverino, Thomas's brother-in-law, fought at the side of Charles, whereas Thomas Aquinas II of Acerra fled from the field of battle.

Foolishly, Urban IV had asked Conradin, Frederick's grandson, to come to Italy in the hope of coming to terms with him. Conradin landed in Italy with his army in 1267 and rallied the Ghibelline forces; in the summer of 1268 he received a triumphal welcome in Rome. But this glory did not outlive the summer, for on August 23 he encountered the army of Charles at Tagliacozzo, a short distance east of Naples. It is often said that Conradin was betrayed into the hands of Charles of Anjou. Whatever may be the truth of this, Conradin was defeated and brought to Naples, where he was publicly executed by beheading on October 29, 1268. Clement IV, protesting the execution, died at Viterbo on November 29 of that same year. By that date Friar Thomas was on his way north from Viterbo to Paris, and the Holy See was vacant for the next three years.

The Popes had reason to regret their invitation to Charles, for the new king of Sicily and Naples ruled with an iron fist to the disillusionment of the papacy. Clement IV could do nothing but repent the action he and his predecessor had taken. It would seem that strong criticism of Charles arose from the Dominicans of the Roman Province, so much so that the provincial chapter of 1266, meeting at Todi in August, strongly rebuked those who spoke ill of King Charles, considering especially that he was protector and patron of the Order everywhere in his kingdom. Those who dishonored the king or made fun of him by words or deed, the chapter declared, were to be severely punished by the prior and visitators, and their names were to be sent to the provincial.[4]

At some date around 1265, either at Orvieto or at Rome, Thomas decided (or was asked) to write a treatise on kingship for the king of Cyprus, called *De regno,* or *De regimine principum ad regem Cypri.* Mandonnet dated this work 1265–66; Walz and Perrier date it in 1266, while Eschmann places its date between 1260 and 1265. Perhaps more than any other writing attributed to Thomas, *De regno* has been heatedly disputed, for it is the only explicit treatise written by Thomas on the relation of Church and state.[5] In the printed versions the treatise consists of four books, each divided into chapters. There have been scholars, such as C. A. Bosone, who maintained the authenticity of the entire text, while J. A. Endres, Ezio Flori, and I. T. Eschmann have rejected the authenticity of all four books.[6] Grabmann and most modern writers believe that the text is authentic up to Book II, c. 4, in the printed editions, ending with the words "ut animi hominum recreentur."[7]

There are many problems connected with the text and its doctrine. First, as to the text, nine out of eleven catalogues examined by Mandonnet[8] list a work entitled *De regno, De regimine principum, De rege et regno,* or some equivalent title. Five of these catalogues are prior in time to Tolomeo of Lucca's catalogue and his own treatise *De regimine principum.* Therefore some work of this title was known to the cataloguers prior to Tolomeo, who himself lists such a work among the authentic writings of Thomas.[9] Among all the early cataloguers, John of Colona is the only one who describes it as a "work he [Thomas] did not complete."[10] Grabmann discovered an Italian translation of the work in the Vatican Library (Chigi MS M. VIII, 168. 2021), which explicitly states that Thomas did not finish the work, and that it was completed by Tolomeo of Lucca, of the same Order, who was later bishop of Torcello.[11] The manuscript evidence is even more convincing. No early MS contains the full four books of the printed version; fourteen of the MSS examined by Grabmann end with what is now Book II, c. 4; O'Rahilly discovered twenty-three MSS that ended in the same place. However, some late MSS do contain the full four books known today.[12] Therefore it is clear that Thomas did write an incomplete treatise called *De regno* (or, to give it the more popular fourteenth-century title, *De regimine principum*); from the manuscript evidence we can say that the authentic portion ended with the words "ut animi hominum recreentur," or some variant, in II, 4. It is possible to say that either Tolomeo of Lucca "continued" and "finished" the original text or someone later combined the two treatises skillfully to form the lengthy treatise that found its way into late MSS and printed books.[13]

We do not know why Thomas left this work unfinished, nor why he undertook the task in the first place. The treatise is clearly no letter of response to a query, for in the prologue Thomas states that it is to be a "gift" to the king of Cyprus. One Vatican MS states that the treatise was addressed to "Henry, King of Cyprus," who died in December 1267. The work could have been terminated when news of the king's death reached Thomas. But we have no idea why Thomas should have wanted to send such a gift in the first place. Grabmann insisted that the intended recipient was Hugh, not Henry, but he was unable to decide whether it was Hugh II or Hugh III.[14] Eschmann suggests that the intended recipient was Hugh II of Lusigan, "the only Cypriote King of the Lusigan dynasty to be buried in the Chuch of St. Dominic's in Nicosia, the main priory of the Preachers' province of the Holy Land."[15]

Eschmann denied the authenticity of even the first twenty-one chapters, i.e., up to Book II, c. 4, because the doctrine contained therein contradicts the earlier teaching of Thomas found in the commentary on the *Sentences*.[16] He insisted that even these early chapters were contaminated by Tolomeo's papalist doctrine, and therefore have to be considered spurious, even though some of the chapters may have been written by Thomas. But, as we have shown, this theory cannot stand, for there are many manuscript copies predating the work of Tolomeo, so the text of these copies could not have been contaminated by him. This point was carefully examined by O'Rahilly, who states:

> I have found that the original treatise was incomplete, that the point where it stops can be definitely settled by manuscript evidence alone, that—apart from chapter headings—there has been no interpolation or revision by the continuator.[17]

In the thirteenth century there were two dominant views of the relation of temporal and spiritual powers. The prevalent view was the papalist or Guelf position, wherein the Pope was said to have the "plenitude of power" embracing both the spiritual and the secular domain. In this view, all authority, even that of kings and emperors, is derived from the Pope in a direct and absolute line in such a way that all temporal power exists only at the sufferance of the Pope. Hence Popes could confer or remove this power at will. Deposition by the Pope of a temporal ruler meant, so it was claimed, that his people were no longer obliged to obey him—in fact, they were not allowed to support a deposed ruler under pain of excommunication and forfeiture. The origin of this power was derived from God through the papacy. In other words, the temporal authority of the Pope was considered an essential part of his power, not an accidental fact of history. Thus, the Pope had full authority over his own temporalities, as well as the power to make or break temporal rulers. The important point from a theoretical point of view is that the Pope's temporal authority over his own papal states and over all rulers of Christendom was considered essential, and not accidental, to his authority as Pope. This papalist view is to be found most clearly in the bull *Unam sanctam* of Boniface VIII.

The imperialist, or Ghibelline, point of view was that all temporal power comes from God through consent of the governed, even in the case of an absolute monarchy or aristocracy. They argued that since all temporal power comes from the Emperor or other legitimate ruler, the Pope's own temporal authority comes from the secular ruler and depends on him for its exercise. In other words, even if the Pope had the fullness

of spiritual power, he could not exercise it in the temporal domain without the authority and consent of the ruler. This view
was strongly argued by Marsiglio of Padua in his *Defensor
pacis,* written in the beginning of the fourteenth century.

A middle position had been taken in the fourth century, when
a clear distinction was made between the temporal and spiritual
domains. The Latin Fathers, and Pope Gelasius in particular,
taught that in temporal affairs the *sacerdotium,* or priestly authority, is subject to the *regnum,* or secular authority, while in spiritual affairs the *regnum* is subject to the *sacerdotium.* This
position is a restatement and application of Christ's own words
to "render to Caesar the things that are Caesar's, and to God the
things that are God's" (Mt. 22:21). The middle position also
maintained that the Pope's temporal power was only accidental,
and could be totally absent without detriment to his spiritual
authority. (Before the fourth century, the Popes had no temporal
power whatever.) Similarly in the nineteenth century, the Popes
lost all dominion over the papal states, leaving only the Vatican
city-state intact, for the sake of practicality; this change in no
way diminished the spiritual power of the Popes. The middle
position was strongly defended by the Dominican John Quidort
of Paris in his treatise *De potestate regia et papali* of 1302.

Eschmann, as I have mentioned, saw a contradiction between
the teaching of *De regno* I, 14, and *Sentences* II, dist. 44. From
this contradiction he concluded that *De regno* is contaminated,
and therefore spurious. In the passage from the *Sentences,*
Thomas had no more than summarized the origin and goal of
spiritual and temporal power, and noted the special case when
the two are conjoined in one person:

> Spiritual as well as secular power comes from the divine power.
> Hence secular power is subjected to spiritual power in those
> matters concerning which the subjection has been specified and
> ordained by God, i.e., in matters belonging to the salvation of the
> soul. Hence in these we are to obey spiritual authority more than
> secular authority. On the other hand, more obedience is due to
> secular than to spiritual power in the things that pertain to the
> civic good. For it is said in Mt. 22:21, "Render to Caesar the
> things that are Caesar's." A special case occurs, however, when

spiritual and secular power are so joined in one person as they are in the pope, who holds the apex of both spiritual and secular powers.[18]

Here Thomas teaches that there are *two* powers with formally two distinct goals, one eternal, the other temporal; one ordained to the salvation of souls, the other to the civic good. Today we might say that the spiritual power is ordained to the supernatural end of man, while the temporal is ordained to the natural good of society. Even when these two powers are joined in one man, they are still two distinct powers accidentally united in one person.

In *De regno,* Thomas seems to speak of only one power from which the other is derived, apparently per se, the lower being ordained to the higher:

> To him [the Roman pontiff] all kings of the Christian people are to be subject as to our Lord Jesus Christ himself. For those to whom pertains the care of intermediate ends should be subject to him to whom pertains the care of the ultimate end, and be directed by his rule. Because the priesthood of the gentiles and the whole worship of their gods existed merely for the acquisition of temporal goods (which were all ordained to the common good of the multitude, whose care devolved upon the king), the priests of the gentiles were very properly subject to the kings. Similarly, since in the old law earthly goods were promised to the religious people (not indeed by demons, but by the true God), the priests of the old law, we read, were also subject to the kings. But in the new law there is a higher priesthood by which men are guided to heavenly good. Consequently, in the law of Christ, kings must be subject to priests.[19]

Here the author seems indeed to speak of *one* power, similar to the "plenitude of power" of the papalists, from which secular power is derived.

Eschmann refused to countenance a change of mind on the part of Thomas. He insisted that in none of his works, "neither the early nor the later ones, excepting text R, is there any trace of that curious theology of the Primacy which includes secular power in its essence."[20] Although Thomas appears never again to have discussed this question, Eschmann sees implicit confirmation of the *Sentences* in passing references in the *Summa theologiae* II–II.[21] But in all these references, as far as I can judge, the only salient feature is that the primary end of the Church is spiritual, and no one would deny that.

In *De regno* I, 14, the author indeed admits that the goal of the king is the care of "the common good of the multitude," a natural right which is his by nature. "The divine law, which is from grace, does not take away human right, which is from natural reason" (*Sum. theol.* II–II, 10, 10). According to Aristotle's dictum (*Ethic.* I, 1, 1094 a 14), the order of ends parallels the order of agents. Therefore the origin of the king's power is not the Pope, but natural reason. The order of grace never destroys or supplants the order of nature. The salvation of souls, which is the concern of the Pope by divine right, cannot destroy or replace the "common good of the multitude," which is the concern of the secular ruler by natural right. The author of *De regno* I, 14, speaks only in broad terms, which can rightly be understood in terms of *In II Sent.*, dist. 44. As far as I can see, the author of *De regno* I, 14, implicitly recognizes these two distinct goals. Therefore there is no contradiction between the two passages. There is no per se order between nature and grace, for nature can in no way merit grace. Hence the jurisdiction of the secular ruler can in no way be at the sufferance of the Pope, and the author of *De regno* I, 14, does not teach this.

Moreover, when we speak of the temporal jurisdiction of the Pope, we mean directly his secular authority over the papal states, not over the whole world. It is true that some Popes and canonists spoke and acted as though the supreme pontiff had temporal jurisdiction over all the princes of Christendom. But this was a misunderstanding, if not an aberration, with a long history. It was never the teaching of Thomas. When the papal states were taken away in the nineteenth century, some dogmatic theologians still maintained that it was a matter of divine faith that Popes had the *right* to temporal authority; but they did not claim that this right extended over the whole of Christendom.

It would seem, then, that *De regno* I–II, 4, can be considered an authentic work of Thomas Aquinas. If the unfinished treatise was indeed intended for King Hugh II of Cyprus, who died in

December 1267, then it must be dated between 1263 and 1267, when Thomas was in Rome.[22]

Regent Master at Santa Sabina, Rome

(1265-67)

In 1265 the provincial chapter of the Roman Province met at Anagni on September 8, following the general chapter at Montpellier. At Anagni the capitular fathers, including Friar Thomas, decided to establish a studium for the Province at Santa Sabina in Rome:

> We enjoin on Friar Thomas d'Aquino in remission of his sins to establish a studium in Rome, and we direct that there be provided for the brethren who are with him for the sake of study sufficient clothing from the priories of their origin. If, however, those students are found negligent in study, we give Friar Thomas full authority to send them back to their respective houses.[23]

Since Thomas attended this chapter in his capacity as preacher general, he would most certainly have taken part in the discussion before a decision was reached. Very likely Thomas himself suggested this turn in the history of the Roman Province. At any rate he was chosen to open the first studium in the Province of Rome at Santa Sabina on the Aventine hill. This priory was one of the oldest in the Order, having been given to St. Dominic by the Holy See in 1221; the spacious basilica was designed by the same architect who designed Santa Maria Maggiore in fifth-century Rome. It would be wrong to call this a general studium in the technical sense of the phrase; Thomas's task was to teach young Dominicans the elements of theology. As far as we know there were no assistant lectors to teach the students philosophy. The students were carefully chosen by the provincial and priors of the various houses of the province. Thomas taught at the provincial studium only for two years; it was the only strictly academic assignment he had during his ten years in the province. The first studium of arts (philosophy) was established in the province four years later.

Before considering the course of studies conducted by Thomas, we must come to some understanding of the new studia that came into existence in the Roman Province. During the four years of growth, 1265–69, the province realized the need to train young Dominicans separately from the usual teaching of the lector for the entire community in the priory. Young men were entering the Order without the advantage of some schooling in philosophy and elementary theology. The general chapter at Valenciennes in 1259, as we have seen, established a commission of five masters in theology to consider a *ratio studiorum* for the Order. In 1265 the Roman Province took an important step when it appointed Thomas to be regent master in theology at Santa Sabina. But this studium was not enough. Four years later, in 1269, when Thomas had returned to Paris, the provincial chapter of the Roman Province established two "general studia of theology," one at Naples, the other at Orvieto. It also established a "studium of arts" in Perugia, where Friar Matteo of Lucca was lector.[24] Three years later, when Thomas returned from Paris in 1272, the capitular fathers at Florence gave Thomas the right to establish a *studium generale theologiae* anywhere he wanted. Thomas, as we will see, chose to go to Naples as regent master of theology. That same chapter established a studium of arts in Pisa, where Friar Ricculdo of Florence was teaching as lector of the priory.

From these assignments it is clear that the capitular fathers had no intention of establishing studia permanently in one or other place; this practice did not come about until later. The fathers of the chapter associated the place of study with the teacher, and not with a particular locality. The closest they came to geographical considerations was in 1269, when there were to be two studia of theology in the province, Naples in the south and Orvieto in the north.

We must emphasize again that the studia established by the provincial chapter were in no way *studia generalia* in the medieval sense of the term; eventually they came to be called *studia provincialia*. The general chapter of Viterbo in 1268 continued to refer to the "four general studia of the Order," when it committed to the master general the appointment of masters, bachelors, and others pertaining to the studium; the same provision is made in the general chapter at Paris in 1269. At that time only general chapters could establish general studia, where all subjects were taught to students sent from any province of the Order. In 1270 two more general studia were to be opened by the Order in the Province of Rome and in the Province of Spain.[25] But, as we shall see, this hope was not realized at that time.

Although the studium opened by Thomas at Santa Sabina in 1265 was not a general studium, it was a new venture for the province. Thomas undoubtedly tried to pattern his studium after those of Paris and Cologne, even to the point of having a bachelor respond at disputations which he held regularly. There is also a suggestion that he may have tried at first to teach part of the *Sentences* before realizing how difficult a book it was for beginners in theology. Although it was not a general studium, such as Albert was asked to open in Cologne seventeen years earlier, we can be fairly certain that Thomas attempted to organize Santa Sabina in much the same way. It is certain that he had a bachelor or senior student, possibly more than one, to respond in disputations, and there may even have been a lector to assist him in reading the Bible; but we must not picture the studium at Santa Sabina as a large operation, or a pretentious school for all young Dominicans in the Roman Province.

When we discussed *De divinis nominibus* by Pseudo-Dionysius in the previous chapter, I suggested that the exposition may have originated as lectures in the provincial studium in Rome. Most authorities date it around 1261 without any compelling reason. However, similarly without any compelling reason, I would suggest that it could more appropriately be dated during this Roman period of Thomas's life. Albertus Magnus had set the precedent when he taught Thomas in Cologne. While the language of *De divinis nominibus* is somewhat difficult, the essential ideas are propounded in a manner suitable for beginners not yet schooled in Aristotelian philosophy. It emphasizes the care that must be taken when talking about God, for He transcends all language and conceptions of Him.

Undoubtedly the select students sent to Rome for training would have been continually exposed to the Scriptures, taught either by Thomas or a lector. There is no indication, however, as to what biblical texts were read.

The most important aspect of the Roman studium was the introduction of disputed questions. The essential nature of scholastic education consisted of both lectures and disputations. It was not enough to hear the great books of Western thought expounded by a master; it was essential that the great ideas be examined critically in the disputation. The finesse, etiquette, and subtlety of the Parisian questions may have been lacking in the smaller studia of Europe, such as at Santa Sabina, but the disputation could not be totally neglected without prejudice to learning.

The disputations Thomas held and determined in the Roman studium can be argued simply from extant catalogues and MSS.

The earliest lists of Thomas's works, which Mandonnet called the "first group of catalogues," were compiled after these works were collected and bound. One criterion of judging authenticity was the exemplars Reginald of Piperno had in his own collection. A Neapolitan scribe indicated the importance of this collection when he appended to an "explicit" the observation that a particular work ends in a definite spot "because no more is found in the exemplar of Friar Reginald of Piperno, who was the socius of Friar Thomas until his death and who had all of his writings."[26] The fact that all the disputed questions were collected and divided into three parts is patent in Nicholas Trevet's catalogue of these questions:

> He wrote the first part of the questions *De veritate* and the rest, which were disputed in Paris. Likewise the second part of the disputed questions *De potentia Dei* and the rest, which he disputed in Italy. Likewise the third part of the disputed questions, the beginning of which is *De virtutibus*, which he disputed when he taught in Paris the second time.[27]

Nicholas Trevet and the other early catalogues specify *De potentia Dei* "and the rest" as Italian productions. There is, of course, some question about the meaning of "the rest." Just as in the case of *De veritate*, the title of the series is derived from the first question, even though it designates the entire series found in all the MSS and printed editions. We may conclude, therefore, that the series of ten questions belonging to *De potentia Dei* was disputed in Italy. But this does not preclude the possibility that other disputations may also belong to the Italian period.

Mandonnet, convinced that Thomas went first to Anagni to the court of Alexander IV in 1259, maintained that the questions *De potentia* were disputed at Anagni and Orvieto (1259–63).[28] But this question has been settled by Grabmann's discovery of *De potentia* in MS 211 of the monastery library at Subiaco, where a rubric on fol. 175^r clearly states: "Questions of Friar Thomas of Aquino which he disputed at Rome."[29] The series *De potentia* consists of ten questions, each divided into numerous articles:

1. God's power considered in itself (7 articles)
2. the generative power within the Godhead (6 articles)
3. creation (19 articles)
4. creation of unformed matter (2 articles)
5. conservation of things in being (10 articles)
6. miracles (10 articles)
7. simplicity of the divine essence (11 articles)
8. relationships in the Trinity (4 articles)
9. divine persons (9 articles)
10. the procession of divine persons (5 articles)

These ten questions contain eighty-three articles. Historians following Mandonnet conclude from this fact that Thomas held eighty-three disputations, each article being considered a distinct academic disputation. But, according to A. Dondaine, some of the articles are so short it is incredible that "an entire faculty would suspend teaching to attend it." Dondaine proposes that each "question" constitutes an entire disputation, each article being a different aspect of a single dispute.[30] Thus there would be two sessions for each question, the first consisting of objections and responses to the various articles proposed by the master for discussion, and the second consisting of the master's determination. Nevertheless a doubt still remains concerning the extremely long questions, such as the nineteen articles on creation, the ten articles on conservation, and the eleven articles on divine simplicity. The same doubt remains for the extremely short questions, such as two articles on the creation of unformed matter.

Admittedly this question does not deserve lengthy disputation; nevertheless, according to Dondaine, two articles constitute an entire disputed question as much as one consisting of nineteen articles. Our understanding of the precise technique of a disputed question is still far from complete, and much more needs to be known. But for our purpose it is sufficient to concede that the "question" was the basic core of the scholastic disputation.

The series of discussions comprising *De potentia* is basically concerned with divine omnipotence in creation and governance, a question of great concern to the Averroists, and with the procession of the Holy Spirit from the Father "and from the Son," a question of great concern to the Greeks. Many of the points discussed here were already discussed in the *Summa contra gentiles*. But in the *De potentia* there is a directness and simplicity of metaphysical thinking that indicate a development of thought. This development stands midway between the *Summa contra gentiles* and the first part of the *Summa theologiae*. In fact, *De potentia* is chronologically and speculatively the immediate predecessor of the first part of the theological *Summa*. No metaphysican or speculative theologian can neglect the disputed questions *De potentia* without detriment to his own understanding of Thomas's *Summa theologiae*, particularly the first part; the second and third parts have unusual characteristics that must be considered later.

The fact that God created the universe and everything in it is of fundamental importance in Aquinas's metaphysics. By faith we know that God created the universe "in time," i.e., "in the beginning" (Gn. 1:1), but we can know by reason that the universe had to be created out of nothing, even if it existed from all eternity. This view was opposed to that of the extreme Aristotelians and Averroists, for whom the universe always existed in time and needed no creation. It was also opposed to the Ultra-Augustinists, like John Pecham and other Franciscans, for whom creation had to exist in time, from which creation itself could be demonstrated.

A paraphrase of some of the ideas contained in *De potentia*, q. 3, on creation, may help to give an idea of the stage of Thomas's development just prior to the composition of the first part of the *Summa theologiae*.

For Thomas an analysis of natural activity cannot explain the coming into being of a whole substance, for every particular being is only partially in act and partially in potency. Each material being is composed of matter and form, and does not exercise causality on another except by reason of its form, which is the active principle of its being. Thus no whole being acts on the whole of another being, but only partially. Moreover, each being in nature is determined in species and genus, and therefore can produce beings that are only similar to it in species and genus. Hence no natural agent can produce being as such (*ens simpliciter*), but only a being that is similarly pre-existent as itself. For this reason all natural agents require already existing matter on which to operate by changing or altering it. If the whole of a being is to exist, what is needed is an agent who is wholly in act within itself and in reference to others. But God is pure act and the font of being. Therefore He can make something out of pure nothing; this "making" is what we call creation (a. 1). The perennial Greek objection is that "nothing can come from nothing." But this axiom is derived from natural changes, which always presuppose some kind of potentiality. In a supernatural agency like God, there can be nothing presupposed (a. 1 ad 1). Therefore God can create something out of nothing. This argument is presented much more simply and directly in *Summa theologiae* I, q. 45, aa. 1–2.

Thomas goes on in article 2 to show that creation and change are not the same, for all change presupposes a subject on which to act, either "prime matter" in substantial change, or substance for one of the three types of motion discussed by Aristotle in the *Physics*. Creation presupposes absolutely nothing common to the non-being "before" creation and the actual being "after" creation. It is only the imagination that pictures something common, a *quid imaginativum*, and a "before" and "after," even though there is no motion, matter, or time.

By creation every creature is related to God as to its source of being, for its very *esse* is from God and from Him alone. Since every creature depends upon God and not vice versa, the relationship on the part of creatures is real and intrinsic, while God's relation to creatures is only a way of speaking, as when we call Him "creator" or "father" (a. 3).

Some philosophers, notably the Neo-Platonists and Avicenna, hold that all reality proceeds from God as from an ultimate source in such a way that He produces the first being, who in turn produces the second and so on, since there is a hierarchy in being. These philosophers think that God produces all things by a necessary emanation. But this is contrary to the faith, which holds that God creates all things immediately according to his free will. Some Christian theologians, such as Peter Lombard, hold that no creature can naturally create another, but that God could communicate this power to a creature as to an instrument; thus God would be the first cause, and a creature could be an instrumental cause of creation (IV *Sent.*, dist. 5). As we saw in chapter 2, Thomas and the majority of Parisian masters rejected this teaching of Peter Lombard. In *De potentia* q. 3, a. 4, Thomas again rejects this idea that creation is communicable to creatures as to an instrument. The activity of everything, even of instruments, must flow from the basic abilities of the thing. Since, however, the abilities of every creature are finite, it is impossible that a creature create anything, for creation requires an *infinite power* to make something out of absolute nothing, because the distance between non-being and being is infinite. When a power is communicated to an instrument of any sort, that power is immediately limited by the capacities of that instrument. In the *Summa* Thomas reduces this argument to the basic truth that only God is His own *esse*, and that therefore only He can create (q. 45, a. 5 ad 1).

In the fifth article of *De potentia* Thomas presents a brief history of metaphysics when he determines the question whether anything exists that is not created by God. He locates the process of this history in the natural process of knowledge. Since all human understanding begins with sense, the earliest philosophers directed their attention to sensible reality. The senses are per se concerned with accidental qualities, not with substance itself. Thus the earliest philosophers claimed that all forms are accidental, and that only matter is substantial. Since substance is a sufficient cause of accidents, for all accidents are caused by the principles of substance, the earliest philosophers felt no need to search beyond matter for a deeper cause. Later philosophers (such as Empedocles and Anaxagoras) gave some consideration to substantial forms, not as universals, but as particular species. They postulated efficient causes, not the kind that universally conferred *esse* on things, but the kind that made matter have this or that form, as the supreme *nous*, or friendship and strife, whose activity consisted in segregating and congregating the pre-existent. Hence even according to them not all things were produced by an efficient cause, since matter was presupposed to the action of the agent. But later philosophers, including Plato, Aristotle, and their followers, arrived at a consideration of universal *esse* itself. Hence they alone postulated a universal cause of things, from which all other things are derived in being.

At this stage of Thomas's development he was not certain whether Aristotle or Plato taught the doctrine of *creation from nothing*. The truth of the matter is that neither of them did, although such a doctrine of creation is not incompatible with their teaching. In *De potentia* Thomas confidently says, "To which doctrine [of Plato and Aristotle] even the Catholic faith agrees." He then proceeds to give three demonstrative arguments. First, whenever there is something common to two or more things, there must be a common cause. *Esse* is common to all things. This common reality cannot arise from one another or from themselves, because each one, precisely because it exists, is divided from the other. Therefore the *esse*, which is common, must be attributed to some single cause of all. Thomas remarks that this seems to be the argument of Plato, who postulated unity prior to plurality, not only in numbers, but also in the very nature of things. Second, whenever some attribute is shared by many things according to different degrees of participation, it belongs properly to the one that has it most perfectly. Thus fire, which is the extreme of heat, is the source of heat in all things that are hot. But there is a unique being that is most perfectly and truly "being," since philosophers can prove that there exists a first mover wholly unmoved and most perfect. Therefore it follows that all other less perfect beings receive *esse* from him. Thomas states that this is Aristotle's proof. Third, everything that is shared "from another" is causally reduced to that which is "per se." Thus if there happened to be heat existing per se, it would have to be the cause of all other heat in bodies participating in it. But there does exist a being that is its own *esse*, since he is pure actuality, in which there is no composition. Therefore from that unique being come all other things, which in no way are their own *esse*, but have it "by participation." This argument, Thomas suggests, is Avicenna's. Thus, he concludes, it is demonstrated by reason and held by faith that all things are created by God (*De pot.* q. 3, a. 5).

In the question of creation, one of the crucial issues concerns the number of ultimate sources, i.e., the number of gods that exist (a. 6). The earliest Greek philosophers, who considered only material reality, saw everything divided into two categories of opposites: good and evil, perfect and imperfect, male and female, etc. Therefore they postulated the existence of two ultimate principles to account for the good and evil existing in the world. The Manichaeans likewise saw a dichotomy and opposition between corruptible and incorruptible, visible and invisible, the Old Testament and the New. They also saw that even good things are easily corrupted by matter. Therefore their whole doctrine of life was based on the warfare between the principle of good and the principle of evil. That is to say, they maintained the existence of two gods, one good, the other evil.

But the Manichaean view is untenable for three reasons. First, whenever one thing is common to many, such as existence, it must come from one source. Existence as such is good, for everything desires to be. Therefore, the source of existence in all things, even in imperfect things, must be unique and good. Even the Greek naturalists, recognizing the great diversity in nature, argued to the existence of a unique first agent, namely the heaven, which is the cause of all diverse motions in the universe. But since the first heaven itself changes position in order to produce the various changes, its motion is reduced to a first mover, who is moved neither per se nor per accidens. Second, an agent acts only insofar as it is in act, that is, only insofar as it is good and perfect. Therefore, evil, which is a privation of act and being, cannot act as an agent. Moreover, since every agent produces something similar to itself, being can produce only good. Therefore the first being of everything cannot be anything but good. Third, there cannot be an order of diverse beings unless one is reduced to another, as when the imperfect is seen in terms of the perfect. But there cannot be any co-ordination without a co-ordinator, except by chance, for spiritual beings move corporeal, the perfect moves the imperfect, and so forth, as is evident in the alteration of the elements by the celestial bodies. This co-ordination cannot be a chance occurrence, for "chance" by definition occurs only rarely and inordinately. Therefore all the diverse things of nature must be reduced to one first principle by which they are all ordered to one.

Thomas's *De potentia* q. 3, a. 7, discusses the difficult but important question of whether God operates in all the activities of nature. If He does not, then He is not the first cause of everything; but if He does, He would seem to eliminate all natural causality and impose determinism in all of nature. For Thomas, God acts not only in all operations of nature, but in all activities of the will.

The Jewish theologian Moses Maimonides, following the Islamic occasionalists, argued that all natural forms are accidents of the subject, and accidents cannot pass from subject to subject; therefore when fire burns, it is not fire that ignites the wood, but God who creates fire in the wood when they are brought together. But this argument, Thomas says, is contrary to sense experience, for the senses perceive only the effect produced by an agent directly acting on it. It is also contrary to reason, for nature does nothing in vain; but if natural forms and powers produce nothing, why does fire need to be applied to wood, if God does the burning? Finally, it is contrary to divine goodness, for things are like God both in being and in operation, both of which are real. When we say that accidents do not pass from subject to subject, we mean "numerically." But when an agent acts upon another, it produces its like generically or specifically. Moreover, it is false to say that all forms are accidents, for this would eliminate all substantial forms that make things to be what they are and to act as they do. The position taken by Moses Maimonides would eliminate all natural science which deals with generation and corruption.

Thomas here adds the view of Avicebron that corporeal bodies themselves do not act, but rather a spiritual force that penetrates all bodies acts through them. He presents three arguments taken from Avicebron and refutes them at considerable length. This view is too subtle to summarize briefly and adds nothing significant to Thomas's doctrine of divine activity. He therefore never refers to it again in later writings, and it could well be passed over here to consider Thomas's teaching on God's causality in creatures.

When we say that God operates in all nature, we should not think that nature does nothing, but rather that within the very activity of nature and will, God is co-actor.

One thing is said to be the cause of another's activity in many ways. When an agent confers on another the power to act, the one is the cause of the other's activity; for instance, when an agent begets a heavy or light body, it is the cause of all the motions that naturally flow therefrom. But God in creating bestows the power to act, not simply in inducing motion, such as gravity in a heavy body, but also in conserving that motion in being. Whatever conserves a body or action is also said to be a cause of motion. Third, a thing is more properly the cause of another's motion when it applies its power to activity. Thus a man is said to saw wood when he applies the saw to wood in continuous action. All natural things are altered when they alter another, while heavenly bodies alter without being altered, even though they are moved movers; only God is the unmoved mover. "It follows of necessity that God is the cause of action in every natural thing as a mover, and the one who applies its power to action" (*De pot.* q. 3, a. 7). In this view, the whole of nature is like an instrument that produces its principal effect not in virtue of its own power, but in virtue of being used by the principal cause. Hence God, who is the first cause of all being, is the principal cause of all action. The higher the cause, the more universal and efficacious it is; and the more efficacious it is, the more profoundly its effects are felt, even in actualizing its remotest potentialities.

Thus God is the cause of the activity of every single thing by giving it the power to act, by conserving that power, by applying that power to activity, and by co-operating with that power in activity. When we consider further that God is His power, and that He is within everything not as part of its essence, but as sustaining the thing in being, it follows that He is immediately acting in everything that happens without replacing the activity of nature and will.

The part of Thomas's teaching most difficult to comprehend is his explanation of how God can move the human will, since it is a free agent. In other works Thomas is more extensive and explicit; here he touches this point only in three of his responses. If God can make a free will, He can certainly move it freely. By free will we have dominion over our own actions; we are responsible for our actions. Dominion and responsibility are taken away only if there is an external force that acts contrary to our determination and produces an action we do not will. But in the absence of such force, whatever we will, we will freely and with responsibility for the action. We know when the action is free or forced. Thomas, however, is more precise in his explanation of free activity. Each type of nature is, of course, determined in a *specific* way without freedom of self-determination. As a nature, the will too is determined toward one specific object, namely, the good or something apparently good. However, in the choice of a particular good at any given time, the will is in no way determined by circumstances; it determines itself and it takes full responsibility for its action. In other words, God as creator and first mover is the assisting power by which the will moves freely. God who moves all things naturally cannot and does not force the will to do anything it does not will to do itself.

Thomas goes on to argue (a. 8) that in the operations of nature there is no element of creation, since nature cannot produce something out of nothing. But in this question Thomas greatly clarifies his understanding of natural change and the importance of potentiality and actuality. Some philosophers, he says, believe that the only way something can come into existence is by coming out of hiding. Anaxagoras held that everything is hidden in everything else, thinking that everything must exist in act. But he failed to distinguish between potential and actual existence. Others thought that matter can only be disposed for a form that comes from some outside agency. Hence Plato postulated a "giver of forms," Avicenna the "tenth intelligence," and some modern Christians call him God. But this is a complete misunderstanding of the natural process and the nature of form itself. Natural forms are not "things"; they are not subsistent in their own right, nor do they have existence of themselves. They are simply actualizations of matter, or that by which a composite is said to exist. Natural forms are not created, but con-created;

they do not exist, but co-exist. They are not the product of natural generation, for the composite alone is such a product. Therefore, properly speaking, one should not say that forms are produced in matter, as though they were implanted, but rather that they are educed from the potentiality of matter. All that is needed is a natural agent to reduce this potentiality to actuality, thus bringing about the natural composite which is the result of natural generation. Therefore, throughout the whole of the natural process there is no element of creation, in the strict sense of the term. Nature cannot create.

At this point Thomas introduces the special case of the human soul (a. 9). Is the human soul created by God out of nothing or is it transplanted with the seed? Some have held that the soul is propagated from the soul of the parents, just as the body is. Others have held that all souls were created in the beginning and incarcerated in a body later, either through their own fault (Origen) or through the will of God. Finally, others say that souls are created out of nothing and immediately infused into the body. The first two positions have been condemned by the Church, but the third is approved. This is clearly stated in the *De ecclesiasticis dogmatibus* (c. 13).[31] In the determination of the question, Thomas concentrates on the absolute need for the human soul to be created by God out of nothing, thereby disproving the first opinion.

First, the rational soul differs from all other forms in nature in that others do not have an *esse* in which to subsist, but rather provide the means by which the composite exists. The rational soul, however, is unique in being able to subsist by an existence proper to its nature, which can be determined by its functions. Since only what exists can act, each thing is related to its functions in the way it is related to its existence (*esse*). But in the operations of all other forms in nature, the form operates only in fusion with the body, which is not the case with the rational soul, whose functions are thinking and willing. Therefore one must attribute to the rational soul an existence that makes it quasi-subsistent. For this reason, too, among forms only the rational soul can be separated from the body. From this it follows that its coming into being must differ from that of all other forms. As we have said, natural forms properly are not generated, since only the composite is generated. If the rational soul cannot come into being by natural generation, it must be created from nothing.

Second, it is impossible that a bodily power be so elevated as to produce an entirely spiritual and incorporeal effect, for nothing can act beyond its own strength. Human generation, however, is brought about by a generative power, which has a bodily organ; likewise the power in the human seed is effective only through heat. Consequently, since the rational soul is an entirely spiritual form, neither dependent on the body nor fused with the body in its function, it can in no way be propagated by generation of the body or produced by some power in the human sperm.

Third, every form that comes into existence by generation or by the power of nature is educed from the potentiality of matter. But the rational soul cannot be educed from the potentiality of matter, since it is a form whose principal functions are not radicated in matter. Therefore, as Aristotle shows, the rational soul cannot be propagated simply by the power of sex.

Article 10 of this question discusses and rejects the notion that the human soul is created outside the embryo and infused at a later date. Those who hold this position assume that the human soul is a complete entity in itself, whereas it is only part of a species and needs the body to constitute a human person. Plato and those who hold for transmigration of souls do not consider man to be composed of body and soul, but to be a soul using a body; so it makes little difference whether it uses this body or that. For Thomas the rational soul is created within the embryo when it is disposed by the powers of sperm and ovum, as well as the living functions of growth, nutrition, and sensation, which are almost immediately evident. Once the embryo is disposed by natural process to receive the human soul, a process which is a matter of days, the soul is created directly by God within the living body and takes over all the functions of embryonic life. This single human soul is consequently unique, contrary to what Plato teaches, receiving its individuation from the unique matter in which it is created. Unlike many of his contemporaries, Thomas refused to admit a plurality of souls in a living organism. Therefore, once the human soul is created, the whole organism is a human person, needing only to be developed.

In article 15 Thomas discusses one of the most crucial problems of thirteenth-century theology in its contact with Moslem philosophy: whether things emanate from God by a necessity of nature or by His free will. Although documentation is lacking in this article, its sources are evident in Avicenna, in Moslem fatalism, and particularly in *Liber de causis*, at this time universally attributed to Aristotle. Here the lengthy arguments of *Summa contra gentiles* are reduced to four. All operations in the universe must have their own end. Nature and will both operate for an end, but nature does not know or will the end that is preordained for it; the will, however, knows the end it desires and freely chooses it. Therefore, all the activities of nature presuppose the activity of intelligence, just as the arrow tends to the spot determined for it by the archer. Therefore the first cause of the universe must create with intellect and free will, not by a necessity of nature. Second, nature is determined to producing one kind of effect similar to itself, as man generates man. But creatures are diverse, unequal, and exceptionally dissimilar. Therefore they cannot proceed from nature, but from free will that creates dissimilarity. Third, every effect must preexist in the agent in some fashion. The kind of pre-existence depends upon the nature of the agent. Since God is intellect, His effects exist in His intellect as ideas, which move the will. Therefore, the things created by God come about by free will. Fourth, according to Aristotle there are two kinds of activities, one immanent, like thinking and willing, which remain in the agent as its own perfection, the other transient, like pushing and heating, which take place in the patient as its perfection. Since God's intellect is His essence, His activity must consist in knowing and willing. Therefore, whatever God does transiently must first of all be in His intellect and will. Hence one must say that all creatures come from God by free will, and not by a necessity of nature.

Only one further point need detain us in *De potentia*. In articles 14 and 17 Thomas discusses briefly a point that would occupy much of his time in 1270 in his controversy with John Pecham, the Franciscan master. The question is whether the universe could have existed from all eternity or whether one can demonstrate that it had a beginning. While the point of controversy with Pecham was not envisaged by Thomas when he wrote *De potentia,* his frame of mind was well established. In article 14, the shortest in the entire question on creation, Thomas argues that since the universe did not come into existence by motion, but by creation, God does not have to exist prior to the effect, but the effect can exist simultaneously with its cause. There is no intrinsic contradiction in saying that a created effect can exist from eternity. Therefore the universe could have always existed, if God had so willed. But we know by faith that God created the universe "in the beginning" (Gn. 1:1). Granting the teaching of faith, we cannot say that it is still possible that the universe existed from all eternity.

At the very beginning of his discussion of article 17, Thomas states that the Catholic faith "cannot be effectively impugned by any physical demonstration." All the pre-Socratics, thinking that the only way anything could come into existence was by motion, postulated the eternity of matter. Even Aristotle held for the eternity of the world in *Physics* VIII, for prior to each moment of motion there must be motion, and prior to each "before" there is a prior time; consequently there can never be a beginning. Although Thomas tries to exonerate Aristotle by saying that he was only disputing "against the position" of Anaxagoras and Empedocles, he does show that no argument of the Greeks disproves the doctrine of faith. What Thomas does not discuss here is the possibility of demonstrating a beginning, which is the crux of the argument with the Franciscans. This he does briefly in *Summa theologiae* I, 46, 2, written before the controversy with Pecham. There he simply says that creation is a free act of God, and we cannot know His will, except in things that happen by necessity, unless He reveals it to us. That the world began in time is believable, but not knowable or demonstrable. He goes on to warn: "And it is useful that this be considered, lest perhaps someone presuming to demonstrate what is of faith, propose inconclusive arguments, which offer an occasion of ridicule to unbelievers who think that it is for such reasons that we believe truths of faith."

Normally in the *Summa theologiae* there is one central article that contains in nucleus the state of the whole question. This is not the case in disputed questions, as can be seen in the question on creation in *De potentia*. In the *Summa* generally the same problems are discussed, but the limits allotted to each question are more precise, and the arguments, though fewer, are more concise. Nevertheless to appreciate the development of Thomas's thought in the *Summa*, one can do no better than examine the appropriate disputed questions chronologically.

One other important series of questions, *De malo*, seems to have been disputed in Rome during the academic year 1266–67 or in Paris in the academic year 1269–70. Both views have their strong partisans, since the question cannot be settled by the early catalogues of Thomas's writings, which list *De malo* under the "et ultra" of either the Italian group or the second Paris group. Defenders on both sides argue their point in relation to the *Summa theologiae*. Mandonnet argued that *De malo* was disputed in Italy between 1263–68 and largely completed before the first part of the *Summa* (1267–68) and entirely completed before the second (1269–70).[32] Dom Odo Lottin strongly argues that *De malo* was written after the first part and before the second part of the *Summa*.[33] Lottin further argues that *De malo* and the *prima secundae* are both posterior to *Quodlibet 1* (Easter 1269). Thus Lottin concludes that *De malo* was disputed in Paris before he began writing the second part of the *Summa*. The problem with this is that most authorities claim that the ⋄ *prima secundae* was begun in Viterbo immediately after the first part of the *Summa* was completed.

Gauthier argues more convincingly that *De malo* was begun after March 1266, that question 16 was completed after November 22, 1267, and before 1269, when Thomas was writing I–II. Arguing that question 8 must have been disputed at the end of ⋄ 1267 or more probably at the beginning of 1267, he concluded that *De malo* must have been disputed in Rome during the academic year 1266–67.[34]

De malo is an extremely important work in sixteen questions covering the nature, causes, and diversity of evil (sin), and a detailed discussion of the seven deadly sins: pride, vanity, sloth (spiritual laziness), anger, avarice, gluttony, and lust. Since *De malo* is, at the earliest, prior to the second part of the *Summa*, and, at the latest, contemporary with it, these disputed quesions are significant for an understanding of Thomas's moral teaching in its early stages. Space does not allow for an analysis of this work here.

While Thomas was regent master in Rome, he may also have disputed the question *De spiritualibus creaturis* in eleven articles. Two MSS explicitly state that this question was disputed in Italy.[35] In article 3 Thomas refers to the commentary of Simplicius on the *Categories,* translated by Moerbeke in March 1266; and in article 10 he quotes Themistius, *In De anima,* translated by Moerbeke in November 1267. Grabmann therefore maintained that the question was disputed between 1266 and 1268 at the court of Clement IV in Viterbo. *De spiritualibus creaturis* is a single question, and therefore most likely a single disputation in two sessions. Grabmann and many other authorities consider it likely that it was disputed at Viterbo between 1267–68, perhaps at the papal curia.

Eschmann reminds us that an Italian origin of a disputation does not preclude a Parisian edition, for we must distinguish between the live performance in a hall and the edition of the text.[36] In the classroom, objections were raised from the floor and answered immediately by the respondent. Both the objection and the reply were taken down by a scribe writing quickly. These transcripts were studied by the master, rearranged, and augmented, and a determination was written out. But even at this stage the disputed question was not yet ready to be copied and circulated among students and masters. The text sent to the stationer's in Paris for public circulation was an edited product, replete with full references, accurate citations, and valid arguments. Consequently it is possible that the important question *De spiritualibus creaturis* was edited in Paris. Nevertheless, it was disputed in Italy, probably at Viterbo in 1267–68, perhaps at the papal curia.

The question *De spiritualibus creaturis* considers the human soul as united to but separable from the body (aa. 1–4), as well as separated substances, generally called angels (aa. 5–11). In article 9 he deals explicitly with the Averroist doctrine of one possible intellect for all men. The problem of Latin Averroism arose in Paris among masters in arts in the mid-1260s, but we cannot be certain how much Thomas was aware of what was happening in Paris. As far as Albert and Thomas were concerned, the error lies in the text of Averroes's commentary on *De anima* III, comm. 5–6; both Albert and Thomas had rejected the doctrine as contrary to the faith and to reason in writings that antecede the Averroist crisis in Paris. In article 9 Thomas argues that the Averroist teaching is contrary to faith "because it takes away reward and punishment of a future life." He presents three arguments from the "true principles of philosophy": (1) it is impossible that one active power be the source of distinct activities; but if two men know the same truth, the same activity would be in two distinct subjects, which is impossible; (2) it is impossible that two individuals of the same species be distinct by reason of their species; but intellection is the specific operation of man; therefore there could not be two distinct men knowing, if there was only one act of intellection; (3) it is impossible that the higher be perfected by the lower, but if one possible intellect were actuated by personal phantasms, that would be the case; therefore there cannot be one possible intellect, i.e., the intellect by which man knows, for the whole human race. Finally Thomas argues that the Averroist doctrine contradicts the text of Aristotle, and that therefore the intellect is not a separate substance, but a faculty of the human soul (a *potentia animae*). Admittedly Thomas's arguments here are weaker than those later proposed. And one might wonder what writings, if any, he had seen of the Parisian Averroists. Nevertheless, this passage and the later disputed question *De anima*, a. 3, are the preliminary efforts for the masterful *De unitate intellectus contra Averroistas* of 1270. Moreover, the question *De spiritualibus creaturis* is the immediate source for the discussion of angels and men in the first part of the *Summa theologiae*, which was completed by 1268, when he left for Paris.

It is often thought that Thomas taught philosophy, i.e., commented on Aristotle, while he was regent master of theology at Rome. This view is based on the statement of Tolomeo of Lucca, already noted in the previous chapter, that while Thomas was directing the studium in Rome he "also wrote commentaries covering almost the whole field of philosophy, both moral and natural, but with particular attention to ethics and metaphysics."[87] Mandonnet not only dated these commentaries during the Italian period, but also thought that they were actually delivered to Dominican students in the classroom. Bourke is particularly insistent that Thomas's commentary on the *Ethics* of Aristotle must have originated as oral lectures "in the vicinity of Rome."[38] Bourke's contention is that Thomas could not have composed during his second Parisian regency all the writings attributed to it. Instead, he asserts, the unpretentious *Ethics*, the simplest and least complicated of all Thomas's commentaries, must be dated early, at least in an elementary form. Bourke rejects outright the Parisian dating acknowledged by most scholars. Gauthier is equally insistent that the *Sententia libri Ethicorum* can in no way be traced to the Italian period, but must have been composed in Paris.[39] The Latin text that Thomas used of Aristotle's *Ethics*, a contaminated version greatly removed from the exemplar, came into existence around 1270. More important, there is no trace of an earlier version, *reportatio*, or classroom notes in the edited version of *Sententia libri Ethicorum*. One would like to think that in imitation of Albert, Thomas also lectured to his Dominican students at Santa Sabina on Aristotle's *Ethics;* but that was not the case.

One must not be misled by the term *lectio* in all the printed versions of Thomas's commentaries on Aristotle. The term is a fourteenth-century usage that means no more than "a small chapter," a *capitulum,* similar to the term *commentum* in the versions of Averroes. In no way does it imply a classroom "lecture." Not only was the commentary on the *Ethics* not given in Rome, but neither were the other commentaries on Aristotle. There is no proof or likelihood that Thomas taught philosophy in "the general studium of theology" that he directed in Rome.

There is only one serious problem about this matter. The catalogue of Nicholas Trevet, undoubtedly copied from a lost exemplar, lists Thomas's commentary on the first book of *De anima* as a *reportatio* taken down by Reginald of Piperno during oral delivery.[40] The second and third books are listed as works written by Thomas. The same curious fact is given in the catalogue of Bartholomew of Capua, presented at the canonization process,[41] as well as in the catalogues of Prague.[42] The problem is: where did Thomas lecture on *De anima,* and what were the circumstances? The catalogues themselves present this as an exceptional case, as Gauthier points out,[43] and one cannot conclude that the first draft of all the Aristotelian commentaries were taken down in this way. In fact, Thomas never wrote an "exposition" of the first book of *De anima,* but only of the second and third. We know also that Thomas "wrote" the commentary on the *Peri hermenias* at the request of Guillaume Bertaut, provost of Louvain. We will explain our view of these commentaries on Aristotle in the following chapter, but the exact origin of the commentary on *De anima* I will have to remain a mystery. The most that can be said is that if *De anima* I was originally presented as a series of lectures, it could have been presented in the Roman studium where Thomas taught young Dominican students.

During all this time in Rome, Thomas continued to work on the *Catena aurea* on Mark, Luke, and John; the gloss on John was completed at Rome in 1267 and dedicated to his former pupil, Cardinal Annibaldo d'Annibaldi. We can say that it took Thomas approximately one year to complete each gloss on the Evangelists (1263–67), while engaged in other writings and his studium teaching. The amount of work that must have gone into the composition of such a gloss is incredible. There is no indication that Thomas had his staff of secretaries in Rome, but it is the type of work for which secretarial assistance would be gratefully appreciated.

Thomas may have tried to teach Peter Lombard's *Sentences* to the young Dominicans sent to him, for at that time it was the beginner's text in theology. He himself had studied it when he was only nineteen or twenty years old during his confinement at Roccasecca (1244–45). If he did try to teach the *Sentences* in the Roman studium, he realized quickly the difficulty of teaching it to young minds, the "beginners" in theology. Therefore, "while teaching in Rome" at Santa Sabina, he conceived a plan to instruct beginners in theology, a plan that was to take form as the *Summa theologiae.*

The "Summa theologiae": First Part

(1266–68)

° There is a strong suggestion that "while at Rome" Thomas revised the first book of his commentary (*Scriptum*) on the

Sentences. This revision would have been the result of his attempt to teach the *Sentences.* Tolomeo of Lucca, the source of our information, claims that Thomas wrote a second version of the first book, to which he adds, "I saw this [book] once at Lucca, but then someone took it away and I never saw it again."[44]   *
Bernard Gui refers to this testimony when he says:

> While at Rome [Thomas] also wrote a commentary on the first book of *Sentences,* as witnessed in the chronicle of the Lord Friar Tolomeo, Bishop of Torcello, who was his disciple and pupil, declaring that he had seen it in the priory of Lucca, but which cannot be found now because it is believed to have been secretly removed and so not multiplied.[45]

Both Tolomeo and Bernard make it clear that the book in question was a revision, distinct from the commentary then in circulation, since they list the well-known commentary in four books separately in their catalogue of works by Thomas. Since this version is apparently lost, not much can be said about it.

However, in 1937 A. Hayen, S.J., proposed a theory that found some acceptance for a short time.[46] Hayen suggested that what Tolomeo saw was the autograph of what was then the full commentary on the *Sentences,* part of which still exists in autograph for Book III. He claimed that the text found in all the MSS and printed books today represents the revised version produced in Rome, while the primitive version derived from his Paris teaching (1252–56) is now lost. This wild theory does violence to all known testimony and cannot be sustained.[47] Nevertheless, the eyewitness testimony of Tolomeo stands as irrefutable; it cannot be contradicted, and it could be confirmed only by a thorough examination of the MS tradition of Thomas's commentary on the *Sentences* and the discovery of a unique MS that was "not multiplied." The point I wish to make here is that Thomas apparently revised the first book of his commentary in Rome (1265–66) and found it unsuitable for teaching beginners.

It would seem that Thomas had the idea of writing a *Summa* for beginners as early as 1265.[48] But many authorities believe that he did not begin it until 1266, before or during his second year of teaching in Rome. According to Tolomeo of Lucca, the three parts of the *Summa* "were written by Friar Thomas almost entirely within the period covered by the pontificate of Clement IV [1265–68] and the vacancy that followed his death, which lasted two years and nine months" (i.e., to December 1, 1271).[49] This information is not entirely correct, for we know that Thomas continued work on the third part of the *Summa* until December 6, 1273.

In the prologue Thomas states that it belongs to the doctor of Catholic truth to instruct not only advanced students, but also beginners, as Paul says in his first letter to the Corinthians: "As to little ones in Christ, I gave you milk to drink, not meat" (1 Cor. 3:1–2). Therefore his intention in this work is "to present those things that pertain to the Christian religion in a manner befitting the education of beginners." He then goes on to indicate the obstacles he hopes to overcome in his new presentation:

> Students in this science have not seldom been hampered by what they found written by other authors, partly on account of the multiplicity of useless questions, articles, and arguments; partly also because the things they need to know are not taught according to the order of learning (*secundum ordinem disciplinae*), but according as the plan of the book might require or the occasion of disputing (*disputandi*) might offer; partly, too, because frequent repetition brought weariness and confusion to the minds of listening students.
>
> Anxious, therefore, to overcome these and other obstacles, we will try, confident of divine help, to present those things pertaining to sacred doctrine briefly and clearly insofar as the matter will permit.

In the mind of Thomas, current works of theology were unsuitable for beginners because (1) they were too verbose and detailed, (2) they were all unsystematic, and (3) they were too repetitious because they were unsystematic. Not only were the *Sentences* of Peter Lombard a prime example of these deficiencies, but the Scriptures themselves lack a logical order. The Sacred Scriptures, while most suitable to proclaiming the Word of God, were not intended to be a systematic presentation of all the divine truths needed for a beginner in theology. The Scriptures, together with the teaching of the Fathers (i.e., the glosses on Scripture), were, of course, the rule of faith, but the training of a theologian requires that beginners in the "science" be aided by a systematic view of the whole of "sacred doctrine."

The *Sentences* of Peter Lombard and the numerous compendia, summas, and treatises of the twelfth and thirteenth centuries tried to reorganize the truths of faith, following the Apostles' Creed, but these too were insufficiently scientific, at least in the mind of Thomas. Melchior Cano, writing in the sixteenth century, found little to praise in Lombard's *Sentences*. "Besides the word 'distinctions,' into which the books are divided, you will find almost nothing distinct, or correctly and orderly distributed. You could call it a congestion of testimonies rather than a disposition and order of discipline." He complained that the three Persons are treated (Bk. I) before the essential attributes of the One God (Bk. IV); the virtues are analyzed in Book III, while some of the vices are discussed in Book IV. "Consequently for scholastics who clung to its vestige everything is confused and almost chaotic."[50]

In his own work Thomas followed a strictly logical and scientific order, inherited from Aristotle's *Posterior Analytics.* Nevertheless he did not reject entirely the order of the Creed or contemporary sentences, summas, and compendia. The three parts of the *Summa* are ultimately divided into two vast visions of God: the *exitus* of all things from God, and the *reditus* of all things, particularly man, to God as to his ultimate goal. The vision of *exitus-reditus*, as we saw, was for Thomas the basic division of the *Sentences,* but it was a division that Alexander of Hales and Thomas forced upon the text, rather than the division supplied by Lombard himself. In dividing the *Summa* into three parts, Thomas states that the first part (*prima pars*) discusses God as one and triune and "the procession of all creatures from Him," the second part (*secunda pars*) discusses "the movement of rational creatures toward God," and the third part (*tertia pars*) discusses Christ, "who as man is the way of our tending toward God" (*Sum. theol.* I, 2, prol.).

In the *Summa theologiae* Thomas follows in broad outlines the order of the *Sentences,* except for the second part, which is the unsurpassed tribute to his genius. Removing the discussion of sins from Book II and the analysis of virtues from Book III, one can readily see that the plan of the *prima pars* and the *tertia pars* falls in line with the distribution of subjects treated by Lombard. The first part of the *Summa* corresponds to Peter Lombard's *Sentences* on the Trinity (Bk. I), creation, the angels, man, and first parents (Bk. II, dist. 2–20). The third part harmonizes with Peter's discussion of Christ the Incarnate Word (Bk. III, dist. 1–22), the sacraments (which Thomas calls "the relics of Christ's passion"), and the four last things (Bk. IV). Thomas, however, completely revised Lombard's discussion of moral questions, synthesizing man's return to God through the virtues (*secunda pars*) in much the same order as Aristotle treats man's search for happiness in the *Nichomachean Ethics*.

Thus the basic divisions of the *Summa theologiae* can be presented briefly as follows:

Sacred Doctrine

I. God, one and triune, and the *exitus* of all creatures from Him (*prima pars*):
   A. God's existence and essential attributes (qq. 2–26)
   B. Trinity of Divine Persons (qq. 27–43)
   C. Procession of creatures from God:
      1. Production of creatures (qq. 44–46)
      2. Distinction of creatures:
         a. In general (qq. 47–49)
         b. In particular:
            i. purely spiritual: angels (qq. 50–64)
            ii. purely corporeal: universe (qq. 65–74)
            iii. composed of spiritual and corporeal: man (qq. 75–102)
      3. Conservation and governance of creatures (qq. 103–19)

II & III. Man's movement toward God (*reditus*):
   I–II. Man's movement toward God by human actions in general (*prima secundae*):
   A. Ultimate goal of human life (qq. 1–5)
   B. Means of attaining this goal:
      1. Human acts in themselves (qq. 6–48)
      2. Principles of human acts:
         a. Intrinsic principles: habits (qq. 49–89)
         b. Extrinsic principles: law and grace (qq. 90–114)

II–II. Man's movement toward God by human acts in particular (*secunda secundae*):
    A. Theological virtues (with vices and gifts):
        1. Faith (qq. 1–16)
        2. Hope (qq. 17–22)
        3. Charity (qq. 23–46)
    B. Cardinal virtues (with vices and gifts):
        1. Prudence (qq. 47–56)
        2. Justice (qq. 57–122)
        3. Fortitude (qq. 123–40)
        4. Temperance (qq. 141–70)
III. Christ, the way to eternal life (*tertia pars*):
    A. Christ, the Savior of mankind (qq. 1–59)
    B. The sacraments as means of salvation (incomplete):
        1. In general (qq. 60–65)
        2. In particular:
          a. Baptism (qq. 66–71)
          b. Confirmation (q. 72)
          c. Eucharist (qq. 73–83)
          d. Penance (qq. 84–90, a. 4)

(Supplement)

          Penance (qq. 1–28)
          e. Last anointing (qq. 29–33)
          f. Holy Orders (qq. 34–40)
          g. Matrimony (qq. 41–68)
    C. The goal of eternal life achieved through Him in rising (qq. 69–99)

As to the chronology of the *Summa theologiae,* most scholars agree that the first part was written in Rome and Viterbo between 1266 and November 1268. The second part, which was later subdivided into two parts, *prima secundae* (I–II) and *secunda secundae* (II–II), occupied the whole of his second Parisian regency, 1269–72, although the first few questions of I–II were probably written while he was still in Viterbo. It is certain that the *prima pars* was complete and in circulation before Thomas arrived in Paris, around January 1269. A detailed chronology of the second part is almost impossible to determine, although many scholars have attempted and are attempting to do this. Eschmann cautiously states that "the approximate latest date of the termination of I–II as well as the approximate earliest date of the beginning of II–II, may be set at the turn of the year 1270."[51] Almost all of the *tertia pars* was written in Naples before December 6, 1273, when Thomas ceased writing altogether; at that date Thomas had reached III, q. 90, a. 4, in the midst of discussing the sacrament of Penance. Whatever was added after question 90, article 4, constitutes the *Supplement,* a work "put together with scissors and paste from pieces cut out of Aquinas's writings on the *Sentences* (especially Bk. 4)."[52]

The *Summa theologiae* is Thomas's longest and most important contribution to the science of theology. It took Thomas seven years to write before he stopped suddenly on December 6, 1273. Of all of Thomas's writings, it was the most widely circulated work both in manuscript and in print. Its influence on Catholic life and thought was enormous, particularly through summaries, paraphrases, and citations in popular manuals written for confessors, preachers, and parish priests. In its material composition, it consists of 512 questions, 2,669 articles, and approximately 10,000 objections with their solutions. In the Leonine edition it consists of nine folio volumes (4–12), together with the commentary of Cajetan. Normally the *Summa* and the *Supplement* are published in five octavo volumes. In its formal structure, it has no equal in the history of theology. The first part is simplicity itself, while being metaphysically profound, concise, and complete. The second part is most original in its discussion of the moral life of man, recognizing its complexity and the primacy of love in all human actions. It has been called Thomas's "real" commentary on the *Ethics* of Aristotle. But it is much more than that, for while following much the same rational order as Aristotle's *Ethics,* it surpasses all authors in its Christian view of man's struggle to reach a supernatural goal, the eternal vision of God Himself. The third part considers the profound mysteries of Christ's Incarnation and His continuing life in the "sacraments of faith," the culmination of which is the Eucharist as both sacrament and sacrifice.

As we have seen, Thomas wanted to present a comprehensive vision of "sacred doctrine" for beginners, a handbook suitable for novices. We can say that in the first part Thomas succeeded admirably. However, the second and third parts are far from being a simple introduction; Thomas himself matured considerably in the writing of these parts. All one need do is compare the fourth book of the *Summa contra gentiles,* where he discusses Christ's Incarnation, the sacraments, and the four last things, with the third part of the *Summa theologiae,* and one will immediately see the development of Thomas's thought in theology. Almost nine years had elapsed between these two writings, and Thomas had learned much during that interval.

The very first question of the *Summa* is an introduction to the whole of "sacred doctrine" that is analyzed throughout the three parts. Strictly speaking, it is not an introduction to the *Summa* itself, but to the subject matter possessed by every Christian and studied by every theologian. This apparently simple question has been the subject of heated debates among theologians and commentators.[53] Thomas himself surely did not think that the first question of a beginner's handbook would cause such controversy and misunderstanding. Every good introduction to a new science, according to Aristotle, must consider three points: its existence (*an sit*), its nature, or definition (*quid sit*), and its modality, or method (*de modo*). That is precisely what Thomas does in the first question of the *Summa.* In this respect it is the same as the first question of the *Scriptum super Sententias.* In the first article of the *Summa,* Thomas demonstrates the existence of sacred doctrine by seeking its necessity, since necessity clearly indicates its existence (*an sit*). In the next six articles Thomas searches for a definition by seeking its proximate genus and specific difference, constituting its species, or definition (*quid sit*). This he does by "dividing the genus" according to the rules given by Aristotle in the *Posterior Analytics.* Finally, in the last three articles, Thomas indicates the modality, or intrinsic method, of sacred doctrine (*de modo*). This "method" has nothing to do with the method employed by a theologian in his personal procedure, but rather with the modality inherent in sacred doctrine, whose existence and nature have been demonstrated.

In determining the existence of sacred doctrine (a. 1), Thomas asks whether besides all the philosophical disciplines there exists another kind of doctrine to be known. He considers two aspects. Since man is destined to a supernatural end, beyond anything that reason can comprehend, he must receive the knowledge of this end "through divine revelation" in order to direct his thoughts and actions to it. Therefore there are certain things that man must know by divine revelation, which transcends all philosophical disciplines. Second, there are, indeed, certain truths about God that can be known by reason. But these too should be revealed, because those truths about God are known only to few men, after long investigation, and even then with much admixture of error. Therefore there exists a sacred doctrine necessary to man's salvation.

As to the nature of this sacred doctrine, Thomas proceeds from the widest possible genus (science), to the proximate genus (wisdom), then to the specific difference, namely "about God." When Thomas asks whether sacred doctrine is a science (a. 2), he is not asking about the scientific methodology of theology, although this question follows, but about the nature of sacred doctrine, whose existence was shown in article 1. The word "science" here simply means "a knowledge through causes." Are there *reasons* for the faith within us? Thomas argues that sacred doctrine is a science, but not an autonomous science such as geometry. Rather it is subalternated to knowledge in God and in the blessed, much as astronomy is subalternated to mathematics. That is, the truths that God and the blessed see directly, we accept on faith. These *reasons* on our part are both intrinsic and extrinsic to the faith we accept. For example, the fact that God became man for the sake of our redemption, and that we will rise on the last day because Christ rose from the dead, etc., are reasons intrinsic to the knowledge we have through revelation. Therefore that knowledge is scientific.

If sacred doctrine is a science, we must ask whether it is one or many (a. 3), whether it is speculative or practical (a. 4), whether it is superior or inferior to the other sciences known by man (a. 5), and whether it merits the title of "wisdom" (a. 6). Thus the immediate genus of sacred doctrine is its character as wisdom, the highest wisdom man can have in this life. The differentiating character of this wisdom is that it is "about God," i.e., it has God as its proper subject (a. 7). Other wisdoms in the speculative and practical sciences may involve some truth about God, as metaphysics and morality, but only sacred doctrine is all about Him as He has been revealed. In other words, sacred doctrine is that wisdom about God by which we lead our life to eternal glory. This is the wisdom of Sacred Scripture; it is the wisdom of saints. There is no higher wisdom in this life.

The last three articles of the first question pertain to the methodology of sacred doctrine. Thomas asks whether sacred doctrine is "argumentative" (a. 8), whether metaphorical termi- nology is inevitable (a. 9), and whether Sacred Scripture has many senses in its presentation of sacred doctrine (a. 10). Commentators have found no difficulty about article 8, for if sacred doctrine is a science, there must be arguments both in- trinsic and extrinsic. But many have found it difficult to fit the last two articles into place, for they seem to be about Sacred Scripture and not about theology. Chenu claims that these articles were discussed by Thomas out of deference to tradition; they would in time disappear from the scene.[54] But in fact, these two articles are about the intrinsic modality of revealed doctrine itself, just as much as is article 8 concerning argumentation. It is not to be identified with the habit of faith, the habit of con- metaphorical language, and many senses. Hence sacred doctrine is the very nature of sacred doctrine to possess arguments, structed theology, the written word of Scripture, or with preach- ing. Rather, it is the revealed content of divine truth accepted by faith, discussed by theologians, written in Scripture and the glosses of the Fathers, and preached to all men. It is the good news of salvation, the *evangelion.*

Van Ackeren rightly points to the essentially active character of sacred doctrine. It is essentially a teaching process (*docere,* from which comes the word *doctrina,* "doctrine"), in which God is the teacher and we the listeners.[55] The Church and theologians have the obligation to study this doctrine and to preserve its purity in transmitting it to each generation; preachers have the obligation of announcing this doctrine to the whole world, since it is the good news of salvation.

The first question, as we said, is not an introduction to the *Summa* itself, for Thomas does not explain his systematic pro- cedure in writing. He does that in the brief prologue to each new section. Thus at the beginning of question 2 he gives the tripartite division of the *Summa* and the division of the first part, the first question of which is the existence of God (*an sit*).

However, before attempting to prove the existence of God, one must know whether or not His existence is self-evident (*per se notum*), for if His existence is self-evident to us, there is no need to prove it (a. 1). But if His existence is not self-evident, then we must know whether it is demonstrable; if it is not demonstrable, it is folly to attempt a proof (a. 2). Finally, if His existence is not self-evident, but demonstrable, then we must give proof of His existence (a. 3).

In analyzing the first query, Thomas explains that there are two kinds of self-evident truths. A truth is self-evident if its predicate belongs necessarily and immediately to the subject, and no proof is needed. One type is self-evident in itself and to our reason, such as definitions and first principles of human reason—such as "God exists," for in itself God's existence is identical with His nature, but this is obvious only to one who sees His nature, which we do not. Therefore, there is need to demonstrate His existence.

Here (ad 2) and elsewhere[56] Thomas considers and rejects the so-called "ontological" argument of Anselm. For Thomas, Anselm was not trying to prove the existence of God, but rather the self-evidence of His existence as "that greater than which cannot be conceived." To the man of faith, God in His necessary triune existence is precisely that greater than which nothing can be conceived, from which must follow His actual existence and not simply His existence in thought alone. It is true that almost all historians, philosophers, and theologians have considered Anselm's argument to be a proof of God's existence. But never once does Thomas consider it such a proof or attempted proof, but always only an assertion of self-evidence. To a man of faith, Anselm is correct: the God of revelation necessarily exists in reality. But to a man without faith, such a definition of God is not necessarily true or acceptable; even if it were, it would not follow that such a God exists outside the mind conceiving such a definition. Whatever may be the historical truth of Anselm's intention, it is significant to note that Thomas never discussed Anselm's argument as a proof for God's existence. In the over-all context of the *Proslogion*, it would seem that Thomas was correct in his view, for Anselm was not writing a systematic natural theology, but rather a clinching argument for monks, that everything revealed must necessarily be so, granting that God is "greater than which nothing can be thought." From this basic truth flows the necessity of the Trinity, the Incarnation, and promised beatitude.

Having settled the question of the self-evidence of God's existence in the negative, Thomas then asks whether His existence can be demonstrated. The problem is that (1) God's existence is a matter of faith, which transcends proof; (2) we do not know the definition of God, only what He is not, but such a definition would be necessary for an apodictic proof; and (3) if His existence were to be proved, it would have to be from His effects, but there is no proportion between God and His finite effects; hence one would be concluding more than the premises allow. On the other hand, St. Paul explicitly says, "The invisible things of Him, from the creation of the world, are clearly seen, being understood by the things that are made" (Rom. 1:20).

In his response, Thomas notes that there are two kinds of demonstration: one through cause, called *propter quid*, the other through effect, called demonstration *quia*. In no way can God's existence be proved through cause, for He has none. But His existence can be proved through His effects, which are evident to us. The existence of any effect demonstrates the existence of its proper cause, which precedes the effect and on which the effect depends in being. Therefore His existence, although not self-evident to us, can be proved through effects that are evident to us.

In response to the problems Thomas says (ad 1) some truths about God can be known by natural reason, as St. Paul says; these truths, strictly speaking, are not "articles of faith" but "preambles to faith"; there is no reason, however, why God's existence cannot be known to one person by faith and to another by reason. In demonstrations *quia* by effect, the effect serves as a medium of demonstration, and only a "nominal" definition of what men mean by God is necessary (ad 2). Through effects that are not proportioned to the cause, we cannot have perfect knowledge of the cause, but we can know the existence of some cause. Thus we can demonstrate God's existence, even though we can never know perfectly His nature (ad 3).

Finally Thomas raises the important question of whether God exists (a. 3). The problems are obvious and perennial. (1) If God exists, how come there is evil in the world? (2) Why multiply entities? Everything in the universe can be explained by natural causes and man's own will. Therefore, there is no need to postulate the existence of God. On the other hand, God Himself says, "I am who am" (Ex. 3:14).

In his solution, Thomas states that the existence of God can be proved in "five ways." These "five ways" have perhaps occasioned more heated debates, doubts, and misunderstanding than any other single article in the *Summa*. Here we do not wish to enter into any controversy, but only to present the arguments as briefly as possible. Formally each argument is distinct from the others, so that any one of them is probative. Thomas was convinced that through them even pagans, notably Plato and Aristotle, arrived at the existence of the true God. Whether any one of these proofs can convince a non-believer, an atheist, or a skeptic is another matter, for emotions easily get into the way of logic. Although each proof is formally distinct from the others, inasmuch as each starts with a particular aspect of the effect, the universe, they are basically the same inasmuch as the nature of the whole effect demands an ultimate explanation, which is God.

The first proof, which Thomas calls the "more obvious way," begins with the fact of change, or motion in the universe. As Aristotle showed, everything that is moved must be moved by something distinct from itself—for instance, as the heating of water requires heat, and the generation of bodies requires an agent, for all change is the reduction of potency to actuality. One cannot proceed ad infinitum in the search for movers, for in that case there would be no "first" and consequently no motion, or change. Therefore one must acknowledge the existence of a first mover, who is unmoved, i.e., a first mover who is outside the condition of moved movers and change. The first mover is what men have called God.

Second, the fact of efficient causality is obvious throughout the universe. Nothing can be the cause of itself, for then it would have to exist before itself. But we cannot proceed ad infinitum in the search for causes that are themselves caused, for there would be no "first" cause and consequently no causality in the universe. Therefore beyond the whole collection of efficient causes that are themselves caused, there must be a first uncaused cause, upon whom all others depend. This uncaused cause is what men call God.

Third, we see in the universe certain things that can be or not, for they are generable and corruptible. But not all things can be corruptible and generable, for then at one time nothing would have existed. But if this is true, then nothing would exist now, for nothing comes to be except by something which is, i.e., in order that possible being exist, there must be something necessary. But every necessary being has its necessity either from itself or from another. There cannot be an infinity of beings deriving their necessity from another, for then nothing would exist. Therefore there must be a being necessary of itself, on whom all others depend. This per se necessary being all men call God.

Fourth, throughout the universe there are gradations of perfection, such as existence, life, beauty, truth, and so on. But gradations of perfection mean a more or less sharing of an absolute on whose nature all others depend. Therefore whatever exists "by sharing" depends upon something that is such by nature. Thus, for example, all living things depend on one that is Life itself, since there cannot be an infinite series of beings that share without that in which they share. Hence all beings "by participation" require a being that is such "by essence." This per se perfection is what all men mean by God.

Fifth, we see in the universe natural bodies that lack intelligence acting intelligently for a purpose. This is clear because they always or normally act in the same way so as to achieve the best end; therefore it cannot be by chance, but by purpose. But things lacking intelligence cannot act for a purpose, or tend to a goal, unless they are directed by some intelligence, just as the arrow is directed by the archer. Therefore there is some Intelligence by whom all natural things are ordered to an end. We call this Intelligence God.[57]

In response to the first objection concerning evil in the world, Thomas simply says that it pertains to the infinite goodness of God to permit evil so as to draw good from it, since Augustine says in his *Enchiridion,* c. 11, "God, since He is the supreme good, could in no way allow any kind of evil in His works, unless He were so omnipotent and good as to produce good even out of evil."

In response to the second objection concerning the self-sufficiency of nature and man's will, Thomas implicitly refers to the fifth way when he insists that all the works of nature presuppose intelligence, since nature does not know or will the end toward which it is preordained; even the functions of man's intellect and will, though free, depend on nature. Moreover all functions of man's mind and will are mutable and defectible, needing an immutable and indefectible intelligence above.

Early in his *Summa* (q. 3, a. 4), Thomas establishes the fundamental principle of his whole philosophy: only in God are essence (*quod est*) and existence (*esse*) identical; in creatures *esse* and *quod est* are really distinct, for creatures share, or participate, in the *esse* that is God. Upon this fundamental principle of his metaphysics Thomas constructs his theology of the One God, creation, and creatures.

We do not know how far Thomas got in writing the *prima pars* before he was assigned to Orvieto. It is certain that question 79, article 4, was written after November 22, 1267, for there he makes use of Moerbeke's translation of Themistius's paraphrase of Aristotle's *De anima,* which was completed on that date.[58] This means that the section on man (qq. 75–102) was written while Thomas was at Viterbo and in the company of William of Moerbeke.

Viterbo with Clement IV

(1267–68)

When the Dominican general chapter met in Bologna on June 5, 1267, the capitular fathers decided that "the provincial of the Roman province should diligently see to it that the priory where the [papal] curia resides, should be provided with suitable friars for the needs of the curia, particularly the prior and the lector."[59] The direct result of this legislation was that Thomas was immediately assigned to the Dominican priory at Viterbo, where Clement IV had been residing since April 30, 1266.

Guy Foulques, cardinal archbishop of Narbonne, was elected Pope at Perugia on October 8, 1264, six days after the death of Urban IV. He was consecrated at Perugia five months later, on February 5, 1265, and took the name of Clement IV. As a Frenchman, he was delighted with the arrival of Charles of Anjou; and after the battle of Benevento in February 1266 he took up residence in Viterbo, which was considerably closer to Rome. Since Guy Foulques was counselor to King Louis of France, Walz argues that he must have known Thomas in Paris.[60] He apparently knew Roger Bacon while they were together in Paris, or at least knew of him through one of his clerics, Raymond of Laon. On becoming Pope, Clement asked Bacon to send him his plan for revitalizing theology, which had become so "decadent" in recent years. This request from Clement eventually resulted in Bacon's *Opus maius* in seven parts, his *Opus minus* summarizing the first work lest the Pope be too busy to read the long version, and his *Opus tertium*, consisting of additional thoughts. We do not know what the Pope thought of Bacon's remedies for the times in its philosophical and theological plight. Certainly nothing came of them.

The provincial chapter of the Roman Province met at Lucca sometime in late June 1267. In the acts of this chapter there is no mention of Thomas's assignment to Viterbo. Presumably, judging from the words of the general chapter, the Roman provincial Aldobrando de Cavalcanti (1262–68) could make such an assignment himself without depending on the provincial chapter at which Thomas was present. One can assume, then, that the assignment came from the provincial and that Thomas went to Viterbo in July or August of that same year. Nothing is even said about the provincial studium that Thomas had opened at Santa Sabina two years earlier. It would seem that if the studium itself were transported from Rome to Viterbo, the provincial chapter would have something to say about the matter. It is easier to think that another Friar was appointed *lector primarius* at Santa Sabina by the provincial, rather than that the studium was transferred with Thomas. However, since there is no documentary evidence of any kind, we can only guess what happened.

No doubt Thomas was sent to Viterbo as lector of the priory with the same obligations he had at Orvieto. At the canonization process at Naples, the seventy-seven-year-old Friar Conrad of Sessa testified that he had known Thomas for a long time and had talked freely with him in Viterbo, as well as in Naples and Rome.[61] Both Bernard Gui and Tolomeo of Lucca note that Clement IV offered Thomas the archbishopric of Naples, together with the revenues of the monastery of St. Peter ad Aram.[62] Bernard Gui added a further note that "Clement, who was very fond of Thomas, actually sent him the bull appointing him to this office, but Thomas utterly refused to accept either it or those revenues, and begged the Pope never to press such things on him again." This offer of the archbishopric of Naples seems to have been made shortly after Thomas arrived in Viterbo.

Although all of the biographers, ancient and modern, speak about a close friendship between Clement IV and Thomas, we do not know of any specific tasks the Pope might have asked of Thomas apart from accepting the archbishopric of Naples. Nevertheless, within that year at Viterbo, Thomas completed the first part of his *Summa theologiae*, and he had the friendship of William of Moerbeke, who was "chaplain and penitentiary" of the Pope. At that time Moerbeke was about fifty-two years old, and Thomas was about forty-two. No doubt when Moerbeke finished translating Themistius's paraphrase of Aristotle's *De anima* on November 22, 1267, he allowed Thomas to read it immediately, for Thomas was then working on the problem of man's soul for his *Summa*, qq. 75–89.

During the revival of Thomism during the nineteenth and twentieth centuries, approximately between 1850 and 1960, an extraordinary number of student manuals appeared for use in colleges and seminaries. Their intent was to teach "Thomistic philosophy" to young students "according to the pure doctrine of St. Thomas," following his order, structure, and terminology. Invariably the manual on "Thomistic psychology" followed the order of the *Summa*, qq. 75–89, without realizing that the philosophical order of investigation differs radically from the theological order followed by Thomas in the *Summa*. In the prologue that opens this section of the *Summa*, Thomas states that "it belongs to the theologian to consider the nature of man's soul (*ex parte animae*), not his body (*ex parte corporis*), except insofar as the body relates to the soul." The theologian, knowing already that man has a soul, begins his consideration with its nature, to be followed with a study of its faculties, and finally its functions, particularly its intellection and volition. The philosophical order followed by Aristotle is the reverse. It begins with an analysis of man's functions, not only intellectual, but also physical and corporeal; only after these have been sufficiently studied does he go on to consider the various faculties of man, and finally his nature as he is in this life. The study of the soul separated from bodily union is beyond the competence of the psychologist. It belongs to the metaphysician, who, however, can say next to nothing about the state of the soul separated from the body; it also belongs to metaphysics to explain how much, if any, knowledge we can have of separated substances. "This question belongs to the metaphysician. However, this question is not resolved by Aristotle, because the complement of that science [of metaphysics] has not yet come to our attention, either because the whole of that book has not yet been translated, or perhaps, preoccupied with death, he never completed it."[63]

For Thomas the immortality of the soul can be demonstrated conclusively from its functions in this life; the natural philosopher, to whom psychology pertains, can know the fact of immortality, even though he cannot know much about the state of its separation from the body. The basic arguments for its immortality, that is, its incorruptibility and continued existence after death, are drawn from the nature of man's knowledge and will. The human intellect, although it depends in this life exclusively on sensation, knows through universal concepts and judgments that are not limited by individuality of matter; therefore intellection, as such, is a human function that is "separated from matter," that is, not restricted to the individualizing characteristics of sensation. For example, the mathematician's knowledge of numbers and figures is not limited to the existent numbers and figures of his experience, which are singular; similarly the natural philosopher devises definitions and judgments that are universally applicable to an infinite number of individual instances; like-wise the metaphysician can discuss the universality of "being" and the existence of substances totally separated from all matter, such as God and angels. Similarly man's free will, even though it considers individual circumstances in its decisions, is not ne-cessitated by any individual thing, but left free to determine itself. Since man's rational functions are thus "separated from matter," the principle, or source, of those functions must itself be devoid of matter, and therefore incorruptible and subsistent in its own *esse*, which is shared by the body when the two are united. Thus, even though the body is corruptible because of its materiality, which is the principle of corruption, the human soul is immaterial, spiritual, and subsistent in its own right.

Nevertheless, the human soul is not an angelic spirit attached to a body (I, 75, 7) but a substantial form informing a partic-ular body with its unique *esse*, which is incorruptible. The human soul is the one and only substantial form man has, since Thomas denied that man or any other composite can have more than one substantial form; the first form a body has is necessarily its substantial form, while posterior forms can only be accidental. From this it follows that the union of the rational soul and its unique body is immediate (I, 76, 1). The union of body and the human soul, therefore, constitutes the human person. Separation of body and soul, though inevitable, is not natural, for the nature of the human soul, unlike the angelic, is to inform the human body. Thus the soul separated from the body is not a person; it cannot think and act as it did in this life. Instead, it must depend on the universal images it acquired in this life, on infused knowl-edge, and on the vision of God face to face in the next. The in-completeness of the human soul separated from the body is used by Thomas to demonstrate the "necessity" of the final resurrec-tion, when each soul will again have its own body to share in its blessedness or damnation.

The uniqueness of Thomas's position in psychology is that he insists on both the immateriality of such specific operations as intellection and will and the essential role of man's rational soul as the one and only substantial form in man. Thus in this life the specific functions of man are "separated from matter," while his soul is intrinsically involved in matter. Siger of Brabant, as we will see in the next chapter, admitted the immateriality of man's thinking and willing, but concluded that the principle, or source, of these activities must itself be physically "separated from matter."

While at Viterbo, Thomas had the advantage of knowing William of Moerbeke himself, who was living at the same priory. The most important work William translated while living with Thomas at Viterbo was the *Elementatio theologica* of Proclus. It was completed on May 18, 1268.[64] Through this translation Thomas came to realize the true Platonic source of *Liber de causis*, which he commented on later. Unfortunately, we do not know the dates on which Moerbeke revised the Latin translations of Aristotle.[65] William was more interested in doing new translations than in revising old ones. Nevertheless, he did revise most of the current translations of Aristotle, checking them carefully against the Greek text. It is not entirely impossible that the idea of revision came from Thomas himself, who was interested in accurate texts. This may be what early biographers of Thomas had in mind when they spoke of "new translations" made at the request of Friar Thomas. But a revision is not the same as a translaton. It would seem that the revision of Aristotle's *De anima* was made in 1268.[66] We know that William spent the whole of 1269 translating the works of Archimedes; the autograph of his translation is in the Vatican Library, Ottob. lat. 1850.[67] Thillet places the revision of Aristotle's *Metaphysics* and the translation of Book Kappa between 1265 and 1268,[68] but this dating is too early. It is generally thought that the revision of the *Metaphysics* with the translation of Kappa occurred in or around 1270. The date of this translation is important, because, with the insertion of Kappa (Bk. 11), Lambda became Book 12; formerly Lambda had always been cited as Book 11. The Lambda numbering is a very important criterion for the relative dating of Thomas's works.

Thomas always had tremendous powers of concentration and insulation from sense distraction. All his early biographers mention this ability as an extraordinary phenomenon. Thomas seems to have had this gift more or less all his life, but it increased considerably as he matured. Bernard Gui noted that while Thomas was writing his commentary on Boethius's *De trinitate*, he was so abstracted that the candle he had held in his hand burned completely down without his having noticed any pain; as we have said, this commentary is an early work dating from around 1258. When Thomas had to have his leg cauterized, he deliberately went into such a deep state of abstraction that he felt no pain, nor did he move his leg once throughout the ordeal. Similarly, when he had to be bled, he "put himself into a state of contemplation" so as not to feel the surgeon's knife.[69] There is a famous story told of Thomas, that in 1269 he was seated next to King Louis IX at a banquet; all the while he was "rapt out of himself," thinking about the Manichees, whose arguments he was then considering. Suddenly in the midst of the meal, "he struck the table, exclaiming: 'That settles the Manichees!' Then, calling his socius by name, as though he were still at study in his cell, he cried out, 'Reginald, get up and write.'" Having been brought to his senses by the prior, Thomas apologized to the king, who ordered a secretary to take down Thomas's thoughts. Thomas explained, "I thought I was at my study, where I had begun to think about the [Manichean] heresy."[70] A similar story is told about his last years at Naples.[71] Frequently (*frequenter*) he was lost in thought or prayer so that tears often rolled down his cheeks when he celebrated Mass or chanted Compline during Lent when the choir sang the versicle "Reject us not in the time of old age." This tendency to be wrapped up in the spirit (*in spiritu rapitur*) should be kept in mind when considering Thomas's second Parisian regency and his last years in Naples.

Meanwhile in Paris the makings of another antimendicant attack started mounting with the secular master Gérard d'Abbeville, a lifelong friend of William of Saint-Amour, who was then living in exile in his native village. The signal for another attack was given by William of Saint-Amour himself in the book *Collationes catholicae et canonicae Scripturae*, which he sent to the new Pope, Clement IV, in October 1266. It was, Eschmann says, "a slightly retouched and considerably enlarged revision of the *De periculis novissimorum temporum*, the writing that had been the occasion for Thomas's *Contra impugnantes*," which was written in the fall of 1256. As early as 1266 Gérard openly attacked the mendicants in his *Quodlibet 7*, q. 7. This attack was continued by Gérard in his Advent *Quodlibet* 5, qq. 5–6, of 1268, and on December 31 of that same year by William of Saint-Amour in his sermon *Postquam consumati sunt*.[72] In the fall of 1268 religious superiors of the mendicant Orders began to worry about another uprising.[73] Clement IV died at Viterbo on November 29, 1268, and the Holy See was vacant for three years until the election of Gregory X on December 1, 1271, and his coronation at Rome on March 27, 1272. During this interval a number of secular masters at Paris, particularly Gérard d'Abbeville, Nicholas of Lisieux, and their followers, called "Geraldini," gave vent to their true feelings about the mendicants.

The minister general of the Franciscan Order, Bonaventure, made his residence in Paris or near Paris and could keep in touch with the rapidly moving sentiments of the secular masters. John of Vercelli, the Dominican master general, felt that the Order should have competent Friars in Paris to refute the charges made against them. At that time Peter of Tarentaise was called back to the chair for France for a second time (1267–69), and it is not certain who was in the Dominican chair for foreigners, the chair Thomas was asked to occupy. Possibly it was the Flemish Dominican Gilbert van Eyen.[74] The charges against the Friars were mainly the mendicants' claim to a higher state of perfection than the seculars, their presumptions care of souls, and their acceptance of young boys into their ranks. It is said that John of Vercelli first of all discussed the matter with Albert the Great, who declined to accept another appointment to the Dominican chair for externs in Paris.[75] Albert at that time was sixty-eight years old and a retired bishop; he could do nothing. If Albert had been consulted, he could have recommended that Thomas Aquinas be sent back to Paris for a second time.

A secondary reason for sending Thomas back to Paris was the growing threat of Latin Averroism among the masters in arts. Mandonnet thought that this was the main reason.[76] But surely Latin Averroism in the arts faculty at Paris was no threat to the Dominican Order, whereas another outbreak of antimendicantism threatened the very existence of the Dominican Order and all other mendicant groups. Latin Averroism under Siger of Brabant and his colleagues had been growing since the early years of the 1260s; if Latin Averroism had been uppermost in John of

Vercelli's mind, he could have ordered Thomas to Paris at the beginning of an academic year. As it was, the academic year 1268–69 had well begun before Thomas was asked to return to Paris in November of 1268. The situation of the Order must have appeared critical to John of Vercelli, since both Thomas and Peter of Tarentaise were asked to occupy the chair in Paris a second time. The immediate effect of a second regency for Thomas and Peter was that the production of Dominican masters at Paris was temporarily suspended. Only grave reasons could have caused such measures to be taken by the master general. These grave reasons would seem to have been the outbreak of new attacks on the mendicants, not the rise of Latin Averroism. On the other hand, when Thomas reached Paris, he realized the significance of Latin Averroism as a threat to Catholic doctrine. He entered this controversy with as much vigor as he did the antimendicant attacks of Gérard d'Abbeville and of the Geraldini.

John of Vercelli, it would seem, informed Thomas in November 1268 that he would have to return to Paris. Thomas, therefore, packed his belongings and traveled the long distance on foot with his faithful companion Reginald of Piperno, the young Friar Nicholas Brunacci,[77] and possibly some other Dominicans. Mandonnet dates the journey from mid-November 1268 to mid-January 1269.[78] Mandonnet tried to confirm this chronology from a *reportatio* of three sermons attributed to Thomas, found in MS A. 11, of the Ambrosian Library in Milan, and originally published by Uccelli in 1875.[79] The rubric of the second sermon declares it to have been preached in the Dominican church in Bologna before clerics of the university on the first Sunday of Advent. The third sermon was delivered in Milan before the people and clergy of the university on the second (?) Sunday of Advent. The first sermon does not concern us here, for it was delivered at Saint-Jacques in Paris on the first Sunday of Advent to clerics of the university. Mandonnet thus argued that the second sermon was delivered at Bologna on December 2, 1268, and the third at Milan on the ninth of December, while Thomas was en route to Paris for a second time.[80] Mandonnet's chronology on this point seems plausible and has been accepted by most modern scholars. Walz, however, followed by Castagnoli, claims that the third sermon must have been preached in Milan on the third Sunday of Advent, i.e., December 16.[81] But this would mean that Thomas and his companions took almost two weeks to travel from Bologna to Milan. Such procrastination would not have been suitable on this occasion, for the situation in Paris was urgent. Whatever must be said about the dating of the third sermon, it is certain that Thomas was told to return to Paris after the academic year had begun, and there was reason for haste. Passing through Bologna and Milan in early December, he arrived at Saint-Jacques sometime in January (or possibly February) to occupy the second Dominican chair in the University of Paris.

Chapter VI

SECOND PARISIAN REGENCY

(1269–72)

When Thomas and his companions entered the Porte Saint-Jacques in the winter of 1268–69, the forty-four-year-old Thomas was, no doubt, cold and tired, but he was at the height of his physical stamina and intellectual vigor. He could not have imagined how productive the next four years would be or the price he would have to pay for his incredible output between 1269 and 1273. He was tall, well-built, somewhat large, and at that time beginning to grow bald, which was noticeable enough to be mentioned, despite his monastic tonsure. He had a large head and always held himself erect, "as men of upright character do." His complexion was healthy, like "ripe wheat." His body had a delicate balance and texture "that goes with a fine intelligence"; yet virile also, "robust and prompt to serve the will."[1]

During the next four years Thomas worked with incredible speed and accuracy with the help of his secretaries. We are told that he ate little and slept little, devoting his energies to writing, dictating, teaching, and praying. What Thomas was able to accomplish between 1269 and 1273 defies imitation. But Thomas not only "wrote and dictated" what he had in mind, he also spent considerable time in reading the works of other authors, ancient and contemporary. Most biographers of Thomas fail to advert to the amount of reading Thomas had to do in order to produce the writings generally attributed to his second Parisian regency. No doubt Thomas read rapidly and retained accurately what he had read; nevertheless, reading does take time, and Thomas did not have much time to spare.

If Thomas had done no more than fulfill his professorial duties and defend the mendicant cause against the attacks of Gérard d'Abbeville, he would have done all that the master general had asked for. But besides these tasks, Thomas completed the entire second part of the *Summa* and wrote part of the third; he wrote detailed commentaries on all the major works of Aristotle, a number of important treatises on polemical questions, and, numerous replies to diverse queries.

It was now almost ten years since Thomas had seen Paris. Much had changed in the university and in the Priory of Saint-Jacques. Of the nine secular masters in theology who had been his colleagues during the first Parisian regency (1256–59), only three were left when Thomas returned in 1269: Eudes of Saint-Denys (1249–84), Robert de Sorbon (1250–74), and Gérard d'Abbeville (1255–71).[2] Nicholas of Orléans was chancellor. Stephen Tempier, onetime master and chancellor of the university, was made bishop of Paris on October 7, 1268. Peter of Tarentaise, the future Pope Innocent V (1276), was in the Dominican chair for France for a second time but was again elected provincial in the summer of 1269. Eustace of Arras was in the Franciscan chair, soon to be followed by the young and brilliant John Pecham. The faculty of arts had grown considerably in numbers and significance. The Averroists among them, led by Siger of Brabant, were of growing concern to orthodox theologians and to ecclesiastical authorities. The Priory of Saint-Jacques not only had a new prior, but also many new faces. Some of Thomas's closest friends were no longer there. However, Thomas did not come back to Paris to renew old acquaintances or to make new friends; he had a job to do, one much bigger than he had anticipated.

Thomas seems to have lost no time in organizing secretaries to help him study and write. He had a secretarial staff during his earlier teaching period, but they seem to have been concerned mainly with copying certain works of Albert and in preparing the *Sentences* and the *De veritate* for publication.[8] We know the names of some of these secretaries for the first Parisian regency: Friars Raymond Severi, Peter d'Andria, and Nicholas of Marsillac.[4] For the second Parisian regency we know the names of only two of his "many" secretaries: Reginald of Piperno and a cleric named Evan Garnit of the diocese of Tréguier.[5] The names of Thomas's other secretaries are unknown. Nevertheless we can say that Thomas's secretaries during the second Parisian regency were concerned mainly with the production of new texts written or dictated by Thomas, and with compiling "instruments of research" such as the alphabetical *Tabula Ethicorum* drawn from Albert's *lectura* on Aristotle's *Ethics*. The fact that Thomas dictated to his scretaries does not mean that he no longer wrote in his "unintelligible hand," for the early biographers always couple "writing and/or dictating." The view that Thomas penned his own works only in the early part of his career when he had no secretaries is doubtful, as we have said. Reginald of Piperno was with him when he "wrote" the major portion of the *Summa contra gentiles,* and William of Tocco testified that he saw Thomas "writing" on *De generatione et corruptione,* which he believed to have been "his last work in philosophy."[6] The highly complex Naples MS of the *Metaphysics* commentary (Bibl. Naz. VIII. F. 16) seems to have been written in seven different hands, the scribes either copying from a previous text or taking down dictation; the portions that were copied could have been from Thomas's own "unintelligible hand" or from an exemplar once removed.

Bernard Gui, depending apparently on the testimony of William of Tocco and Reginald of Piperno, notes that Thomas "used to dictate in his cell to three secretaries, and even occasionally to four, on different subjects at the same time."[7] Both biographers note that "one of his secretaries, a Breton called Evan [Garnit] from the diocese of Tréguier, relates that Thomas, after dictating to him and two other secretaries, would sometimes sit down to rest from the work and, falling asleep, would go on dictating in his sleep; Evan meanwhile continuing to write just the same."[8] There can be no doubt, then, that Thomas had a staff of secretaries in Paris.[9] Apart from his last years in Naples, when he most probably had secretaries, we do not know whether he had any secretarial help except Reginald during his ten years in the Roman Province. Most likely he did not, but this cannot yet be proved or disproved.

The fact that Thomas could dictate to three or four secretaries at the same time on different subjects is astounding, but we know that Julius Caesar and Napoleon Bonaparte also had the same gift, requiring extraordinary concentration and ability to switch from one train of thought to another rapidly.[10] Also astounding is the fact that Thomas could sleep and still continue a train of thought; but that is not humanly impossible, for the mind continues to function even in sleep, and one sometimes awakes suddenly to an original idea that must be put on paper immediately lest it be forgotten by morning. Rare, however, is the ability to dictate coherently in sleep. Aristotle calls sleep "a suspension of the common sense," or consciousness, which is a sense faculty. The body, since it is material, needs rest and sleep. The immaterial intellect, though dependent on sense images, is free to drift; sometimes one can recall dreams and even talk intelligently during sleep. The point being made here is that Thomas had such an extraordinary gift of intense concentration that he could dictate to three or four secretaries on different subjects at the same time. The testimony of Evan Garnit leaves no room for doubt.

With cautious rein on the imagination, we should note that during Thomas's second regency, there was an unusual development in his mentality, some profound, personal, psychic experience that affected his writing. A number of modern authorities have adverted to it in their examination of particular doctrines. I. T. Eschmann could not account for the conspicuous difference between the first and second parts of the *Summa*. The first part is coldly metaphysical, precise, and curt, even in the discussion of man and divine providence; the second part, on the other hand, from early in the I–II onward, is impressively human, considerate, and complex. Speculative theologians would, no doubt, attribute this contrast to the different kind of material discussed in the two parts. However, the problem seems to lie deeper than that, for it affects all of his later writings. Gauthier, discussing a significant change in Thomas's doctrine of continence—placing this virtue in the will instead of in the intellect—claims that Thomas was induced to "mitigate the excessive intellectualism that he had earlier displayed."[11] Dom Odo Lottin also noted a change of this kind when he examined the question of free will, but he attributed the change to the condemnation of Averroist theses in 1270.[12] Santiago Ramirez, studying the problem of faith and the gifts of the Holy Spirit, also noted an over-all development and attributed it to the growing influence of St. Augustine on the mind of Thomas.[13]

It might have been a kind of mystical experience or it might have been a sudden, new realization of the apostolic character of all his work. Like the young Macedonian in St. Paul's vision, who beckoned Paul to come to Macedonia to help them (Acts 16:9), so too young students, both Dominican and non-Dominican, beckoned Thomas to come into their world and help them. The *Summa theologiae* was begun for young students in theology. Similarly the commentaries on Aristotle were destined for young masters in arts. Gauthier seems to be right: Thomas was induced to mitigate the excessive intellectualism that he had earlier displayed. Whatever was the specific cause of this change in Thomas, it must have occurred during the early years of 1269-70. It was of sufficient magnitude to affect all of his later writings. Whatever the cause was, it in no way decreased his productivity, but rather increased it. This is a very important point, for some kinds of experience, mystical or natural, tend to decrease productivity rather than encourage it. In Thomas's case, the experience reinforced his already intense apostolic life and full program.

Since Thomas worked on so many diverse problems at the same time during his second Parisian regency, it will not be feasible or even possible to proceed in a strictly chronological order. Therefore we will select certain essential aspects, and discuss each of them chronologically insofar as it is possible. Basically, Thomas was a regent master in theology at Paris; he had, therefore, certain professorial duties in the university. This position served as the basis of all his work in Paris.

Professorial Duties and the "Summa"

Thomas arrived in Paris in January 1269, when the academic year was half over and apparently at a time when the masters in the university were on strike. According to Glorieux's reckoning, Thomas was the only master who taught despite the suspension of teaching in the university; at least this is the impression one gets, even though there seem to have been no repercussions.[14] Thomas not only taught during the half year, January to June, but he continued to teach during the next three academic years. The basic duties of a master in theology, as we indicated earlier, were lecturing on the Bible, holding public disputations both ordinary and quodlibetal, and preaching to the academic community.

There are only two scriptural commentaries that can safely be identified with Thomas's Paris teaching: the commentary on John and the Pauline letter to the Romans, together with one on part of the first letter to the Corinthians up to chapter 10 inclusive.

The "primitive" catalogue of Thomas's writings as represented by Bartholomew of Capua, Nicholas Trevet, and the two Prague catalogues lists the commentary on John ("better than which none can be found") as a *lectura*, that is, a *reportatio* taken down by Reginald of Piperno during actual delivery in the classroom, but "corrected" by Friar Thomas himself.[15] Because Thomas "corrected" the *reportatio*, the *lectura* on John holds a special place among his writings, almost equivalent to an edited exposition of the text. Among all of Thomas's writings on Scripture none surpass the *lectura* on John's Gospel. It is sublime in its theological profundity, particularly in its discussion of the last discourse of Jesus (Jn. 14–17). Here the trinitarian doctrine expounded by Thomas in the first part of the *Summa* comes to life vividly; the intensity of God's love for man and the vast extent of Christ's love for his disciples and for us is poured forth line after line with theological accuracy and poetic beauty. Modern biblical studies have, of course, surpassed the work of earlier generations, and there are a number of excellent modern commentaries on the Gospel according to John. Nevertheless no modern work has surpassed or replaced the sublime theological dimensions of Thomas's *lectura*. It is a mature work for theologians as well as for students of Scripture. The lively classroom presentation can be seen in the brief questions disputed in the course of the commentary, notably on the "natural desire" to see God, the immediacy of man's beatific vision of God face to face, the triune unity of the Godhead, and the procession of the Holy Spirit from both Father and Son. In an address to the students of the Angelicum in Rome, Pius XII said that no man can truly consider himself a Thomist who is not familiar with the scriptural commentaries of Thomas; this is particularly applicable to the *lectura* on John and the Pauline epistles.

Tolomeo of Lucca notes that Thomas wrote the first five chapters on John himself, but the rest is a *reportatio* "corrected by him."[16] No doubt the revision of Reginald's notes was due to the desire of a close friend of Thomas, Adenulf of Anagni, provost of Saint-Omer since 1264, master in theology (1282–85), canon of Notre Dame, and later chaplain to two Popes.[17] Adenulf was not only a friend and student of Thomas's during the years 1269 to 1272, but he offered a considerable amount of money to have a fair copy of the *lectura* on John made by professional scribes. Without Adenulf's enthusiasm and money, the *lectura* on John would have remained a simple *reportatio*.

It is certain that the lectures on John were delivered during the second Parisian regency, 1269–72, since it was Reginald who made the transcript, but it is, at present, impossible to determine the exact year. Most authorities are willing to leave the precise year undetermined, but C. Spicq argues in favor of the academic year 1270–71. This dating does not eliminate the need of further research.

Thomas had particular affection for St. Paul, as did St. Dominic before him. However, his commentaries on Paul present many difficulties, and the current editions are badly corrupted. The earliest catalogues present the commentaries on Paul in two distinct groups: those written by himself, namely, Romans to 1 Corinthians 10, and those recorded by Reginald of Piperno, namely, 1 Corinthians 11 to Hebrews, in the order presented by the Latin Vulgate. It is certain that Thomas lectured on some of the Pauline epistles in Paris. This is clearly stated by Bernard Gui, who says, "Once at Paris, when writing on Paul's epistles, he came to a passage which quite baffled him until, dismissing his secretaries, he fell to the ground and prayed with tears; then what he desired was given to him and it all became clear."[18] William of Tocco attributes the enlightenment to a visit from the Apostle: "He wrote on all the epistles of Paul, which he valued above all writings, the Gospels alone excepted; and while engaged on this work at Paris, he is said to have had a vision of the Apostle."[19] The fact that both Tocco and Gui specify the place as Paris is significant.

According to Mandonnet, however, Thomas never lectured on St. Paul in Paris. Instead he lectured twice on Paul while in Italy, the first time being between 1259–65, when he was in Anagni and Orvieto; the second time being in Naples between 1272–73. Mandonnet suggests that when Thomas lectured on Paul in the first period, he commented on the entire Pauline corpus; and that the second time he lectured on Paul, in Naples, he covered only Romans to 1 Corinthians 10. The first series was reported by Reginald, as the catalogues state, and the second was an edition of the commentary by Thomas himself. The abrupt ending of the second series, according to Mandonnet, is explained by Thomas's cessation of all work on December 6, 1273. Finally, the first version of Paul, a *reportatio*, was replaced by the *expositio* of Romans to 1 Corinthians 10. The resulting compilation is found in the Pauline commentaries we have to-day. However, a fragment of 1 Corinthians 7:10 to 10:33 of all the printed versions was lost and replaced by the parallel passage of Peter of Tarentaise in the version of Nicholas Gorran.

In other words, according to Mandonnet, Thomas lectured on the entire Pauline corpus when he was in Italy between 1259–65. These lectures were taken down by Reginald of Piperno, as the catalogues state. Later, at Naples, Thomas again lectured on Paul (1272–73), beginning with Romans and reaching 1 Corinthians 10 before suspending all teaching. This latter commentary was the *expositio* edited by Thomas himself, as the catalogues testify. This new section replaced its corresponding text in the earlier version, which was discarded or destroyed. Even so, the final version of 1 Corinthians 7:10 to 10:33 was somehow lost and the lacuna filled by Peter of Tarentaise's text in the version of Nicholas Gorran, another Dominican. This is the state of the current "vulgate" text of Thomas's commentary on Paul.

Thomas's commentary on Romans is a magnificent, superb piece of work. It is a highly polished version, replete with quotations from the Latin and Greek Fathers, an explanation of all the main heresies in the early Church, particularly Pelagianism, and numerous citations of Aristotle, particularly the *Ethics*. On the other hand, the commentaries on all the other epistles seldom refer to anything but the *Glossa* and the Bible itself; however, they do contain extensive discussions of theological points. It is difficult to see how Thomas could have edited in full his commentary on Romans at Naples, since he ceased writing abruptly so soon after lecturing on it. Moreover Mandonnet's theory excludes the testimony of Bernard Gui and William of Tocco, both of whom state that Thomas expounded the words of St. Paul at Paris.

While admitting the double redaction of the commentary on Paul, Glorieux argues that the edited version, the *expositio* of Romans to 1 Corinthians 10, must be dated during Thomas's second regency in Paris, between 1270–72; the *reportatio* of 1 Corinthians 11 to Hebrews, together with a now lost commentary on Romans, is an early version delivered while he was in the Roman Province between 1259–65.[20]

In any case, Thomas's edited commentary on Romans reveals how deeply he was committed to the Pauline doctrine of justification by faith, gratuity of grace, predestination, merit, good works, and the doctrine of original sin. St. Augustine is the most frequently quoted Father of the Church, but there is frequent use of the *Glossa*, Jerome, Ambrose, Gregory, Athanasius, and others. In the course of his commentary Thomas refers to almost all the books of Aristotle's *Ethics*. Despite the corrupted state of our printed editions, Thomas's commentary on Romans should be read by everyone who hopes to understand his doctrine of grace, as well as Pelagianism, under which name Thomas includes not only the authentic teaching of Pelagius (through the eyes of Augustine) but also what later centuries would call semi-Pelagianism. Throughout this commentary Thomas raises problems on the text—a kind of miniature disputation—which he resolves immediately. Moreover, there are frequent diversions from the text to elucidate the theological problems involved; he does not hesitate to explain the heresies of Arius, Nestorius, Sabellius, Pelagius, and the Manichees. Nor does he have any qualms about quoting pagan authors in order to bring out the truth more clearly and decisively.

Glorieux would add the commentaries on Job and Isaiah to this second Parisian regency. However, according to our interpretation, the commentary on Job, with all of its adroit use of Aristotle, is to be dated at Orvieto during the pontificate of Urban IV. The commentary on Isaiah, of which an autograph fragment has been preserved, raises a special problem, which we will not go into here. Eschmann eliminates this from either Parisian period and prefers to give it an Italian dating.[21]

Briefly, then, it would seem that while Thomas was in Paris for a second time as master, he expounded and edited the commentary on John, a *lectura* which was recorded by Reginald of Piperno and "corrected by Friar Thomas." Second, he expounded and edited the commentary on Romans to 1 Corinthians 10, the rest being an early *lectura* reported by Reginald in the Roman Province, but not corrected by Thomas.

As to the disputed questions that were held during the second Parisian regency, there is no unanimity of opinion. The earliest catalogues of Thomas's writings merely state that when Thomas was in Paris for the second time, he disputed *De virtutibus* "and the rest" (*et ultra*). The problem is to determine what is included in the *et ultra*.

We can be certain that the disputed question *De anima* took place in Paris during his second regency, since two reliable MSS give Paris as the origin of the dispute (Klosterneuburg Stifsbibl. 274 and Angers 418).[22] Glorieux argues that the questions *De anima* must have been disputed at Paris in the spring term (January to June) 1269.[23] *De anima* has twenty-one articles, or questions, some of them quite lengthy. If each article represents a distinct disputation, as Mandonnet claimed, Thomas would have had to hold them once a week for the remaining half year. Dondaine, as we have mentioned, would consider this too frequent.

Without discussing details of the exact date of the questions *De anima*, it is sufficient to know that they were disputed in Paris shortly after he arrived. The choice of disputing first on *De anima* was most appropriate for Thomas's second regency. Undoubtedly Thomas knew a great deal about the Averroist view proposed in the arts faculty. There was no better way to declare what he maintained on the nature of man's soul, particularly his intellect, than by a disputation open to the entire academic community. The questions *De anima* were disputed shortly after Thomas completed his discussion of man in the *Summa theologiae*.[24] Nevertheless it is far more extensive and in many ways superior to the earlier discussion proposed for beginners in theology. The entire question deals with problems then being disputed in the schools. The first five questions deal directly with the errors of Avicenna and Averroes. The third question in particular discusses the problem of the separated single intellect for all mankind, while question 14 takes up the question of personal immortality after death as opposed to the Averroist doctrine of immortality only for the separated possible intellect.

The first question of *De anima* takes up the problem of wider import, for it discusses the nature of the human soul as both the substantial form of man and a *hoc aliquid*, i.e., an individual, substantial reality having *esse* in its own right so as to be subsistent. The second objection sets forth the problem in this way: In order to be a *hoc aliquid*, the soul would have to be an individual, since universals cannot be a *hoc aliquid*. But if the soul is individuated, it would have to be such either by itself or by reason of something else. If it is individuated by something else, it would have to be by reason of its body, for matter is the principle of individuation. In this case, when the body corrupts, individuation of the soul must also cease. If, on the other hand, the soul is individuated by itself, then each soul would have to be a species, like an angel, and hence could not be the substantial form of man. If the soul is taken to be composed of matter and form so as to remain individualized, it could not be a substantial form, for matter is not the form of any composite. Hence it is impossible for the soul to be both a substantial form and a *hoc aliquid*.

This formulation of the problem involves a basic tenet of the Averroists: either the human soul is a *hoc aliquid*, in which case it cannot be the substantial form of man, or the human soul is the substantial form of man, in which case it cannot be a *hoc aliquid*. Thomas responds to the objection briefly when he says that everything has *esse* in the same way as it is individuated. Just as the soul receives *esse* from God and is in the body as in matter, so, since the soul cannot corrupt, neither can it lose its individuation. The very nature of the soul, according to Thomas, is to animate the body; even when it is separated from matter in death, its nature is still to inform the matter to which is is related. The basic question, as Thomas saw it, was not individuation, but rather the compatibility of the soul being the one and only substantial form of man and at the same time possessing *esse* in its own right. Angels are admittedly separate substances, each having *esse* distinctly and properly, but no angel could ever be the substantial form of a body. Its nature is not to inform matter of any kind; it can only "possess" a material body and use it as an instrument. Thomas even goes so far as to call the "body" assumed by an angel or a demon nothing but compressed air.— The main point is that each angel is a *hoc aliquid* and a distinct species, while the intellective soul, because of its unique position in nature, is at the same time the substantial form by which man is constituted in the species "man" and a *hoc aliquid*. Since its principal functions are not rooted in matter, the soul somehow has subsistent *esse* in which the body participates.

In the doctrine of Thomas the intellective soul of man occupies a unique position in the whole of creation; it is at the same time the substantial form by which man is rational and an immaterial *hoc aliquid* in whose *esse* the body participates. Because the soul is immaterial, not composed of matter and form, it cannot corrupt.

In the third question Thomas discusses the crucial point for the Averroists, namely, that if the intellect is immaterial, knowing the species of all things, it must be separate in being, subsisting apart from human phantasms that would individualize it. If the human intellect is separated from body, it can only be one, just as the color "white" if it existed apart from all matter would be one. When discussing this question with the Averroists, Thomas is careful to use the expression "intellective soul" rather than "human soul." The Averroists, such as Siger of Brabant, were willing to admit that man has a unique substantial form, which is the human soul, multiple, personal, and corruptible. Since the problem deals with the human intellect, Thomas prefers to insist that it is the intellective soul that is the substantial form of man, and immortal.

In his response, Thomas admits the principle that if the possible intellect is a substance separated from matter in being, it must necessarily be one for all mankind. "But," he says, "the unicity of the intellect requires special consideration, since it involves a special difficulty."

The basic problem of the Averroists involves the "possible intellect" (*intellectus possibilis*), not the "agent intellect" (*intellectus agens*). It is important to understand the terminology involved, for some recent authors seem to confuse the two, making the problem hopelessly unintelligible. For Thomas, the "possible," or "passive," intellect is the immaterial faculty so called by which man thinks or knows by receiving universalized concepts from the phantasm. While this intellect needs sense images for its thinking in this life, its universalized concepts, once received, are not lost, forgotten, or corrupted; as an immaterial faculty it cannot know singulars as such, but universalizes what it receives through sense faculties. Thomas calls this thinking intellect a "faculty of the soul" (*potentia animae*) precisely to distinguish it from the Averroist conception of a separated intellect, one for all mankind. On the other hand, man also has an agent "intellect" by which thoughts are universalized by abstraction. It is a distinct, "active," spiritual power of the soul, to distinguish it from the Avicennian agent intellect, subsisting apart and one for all men. For Avicenna the active "intellect" was the tenth intelligence, separate from matter, that bestows the forms of other things (concepts and truth) into the human passive intellect. Early scholastic writers found no difficulty in accepting and adapting the Avicennian view, preferring to call it God, or the "light that illumines every man that comes into the world" (Jn. 1:9). Thomas rejected the Avicennian view and the Augustinian version of illumination, calling the agent intellect also "a power of the soul," i.e., an active, illuminating faculty that each man must have in order to understand. The Avicennian view was made compatible with Christian doctrine, so nothing was lost by it. The Averroist view, on the other hand, was completely disrupting, for it denied personal immortality, responsibility, and reward, as well as punishment, in the life to come. For Averroes, not only was the agent intellect separate from all matter, but the possible intellect as well was separate and one for all men. Thus, for Averroes, the separate possible intellect was a "kind of separate substance."

Thomas's rejection of the Averroist doctrine in *De anima,* q. 3, is based on the observed difference between men in their process of knowing. Trying to explain the unicity of truth and knowledge, Averroes postulated a unique intellect; whereas Thomas, trying to explain the diversity of knowledge among men, insisted on the diversity of human intellects.

More will be said of Latin Averroism later. Not all of the questions in *De anima* deal with the Averroist problem. It also discusses and rejects the multiplicity of substantial forms in man, the existence of a spiritual matter in the composition of angels and the human soul, the identity of human faculties with its substance, the identification of the human soul with angelic natures, and the denial of the soul's knowledge after death.

Thomas disputed the questions *De virtutibus* "and the rest" during his second Parisian regency, as we know from the earliest catalogues. This group undoubtedly contained the series *De virtutibus in communi* (thirteen articles), *De caritate* (thirteen articles), *De correctione fraterna* (two articles), *De spe* (four articles), and *De virtutibus cardinalibus* (four articles). These short disputations parallel the second part of the *Summa,* on which Thomas was working at the time.

Many authorities, if not most, prefer to list the disputed questions *De malo* during this same period, because they conveniently parallel the *Summa,* not in similarity of doctrine, but in relevance. However, Lottin has presented some strong arguments that place *De malo* prior to the second part of the *Summa.*[25] Lottin has also argued that *De malo,* qq. 6 and 16, were originally separate disputations. Question 6 on free will is one of the best and most profound discussions of the complex problem of human freedom. It seems to have been discussed in Paris during Thomas's second regency prior to *Summa theologiae* I–II, qq. 9–10. Question 16 on demons is also an extra-serial disputation, discussed separately from the series *De malo.* However, the earliest manuscripts of *De malo* all contain question 6 and question 16 in their present position.

In my view the chronology of the disputed questions can be expressed briefly in the following way:

I. Paris (1256–59)   *De veritate*   (qq. 1–7)
(qq. 8–20)
(qq. 21–29)

II. Italy (1265–68)   *De potentia* (Rome)
                      De malo   (Rome)
                      De spiritualibus creaturis (Viterbo)   °
III. Paris (1269–72) *De anima*
                      De virtutibus (*in communi; De caritate;*
                          De corr. fraterna; De spe; De
                          virt. cardinalibus)
                      De unione verbi incarnati

As regent master at Paris, Thomas held quodlibet disputations. These were held during Advent and Lent of each year at the will of the master. However, as the word "quodlibet" signifies, they could be on any subject and posed by anyone, the master being obliged to dispute the point and determine the question as he saw fit. Eleven such quodlibets were edited and submitted to the university stationer's office for copying and circulation. The entire collection of his quodlibets appeared in the stationer's list of 1286 and again in 1304.[26] Shortly after 1300 another quodlibet was discovered and added to the collection as *Quodlibet 12*. This last item is a *reportatio* (or possibly notes) in view of a determination by the master; it raises many difficulties besides that of chronology. Nothing would be gained by discussing these quodlibets here. Let it suffice to say that generally *Quodlibets 1–6* and *12* are attributed to Thomas's second Parisian regency, while *7–11* are attributed to the first.[27]

Historians of thirteenth-century scholasticism often refer to a "famous debate" between Thomas and Friar John Pecham, later archbishop of Canterbury, on the unicity of substantial form in man.[28] One version of this encounter is based on the testimony of Bartholomew of Capua at the canonization process in Naples in 1319. Bartholomew, claiming to have heard this "from many Friar Preachers, worthy of belief," states that at Paris once when Thomas was "conducting a disputation," at which the Franciscan John Pecham was present, the latter attacked Thomas "with bombastic and arrogant words," whereas Thomas remained unalterably humble, gentle, and courteous.[29] The other version is presented by John Pecham himself, who, in a series of letters to various persons, protested his innocence from the charges of the Dominicans. He declared that he had not persecuted the opinion concerning the unicity of form with arguments from reason and from the authority of the saints to the very death of Thomas. Nor was he the "first" to censure that opinion. Nay rather "when [Thomas] argued this position [against] the Bishop of Paris, many masters in theology, and his own brethren, we alone stood by him, defending him as much as we could within the bounds of truth, until he, like a humble doctor, submitted all his positions, which correction could weaken, to the judgment of the Parisian masters."[30] Perhaps Pecham was a bit pompous. Nicholas Trevet describes Pecham as "the principal zealot of his Order, an outstanding poet, pretentious in his carriage and speech, but kind in soul and very liberal in spirit."[31]

The occasion of which Pecham speaks could not have been a disputation at which Thomas presided. Rather it must have been at the inception of a new master or at a convocation of regent and non-regent masters in theology assembled to discuss propositions proposed for condemnation. Bartholomew, not being familiar with academic procedures, and not being present at the event, presented an unlikely picture that was, perhaps, unjust to Pecham. Nevertheless Pecham's teaching was directly opposed to that of Thomas, which he characterized as "profane novelties" that originated in the schools not more than twenty years earlier, i.e., around 1265.[32] The incident referred to by Bartholomew and Pecham must have taken place in the academic year 1269–70, for Pecham became master in 1269 or early 1270.

While Thomas performed his regular duties as a university master, conducting his classes at Saint-Jacques, he was also intently busy composing the second part of his *Summa theologiae*. The *secunda pars* is Thomas's most original contribution to theological literature. Neither Thomas nor his contemporaries considered this part to be a "moral theology." For Thomas there is only one science of theology, embracing both the speculative and the practical, the "dogmatic" part as well as the "moral." Only in recent times has theology been fragmented into dogmatic, moral, mystical, positive, apologetical, etc. In the mind of Thomas such divisions are strictly academic and do not constitute separate parts of theology. The teaching of theology, however, does require a detailed discussion of man's moral actions needed to arrive at his true beatitude, which is the contemplation of God through grace in this life and through glory in the next.

Thomas introduces the second part by saying that man is made to the image of God in that man is an intellectual being endowed with free will and is per se responsible for his actions. After discussing God the exemplar and all things that He has freely made, "we must consider His image, i.e., man, according as he is both the source of his own actions, having free will, and responsible for his actions." The first five questions of the second part discuss in detail man's ultimate goal. The rest of the second part considers man's personal striving for the goal, while the third part discusses Christ and His sacraments as the means through which salvation is achieved. In human affairs the ultimate goal desired, though first and uppermost in one's mind, is the last thing attained. The final cause precedes the efficient, as expressed in a scholastic axiom, "The first in intention is the last in execution," meaning that the final cause *cuius gratia* is the motivating force for activity through which man attains his desired end as an effect.

Thomas intended to discuss the ultimate goal as achieved, but he died before such a program could be completed. Thomas himself divided the second part of the *Summa* into general considerations and special considerations. Shortly after his death, his disciples found it more convenient to specify the first part of the second *prima secundae* (I–II), and the second part of the second *secunda secundae* (II–II).

The first five questions of I–II—most likely composed in Viterbo—are discussed in logical sequence: (1) is there an ultimate goal for man, (2) in what does it consist, (3) what is man's beatitude, (4) what circumstances are involved in man's happiness in this life and the next, and (5) how does man go about achieving such happiness?

For Thomas, every creature by its very nature must act for an ultimate end proportioned to itself, for nature is the source of all motion and rest. However, different natures have different ways of acting for an end proportioned to itself. Man has rational dominion over his actions, while all other things in the world are moved to ends by their nature, like the arrow that is directed toward the target by the archer. Since man has dominion over his actions, he is responsible for the goal he chooses as well as all actions tending to that end, for it is the end that determines, specifies, and justifies the means to that end. Every man must have some goal in life (chosen at puberty and subject to rejection), otherwise he could not act at all. No doubt, most men do not think in terms of some ultimate goal, but rather about immediate goals to be achieved throughout the day. His way of thinking about these immediate ends is, in fact, dominated by the over-all goal he has set for himself, whatever that may be; but because of indifference, mental laziness, or the demands of everyday living, he may not wish to think about something so abstract as an "ultimate goal."

Man, having free choice and dominion over his actions, may think that his ultimate goal consists in riches, honors, fame, power, physical well-being, sex, learning, or some other personal fulfillment, whereas in truth only God, the uncreated goodness, can satisfy all of man's highest desires. God, therefore, is the true object of man's happiness. Here St. Augustine could say: "Thou hast made us for Thyself, O Lord, and our hearts are restless until they rest in Thee."

Having discussed the true object of man's happiness (q. 2), Thomas goes on to discuss the nature of happiness itself (q. 3), since happiness seems to be some kind of personal achievement or function. Although God is the *object* of human happiness, the means by which we attain Him cannot itself be God, but rather some personal and created function. Happiness is not a function of the senses, even though sensation can prepare the mind antecedently and share consequently in the overflow of joy. Happiness itself is so profound that it must be attained through the highest functions of man. The Franciscan tradition would ground true happiness in love, which is a function of the will. Thomas, however, here and elsewhere, insists that love is a derivative of knowledge. Lest love be blind, it presupposes knowledge in the intellect. Therefore, happiness consists in contemplation, which overflows into love and joy. While recognizing the importance of love, which is rooted in the will, Thomas's intellectualism contrasts sharply from the voluntarism of the Franciscans. For him the root of all true happiness consists in contemplation of God, here through faith, and hereafter through actual vision of Him face to face. Thomas insists that man can be happy in this life, but only if he fixes his goal in knowledge and love of God. One must not think that happiness belongs exclusively to knowledge, a function of the intellect, least of all in this life. In this life love can far outstrip the degree of our knowledge, but without some knowledge, love is blind. Therefore the primary, personal, formal element of eternal happiness is the beatific *vision* of God, which is a function of the intellect.

Knowledge of God, though the formal element in happiness, is not the only element, for happiness is a total fulfillment in heaven and a partial fulfillment in this life. One important element for happiness is delight, or a sense of well-being in the object possessed. It is a state of euphoria of mind and body, which man enjoys only imperfectly and sporadically in this life, but fully in the next. Moreover, true happiness requires "rectitude of the will," i.e., the life of virtue, antecedently, in order for man to attain happiness and consequently in order for him to rejoice in the goal achieved, or attained. A life of virtue is absolutely essential to achieving happiness in this life and in the next. This principle seems to suggest that man needs his body for true happiness. In one sense that is true, for in this life man needs phantasms in order to know, and in the final resurrection of the body the individual personality of each man will be reconstituted in its specific nature. But it would be wrong to suggest, as some Greek writers have, that between death and resurrection of the body the separated intellective soul cannot rejoice in the fruits of the redemption. The essence of happiness in heaven consists in the vision of God, for which he does not need his body.

Thomas then goes on to explain that happiness in this life needs health of body (a. 6), a sufficiency of temporal goods to enable man to live virtuously (a. 7), and the company of friends (a. 8). Both for Aristotle and Thomas, man has a profound need of friends. Friendship, though ardently desired by all men, is a gift of God and cannot be forced, purchased, or demanded. It must be accepted and treasured, for it is part of man's happiness on earth and in heaven, where we will enjoy the companionship of the saints.

In the fifth question Thomas discusses the attainment of happiness. For him, happiness is an attainable reality (a. 1), one that can be shared in various degrees, depending upon the

capacity and disposition of the individual (a. 2). Thomas clearly
holds that some degree of happiness is attainable in this life
(a. 3), but happiness in this life can easily be lost in the changing conditions of life, but even in this case man can enjoy a
modicum of happiness, for it is grounded in intellect and will
(a. 4). That is to say, man can be truly happy even with the
loss of health, insufficiency of temporal goods, and the lack of
friends in this life. The attainment of temporal happiness is
possible, for it is within the powers of man and nature; however, attainment of ultimate happiness, the eternal vision of God,
is beyond the powers of pure nature (a. 5). The true ultimate
happiness of man is a gift of God, attainable only through grace.
Not every man desires this ultimate beatitude, "which God has
prepared for them that love Him," either because they do not
know about it or dismiss it as of little consequence (a. 8).

The rest of the second part of the *Summa* is devoted to understanding the means of attaining happiness. Since the attainment
of happiness is a human achievement, Thomas discusses the
nature of human acts, that is, acts which belong to man as a
rational and responsible person (qq. 7–21), then the emotional
life of man (qq. 22–48), virtues and vices in general (qq. 49–
70), and sin (qq. 71–89)—all of which have to do with personal
achievement in general. However, in order to direct one's self
in the personal attainment of these means to happiness, one
must examine two external guidelines: law (qq. 90–108) and
grace (qq. 109–14). Thomas's insight into the nature of law,
particularly the new law of grace, is surpassed only by his discussion of grace itself. Unfortunately many modern commentators have wrenched Thomas's teaching on natural law out of
context and have distorted it; similarly certain aspects of his
teaching on grace have been distorted. Frequently they fail to
see that Thomas's approach is derived from St. Augustine's *De
spiritu et littera,* and *De natura et gratia.* The discussion of law
in general and of the natural law in particular does not constitute
Thomas's full teaching on the foundations of natural law. In
I–II, these are only preliminary questions for his principal interest, which is the Old Law and the New Law of the covenant
which God made with His people.

Having discussed virtues and vices and all other things that pertain to moral matters in general (I–II), Thomas then devotes the largest part of the *Summa*, the *secunda secundae* (II–II), to a detailed discussion of each virtue in particular, together with its corresponding vice and concomitant aspects. First he discusses virtues in detail as they pertain to all men in society (qq. 1–179), and then as they pertain to man in different states of life, namely episcopal and religious life, both contemplative and active (qq. 179–89).

In the whole of his moral teaching, Thomas sees the life of virtue as the foundation of man's happiness. Instead of emphasizing the "seven deadly sins," the ten commandments, or the vices to be shunned, he constructs his theology of happiness in a positive way through virtue vivified by love. A habit, for Thomas and for the ancients, is an active quality acquired or infused into the soul whereby man performs actions easily and assuredly in a given area of activity. Habits, good or bad, constitute a second nature; once acquired, they are difficult to shake. Whereas many personal idiosyncrasies would be called "habits" in English, they would not be called "habitus" in scholastic language. Good habits are called virtues, whereas bad habits are called vices. For Aristotle and Thomas, virtue is a *mean* between two extremes that are vices. The English expression "virtue lies in the middle between two extremes" can be misleading; the virtue of charity, or love, for example, is itself an extreme, and justice knows no extreme—only deficiency. After a detailed discussion of the three theological virtues, faith, hope, and charity, he analyzes the four cardinal virtues, prudence, justice, fortitude, and temperance. Since the cardinal virtues have an extraordinary number of aspects, integral parts, as well as potential parts that must be considered in detail in order to appreciate the true condition of man, this part of the *Summa* is understandably the longest. It reveals Thomas's profound insight into the human condition. Without fear of contradiction, one could say that II–II far surpasses anything written by earlier and many modern theologians or philosophers. But it would be a mistake to study II–II apart from the basic principles established in I–II.

The last eleven questions of II–II deal with the contemplative and active life, their comparison, and the "states" of religious perfection. This is not to ask who is higher than who in spiritual perfection. It is, rather, to ask about the theological implications of canonically established states, such as one finds among religious Orders and the episcopal state. Although Thomas does not mention the point, his theological analysis would also apply to the Pope as bishop of Rome. For Thomas, religious Orders, both contemplative and active, share in the perfection of the episcopal authority. The place of mendicant friars in such a hierarchy was the main point of dispute in the antimendicant controversy.

Thomas composed this section of the *Summa* when the controversy, under the leadership of Gérard d'Abbeville (d. 1272), was fection. It is, rather, to ask about the theological implications of at its height. For Thomas, religious Orders are distinguished primarily by the end intended and secondarily by the means employed in its attainment. Thus contemplative Orders, such as the Cistercian and the Benedictine, are intended primarily for personal salvation through work and contemplation of eternal truth. Active Orders, those devoted to external activity (such as hospitalers, those founded for ransoming captives, etc.), are directed to temporal and spiritual works of mercy. Orders having the same final goal must be distinguished by the means (*exercitii*). Since contemplation is more perfect than external works, the contemplative Orders are higher in perfection than active Orders. But there are two kinds of external activity: those involving preaching, teaching, and the salvation of souls, and those involving temporal activity. The highest state, therefore, is one devoted to contemplation and directed toward giving the fruits of one's contemplation and study to others by preaching, teaching, and hearing confessions. "Therefore those [Orders] ordained to preaching hold the highest state among religious orders; and they are the closest to the perfection of bishops, . . . for just as it is better to illumine than to shine, so it is better to give to others the fruits of one's contemplation, than simply to contemplate" (II–II, 188, 6). Therefore, for Thomas, the Order that is dedicated to preaching is the highest state of religious perfection, sharing the highest perfection of bishops. There can be no doubt that Thomas had in mind the Dominican Order, which has as its goal the salvation of souls through preaching, involving, as it does, the means of study, community life, choral office, and the solemn vows of poverty, chastity, and obedience.

The last three questions of this part encompass all the theological arguments of the secular masters against the mendicant friars: their right to preach, teach, hear confessions, beg, and receive boys into the Order. These three questions, in fact, summarize all the arguments of the secular masters, who believed that friars had no right to exist, least of all for preaching and teaching. Without condescending to polemics in the controversy, Thomas considered and refuted each point soberly.

Gérard d'Abbeville was still alive when this part of the *Summa* was being written. Modern Thomists, for the most part ignorant of the antimendicant controversy, dismiss these questions as irrelevant and insignificant. However, they were very relevant and significant when Thomas wrote them. To understand these questions fully one must know the arguments of the opposition and read them in conjunction with the larger polemical treatises against William of Saint-Amour and Gérard d'Abbeville.

According to I. T. Eschmann, Thomas began the *secunda secundae* late in 1270 or early in 1271; it seems to have been completed before the end of the academic year 1272. But Thomas did not stop there for long. Rather, he seems to have begun the third part, on Christ and the sacraments, in 1272 and to have stopped abruptly on December 6, 1273. Eschmann estimates that Thomas could have finished as many as the first twenty questions of the third part before his departure for Naples. This will be discussed in the following chapter. However, it would seem that the disputed question *De unione verbi incarnati* was held at Paris early in 1272 when he was beginning the section on the Incarnate Word for the third part of the *Summa*. These questions will be discussed in the next chapter when we come to consider the last years of Thomas's life, in Naples.

For the moment we must retrace our steps and consider the real reason for Thomas's return to Paris in the winter of 1268–69.

Mendicants and Renewed Opposition

The second phase of opposition against the mendicant Orders was well under way by the time Thomas arrived in Paris. We have already argued that this growing opposition was the real reason why Thomas was sent back to Paris for a second time—not

Latin Averroism. It was also the reason why the authorities decided to send Peter of Tarentaise back to his chair in the fall of 1267. Opposition was triggered when William of Saint-Amour, exiled to his native village since summer of 1257, sent his *Collationes catholicae* to the new French Pope, Clement IV, by October 1266. William obviously felt that a French Pope would be sympathetic to the claims of the French hierarchy, who resented the encroachment of mendicant friars on their rights, specifically of preaching, hearing confessions, caring for souls, and collecting fees and donations within their own dioceses. Above all, the French bishops resented papal authority in their own dioceses in the guise of mendicant friars, who claimed exemption from local bishops. Eschmann frequently referred to this attitude of the French hierarchy as Gallicanism "ante nomen."[33]

In response to William of Saint-Amour's charges, which were the same as those made eleven years earlier in his *De periculis*, Clement IV renewed the privileges of Alexander IV in a bull issued on February 28, 1267. These privileges were the very ones that the French hierarchy and the French masters at the university wanted suppressed, for they infringed on the rights of seculars.

One interesting feature of the second phase of the controversy, which continued until December 1271, is that it did not arouse the populace of Paris; there were none of those riots, physical assaults, and insults that characterized the first phase, which required royal archers to protect Saint-Jacques. The second phase, though extremely bitter and vociferous, was conducted through the university media of Advent and Lenten quodlibets, sermons, and polemical treatises. The charge of being false preachers and false prophets announced by the Abbot Joachim was dropped from the list of charges, while a new charge was added, namely, the acceptance of young boys into religious Orders. The main issue, however, remained the same: the right of mendicant friars to exist in the Church. Basically the seculars maintained that no Order in the Church can be established on mendicancy, for begging is sinful for anyone who can work with his hands. No Order can be established whose goal is preaching and the care of souls, for this right belongs to the bishops and their clergy. Finally, no one can hear confessions in any diocese without faculties from the local bishop; no one, not even the Pope, could overrule the divine law in this matter. On more practical grounds, the seculars resented the loss of revenue that was diverted from them to the mendicants. Frequently it happened that a dying man would give all his possessions to the priest who heard his last confession. Generally the laity were more generous with the mendicants, whose evangelical poverty they admired and whose counsel they consequently sought.

Intrinsic to the main issue was the question of spiritual perfection and the role of evangelical poverty. Both Bonaventure and Thomas realized that the question was not who is more perfect than who, but who is in the *state* of perfection, canonically established by divine law and the Church. Because of this state every member was obliged to seek perfection always; it did not presuppose that men were already perfect when they professed the life of poverty, chastity, and obedience, but it did impose on all members an obligation to seek personal sanctity. The role of poverty in this perfection was controverted not only by the seculars against the mendicants, but also among the mendicant Orders themselves. Not only did the seculars feel that "evangelical poverty" was an attack on the wealth of the Church, but also that it was heretical to claim or imply that Jesus and his companions had no money in common. This last point was heatedly controverted among the Franciscans. Some of them maintained that evangelical poverty was of the essence of perfection to such an extent that not even the community could claim anything as its own; they claimed that they could not profess this kind of poverty unless all possessions were "owned" by the Holy See. These "brown" Franciscans eventually became known as the spirituals. Others sided more with the Dominican view of poverty, declaring that while no member could claim anything as his own, temporal goods could be held in common by the Order as such. These "black" Franciscans eventually became known as the conventuals. The Dominicans, on the other hand, never experienced this kind of rift in the Order. For them, evangelical poverty, while basic to the life of the counsels, was not the essence of spirituality. Thomas echoed the Dominican spirit when he insisted that charity alone is the essence of perfection.

On New Year's Day 1269, Gérard d'Abbeville preached a sermon in the Franciscan church in Paris defending the wealth of the Church and the original donation of Constantine to Pope Sylvester, whose feast had been celebrated on the previous day. He took this opportunity to denounce one theory of evangelical poverty—actually one of the Franciscan views—as a veiled and heretical attack on the Church, its possessions, and wealth. Thomas had not yet arrived in Paris, but Bonaventure and John Pecham were undoubtedly in the congregation.

From the beginning of March 1269, when Thomas held his first Lenten quodlibet, until December 1271, when he held his fifth, the controversy continued in the schools between Thomas and Gérard d'Abbeville in the Lenten and Advent quodlibets. Bonaventure and John Pecham wrote treatises defending the mendicant Orders and attacking the arguments presented by Gérard and Nicholas of Lisieux.[84] Although Gérard d'Abbeville did not die until November 8, 1272, the open controversy in the schools came to an end in December 1271; Thomas was then free to return to Italy in the following summer. William of Saint-Amour died on September 13, 1272; and the young Gérard d'Abbeville died two months later. During the three and a half years Thomas was in Paris, he was constantly involved in this polemic.

In the summer of 1269, Gérard published a book called *Contra adversarium perfectionis christianae*, composed twelve years earlier against the Franciscan Thomas of York, who had entered the controversy during its first period. Gérard did not publish this work at that time because of the condemnation of William's *De periculis*. However, with the death of Clement IV on November 29, 1268, the Holy See was vacant, and Gérard took the opportunity to publish his early work without fear of condemnation. Bonaventure replied to this work in his *Apologia pauperum* in the fall of 1269.

During the last few months of 1269 and the first few months of 1270, Thomas Aquinas composed a sober work entitled *De perfectione spiritualis vitae*, an apology of religious Orders, in which he explained the nature of perfection, the nature of the three monastic vows as aids to perfection, the meaning of various states of perfection, and the insistence that only bishops and religious can be in a state (*status*) of perfection, while parish priests, curates, and archdeacons cannot be. Gérard d'Abbeville, archdeacon of Ponthieu and Cambrai, did not take kindly to this denigration of the lower clergy.

For Thomas, perfection consists in charity, in loving God above all things and one's neighbor as one's self. This is a precept of the divine law, binding on every Christian, whether he belongs to a state of perfection or not. The means of perfection are available to all Christians, and all must make use of them. However, for Thomas, there are three areas in life that make the attainment of perfection difficult: wealth, sex, and one's own will. To obviate these difficulties, the Lord counseled poverty, chastity, and obedience, not for all Christians but only for those who want to bind themselves by public and solemn vows to the constant pursuit of perfection in a religious "state." "Thus it is evident that some people are perfect, who do not have a state of perfection, while others have the state of perfection, but are not perfect" (c. 15).

To take on a state of perfection means to bind one's self totally and permanently to the pursuit of perfection with the aid of the three vows. Since all religious take these three vows, they are constituted in a permanent *status*.[35] Bishops too are in a state of permanent dedication by their consecration, for as bishops they are obliged to love their enemies, as Christ and the Apostles did, to lay down their lives for their brethren, either by exposing themselves to the danger of death or by devoting their whole life to the service of others, and by administering spiritual goods to their neighbor, as true mediators between God and man. According to Thomas, this threefold service to the people of God constitutes a *state* higher than that of religious. While all Christians should serve others, the bishop by reason of his consecration is bound to give his whole life to the service of others, as Christ and the Apostles did. This is the *officium*, the duty, of bishops. Hence they are constituted in a state of perfection, whereas parish priests, curates, and archdeacons are not, precisely because they lack the permanence and stability of consecration or religious profession.[36]

Thomas's treatise *De perfectione* in twenty-three chapters was written within a few months in either 1269 or 1270. Within a matter of a few weeks, a list of objections and counterarguments came to Thomas's attention, which he felt should be answered immediately. These objections, undoubtedly raised by Gérard d'Abbeville, tried to prove that parish priests, curates, and archdeacons are in a higher state of perfection than religious. The list of these objections and Thomas's replies constitute chapters 24 to 30 of the new "edition" of *De perfectione,* added in January or February 1270.

Throughout the spring and summer of 1270 the debate raged in the schools and in polemical treatises. Between April and June, Nicholas of Lisieux replied to Thomas in his *De perfectione status clericorum,* and at the same time he culled twenty-three errors that he found in the works of Thomas. Between February and July, John Pecham defended the role of poverty in the spiritual life in his *Tractatus pauperis,* and again in *De paupertate,* written in November.

Already by 1269 a new charge had entered the controversy, namely, the acceptance of boys into religious life. In January 1270, John Pecham defended this practice in his *De pueris oblatis;* throughout spring and summer this became one of the crucial points of debate. Even Roger Bacon decried the fact that mendicant Orders were accepting mere "boys" (*pueri*) into their ranks, but it is not clear what is meant by "boys" or the way in which they were "accepted." Possibly both Thomas and John Pecham were defending a common practice over which they had no control. Although the Dominican constitution of the day expressly forbade the reception of boys under the age of eighteen, it would seem that some boys under this age were received, at least without vows. A statute of Innocent IV commanded that a year's probation be enjoined on anyone who wanted to enter religious life, and prohibited anyone being bound by vows before the age of fourteen, the commonly accepted age for puberty among boys.

At the beginning of Lent 1271 Thomas discussed the question of "boys" entering religious life (*Quodl. 4,* aa. 23-24). Shortly after this, probably in the summer of 1271, Thomas wrote his second major treatise "against Gérard," called *Contra doctrinam retrahentium a religione,* commonly known as *Contra retrahentes.*[37] This treatise is a refutation of all those arguments used to deter young men from entering religious life. Gérard d'Abbeville used three basic avenues of attack: (1) no one should enter religious life and the practice of the counsels until he has first mastered the precepts of the law; (2) no one should enter until he has deliberated a long time and taken counsel of many friends and relatives; (3) no one should bind himself by *vow* to embrace the religious life.

As to the first point, Gérard misunderstands the relationship between the counsels and the commandments, for the observance of the commandments and counsels are ordained to the same end, the love of God above all things and one's neighbor as one's self. The counsels are a means of increasing this love, and so are a means of observing the commandments. Since by means of the counsels, the precepts can more easily and more perfectly be kept, it follows that by means of the counsels, men can attain to the perfect love of God and of their neighbor. "Hence we see that, although in intention, this precept [of love] precedes the counsels, yet in prosecution, the counsels precede this precept" (c. 7).

As to the second point, if the inspiration to enter religious life is from the Holy Spirit, it must be followed as quickly as possible. At the command of Jesus the Apostles left everything to follow Him. Too much advice from friends can be detrimental; and the advice of relatives especially is not to be trusted.

As to the third point, the assumption is that it is better to perform good works without being bound by any obligation, such as a vow, whereas the truth is that good works done under vow are more meritorious than those performed without any such obligation. By vows religious strengthen their wills in constancy and resolution so as to observe the commandments more faithfully. A vow is an act of *latria*, that is, a promise made to God concerning those things which relate to His worship. Hence all lower acts of the will are rendered more perfect and meritorious by being motivated by the higher act of religion.

The case of children taking vows is a special question because it involves responsibility for their action or the action of their parents. Thomas distinguishes two kinds of vows to enter religion: simple and solemn. A simple vow, for him, is no more than a promise to enter religious life when the time comes. A solemn vow, by which a man becomes a monk or friar, is religious profession, which must be preceded by a year's probation (*Sum. theol.* II–II, 189, 2 ad 1). A simple vow, being no more than a promise to God that proceeds from an interior deliberation of the mind, can be invalid for one of two reasons: by a defect of deliberation on the part of the one promising, such as insane persons or children, who have not reached the age of reason, or by a defect of the subject promising something that is not his to give, such as slaves and children before the age of puberty. For Thomas, children before the age of reason, or moral discretion, belong to the father, who can accept or reject the promise made. Likewise a child on reaching the age of reason can accept or reject a promise made by the parents, as was the case in Thomas's own childhood and youth. The age of moral discretion for the most part (*frequentius*) occurs at the time of puberty, which for boys is generally fourteen, and for girls twelve. In certain instances the age of moral discretion can be advanced or retarded by a few months, depending on the disposition of nature. The important point is that only a person who has reached the age of reason, the age of moral discretion, or the age at which he is capable of doing wrong deliberately (*doli capaces*), is capable of making a true solemn vow to enter religion (*Sum. theol.* II–II, 189, 5). Since it is difficult to know the precise time at which a boy reaches the age of reason, the practice of the Church is to recognize puberty as the critical moment of responsibility, which is generally the age of fourteen for boys. Consequently boys who have reached the age of moral discretion are capable of making solemn profession in a religious Order. The question is not whether boys of fourteen should be admitted to religious life, but whether they *can* be, according to the laws of the Church and sound philosophy.[38]

Thomas concludes his *Contra retrahentes* by saying that this is all that occurs to him at the moment against the "pernicious and erroneous teaching" which deters young men from entering religious life. "If any man desires to contradict my words, let him not do so by chattering before boys, but let him write and publish his writings, so that intelligent persons may judge what is true, and may be able to confute what is false by the authority of the Truth." These are indeed strong words coming from Thomas. Evidently Gérard d'Abbeville and the Geraldini promulgated their views among students of the arts faculty in Paris and deterred some from entering the mendicant Orders.

An interesting light is shed upon Thomas's view of boys in "religious life" in two questions he disputed at the beginning of Lent 1271, *De ingressu puerorum in religione;* these two questions have been attached to *Quodlibet 4* as articles 23 and 24. In these two questions Thomas defends the acceptance of boys before the age of puberty, because the things we learn in childhood are more firmly inculcated within us. Thomas undoubtedly had in mind his own experience at Monte Cassino where he had been an oblate. In *Quodlibet 4,* a. 23, Thomas says nothing about the mendicant Orders, but answers the question in general with special reference to the immemorial custom of the Benedictines. For Thomas it was admirable for parents to send their youngest son to a monastery to be taught the ways of sanctity. But when the youth has reached the age of puberty, he must make up his own mind whether to take vows in the community or not. As we have seen, Thomas was about nineteen years old when he received the Dominican habit. We do not know for certain what his religious status was between the ages of fourteen and nineteen. But, following Eschmann, I have argued that he was simply a layman; all indications, even though circumstantial, seem to suggest this to have been the case. One thing is certain: Thomas never regretted having been a Benedictine oblate. But again in *Quodlibet 4,* a. 23, Thomas makes it clear that when such an oblate reaches the age of reason, i.e., puberty, he must ratify the offering made by his parents or withhold it. Unfortunately Thomas gives us no autobiographical information.

Only briefly and in passing does Thomas refer to the antimendicant controversy in his Advent quodlibet of December 1271. By this date the controversy was over, but no real solution was found to the main problem. The mendicants still clung to their privilege of preaching, hearing confessions, caring for souls, and begging for sustenance. A partial solution was found in 1300, when Boniface VIII in his bull *Super cathedram* declared that mendicants working in a diocese should first obtain a formal license from the local bishop. By this time it was becoming evident that papal privileges given to the mendicants in the early thirteenth century were impractical and a serious detriment to the rights of the bishop. The right of exemption from jurisdiction of the local ordinary eventually was limited to internal affairs of individual priories.

While such momentous problems were argued in the faculty of theology at Paris, the faculty of arts had its own serious problems.

Latin Averroism and the Aristotelian Commentaries

"Latin Averroism" is a modern label given to a complex of doctrines arising from the teaching of Averroes and accepted by certain members of the arts faculty at the University of Paris in the second half of the thirteenth century concerning certain radical teachings of Aristotle, even when those teachings contradicted the true doctrine of the Catholic faith. The term "Latin Averroism" was introduced by Mandonnet in his pioneer work of 1899, *Siger de Brabant et l'Averroïsme latin au XIIIᵉ siècle,* revised during the following decade. That Siger of Brabant (in what is now Belgium) was the leader of such a movement is evident from his own works and his involvement in the Parisian condemnations of 1270 and 1277. Some modern historians of thirteenth-century scholasticism, such as F. Van Steenberghen, object to the title "Averroism," claiming that Averroes was not the sole influence on the thought of such leaders as Siger of Brabant and Boethius of Dacia; but this objection is not to the point. The point is that the critical doctrines involved, such as the unicity of the intellect for all men, the denial of free will, the restriction of divine providence, and the eternity of the world, were, in fact, derived from the commentaries of Averroes on Aristotle. These men, according to Albert, so deified Aristotle that his teaching was considered identical with the whole truth attainable by human reason, while Averroes was considered, on the whole, his best interpreter. Averroes was "the Commentator" on Aristotle—a title Averroes had even before the rise of Latin Averroism. Thomas in his polemical treatise of 1270 "against master Siger" on the unicity of the intellect calls his opponents "Averroists," at least in some MSS; this seems to be the earliest use of the term. There is little use in arguing about the name, as long as the reality intended is understood.

Very little is known about Siger of Brabant, the leader of this movement to free philosophy from the directives of faith. Literary posterity would remember Siger from Dante's *Divine Comedy*. In the fourth heaven, the abode of the wise, Dante depicts a circle of twelve wise men of the past, the youngest of whom is Siger, whom Thomas Aquinas introduces: "This figure, which your eyes encounter as they return towards me, is the light of a spirit, who, wrapt in grave thoughts, found death slow in coming. This is the eternal light of Siger, who, when he taught in the Street of Straw, established unwelcome truths" (*Paradiso* X, 133–38). This last is a reference to the rue de Fouarre (*vico straminis*), where Siger and all the masters in arts taught. His "unwelcome truths" refer to the propositions condemned by the bishop of Paris in 1270 and again in 1277. Historians and literary critics still argue about the significance of Siger's presence in heaven in the circle of wise men in the company of Thomas Aquinas, Albert the Great, Peter Lombard, Solomon, Dionysius the Areopagite, Orosius, Boethius, Isidore of Seville, Venerable Bede, and Richard of Saint-Victor. We will make no attempt to resolve this problem.[39]

The first mention of Siger in the documents occurs in 1266, when he was cited as one of the leaders of dissension among the four nations making up the faculty of arts at Paris; terms of reconciliation were imposed by the cardinal legate Simon of Brion.[40] By that time he was a young master in arts belonging to the Picard nation, not past his middle twenties. The thirteen propositions condemned on December 10, 1270, are clearly from his writings and public teaching.[41] In 1271 he was again involved in a dispute in the faculty of arts, this time over the election of a rector. On April 1, 1272, masters in arts were forbidden to discuss theological questions or to determine anything in philosophy that is contrary to the faith.[42] All of these facts were known to Friar Thomas d'Aquino, who took a special interest in Siger. Later, on November 23, 1276—after the death of Thomas—Siger was summoned along with two other masters from Brabant, Goswin of La Chapell and Bernier of Nivelles, to appear before the inquisitor of France, Simon du Vale, to answer the charge of heresy. From this point on, events become hazy. One chronicler wrote: "At that time there flourished Albert of the Order of Preachers, extraordinary in doctrine and knowledge, who refuted master Siger extensively in his writings. This Siger, a native of Brabant, not secure enough to remain in Paris, since he held certain opinions contrary to the faith, went to the Roman curia [in Viterbo] and perished there after a short time, stabbed by his almost demented assistant."[43] Although John Pecham was confused about the facts in the case, he seems to refer to Siger's "miserable" death in a letter to the Oxford chancellor on November 10, 1284.[44] Because of this letter, many historians state that Siger died before November 10, 1284. But Pecham refers to the "two principal defenders or perhaps inventors" of the heresy, who died miserably in transalpine territory; this second person is commonly thought to be Boethius of Dacia, about whom even less is known. It is also said that Boethius became a Dominican to escape the censure of excommunication by becoming a member of an exempt religious Order.[45] After the discovery and publication of the De aeternitate mundi by Boethius of Dacia, there is no doubt that he too was envisaged in the condemnations of 1270 and 1277, where he is explicitly implicated.[46]

Siger of Brabant, Boethius of Dacia, "and the others" were cited to appear before the ecclesiastical authorities on the charge of *heresy*, not just bad philosophy. They dared to hold conclusions of philosophy which were directly opposed to the teaching of faith. If it were only a matter of philosophy, the Parisian authorities would not have bothered too much, nor would Thomas have taken the whole situation so seriously. As it was, the tenor of Latin Averroism was directly contrary to the faith and to the basic assumption of thirteenth-century theologians that there can be no contradiction between the truths of faith and the conclusions of philosophy. Throughout his whole life Thomas maintained that every argument presented against the faith could not be a true demonstration, but a sophism which contains within itself a philosophical error. In other words, for Thomas and most thirteenth-century authorities, the harmony between faith and reason is a reality, since both come from God, and God cannot contradict Himself. The Latin Averroists, on the other hand, proposed arguments from Aristotle and Averroes, such as the eternity of the world, unicity of the human intellect, denial of personal immortality, denial of human responsibility for decisions made, etc., that were proposed as necessary conclusions of true philosophy, even though they happened to contradict truths of faith. Both Siger and Boethius, however, were careful not to call these conclusions "truths" of reason, but fruits of reason. At the critical moment they maintained that only doctrines of faith, based on "miracles and revelation," are, strictly speaking, true. Nevertheless they vehemently defended the right of the philosopher to go as far as he can within his own domain without the supervision of faith. They perhaps did not maintain that there were two contradictory "truths," one for philosophy, the other for faith, but they came very close to believing it, since for them philosophy is the highest happiness attainable by man in this life, and according to philosophy there is no life hereafter. The bishop of Paris was careful to say in 1277 that these philosophers spoke "as though they were two contrary truths." Surely, if philosophy is the highest goal of man, it must reach truth, not just necessary conclusions that were probable! In any case, Siger and Boethius were careful to state that absolute truth belongs to faith, which was beyond their properly philosophical premises. Nevertheless they demanded the right to philosophize and maintain conclusions drawn from their own principles of philosophy.

The catalyst that triggered the controversy was Averroes's exegesis of Aristotle's *De anima* III, 5, 430a10-25, where he speaks of the intellect as "separable, impassible, unmixed," as well as "immortal and eternal." This passage is difficult, and many commentators have puzzled over it, from the time of Alexander of Aphrodisias (c. A.D. 200) onward. Alexander in his commentary spoke of three kinds of intellect: the active intellect (*noûs poietikos*), which is distinct from man and to be identified with God the supreme light; the material or potential intellect (*noûs physikòs*), which belongs to each man, a *vis cogitativa* that corrupts at death; and an acquired intellect (*noûs 'epíktetos*), which is the conjunction or continuation of the other two in knowing eternal truths (*intellectus adeptus*). For Averroes this last is the possible intellect, a "kind of separate substance," which knows; it is physically separated from all matter, one for all men, and immortal. In the view of Averroes, knowledge and human happiness consist in the union of man's *vis cogitativa* with the possible intellect by means of the agent intellect illuminating the phantasms. From this it follows that such an intellectual power cannot be the substantial form by which man is constituted what he is; this function must be fulfilled by the "human soul," which is corruptible. From this it follows that man's soul is not immortal, nor is it really responsible for its actions, which are determined necessarily by intellect and by circumstances. From this it also follows that man is not subject to reward or punishment in this life or the next. Clearly such conclusions were contrary to the faith and had to be condemned as heretical.

Stephen Tempier, bishop of Paris, condemned thirteen propositions that constituted the heart of Latin Averroism on December 10, 1270, when Thomas was in the middle of his second full academic year in Paris:

1. That the intellect of all men is one and numerically the same.
2. That it is false or improper to say, "Man understands."
3. That the will of man wills or chooses necessarily.
4. That everything that happens here in the sublunar world is governed by the necessity of celestial bodies.
5. That the world is eternal.
6. That there never was a first man.
7. That the soul, which is the form of man inasmuch as he is man, corrupts on the corruption of the body.
8. That the soul separated after death does not suffer from corporeal fire.
9. That free will is a passive power, not an active one; and that it is moved necessarily by the appetible object.
10. That God does not know singulars.
11. That God does not know anything other than Himself.
12. That human actions are not governed by the providence of God.
13. That God cannot grant immortality or incorruptibility to a corruptible or mortal thing.

This list of propositions, unlike the hasty list of 1277, is carefully and logically drawn up with the fundamental error listed first, and the rest flowing more or less logically therefrom.

It would seem that this list of propositions was in circulation in the faculty of theology for some time before the actual condemnation. A list of fifteen propositions taught in the schools of Paris by those "who are reputed to be the foremost in philosophy" was sent to Albert the Great by Friar Giles of Lessines, a Dominican, who had studied under Albert. Of these fifteen propositions, thirteen are identical with the list condemned by Tempier, while the last two are new:

1. That the body of Christ lying in the tomb and hanging on the cross is not, or was not, numerically the same absolutely (*simpliciter*), but only relatively (*secundum quid*).
2. That an angel and a [human] soul are simple, but not with an absolute simplicity, nor by increase in composition, but only by decrease from the highest simple being.[47]

Mandonnet was under the impression that these two propositions reflect the teaching of Thomas and were somehow expunged from the final list of thirteen. Van Steenberghen, however, notes that these two were rejected by Albert just as the others were, and that the compilation belongs to the years 1273–76. Moreover he rejects the thesis that these last two propositions belong to Thomas.[48] Whatever must be said about the fifteen theses sent to Albert, we can be certain that the last two do not belong to Latin Averroism, nor do they have anything to do with Thomas's teaching. Albert even observes that the fourteenth proposition, concerning Christ's body on the cross and in the tomb, does not belong to the realm of philosophy.[49]

Before the condemnation of 1270, Thomas wrote a tightly argued refutation of Siger's arguments concerning the nature of the human intellect. In the early catalogues it is called *De unitate intellectus, contra Averroistas Parisienses*.[50] Grabmann notes that the Oxford Corpus Christi College MS 225 concludes with the statement: "Thomas wrote this [work] against master Siger of Brabant and many other regents in philosophy at Paris in the year of our Lord 1270."[51] Many attempts have been made to identify the particular treatise Thomas refuted, and thus far this work has not been identified. The lost work of Siger *De intellectu*, known to A. Nifo, seems to have been a reply to Thomas; and Siger's questions *De anima intellectiva*, published by Mandonnet, seem to have been written later. Judging from the concluding paragraph of *De unitate*, one might say that

Thomas's work was directed to the oral teaching of Siger and his colleagues.[52]

In five well-constructed chapters Thomas argues (1) that the possible intellect is not a substance separate in being by the authority of Aristotle (c. 1) and of other Peripatetics (c. 2), and by arguments from reason (c. 3); and (2) that the possible intellect is not one for all men by arguments especially from Aristotle (c. 4), and by refutation of the adversaries' arguments (c. 5). This kind of literary exegesis of Aristotle's text was exactly what was needed to undermine the assumptions made by Siger. Thomas concludes: "from this careful examination of almost all the words of Aristotle concerning the human intellect it is clear that he was of the opinion that the human soul is the act of the body [i.e., the substantial form of man], and that the possible intellect is a part, or power of that soul." In reply to appeals from authority, Thomas was able to show that neither Themistius nor Theophrastus supported the conclusion of Averroes; this Thomas was able to show by his own reading of Themistius' commentary on De anima translated by William of Moerbeke toward the end of 1267. In his rational arguments Thomas was able to show that the intellective soul of man is the unique substantial form of each man, and that the intellect is a "power of the soul," a potentia animae, one for each man.

The crux of the problem is a metaphysical one, and a very difficult one. In the eyes of Siger, "the two leading men in philosophy, Albert and Thomas,"[53] hold that "the substance of the intellective soul is united to the body, giving it being [esse], while the power of the intellective soul is separate from the body, since it does not operate through a corporeal organ." The decisive argument for Siger was: "If a substance is united with matter, its power to operate cannot be separated from matter."[54] This argument is based on one of the fundamental principles of metaphysics: agere sequitur esse—the manner of acting (agere) depends on the manner of being (esse). Thus, if the structure of esse depends upon matter, so must its activity (agere), and conversely, if its activity is separated from matter, so must its being (esse). In the face of this metaphysical argument, all one can say is that the facts of the case prove that man is unique in all of creation: he has a spiritual soul that informs the body giving it human existence, and at the same time he has functions, such as thinking, that transcend the organ he uses, the brain. This transcendence for Thomas proves that the soul is *separable* and immortal, but not here and now *separate*.

Thomas concludes his vigorous treatise *De unitate* by noting that he has not attacked the error of Averroes "by the teaching of faith, but by arguments and words of the philosophers themselves." He goes on to say that if anyone wishes to attack the arguments presented, "let him not speak in corners, nor in the presence of boys who do not know how to judge about such difficult matters, but let him write against this treatise, if he has sufficient courage." This statement suggests that Thomas was not writing against a particular work written by Siger, but against the best arguments proposed by the Averroists themselves in their classroom teaching, *reportationes,* and the like. Thomas clearly showed that the error stems not from Aristotle, nor from the Peripatetic school, nor from true reason, but from Averroes, who must be called "not so much a peripatetic as a perverter of peripatetic philosophy." Thus Siger and his followers must be called not so much Aristotelians as perverters of Aristotle and followers of Averroes.

Unfortunately the *De unitate intellectus* of Thomas, brilliant though it was, came too late; it did not convince Siger of Brabant of his error. As far as we can tell from the extant authentic writings of Siger, he did not become a Thomist, as some have claimed. Perhaps Thomas's *De unitate* deterred some younger masters in arts from becoming Averroists. But it would seem that neither the *De unitate* nor the bishop's condemnation of December 10, 1270, prevented the growth of Averroism; it was still vigorous enough to be condemned again in the hasty proclamation of March 7, 1277.

All the condemned propositions of 1270 had been rejected by Albert and Thomas during the preceding two decades. Both Albert and Thomas had examined and rejected the critical Averroist interpretation of Aristotle, as well as of the eternity of the world, throughout the 1250s and 1260s, well before Siger of Brabant promulgated his views on the unicity of the human intellect. Why was it that Siger seems not to have been influenced by "the two leading men in philosophy, Albert and

Thomas"? The explanation seems to be (1) that Albert's philosophical paraphrases avoided the exegesis of the text, and (2) that Thomas's teaching was mainly confined to works of theology, which most masters or students in arts were not likely to read. What was needed was an exegetical guide to Aristotle. The only one available was the one composed by Averroes, who in many passages was not so much an Aristotelian as a perverter of Aristotle.

The shocking truth was that young men, trying to understand the Philosopher, and using the only exegetical guide available, were led into heresy and thereby incurred excommunication. Here was a situation that cried out for help early enough in the philosophical formation of young men. In the 1270s there could no longer be suppressions and proscriptions of Aristotle's works. As late as 1263 Urban IV renewed the ancient prohibition against the study of Aristotle's writings, but to no avail; the study of Aristotle was mandatory for students in arts from at least 1255 onward.[55] The text of Aristotle had been circulated far too widely to be stopped, and all masters in theology as well as in arts were rightly or wrongly influenced by his teaching.

In the 1270s there was growing hostility to an Aristotle that could not be suppressed, particularly from such a man as Bonaventure, who himself was once a master in arts in the University of Paris. As the Averroist movement increased in Paris, so did Bonaventure's denunciations of the Philosopher increase in vigor. For him the use of Aristotle in theology was mixing darkness with pure light, water with wine, error with truth. Bonaventure was not the only theologian inveighing against the invasion of pagan philosophers. There was a large group of conservative and Augustinist theologians, who triumphed in 1277, but who could not suppress the reading of Aristotle or any other pagan philosopher.

Not only the condemnation of 1270, but the whole build-up of forces leading to it, came as a great shock to Thomas, as Lottin has pointed out.[56] Thomas's love of youth and their education in truth could not have allowed the situation to remain as it was in 1269–70. The plight of young masters who had to teach Aristotle in the schools and who were always subject to being led astray into heresy, especially by Averroes, could not have been ignored. For this reason Thomas considered it his duty to young men in arts to supply them with commentaries that would be true to Aristotle, even when the latter's teaching had to be rejected, and free from error in philosophy. I am convinced that Thomas felt this apostolate to be urgent upon him, and one that he could minister to.

The apostolate was indeed there, but one might wonder whether Thomas had to burn himself out trying to supply the need. He was already working on a *Summa theologiae* for young students in theology, and now he would undertake to guide young students in arts through the intricacies of Aristotle's thought, the "intention of Aristotle" (*intentio Aristotelis*) as well as the text (*littera*). Thomas supplied the much-needed exegetical guide to Aristotle through his *sententiae*, or commentaries, on the major works of Aristotle. One cannot know whether Thomas would have written *sententiae* on all the books of Aristotle if he had not broken down physically and died so young. As it was, Thomas left many commentaries unfinished upon his untimely death at the age of forty-nine.

Among Thomists there is no unanimous opinion why Thomas commented on Aristotle or how these commentaries should be evaluated. Some say that they are no more than paraphrases of Aristotle and of little importance to anyone. Others say that they are the outcome of his lectures to Dominican students. Still others say that these philosophical exercises are of little use to theologians, since all of Thomas's own philosophy is to be found in his theological writings, such as the two *summae*. Naturally those Thomists who neglect the Scripture commentaries and disputed questions of Thomas would also neglect the Aristotelian commentaries. In my opinion Thomas commented on Aristotle because he felt an apostolic need to help young masters in arts to understand Aristotelian philosophy correctly in harmony with the actual text and the guideline of faith, where necessary. Similarly I consider these commentaries to have a great philosophical value, as well as great significance, in the development of Thomas's theology. The least one can say is that Thomas must have considered the valuable time and energy expended on their composition, at the very height of his maturity, worthy and necessary. In other words, Thomas must have thought that they were of sufficient importance for someone to labor over them. If Thomas thought they were important, why should we consider them unimportant? If Thomas had lectured to Dominican students on these books, which he did not, it would be easier to dismiss them. As it was, there was no compulsion to write them other than a deep personal motive to help others in need, namely, the young masters in arts.

There is no unanimity among scholars on the dates of the Aristotelian commentaries; a more detailed discussion of each of them will be found in the brief catalogue at the end of this volume.

With the possible exception of the commentary on *De anima*, which may have been started in Italy around 1268, all the others seem to have been written between 1269 and 1273. There are four general criteria used by scholars to date these commentaries in lieu of an absolute date given in the manuscripts. First, there is the criterion of *Metaphysics* Lambda, that is, the date when Book K (XI) was newly translated from the Greek by Moerbeke and inserted in the *Metaphysics* as Book XI, whereby Lambda, formerly Book XI, became XII. Second, there are certain sources used by Thomas, especially Greek sources, which can be dated directly. Third, there is the Latin version of Aristotle used by Thomas. Finally, there is the development of doctrine; this is the most difficult criterion of all, but one of great importance.

One of the earliest commentaries composed by Thomas was the *Sententia super Physicam* (1269–70). In it Thomas followed closely the commentary of Averroes, rejecting strongly his explanations of local motion and the role of resistance (Bk. IV), and rejecting also the eternity of the world as held by Aristotle and Averroes. Answering the argument that before motion, there must be motion, and before time, there must be time, and consequently an eternal world, Thomas replies that the term "before" must be taken as a *quid imaginativum* in this context, just as the word "beyond" used in the phrase "beyond the heavens." F. Pelster has argued that in the course of composition Thomas changed from an earlier version of Aristotle, the *Physica veteris translationis*, to the Moerbeke version, whose date is unknown.[57]

Early also is the commentary on *Peri hermenias*, dedicated

to the provost of Louvain, and composed in Paris betwen 1269 and 1270 or 1271. Lambda is referred to as XI, while the only sources used by Thomas were the second commentary of Boethius on the *De interpretatione* and Ammonius's commentary, completed by Moerbeke on September 12, 1268. After the long journey from Viterbo to Paris, Thomas reached Paris in January 1269, and could have begun his own commentary on the *Peri hermenias* in the spring of 1269. This work is particularly important for Thomas's views on future contingent propositions and the basis of their veracity. The Aristotelian text used by Thomas was that of Moerbeke, date of revision unknown. Thomas's commentary is unfinished, ending with Book II, lect. 2 (19b26).[58]

The *Sententia super Posteriora Analytica* must also be dated 1269-71. The basic Aristotelian version is that of James of Venice, but Thomas also had at his disposal the revision by Moerbeke.[59] This work is especially important for understanding Thomas's appreciation of the "scientific" process as opposed to dialectical or probable knowledge, and sophistry. Thomas cites a passage from the *Meno* of Plato in I, lect. 3, n. 2, but it is difficult to know whether he had access to the translation by Henricus Aristippus or learned of it from Albert, whose commentary precedes that of Thomas.

In a remarkable study on the *Sententia libri Ethicorum*, R.-A. Gauthier has shown that this commentary was written at the same time as II-II, begun very late in 1270 or early 1271. He further shows that Thomas learned of *Metaphysics* K between lect. 1 and lect. 4 of the first book of the *Ethics*, and that this discovery parallels II-II, qq. 80-81. Furthermore, *Ethics* IV, lect. 8-9, were written shortly before II-II, q. 129, and *Ethics* VII, lect. 10, corresponds to II-II, q. 155. Therefore the *Sententia libri Ethicorum* was composed in Paris at the time that he labored on II-II, which must be placed in the years 1270/71-72. Thus the commentary on the *Ethics* was written during the years 1271-72.[60]

Thomas understood the Platonic nature of the *Liber de causis*, generally attributed to Aristotle, when he read the *Elementatio theologica* of Proclus, translated by Moerbeke and completed on May 18, 1268. Thomas's commentary on *De causis* seems to have been written in the first half of 1272, while he was still in Paris.[61]

The *Sententia super Metaphysicam,* one of the most important commentaries of Thomas, is a textual challenge, since various books were commented on at different times.[62] The commentary on Books II–III was composed after V, lect. 5, to VII, lect. 16; and only from Book V, lect. 20–22, is the Moerbeke version definitely preferred. In any case, the commentary on *Metaphysics* Lambda is prior to the commentary on *De caelo,* which corrects many previous misconceptions, particularly in astronomy.

The commentaries on *De caelo, De generatione,* and *Meteora* were written late in Thomas's career and left unfinished at the time of his death. We know that Thomas refused to comment on *De caelo* until he had seen the commentary of Simplicius on this work; this commentary was translated by Moerbeke and completed on June 15, 1271. Therefore it is said that these three works may have been begun in Paris and been continued in Naples together with the *Metaphysics.* Thus Thomas worked on these commentaries at the same time as he was laboring on the second and third parts of the *Summa.*

In all of these commentaries Thomas carefully observes both the "words" (*verba*) of Aristotle and the "intention" (*intentio*) of Aristotle. When the words were obscure, he relied on parallel passages to determine the *intentio Aristoteles.* The interpretation of Averroes, always carefully kept in mind, is frequently rejected as "fatuous," "erroneous," or "less sound." It is hard to see how these Aristotelian commentaries could be considered a "mere paraphrase of Aristotle," as many authors maintain, or a simple exercise to understand the Stagirite more accurately. Thomas knew the text of Aristotle from his earliest youth, and he had read the commentaries of Averroes even before commenting on the *Sentences,* in which he differed strongly from certain views of the commentator. There was no need for Thomas to comment on Aristotle for his own amusement. He must have seen an academic apostolate demanding his best efforts. This apostolate, as we have said, was the plight of young masters in arts who needed an exegetical guide in order to understand

and teach the Aristotelian books accurately without being led into heresy.

It is interesting to note that all of Thomas's Aristotelian commentaries served their purpose. They were available from the university bookstore even as late as 1304, and early masters in arts relied heavily on them in the fourteenth to the sixteenth centuries.

But not all of his colleagues at Paris sympathized or approved of Thomas's apostolate or of his attempt to utilize Aristotle in theology. Strong opposition came from thirteenth-century Augustinists, not all of whom were Franciscans. This thirteenth-century wing of theologians not only feared an Aristotelianism that could lead to Averroism and its heretical consequences, but they also rejected the use of the pagan to dilute the pure steam of theology. As extreme conservatives, they appealed to the authority of St. Augustine in matters philosophical as well as theological. Probably there would not have been a thirteenth-century Augustinism if there had not developed on the scene a Latin Averroism derived from Aristotle. There certainly would not have been a thirteenth-century Augustinism if Thomas had not used the pagan Aristotle in the service of his theology.

Thomas and Scholastic Augustinism

Augustinism was the refuge of thirteenth-century conservatives in the face of a growing Aristotelianism, particularly in theology. As a group, the strongest opponents of Thomas were the Franciscans, but they were not alone. There were some secular masters, one of whom was certainly Stephen Tempier, bishop of Paris; and there were some of Thomas's own *confrères*, notably Robert Kilwardby, later archbishop of Canterbury. But as a group, the Franciscan masters claimed a tradition of orthodoxy loyal to the real or imagined authority of Augustine. The spokesman for this group during Thomas's second Parisian regency was a Franciscan master, the young and brilliant John Pecham, later archbishop of Canterbury. But Pecham was not alone. Behind him stood the towering figure of Bonaventure, minister general of the Order of Friars Minor. While it would seem that Bonaventure and Thomas respected each other, even though they did not share the same ideas, John Pecham and Thomas frequently stood in open conflict. Pecham's terminology was Aristotelian, but his ideas were often those of Bonaventure in the spirit of true Franciscan theology.

It is said that when St. Francis allowed the Portuguese Friar St. Anthony of Padua to lecture on theology to the Friars, he clearly stipulated that such permission was granted "as long as the study of such did not extinguish the spirit of holy prayer and devotion, as contained in the *Rule.*" Whatever must be said of Duns Scotus or William of Ockham at a later period, we can say that all of the great Franciscan masters of the thirteenth century were loyal to the spirit inspired by Francis. Their theology was more in harmony with monastic theology than with the Aristotelian rationalism of the Dominicans, and differences in thought patterns were inevitable within the confines of fraternal charity.

It used to be thought that Thomas's short treatise *De aeternitate mundi* was directed against the Averroists, who maintained that the world is eternal. However, recently Ignatius Brady has shown beyond any reasonable doubt that it was directed against John Pecham shortly after he incepted in theology.[63] Pecham maintained, contrary to both the Averroists and Thomas, that the world could never have been eternal, since reason can demonstrate that God pre-existed before creation. This is directly contrary to what Thomas had said in his *Summa theologiae* I, 46, 1–2. Thomas must have composed the treatise *De aeternitate mundi* between 1270–72, for it was copied in the notebook of Godefroy of Fontaines. The point at issue is whether God and the universe could have co-existed from all eternity with God as the creator. Thomas saw no repugnance between the eternity of God and an eternal created universe. After citing various passages from St. Augustine, he notes that Augustine never saw any contradiction between an eternal creator and an eternal effect. If there is some intrinsic contradiction, how is it that Augustine never saw it? Therefore it must be that the "murmurers" against whom the treatise was written "speak as though they alone were rational beings and wisdom had originated in their own brains" (cf. Job 12:2).

To show Thomas's humility, William of Tocco narrates an incident that has often been quoted in whole or in part.[64] According to William, a certain religious held his *vesperies* for the magisterium in Paris and defended a view contrary to the position Thomas had determined in his school, but Thomas allowed the matter to pass unperturbed. On the return journey to Saint-Jacques, the students accompanying Thomas were most indignant that the new master should defend such a position contrary to Thomas's and that Thomas should have allowed such an injury to truth to go unchecked before all the masters of Paris. Thomas replied, more in effect than in words, "Children, it seems to me that one should be indulgent to a new master at his *vesperies*, lest he be embarrassed in the presence of all the masters; as far as my doctrine is concerned, I do not fear contradiction from any doctor, since with the help of God I have established it firmly on the authority of the saints and the arguments of truth. However, if you think otherwise, I will try to make up for it tomorrow." On the next day, in the *aula* of the bishop, the young master maintained the same position without any change. Then Friar Thomas got up and said modestly, "Master, that opinion of yours, with all due respect to the truth, cannot be maintained, for it is contrary to such and such a Council, and if you do not wish to oppose the Council, you will have to take another stand." But when the young master changed his wording, but not his opinion, Thomas again adduced the authority of the Council, and "forced him to confess his error, and humbly to ask the aforesaid doctor to elucidate the truth more fully," which Thomas is supposed to have done. Tocco goes on in great rhetorical style, noting the amazement of all the masters at such a display of learning. But to this day no one has been able to name the Council in question or the point of the argument.

Despite the rhetoric and slight discrepancies from the actual ceremony of inception (for Tocco was not a university man), this incident, as many claim, could refer to the inception of John Pecham in the early months of 1270. Pecham replaced Eustace of Arras as regent master when the latter left Paris with King Louis IX on March 15, 1270. As has been explained earlier, the incepting master passed around four questions to be debated in the inception ceremony, the second and third of which had to be settled definitively by the young master at his *resumptio*. Brady has recently discovered and published the two questions Pecham determined in his *resumptio* following inception. They are attempts to prove that the world had a beginning, and therefore could not have existed from all eternity even with God as its cause. The basic argument used by Pecham in his *quaestio* is that the universe by its very nature is mutable, and that nothing mutable can be co-eternal with the immutable. Pecham also relied on the authority of Augustine in *De civitate dei* XII and *Super Genesim* VIII, as well as on the perennial argument that an actual infinity of souls, implied in an eternal world, is impossible. Therefore, Brady concludes, "the opuscule of Aquinas was indeed provoked by the disputation of the Franciscan," i.e., John Pecham. Thus in his *De aeternitate mundi* Thomas replied to all the arguments adduced by Pecham and to all the authorities cited, probably without having a transcript of Pecham's disputation. Thomas argued accurately from memory against the arguments used and the authorities cited by Pecham at his inception. Therefore it would seem that Thomas's *De aeternitate mundi* was written against Pecham in the early spring of 1270.

Pecham's personal attitude toward Thomism, after years of experience, was summed up in his letter to the bishop of Lincoln, dated June 1, 1285:

> I do not in any way disapprove of philosophical studies, insofar as they serve theological mysteries, but I do disapprove of irreverent innovations in language, introduced within the last twenty years into the depths of theology against philosophical truth, and to the detriment of the Fathers, whose positions are disdained and openly held in contempt. Which doctrine is more sound, the doctrine of the sons of St. Francis . . . or that very recent and almost entirely contrary doctrine, which fills the entire world with wordy quarrels, weakening and destroying with all its strength what Augustine teaches concerning the eternal rules and the unchangeable light, the faculties of the soul, the seminal reasons included in matter, and innumerable questions of the same kind.[65]

Here John almost identifies the conflict in doctrine with the distinction of the two Orders, Franciscan and Dominican, the Augustinism of the one and the Aristotelianism of the other. Gilson has pointed out that the innovations Pecham refers to "within the last twenty years" seem to have come about with the *Summa contra gentiles* of Thomas. As Gilson further points out, when Pecham wants to list some of the points on which the two groups are opposed, the first three that come to his mind are: the doctrine of divine illumination, the identity of the powers of the soul with the essence of the soul, and the seminal reasons in matter.[66] Thomas did, in fact, reject or modify these three Augustinist doctrines.

But most of all, Pecham's target was the Thomistic doctrine of the unicity of substantial form in material composites. Not only at Paris, but also in the Roman curia and in England during Pecham's conflict with the early Dominican Thomists, the most pernicious doctrine in his eyes was Thomas's outright rejection of the "traditional" doctrine of plurality of forms.[67] Following the principles of Aristotle, Thomas time and time again argued that the first actualization of prime matter (*materia prima*) is the substantial form of that composite; whatever is posterior is non-essential and "accidental" in the technical sense of the term. If the first actualization of matter is a certain "form of corporeity" (*forma corporeitatis*), then man is not essentially a man, but only accidentally so. For Thomas, no composite can have more than one substantial form. Pecham, on the other hand, following the supposed teaching of Augustine and even of Bonaventure, insisted that man is a composite of many substantial forms, one following upon the other in logical succession. For Pecham this was not simply a philosophical issue, but one that touched the roots of Christian faith. If man has only one substantial form, he argued, then the living body of Christ on the cross cannot be the "same body" of Christ in the tomb. Pecham argued that there must be a "corporeal form" that is identical for both bodies. He and others even argued that if Mass had been celebrated while Christ was dead, it would not be true to say, "This is my Body," or "This is my Blood." Therefore, in the eyes of Pecham and others, the doctrine of unicity led to heresy, and had to be condemned, as it was by Robert Kilwardby, his Dominican predecessor in the chair of Canterbury, in 1277. Pecham, claiming that his doctrine was the teaching of Augustine, which "the whole world had held up to this time,"[68] denounced the doctrine of unicity as a presumptuous novelty that leads to heresy. On this point Pecham was adamant.

D. A. Callus has pointed out in numerous studies that the doctrine of plurality is not found in Augustine, and that it was not held by "the whole world up to this time."[69] It was, in fact, an innovation of the twelfth century, introduced by the Latin translation of a work by the Jewish philosopher Ibn Gabirol, the *Fons vitae*. Moreover, the doctrine of unicity of form does not lead to heresy, as Thomas argued (*Sum. theol.* III, 50, 2 and 5), and as his followers kept pointing out in the *Correctoria* literature, as we shall see in the next chapter. For Thomas, the Divine Person of the Word assumed an entire human nature united to Himself in His person; the body of Christ was hypostatically united to the Person just as the soul was. Therefore, even in death the body of Christ remained His as much as His soul remained His in Limbo. The real reason for the identity of Christ's body dead or alive was thus the hypostatic union and not a "corporeal form" that remained after death. Consequently Thomas's teaching on the unicity of form in no way led to heresy, but rather pointed out a basic flaw in Pecham's doctrine of the Incarnation.

During the three and a half years Thomas lived in Paris, he was frequently called upon to give his expert opinion. One of the more interesting occasions was in April 1271, when the master general John of Vercelli sent a list of forty-three propositions to be examined independently by Thomas in Paris, Albert the Great in Cologne, and Robert Kilwardby in London.[70] These propositions have nothing to do with any of the major issues debated at Paris, but originated in the Dominican studium in Venice. At an earlier date Thomas had replied to almost all of the questions sent by the lector of Venice but to no avail. Eventually the Venetian dispute reached the master of the Order, who called upon three outstanding theologians in the Order to give their opinion on each of the propositions. The response was to be given as quickly as possible according to three criteria: (1) Do the *Sancti* (Fathers of the Church) maintain the doctrine or opinion contained in the articles listed? (2) Whether or not the *Sancti* support the doctrine or opinion contained in the articles, does the consultor maintain the aforesaid doctrine or opinion? (3) If the consultor does not personally hold the view, could such a doctrine or opinion be tolerated without prejudice to the faith? Unfortunately none of the articles have far-reaching significance, but they provide an opportunity to evaluate the reaction of three outstanding theologians. Thomas was brief and to the point; Albert was irritated and annoyed, for he had discussed many of the same issues in his philosophical writings; Kilwardby was lengthy and magisterial, revealing many differences from the other two. None of the consultors saw the reply of the others, but each replied as he saw fit to the general of the Order.[71] The general's letter reached Thomas on Wednesday, April 1, 1271, during the celebration of Solemn Mass. Immediately on the following day, Holy Thursday, Thomas wrote his reply to the master general.

During this same period Thomas wrote numerous letters to various persons involving points of doctrine. Today the formalities of the "letter" have been lost, and all that survive are the contents presented as treatises. Such is the treatise on the motion of the heart, originally a letter written to master Philip of Castrocaeli, a physician, professor first at Bologna and later in Naples. To the same master he wrote on the mixture of elements. Twice he wrote to Friar Bassiano of Lodi, the lector at Venice, concerning the troublesome queries that eventually reached the master general and involved the three masters in sacred theology. In all of these replies Thomas gave his full attention to the problem submitted for his consideration. No doubt Thomas wrote his replies quickly, but always with care and consideration.

By summer 1272, Thomas's work in Paris was finished. Nothing was settled. The antimendicant controversy, Latin Averroism, and opposition from Augustinists would continue long after his death, but there was nothing more that could be done. With the inception of Romano of Rome, a member of the Orsini family and a Dominican of the Roman Province, Thomas could relinquish his professorial chair and return to Italy.[72] Though

Thomas worked very hard and accomplished much at the height of his genius while he was in Paris, he still had his *Summa* to complete, as well as numerous commentaries on Aristotle, begun in Paris but not yet finished. But the three and a half years in Paris were clearly the most productive of his life.

Chapter VII

LAST YEARS AND AFTER
(1272–1323)

Thomas had no need to wait until the end of the academic year to return to Italy. Since December 1270, when thirteen Averroist theses were condemned, the faculty of arts had been in turmoil. Violent opposition broke out between the minority followers of Siger of Brabant and the majority followers of Alberic of Rheims; the faculty of arts was divided not only in doctrine, but also in the election of the rector and proctors.[1] The bishop of Paris, it would seem, tried to interfere; but in protest, by authority of a privilege granted by Gregory IX in 1231, the entire university suspended all lectures and other academic acts from Lent 1272 until the feast of St. John the Baptist, June 24.[2] Nevertheless Thomas held his Lenten quodlibet (6) that year, as well as disputed questions, and apparently presided over the inception of his successor, Romano Orsini of Rome, brother of Cardinal Matteo Rosso-Orsini.[3] Thomas could not have left Paris without providing a successor, but once that was done, there was no need to delay. It was, no doubt, the master general John of Vercelli who recalled him after the antimendicant controversy had subsided. Therefore after Easter, April 24, 1272, Thomas and Reginald of Piperno left Paris on the long journey back to Italy.

However, it must be noted that during Thomas's last years in Paris a strong bond of mutual understanding and friendship had developed between Thomas and a large number of masters and students in arts. Some, like Peter of Auvergne, could be called disciples; others had been won over after the Averroist

crisis of 1270; many others came to appreciate Thomas's apostolate toward them. Members of the arts faculty tried to forestall
his departure or at least to have him returned; the rector and
masters in arts even wrote an official letter to the general chapter
meeting in Florence that year to ask for the return of Thomas to
Paris—for their sake—but to no avail. This letter, now lost, is
referred to in the letter of 1274 which the rector and arts faculty
wrote to the capitular fathers meeting in Lyons after the death
of Thomas. It is certain that Thomas had a strong following in
the faculty of arts from 1270 onward. That does not mean, however, that these young masters and students in arts could be
called Thomists in the sense of understanding, promoting, and
developing the teaching of Thomas. In twenty to forty years
these young scholars presumably became the intellectual leaven
of their generation, but there is little evidence of their intellectual
influence. It is doubtful that they understood even what is called
today the "essentials" of Thomas's thought. The most perhaps
that can be said is that they were full of admiration for Thomas
and as teachers and administrators they were able to soften or
repress attacks on him or his doctrine. Nevertheless it can be
said that these young men respected and appreciated Thomas
as a saintly and impressive man and as an outstanding teacher
and writer, whose works they read.[4]

The general chapter of the Order met in Florence at Pentecost,
June 12. The fathers of the chapter held their meeting in the
spacious Priory of Santa Maria Novella, founded in 1219 during
the lifetime of St. Dominic; the more famous Priory of San
Marco was not established until the fifteenth century. As was
customary when the general chapter met in the Roman Province,
the provincial chapter was held in the same place immediately
after. As a preacher general in the Roman Province, Thomas
had a right to be present at the provincial chapter. It would
seem that Thomas and his companion Reginald reached Florence by Pentecost or shortly after. Following Davidsohn, Walz
pictures Thomas in the assembly of Dominicans present when
John of Vercelli addressed the citizens of Florence, exhorting
them to make peace with the other Tuscan cities.[5] This exhorta-
tion on behalf of the new pontiff, Gregory X (1271–76), was

presumably made at the opening of the chapter, on Pentecost, in which case Thomas arrived in Florence by June 12.

One of the issues voted upon by the general chapter of 1272 was the establishment of two more *studia generalia* in the Order in addition to the four existing studia. The two new general studia were to be in Spain and in the Roman Province. This legislation was introduced at the chapter in Milan in 1270 and repeated in the Florence chapter of 1272. The chapter at Pest (now Budapest) in 1273 approved it, but the following chapter at Lyons did not confirm the new legislation. However, the situation looked promising in 1272 when the fathers voted upon it at Florence. It is not correct to say, as Walz does, that the general chapter of 1270 ordered that the *studium generale* be set up in Naples.[6] In no case was a specific priory ever designated by the general chapter, neither here nor in the earlier erection of the original four. In fact, in 1272 it was entirely up to Thomas to select a location. In any case, it looked as though the Roman Province would soon have a general studium of the Order to which every province could send students for training in philosophy, theology, and law.

The chapter of the Roman Province was held at Santa Maria Novella immediately following the general chapter. Among its provisions, the fathers declared: "We entrust entirely to Friar Thomas d'Aquino the general studium of theology as to place, persons, and number of students."[7] In 1265, when Thomas had been chosen to establish a studium, the place was designated by the fathers of the chapter; it was to be in Rome at Santa Sabina, as we have explained. In 1272, however, the choice of place was to be entirely in Thomas's hands. No one city in the entire Roman Province presented itself as an inevitable choice. Rome, no longer the residence of the Roman pontiff, was largely dominated by wealthy Ghibelline families; Naples was in a separate political kingdom and the future was uncertain; and Viterbo, Orvieto, and other papal residences had nothing to offer except the temporary residence of the Pope, and the new studium envisaged was not to be a studium of the curia, but a permanent studium of the entire Order, just like those at Paris, Bologna, Oxford, and Cologne, or so it was hoped at the time.

For many plausible reasons at the time, Thomas chose Naples

as the place of his theological studium. San Domenico in Naples had once before been chosen by the fathers as a place for the theological studium of the province—which was still functioning, as far as we know. Whatever the future of kings may hold, King Charles I was a protector of the Order and on good terms with the Holy See. He had established peace in his kingdom and he was seriously interested in renovating the "university" founded by Frederick II. On July 31, 1272, Charles sent a general invitation to all the masters and students of Paris and Orléans to come to Naples, where they would find not only peace, but also healthy air, conspicuous amenities, an opulent abundance of all things, as well as the sea to refresh them in their studies.[8] There was a vitality about Naples that was absent from Rome or any other city in the Roman Province. Thomas was not being sentimental in choosing Naples, but thoroughly objective in his decision. Naples offered stability, vitality, and the best possibilities for the immediate future.

We must remember, however, that Thomas was not chosen to open a general studium of the Order, but only a theological studium of the province. The same provincial chapter that appointed Thomas regent of theology established the studium of arts in Pisa where Friar Ricculdo of Florence was teaching. It was not until 1303 that the general chapter agreed to establish a general studium at Naples "at the insistence of the King of Sicily."[9] But by that time Naples was the center of a new province of the Order, for in 1294 Naples and Sicily were cut off from the Roman Province to constitute the *provincia Regni*. This development will be considered later, for it was the Province of Naples that initiated the cause of Thomas's canonization.

On his way to Naples, Thomas seems to have stopped in Rome to visit his sister Theodora and her husband, Count Roger of San Severino, who was King Charles's representative in Rome.[10] Continuing their journey to Naples, Thomas and Reginald were accompanied by the young Friar Tolomeo of Lucca, who was to be one of Thomas's students in Naples.[11] Traveling south of Rome on the Via Latina, Thomas and his companions turned west a short distance to visit his dear friend, Cardinal Richard d'Annibaldi, at the castle of Molara just south of Rocca di Papa. On arriving at the castle, however, they were told that the cardinal had died just a few weeks earlier, on June 1, 1272. While there, Thomas and Reginald both fell ill with a fever. Thomas recovered after the usual three days of "tertian fever," but Reginald's condition became very serious and the cardinal's doctors gave up hope, for the "critical signs" of life were weak. According to Tolomeo, writing forty-five years after the event he witnessed, Thomas "took some relics of Blessed Agnes, which out of devotion he brought from Rome, telling [Reginald] to place them on himself and have full confidence. Reginald did so and was cured, although the doctors had given up all hope." Tolomeo goes on to say, "To commemorate the event, Friar Thomas decided to arrange that every year, on the feast of St. Agnes [January 21], the brethren should celebrate it with special solemnity and a good dinner. This they did that same year [January 21, 1273] at Naples, but the next year Friar Thomas passed away."[12] Agnes was a very popular saint in the Early and High Middle Ages; she was a Roman martyr who died c. 304, and devotion to her was widespread, particularly in Italy; even the octave day of her feast was observed on January 28. But there is no other indication that Thomas had a personal devotion to her in particular.

Walz suggests that after leaving Molara, Thomas and his companions may have stopped at the castle of Ceccano, a few miles southwest of Frosinone, to visit one of his nieces, Francesca, who had married Count Annibaldo; he may also have stopped at the family castle of Roccasecca, and perhaps at the Abbey of Monte Cassino.[13] In 1269 Thomas had interceded with Abbot Bernard Ayglier to allow the Dominicans to open a priory at San Germano at the foot of Monte Cassino, which he did on December 27, 1269, out of love and devotion to Friar Thomas d'Aquino. Walz thus considers the proximity of Monte Cassino to the Via Latina an opportunity for Thomas to express his gratitude to Bernard Ayglier.

In any case, the traveling Friars must have reached the Priory of San Domenico in Naples by early September. Thomas could have begun the academic year on September 14, the feast of the Exaltation of the Holy Cross, as was customary at Paris, or on September 29, the feast of St. Michael, as was customary in religious houses.

At that time there were many very eminent Friars living at San Domenico, mentioned by Walz. Only one of them need here be mentioned for his deep influence on Thomas's youth, Friar John of San Giuliano. Among the many students known to have attended Thomas's lectures[14] was William of Tocco, who was born in the family castle of Tocco in the Province of Benevento. Later Tocco became prior of the Dominican house in Benevento and inquisitor for the Kingdom of Naples under Charles II. Having been appointed promoter of the cause of Thomas's canonization, he was indefatigable in his search for information concerning Thomas, and is now regarded as the most reliable of Thomas's biographers. Tocco knew Thomas only for the year and a half they were together at San Domenico; at that time Tocco was only a student, but Thomas made a deep impression on him, as can be seen from his biography and his testimony in the process of canonization.

Regent at Naples and the "Tertia Pars"

(1272–73)

If Thomas began his lectures on September 14, as some suggest, he had to interrupt them almost immediately to deal with secular matters of some importance. Thomas's brother-in-law, Roger of Aquila, Count of Traetto and Fondi, the husband of Adelasia d'Aquino, died at his castle on Friday, August 26, 1272. Before his death the count had drawn up his last will and testament, appointing Thomas its executor. It is debatable whether Thomas was at the castle of Traetto when Roger died or at the funeral; the castle was just off the Via Appia near Minturno, about fifty miles north of Naples. Count Roger had hoped to entrust the upbringing of his four small children to another of his wife's relatives, Count Roger of San Severino. On September 1, King Charles appointed the procurator of Terra di Lavoro to be responsible for these young children, provided that a relative of the count's be chosen to supervise their upbringing. On September 10, having learned of the will of Count Roger and that Thomas was its executor, Charles ordered the procurator to provide all necessary aid to the expeditious execution of the will.[15]

By September 20, Thomas was at Traetto disposing of the Count's possessions according to his will; the disposition of all movable goods by Thomas is recorded in a document of September 20, 1272.[16]

However, there was a small matter of "restitution" for certain "incorrectly appropriated" goods from various places and persons indicated in the will. Apparently Thomas decided that a royal license was necessary for this transaction, and on September 27 Thomas visited the king at Capua, midway between Traetto and Naples, to obtain it. On this occasion Thomas also asked the king to remove Richard, Count Roger's eldest son, from the care of the royal procurator of Terra di Lavoro and to put him under the care of Count Roger of San Severino, as was the expressed wish of the deceased; this favor was also granted. According to Walz and Scandone, "Charles was so impressed with Master Thomas that henceforth he looked upon him as a dear friend."[17] On October 2 the king wrote to the procurator of Terra di Lavoro to provide the necessary assistance and co-operation, allowing Thomas, "our dear friend," to make the necessary arrangements.[18]

On October 15, 1272, King Charles ordered the same procurator of Terra di Lavoro to pay one ounce of gold to the prior at Naples for every month that Thomas was "at Naples for the sake of teaching."[19] In effect, this meant that the priory received twelve ounces of gold each year for Thomas's teaching. This is the earliest indication that Thomas's lectures were paid for by the king. It leads us to believe that Thomas was the official teacher of theology in the Neapolitan "university" founded by Frederick II. We have already seen (chapter 1) that Frederick II paid twelve ounces of gold annually to Master Peter of Isernia, who taught law at the university in the 1220s; King Conrad paid the same amount annually to a lecturer at the university in the 1250s.[20] Later, during the years 1302-6, when three masters taught theology, a Dominican, a Franciscan, and an Augustinian, King Charles II disbursed annually 150 ounces of gold to the three religious houses, San Domenico, San Lorenzo, and San Agostino, for instruction given in their respective houses as university lectures. It would seem that in the 1270s, as in the 1220s, there was only one regent master of theology in the university. The Dominican Priory was adjacent to the original site of the University of Naples until the seventeenth century. Thomas, of course, lectured in the Priory of San Domenico, but his lectures were university lectures open to all qualified to attend. Thus it would seem that credence must be given to the ancient tradition that Thomas was regent master in theology at the University of Naples, paid annually by the king. However, it is highly doubtful that Charles requested the Dominican authorities to recall Thomas from Paris in order to teach at the university, as has been claimed. The academic arrangement is therefore clear: Thomas taught in the Dominican Priory of San Domenico as regent master of both the provincial studium and the University of Naples.

Thomas was forty-seven years old when he began teaching at Naples. From all that we know, he was still in excellent health and full of vigor, as he had been in Paris. While his teaching load was light—there are no extant disputed questions from this period—his writing was extensive and meticulous. All of his energies, it would seem, were directed to completing the *Summa theologiae* and the Aristotelian commentaries. Most likely Thomas had some secretaries besides Reginald to assist him in his writing, judging from the seven scribal hands appearing in the Naples MS of Thomas's *Sententia super Metaphysicam*. One of these scribes at Naples seems to have been Friar Jacobinus of Asti, who, after the death of Thomas, "transcribed into legible writing" the commentary on Isaiah.[21] Dondaine tentatively identified hand A in the Naples MS of the *Metaphysics* as Jacobinus of Asti, thus evidencing that Jacobinus was one of Thomas's secretaries at Naples.[22] In the process of canonization, Bartholomew of Capua testified that at Naples Thomas dictated "to many secretaries" (*pluribus scriptoribus*).[23] When one considers that Thomas's intellectual activity in Naples extended only to fourteen or fifteen months, one must conclude that these were highly productive months. The *tertia pars* of the *Summa*, covering the Incarnation and the sacraments, particularly the Eucharist, stands out as a monument of his genius, industry, and scholarship.

Nevertheless during these highly productive months Thomas became more and more absorbed in thought and in contemplative prayer. His *abstractio mentis* seems to have overtaken him without effort and under varied circumstances, but most notably at Mass and the Divine Office. William of Tocco records one such incident that took place on Passion Sunday, March 26, 1273, while Thomas was celebrating a public Mass attended by many noble gentlemen of the city; he became so completely absorbed in the sacred mysteries that he stood for a long time as though in a trance, "his face bathed in tears." Finally one of the brethren approached him, shook him, and asked him to proceed with the Mass. Afterward when some of the laity asked Thomas about the incident, he dismissed the matter as of no importance.[24]

Another incident happened in Naples, which was recorded by Tocco and copied by Bernard Gui.[25] Once when a certain cardinal legate wished to meet Thomas, about whom he had heard much, he asked the archbishop of Capua, "formerly one of Thomas's pupils," to arrange a friendly meeting with him. Thomas was thus called away from his studies to talk to the two prelates who had come to the priory, but he "remained in his abstraction." They made him sit down between them, but his mind was miles away and he said scarcely a word to them. After a long silence, while they waited for him to speak, his face suddenly beamed and he exclaimed, "Ah, now I have it!" Meanwhile the cardinal legate was becoming annoyed and indignant that this friar gave him and the archbishop no sign of reverence; "and in his heart he was beginning to despise him." But the archbishop said to him, "My lord, do not be surprised, he is often like this; with a mind so abstracted that he cannot be got to talk whatever the company he is in." Then he took hold of Thomas's *cappa* and tugged it sharply. Thomas came to himself and, noticing the prelates on either side of him, bowed his head reverently to the cardinal and begged his pardon, saying, "My lord, please excuse me; I thought I was still in my cell." Asked why he should express such exuberance in the state of his abstraction, Thomas said, "A beautiful idea has just occurred to me for the work on which I am engaged at present. My pleasure in this simply burst forth in delight." The cardinal was taken aback, but he was very pleased all the same by the encounter. The archbishop enjoyed telling this story afterward, and often did so.[26]

One of the many interesting points in this story is that the archbishop of Capua, Marino of Eboli, is supposed to have said, "He is often [*frequenter*] like this." In the process of canonization, Marino of Eboli is mentioned as being on intimate terms with Thomas, and Tocco explicitly states that he was "a pupil of the aforesaid doctor."[27] If Marino had in fact been a pupil of Thomas's, he would have had to study under him either at Paris or Rome. Marino of Eboli was not a Dominican, so it is more likely that he studied at Paris and attended Thomas's lectures there.

From what has been said it would seem that Thomas began his academic year in Naples on September 29, the feast of St. Michael the Archangel. He lectured as regent master throughout the academic year 1272–73 and during the first two months of the following academic year, that is, until December 6, 1273. We have already said that there are no known disputed questions from this period, although we can be certain that disputations were held by Thomas at Naples.

The only academic work that can be attributed to this period with certainty is his series of lectures on Psalms 1–54. The catalogue of Bartholomew of Capua, inserted into the process of canonization, refers to this work simply as "On four nocturns of the Psalter," reported by Friar Reginald. Nicholas Trevet includes it among the *reportata* made by Reginald and calls it "On three nocturns of the Psalter." Bernard Gui says, "Friar Reginald, his socius, is said to have reported a postille on three nocturns of the Psalter, while Thomas was lecturing."[28] The commentary on Psalms 1–51 is to be found in all the printed editions of Thomas's works; the commentary on Psalms 52–54 was discovered by Uccelli and published in Rome in 1880.

Psalms 1–51 comprise the nocturns for the ancient Office of Matins: Sunday (Ps. 1–20 with the exception of 4 and 5), Monday (Ps. 26–37 with the exception of 21–25, which were sung at Lauds), Tuesday (Ps. 38–51 with the exception of 42 and 50), and Wednesday (Ps. 52–67, excepting 62, 64, and 66). Hence medieval usage referred to Thomas's work as a postil on the first three nocturns of the Psalter. Bartholomew of Capua, however, directly or indirectly knew the commentary on the first three Psalms for Wednesday (Ps. 52–54), and he referred to it as a postil on the first "four nocturns of the Psalter."

While the description of this work as a postil on a given number of nocturns would be self-explanatory to a historian of the liturgy, it would not describe the work had Thomas lived to complete his commentary. It would be better to describe it as *Super Psalmos* or *Super Psalterium*, since Thomas's commentary follows exclusively the order of the Vulgate, and not that of the Divine Office as such.

Since the earliest centuries of Christianity, the Psalter was taken over into Christian worship as the official liturgical song of the Church. By the second century the whole Psalter of 150 Psalms was recited once a week by clerics obliged to full liturgical worship, and by monks, who by profession were obliged to the Divine Office in choir. By the time of St. Benedict, it had long been the custom to sing the whole Psalter every week. In his *Rule* St. Benedict stipulated that the distribution of the Psalms may be altered by the monk in charge, provided that "every week the whole number of 150 psalms be sung" (*Regula*, 18). By the time of Charlemagne the whole Psalter was divided into two parts: Psalms 1–108, with a few exceptions, comprised the noctural Office of Matins, and Psalms 109–150, with the exception of Psalm 118, comprised the diurnal Office of Vespers.[29] By the thirteenth century, religious Orders, including the Dominicans, adopted this basic division, but stipulated, as was the ancient custom, that certain Psalms could be omitted in the singing of Matins and sung instead for Lauds and the minor hours.[30] Thomas's commentary does not follow strictly the Psalms sung in choir or recited in the Breviary, but rather the distribution of the Psalms in the Vulgate Bible. Moreover, if Thomas had completed his commentary, it would have included the diurnal office as well as the nocturnal. Therefore, the more proper designation of Thomas's commentary would be simply *Super Psalmos* (incomplete).

In the prologue to his commentary on the Psalms, Thomas notes that there are "three translations" of the Psalms into Latin known to all. In apostolic times there was an old Latin translation that had become "vitiated by scribes" by the time of St. Jerome. Hence at the request of Pope Damasus, Jerome "corrected the psalter, and this version is used in Italy." This "corrected version," we know, was made in 383 by Jerome, and became known as the "Roman Psalter," because of its use in Italy. Thomas goes on to say, "Since this translation was at variance with the Greek text, Jerome again translated the psalter from the Greek into

Latin at the request of Paula, and Pope Damasus ordered this version to be sung in France; and it agrees word for word with the Greek." In reality this version was made at Bethlehem in 392 from the Septuagint with the aid of Origen's Hexapla. It was adopted at Tours in the sixth century, and became known as the "Gallican Psalter"; eventually this second version by Jerome was adopted by the whole of Latin Christendom, and became the standard text of the Vulgate. Thomas recounts the origin of the third version as follows:

> Later a certain Sophronius, occasionally disputing with the Jews —since the Jews would say that something was not the case when he introduced a text from the second version of the psalter—asked Jerome to translate the psalter from the Hebrew into Latin. Jerome acceded to this request. This translation agrees fully with the Hebrew, but is not sung in any church. Nevertheless [this version] is possessed by many.

Thomas did not specify which version would be the basis for his lectures. However, a comparison of the Roman and Gallican Psalters (PL 29, 123–420) clearly indicates that his basic text was the Gallican Psalter, while the Roman Psalter was introduced as the *alia littera*.

The Dominican liturgy was adopted from the rite then in use in the Roman basilicas in the thirteenth century. Their distribution of the Psalms was identical, but the Dominicans adopted the text of the Gallican Psalter. The Franciscans followed the rite of the Roman curia, but they too adopted the Gallican Psalter. Eventually the Franciscan rite of the liturgy was accepted by the Roman curia for its own use.[31] In the standardization of liturgical rites under Pope Pius V, all those Orders and dioceses not having a proper rite in continual use more than a hundred years had to conform to the rite of the Roman curia; this became the "Roman Rite" in common use after the Council of Trent, distinct from the "Dominican Rite," which had been adopted by many other Orders, congregations, and dioceses in the Scandinavian countries. Only fragments of the old Roman Psalter continued to be in liturgical use from the thirteenth century to the mid-twentieth, e.g., in the Responds, Gradual, and Invitatory.

The Vulgate text was the Gallican Psalter. It is not at all surprising that Thomas should have lectured on the Gallican Psalter at Naples in 1272-73.

All authorities agree that Thomas's commentary on the Psalms is to be dated at Naples 1272-73. It ends abruptly in Psalm 54, no doubt, because of the extraordinary experience of December 6, 1273, when Thomas was forced to cease all work. The unique MS of the portion of the commentary on Psalms 52-54, which Uccelli discovered in the Grand Archives of Naples (Regio Archivio 25), ends with the following scribal note:

> Here ends the postille on part of the psalter according to Friar Thomas d'Aquino of the Order of Preachers, because no more is found in the exemplar of Friar Reginald of Piperno, who was the socius of Friar Thomas until his death, and who had all his writings.[32]

Mandonnet, as we have seen (chapter 6), argued that Thomas also commented at Naples on Paul's letter to the Romans and part of his first letter to the Corinthians. This commentary likewise ends abruptly in chapter 10. Following Glorieux, we rejected this view, and maintained that these Pauline lectures were given in Paris; they were abruptly terminated by Thomas's premature departure from Paris in spring 1272. Mandonnet's a priori principle that masters lectured alternately between books of the Old and New Testaments cannot be sustained by the known facts. Thus, following the majority of modern scholars, we must say that Thomas lectured at Naples on the Psalms exclusively.

The subject matter of the Psalms, for Thomas, is the whole of theology, in contrast to the other books of canonical Scripture, each of which has a special subject. The Psalms praise all the works of God, the opus Dei, which embraces creation, governance, reparation, and glorification. Since all of these works of God pertain to Christ, the subject matter of this book is "Christ and His members." "Everything pertaining to the purpose of the Incarnation is clearly conveyed in this work, so that it would almost appear to be a gospel, and not a prophecy." Because the work of glorification and the other works of God are so clearly recognized in the Psalms, it is most frequently sung in the

Church: "The Psalter contains the whole of Sacred Scripture."
Thomas notes that in expounding the Psalms, as well as the
prophets, we must avoid an error condemned in the fifth ecumenical council of the Church, namely the Second Council of
Constantinople in 553. According to Thomas, Theodore of Mopsuestia maintained that nothing in the Old Testament refers expressly to Christ, but to other things, and only later was the Old
Testament adapted to Christ. Thomas explicitly states that he in-
tends to expound the Psalms following the general rule given by
St. Jerome in his commentary on Ezechiel, "namely, that all actions narrated [in the Old Testament] are to be expounded in
such a way that they prefigure something of Christ or His
Church." Modern exegetes perhaps would not accept this principle, but it is a most salutary way of viewing the Psalms in Christian worship. Thomas does not deny that the Psalms have a literal
sense pertaining to people and events in Jewish history, but he
concentrates on what he usually calls "the spiritual sense," in
which persons, things, and events narrated signify Christ or
His Church on earth or in heaven (see chapter 3 above). For
him, the spiritual sense of the Old Testament is more relevant
than the literal in Christian worship and in the personal lives of
Christians.

The main sources of Thomas's commentary on the Psalms are
the other parts of Scripture, Jerome's translation from the Hebrew, the *Glossa,* and Augustine's commentary on the Psalms. In
referring to Jerome's translation of the Psalms from the Hebrew
(PL 28, 1189–1306), Thomas always refers to it under the name
of Jerome, e.g., "according to Jerome," "Jerome has," "Jerome's
version is," "Jerome says," etc. Therefore when Thomas commented on the Psalms in class, he had before his eyes all three
versions made by Jerome: the "corrected" version known as the
Roman Psalter, the version made from the Septuagint known as
the Gallican Psalter, and the version made from the Hebrew.
Commenting on Psalm 8:3, he refers to a text of Aristotle, "even
though it is not found in any of his books that have come down
to us"; such a statement could be made only by one who knew all
the extant writings of Aristotle thoroughly. There are also numerous references to the known works of Aristotle (*Rhetoric, Politics,
Ethics,* and *Meteora*), as well as to Cicero, Seneca, Boethius,

Liber de causis, and others. It is a remarkable work in which the Psalms are seen in relation to Christ and His Church. For Thomas, "Christ and the Church are one person" (Ps. 30:1). This Christocentric view of the Psalms parallels the Christology of the third part of the *Summa theologiae,* written in large part while Thomas was in Naples, lecturing on the Psalms. The lectures on the Psalms and the *Summa* both ended abruptly on December 6, 1273, as did some of his commentaries on Aristotle.

Eschmann suggests that Thomas may have written as many as the first twenty questions of the third part of the *Summa* while he was still in Paris. There is no proof of this, and it is most improbable that there was sufficient time, since Thomas left Paris shortly after April 25. But it seems likely that Thomas finished the *secunda secundae* early in the spring of 1272, and was able to begin the *tertia pars* immediately. However, considering that Thomas left Paris late in April, I do not think Thomas could have written more than the first two or three questions of the *tertia pars* before leaving Paris. However, Thomas was certainly thinking about the mystery of the Incarnation in the early spring of 1272, for Thomas's last disputation in Paris was *De unione verbi incarnati* in five articles, the third and fourth of which are certainly prior to III, q. 17, aa. 1–2, dealing with theological grammar and the problem of *esse* in Christ. Therefore it is still uncertain how many questions Thomas wrote of the third part before leaving for Florence and then Naples.

The five articles of the disputed question *De unione verbi incarnati,* admitted by most historians to be of Parisian origin, were discussed by Thomas more succinctly and definitely in the *tertia pars.* The first two articles of *De unione,* on the manner of the union between the divine and human natures in Christ, parallel question 2, articles 1–3, of the *Summa,* while the next two, on the *esse* of Christ, parallel question 17, articles 1–2. Although there is no serious contradiction between the disputed question *De unione* and the *tertia pars,* the former seems to be rather preparatory for the definitive presentation in the *Summa.* There is clearly a development of thought between the two passages.

The first article of *De unione* asks whether this union is brought about in the person or in the nature. Seventeen arguments, mainly philosophical, are introduced to prove that the union must be in the nature, that is, in the human and divine nature of Christ. These arguments are heterogeneous, some directed against a personal union, and others in favor of a natural union; the two arguments *sed contra* are from the authority of St. Augustine. In the *Summa,* arguments defending the natural union are distinct from those against a personal union; all the arguments are taken from patristic sources, and the single argument *sed contra* is the definitive statement of the Council of Chalcedon in both articles 1 and 2 of question 2.

In *De unione* Thomas first defines what is meant by "nature" and "person" in this context, taking his definitions from Boethius's treatise *De persona et duabus naturis in Christo.* Since the meaning of "nature" as "the informing specific difference in each and every thing" is distinct from "person" as "an individual substance of a rational nature," there is no reason why something cannot be united in person that is not united in nature. Since human nature does not pertain to the divine nature, but does belong to Christ, the union of these two natures, human and divine, must be personal. This argument is not used in the *Summa.*

In *De unione* Thomas says that among created things there are two ways in which distinct things can be united: accidentally or essentially. But in neither of these ways is the truth of the Incarnation made manifest. Nestorius (d. 451) and Theodore of Mopsuestia (d. 428) had believed that the union of the Godhead and Christ was accidental, that is, by means of the grace of adoption, thus permitting the distinction of two persons. This position was condemned by the Council of Ephesus in 431. Others, wishing to avoid the duality of persons in Christ, maintained that the Divine Word adopted a human soul and a human body that were not naturally united. In this accidental union, however, the Word would not have assumed a true human nature, even though such a separation of body and soul would avoid the formation of a human "person." This teaching was condemned under Alexander III in the Council of Tours in 1163. Others, such as Apollinaris and Eutyches, maintained that the union was essential as if there were a conflation of the human and divine in one nature, or essence. Thus according to Apollinaris, Christ had no human soul, its place being taken by the Divine Word. Secondly, Apollinaris maintained that Christ had, at most, a sensitive soul, but not a rational one, since the divine nature took its place. Thirdly, he held that the body of Christ was not begotten of a woman, but formed directly by the Word from matter that was changed and converted into the Godhead. These three heretical points were brought against Apollinaris in a certain letter written by Pope Leo to the council fathers meeting in Constantinople. Thus the doctrines of Apollinaris were condemned at the Second Council of Constantinople in 553, while Eutyches's doctrine had been condemned in the Council of Chalcedon. This section of *De unione* is the earliest indication we have that Thomas was familiar with the conciliar acts of Constantinople II. Thomas concludes that the union of the Divine Word and human nature cannot be "accidental," nor "essential," but "substantial" (i.e., hypostatic or personal) in the sense that substance signifies a hypostasis. In *Summa* III, q. 2, the various heretical positions are discussed separately according to reason in the service of faith and extensive quotations from the Councils of Ephesus, Chalcedon, and Constantinople II.

In *De unione*, a. 2, Thomas asks whether there is only one hypostasis (or suppositum) in Christ or two. This question parallels question 2, articles 3 and 6, in the *Summa*. This article considers the opinion of those who maintain that Christ has one person (in order to avoid the heresy of Nestorius), but two hypostases, or two supposita. This is the first opinion listed by Peter Lombard in *Sentences* III, dist. 6. According to this opinion, widely discussed in the twelfth century, because it seems to have been defended by an archbishop of Sens,[33] the phrase "this man," pointing to Christ, refers to a suppositum of human nature, and not divine. The expression "this man" implies nothing more than a certain particular substance composed of body and soul. This human suppositum or hypostasis was assumed by the Person of the Word. Therefore although the person is divine, the suppositum assumed by Him was human and distinct from the divine suppositum. Thomas refutes this simply by pointing out the ignorance of terms used, and reducing this opinion to the heresy of Nestorius. In the *Summa* he considers this opinion under the general heading of "accidental union." He insists that this view should no longer be listed as an "opinion," but as a heresy condemned by the councils of the Church.

Although question 2 of the *Summa* is better organized and depends more heavily on conciliar texts, it could be considered contemporary with *De unione,* aa. 1–2. However, *De unione,* aa. 3–4, seems to be earlier than the parallel discussion in *Summa* III, q. 17, which is in two articles. The problem discussed in these parallel places is identical, but the intricate development of the argument in them is quite different.

De unione, a. 3, and *Summa* III, q. 17, a. 1, are essays in theological grammar. A major part of theology, at least of scholastic theology, consists in knowing what man can say and cannot say to preserve the truth of revelation. The problem under consideration is whether we can say Christ is one or many in the neuter gender. This debate was occasioned by the opinion of the archbishop of Sens, considered in the previous article in *De unione,* namely, that there are two hypostases or supposita in Christ, but only one person. Since the masculine form of "he" or "him" always refers to the person, Christ is said to be "one" (*unus*) in the masculine gender. But if Christ has two supposita, as claimed by the archbishop of Sens, can the human suppositum be referred to as "it" (*unum*) in the neuter? This problem is most difficult to discuss in English, for it is a problem of Latin grammar in the service of the faith. We cannot do justice to the problem here, but only indicate the line of argument.

In *De unione* the argument involves the different ways in which things are said to be "one" absolutely and relatively, i.e., *simpliciter* and *secundum quid.* Since "one" is convertible with "being," there are as many ways of saying "one" or "many" as there are modes of being, namely, substantial and accidental. There are many things in nature which are "one" substantially and "many" accidentally, at least in Latin. A man who is white of skin and musical of talent can be said to be "one" *simpliciter* (for there is only one substance involved) and "many" *secundum quid* (because there are many accidents involved). So it is with Christ, who can in a certain sense be called *unum* in the neuter, because there is only one suppositum, and in a certain sense, He may be called "many" or "two" because He has two natures. Consequently, "since Christ is a single supposite having two natures, it follows that Christ is 'one' [*unum*] *simpliciter* and 'two' *secundum quid.*"

The argument in *Summa* III, q. 17, a. 1, is quite different. Thomas no longer speaks of Christ as "two," even *secundum quid*. The basic principle is that unity and plurality depend entirely on *esse*, which is discussed in the following article. Since, as we shall see, Christ has only one *esse*, reference to Him must be not only *unus* in the masculine but also *unum* in the neuter. The argument in the *Summa* is based on the distinction of abstract and concrete names used as predicates in human speech. Only in the Godhead can abstract names be predicated, such as "God is love," "God is truth," etc. In all creatures, names must be predicated in the concrete. Thus we can say "Christ is man," but not "Christ is humanity." The question of duality in Christ is raised only in terms of His two natures. If both of these natures could be predicated of Christ in the abstract, we would be justified in saying that Christ is twofold, just as we say the Godhead is triune. However, since the two natures are predicated of Christ precisely as they are signified in His person or hypostasis, the terms "one" and "two" are predicated of Christ *secundum rationem suppositi*, that is, precisely as they relate to the suppositum, or Person. Since Nestorius postulated two persons in Christ, he could say that Christ is "two" both in the masculine and in the neuter. "But since we postulate only one person and one suppositum in Christ, it follows that we can say not only "one" in the masculine gender [*unus*], but also "one" in the neuter gender [unum]." In other words, there is a radical difference between predicating divine terms of Christ and predicating human terms; divine terms are predicated in the abstract, while human terms must be predicated in the concrete with all their determined, individual properties. This is to say that duality does not arise from the two natures in Christ, but only from the way in which they exist in the one Person of the Word. Thus it is not correct to speak of Christ being "two" *secundum quid*, but rather "one" having two natures.

This brings us to the most controverted question in *De unione* in relation to the *Summa*: whether there is only one *esse* in Christ. This question follows logically upon the previous discussion. The arguments proposed in these two works are profoundly different and must be considered a development of doctrine.

In *De unione*, a. 4, Thomas utilizes the distinction made in the previous article between *simpliciter* and *secundum quid* and gropes for a solution that would allow Christ to have a human "*esse*" *secundum quid*. Thomas argues:

> Just as Christ is "one" *simpliciter* because of the unity of the supposite, and "two" *secundum quid* because of the two natures, so he has one "*esse*" *simpliciter* because of the eternity of the divine supposite. But there is another *esse* belonging to the supposite, not insofar as He is eternal, but insofar as He became man in time. Although this *esse* is not accidental to the Son of God—for the term "man" is not predicated accidentally of Christ, as already demonstrated—it is not the principal *esse* of the supposite, but secondary.

Thomas agreed that if Christ were two persons, one human and the other divine, there would be a twofold *esse*, each of which would be principal in its own right. In this argumentation Thomas allowed the human nature of Christ to have an *esse* proper to itself, distinct from the divine *esse*.

In the *Summa* (q. 17, a. 2), Thomas in no way allows the human nature of Christ to have an *esse* proper to it. *Esse* belongs properly to the suppositum as that "which" has *esse*, and to the nature as that "by which" a suppositum exists in a given way. "If there were a form or nature which did not pertain to the personal *esse* of the subsisting hypostasis, that *esse* would not belong to the person *simpliciter*, but *secundum quid*, just as "to be white" is the *esse* of Socrates, not insofar as he is Socrates, but insofar as he is white." Such an *esse* would be accidental to the person. Since human nature does not belong to Christ accidentally, its *esse* must be that of the supposite, and not distinct from it. Thomas might have alluded to the case in creatures: the *esse* of man's human nature is not other than the *esse* of his person. Since Christ's human nature is hypostatically united to the Divine Word, its existence cannot be distinct from the divine *esse* of the Word. Thomas again acknowledges that if there were two supposites or persons in Christ, one human and the other divine, accidentally united, the *esse* of the human person would be distinct from the *esse* of the Divine Person. But for Thomas, the human nature of Christ is united to the Word hypostatically—not accidentally or essentially. Therefore there can be only one *esse*, the divine *esse*, in which the human nature subsists.

In the *Summa*, Thomas no longer admits a secondary *esse* for the human nature of Christ. He no longer holds that the human nature of Christ has unity and "esse" *secundum quid*. The expression *secundum quid* is applied only to accidents, of which there are many, and no longer to the human nature of Christ. It is clear that in the *Summa*, Thomas realized more fully the implications of a hypostatic union, which demands that there be only one *esse* for both the human and divine natures, an *esse* that is not distinct from the Person. In other words, the Divine Word became incarnate, assuming to Himself a complete human nature, which exists by reason of the eternal *esse* of God.

Thomas disputed the question *De unione verbi incarnati* in Paris before Easter 1272, perhaps early in April. His interest in this problem was aroused by the fact that he had begun work on the *tertia pars* of the *Summa*. But we do not know how much of the *tertia pars* was written before he left Paris; in all probability Thomas wrote no more than the first few questions. Question 17 is certainly later than the disputed question *De unione*. If Thomas resumed work on the *Summa* when he reached Naples, there would have been an interval of four or five months between *De unione* and *Summa* III, q. 17. If, however, Thomas dictated on the journey, the interval would have been shorter, but still enough time to rethink the implications of the hypostatic union in Christ. In any case, Thomas composed most of the *tertia pars* in Naples, 1272-73.

When Thomas wrote his prologue to the third part of the *Summa*, he intended to divide the work into three parts: Christ the Savior of mankind (qq. 1-59), His sacraments, through which we attain salvation (q. 60-*Suppl.*, q. 68), and the goal of life eternal, to which we arrive through Him in rising again. From this point of view we can say that the whole of the *tertia pars* is about the "Savior." In his prologue to question 60, Thomas states, "After considering all those things pertaining to the mystery of the Incarnate Word, we must consider the sacraments of the Church, which have their efficacy from the Incarnate Word Himself." However, Thomas did not live to complete his projected plan. By December 6, 1273, he was in the midst of his detailed discussion of the sacrament of Penance; he completed question 90, which discusses the parts of Penance in general, when he "could not" go on.

Thomas divides his discussion of the Incarnate Word into two parts: the mystery of the Incarnation by which God became man for our salvation, and those things which were done and suffered by the Savior for our sake. Under the heading "mystery of the Incarnation," Thomas discusses three major points: the appropriateness of God's becoming man for our salvation (*an sit*), the manner in which God became man in the Incarnation (*quid sit*), and the consequences of this union (*quale sit*).

For Thomas, God could have redeemed mankind in an infinite number of ways, but He chose to reconcile man by communicating with him in the most intimate way imaginable, namely, by becoming man and shedding His own Blood for us. God became man to save us from sin, principally original sin, but from all personal sins as well. Many of Thomas's contemporaries maintained that even if Adam had not sinned, God would have become man because of His great love for us. For Thomas, however, we can know God's motive only through His revelation to us, and the only motive revealed in Scripture and the Creeds of the Church is "on account of our salvation." Thus the principal reason why God became man was to save man from sin, so that if Adam had not sinned, God would not have become man. Consequently in the blessing of the paschal candle the Church sings, "O happy fault (*felix culpa*), which merited to have such and so great a Savior."

In the *tertia pars* Thomas discusses not only the mystery of the Incarnation, which we have considered briefly, but also the mystery of the sacraments, which he calls the "relics of the passion of Christ," because through them the fruits of the Redemption pour into our hearts. For Thomas, the sacraments of the New Law not only symbolize the covenant between God and man, but actually effect the infusion of grace symbolized by the sacramental action. Thus in the *tertia pars* the sacraments do not merely dispose man for the infusion of grace, as he had previously held, but actually *cause* grace. In Thomas's earlier writings, he thought that grace must be created from nothing, and only God can do this upon the application of the sacraments. In the *Summa*, on the other hand, Thomas clearly states that the sacraments, as "instruments" of Christ's passion and death, educe grace from the potentiality of man; later this potentiality came to be called "obediential potency," but we are not concerned with this at the moment.

Among all the sacraments, the most sublime is "the sacrament of the altar," the Holy Eucharist, for it not only causes grace, but also contains the author of grace, Christ Himself. The sacramental action of consecration, namely, the words "This is my Body" and "This is my Blood," effect the real presence of Christ's Body and Blood, the *res* signified by the action and visible species of bread and wine (*sacramentum*). Sacramentally by reason of the words of consecration, the Body and Blood of Christ are present distinct from one another as in the sacrifice of Calvary. By reason of this sacrament it is the dying Christ who is present in the sacrifice, i.e., in the separation of Body and Blood; even the consecrated host held up for adoration and reserved on the altar contains the Body of Christ sacramentally separate from His Blood, that is, the dying Christ. However, since the actual Body of Christ is no longer dying (except sacramentally in the Eucharist), the whole Christ is present by "concomitance," and even the entire Trinity is present by "circumincession." Hence for Thomas the sacramental aspect of the Eucharist is not something other than the sacrificial; the sacramental presence of Christ by transubstantiation is identical with the sacrifice of the altar, an unbloody representation of Calvary.

Unfortunately space does not permit us to dwell longer on the sacraments of Christ as discussed in the *tertia pars* of the *Summa*. We can only point out that Thomas's discussion of the Eucharist, questions 73-83, is among the most sublime and the most perfect treatises produced in the Middle Ages. Thomas seems not only to have worked most diligently on the mystery of the Eucharist, but also to have prayed most fervently.

William of Tocco recounts a story, which he heard from Friar Dominic of Caserta, the sacristan of San Domenico, "who [also] on other occasions had miraculous visions."[34] Friar Dominic, apparently, became curious about Thomas's frequent visits to the chapel of St. Nicholas in San Domenico before Matins. One night Friar Dominic concealed himself to watch Thomas in prayer. He saw Thomas elevated "almost two cubits in the air," and he heard Thomas praying fervently and weeping. Then he heard Thomas speaking to the crucifix on the wall of the chapel. The figure on the cross said, "Thomas, you have written well about me. What reward will you have?" To which Thomas replied, "Lord, nothing but yourself." Tocco adds that at that time Thomas was writing the third part of the *Summa* on the passion and resurrection of Christ. It could very well have been the treatise on the Eucharist. To this day the friars of San Domenico point out the crucifix that spoke to Thomas in the chapel of St. Nicholas. Whatever credence must be given to this story of Friar Dominic of Caserta, one must admit that it could have happened and that it perfectly expresses Thomas's anxiety over the third part of the *Summa*.

Besides composing this remarkable part of the *Summa* at Naples, Thomas also worked on his commentaries on Aristotle, some of which were left unfinished when he left Paris. All of the Aristotelian commentaries are difficult to date, but there are three or four that can be attributed to Thomas's last years in Naples: part of the *Metaphysics, De caelo* (unfinished), *De generatione* (unfinished), and possibly the unfinished commentary on the *Meteora*. The largest and most important of these is undoubtedly his *Sententia super Metaphysicam*. It seems to have been begun in Paris and completed in Naples. This may very well have been one of the works referred to by the faculty of arts at Paris after Thomas's death when the rector and procurators requested that certain writings of a philosophical nature be sent to them, works that were "begun by him at Paris, left unfinished at his departure, but completed, we have reason to believe, in the place to which he was transferred."[35] In *Metaphysics* XII, lect. 10, Thomas quoted three passages from Simplicius's commentary on *De caelo,* which was completed by Moerbeke at Viterbo on June 15, 1271.[36] Similarly Thomas's commentary on *De caelo* utilizes Simplicius throughout, but Thomas's unfinished commentary terminates in Book II, lect. 8, the rest being by Peter of Auvergne. Eschmann, however, suggests that the commentary on *De caelo* is not "unfinished," but completed as far as it goes: Thomas "knew no more Aristotelian

text of *De caelo* than [that] which he explained."[37] This important commentary, in the words of Eschmann, "represents the
high-water mark of St. Thomas's expository skill." The commentary on *De generatione* is unfinished, terminating with Book
I, lect. 17, the remainder being written by Thomas Sutton and
others. William of Tocco himself saw Thomas writing this commentary on *De generatione*, and testified that he believed this to
have been Thomas's "last work in philosophy."[38] The unfinished
commentary on the *Meteora*, terminating with Book II, 8, 369a9,
might also have been written in Naples, although Mandonnet
and Grabmann believe it to have been composed in Paris, 1269–
72, while Pelster believes it to be of Neapolitan origin. The
Leonine text ends with lecture 10 in Book II, c. 5, 363a20,
but A. Dondaine has discovered the commentary on chapters 7
and 8; the commentary on Book II, c. 6, seems to be lost.[39] The
rest of Book II and all of Book III were written by an anonymous
master in arts, as well as by Peter of Auvergne, while the commentary on Book IV is by James of Douai.[40] The *Meteora* of
Aristotle was utilized in detail by Thomas throughout his lectures on Psalm 17.

Not all of the unfinished works of Thomas should be attributed
to his last years in Naples. Some of them, including the commentary on *Peri hermenias*, were begun in Paris and never finished at all. Further research is needed to determine the sources
and dates of the Aristotelian commentaries.

Two more important writings, listed among the *opuscula*,
should be considered briefly, because most historians tend to
date them toward the end of Thomas's stay in Paris or during
his last years in Naples. These are the *Compendium theologiae*
and *De substantiis separatis*, both unfinished and both dedicated
to his faithful companion Reginald of Piperno.

Thomas's *Compendium theologiae* was of particular interest
in the late Middle Ages, and it was frequently copied, as the
eighty-two extant MSS testify. It is a brief and succinct presentation of the whole of Christian life, divided into three parts:
faith, hope, and charity. According to Thomas, St. Paul teaches
in 1 Corinthians 13:13 that "the whole perfection of the present
life consists in faith, hope, and love." Therefore the treatise
for Reginald was to be divided into these three parts so that he

could always have before his eyes the teaching of the Christian religion in a brief manner (*doctrina compendiosa*). The first part on faith treats all the basic truths of faith in 246 chapters, from the existence of the one God, the Trinity, creation, souls, the Incarnation, and the passion and death of Christ, to the final judgment. Although the doctrines discussed parallel those of the *Summa*, the style of presentation is more reminiscent of the *Summa contra gentiles*, the only section missing being that on the sacraments. Thomas began the second treatise on hope and prayer, but ended abruptly within chaper 10. One MS of Bologna has a colophon, which states: "Friar Thomas d'Aquino wrote thus far, but alas prevented by death, he left it incomplete."[41] Despite this and other indications, some modern scholars tend to date the *Compendium theologiae* much earlier.

The important treatise *De substantiis separatis*, or *De angelis*, was written, according to the Leonine editors of this "philosophical opusculum," between 1270 and 1273.[42] It is a personal evaluation of the relative merits of what Plato, Aristotle, Avicenna, Avicebron, Origen, and other ancients had to say about separate substances. Thomas clearly evaluates the acceptable points of their teaching and points out their erroneous views. Despite the fact that Thomas had access to practically nothing of Plato's writings, he saw the major points on which Plato and Aristotle agreed, as well as the major points on which they disagreed. This personal evaluation of Plato and Aristotle is of great interest to philosophers, even though this "philosophical opusculum" is clearly a theological treatise. For Thomas, Plato and Aristotle agree on three points: all immaterial substances participate in the supreme Being, who is God; they are completely devoid of matter; and they share in the governance of the world through divine providence. On the other hand, Plato and Aristotle differ on three points: for Plato the separate substances are species of all things, while for Aristotle they are intellectual beings who know themselves and move the spheres; Plato does not limit their number to the number of celestial motions, as does Aristotle; Aristotle does not postulate any souls intermediary between the "souls of the spheres" and the soul of man, as does Plato when he acknowledges demons. If Thomas had lived to complete this work, the theological character of the treatise would have become

most evident. As things happened, the treatise ends with chapter
20, which discusses the grades of angelic spirits.

At Naples, Thomas not only studied, lectured, wrote, and held
disputations, but he also preached, notably throughout the whole
of Lent 1273. As preacher general for Naples, he had the obligation of providing a Lenten preacher. He undertook the task
himself and preached daily in the Neapolitan vernacular from
Septuagesima (February 12) until Easter (April 9) on two
precepts of charity, the ten precepts of the law, the Apostles'
Creed, the Our Father, and possibly the Hail Mary. This Lenten
cycle of fifty-seven or fifty-nine sermons (if one includes the Hail
Mary) has always been published among the *opuscula* of Thomas,
whereas it should have been listed among the sermons. In their
published Latin form, they are simply summaries of the particular points made by the preacher; they are not the full sermon
text. In the canonization inquiry a great number of laymen and
religious testified that they heard Thomas's sermons during Lent,
and were deeply moved by that memorable experience. Among
those who had heard them were John Coppa of Naples (who said
that "almost the whole population of Naples went to hear his
sermons every day"), John Blasio, a Neapolitan judge, Peter Bran-
chatius, and John of Caiatis, as well as many religious.[43] In the
words of William of Tocco, "He was heard by the people with
such reverence that it was as if his preaching came forth from
God."[44] The sermon summaries we have in our printed works are
reportationes by Reginald of Piperno, except that the sermons on
the ten precepts of the law were taken down by Friar Peter
d'Andria.

Thomas had been working at a high pitch for the preceding
five years, ever since his return to Paris in 1269, when he seemed
to realize in a new way the great need for his apostolate. A kind
of fever seemed to possess him, so that "he was continuously
occupied in teaching, or in writing, or in preaching, or in praying, so that he devoted the least possible time to eating or to
sleeping."[45] The quality of his work never suffered. On the contrary, he continued to mull over problems and their solution,
trying to improve his grasp of the truth. In the odyssey of his
thought he progressed from imperfect solutions to more perfect
expressions of the truth. He modified earlier opinions and some-

times changed them significantly. He was never satisfied with a simple repetition of a view he expressed earlier, even when he was answering letters from those who sought his expert opinion on various problems, but had to rethink every problem anew. Perhaps this was the secret of his originality and freshness: rethinking every problem anew, and presenting newer and more accurate solutions to old problems. His was constantly an apostolate of service to others: "always studying, lecturing, or writing for the good of his fellow Christians."[46] "It was the common view," according to Bartholomew of Capua, "that he had wasted scarcely a moment of his time."[47]

Obviously Thomas could not keep up this pace forever. Something had to give way after five years of driving himself day in and day out. Before he was forty-nine years old, he had written more than forty substantial volumes that benefited the Church and mankind. Judging from the available evidence, we can say that Thomas's health was generally excellent throughout life; his resistance and stamina were considerable. However, something happened to Thomas on December 6, 1273, that changed his whole life; three months later he died, on March 7, 1274.

Breakdown and the Last Journey

(December 6, 1273–March 7, 1274)

The best source of our information about the last months of Thomas's life is Bartholomew of Capua, a layman prominent as *logotheta* and prothonotary in the service of the king; there can be no doubt that the source of his information was Reginald himself, who died less than thirty years before the process of canonization began. Reginald is also the source of much information in the biography and witness of William of Tocco.

According to Bartholomew, Thomas adhered to a strict regimen. He arose early every morning to confess his sins to Reginald and celebrate Mass in the chapel of St. Nicholas, served by Reginald and attended by at least one layman, Nicholas Fricia. After his own Mass, Thomas made his thanksgiving while attending another Mass, usually said by Reginald. Then he immediately began his teaching. "After descending from the [professorial] chair, he set himself to write or dictate to his many secretaries until the time for dinner." After dinner he went to his cell to pray until siesta time, after which he resumed his writing and dictating. After working late at night, he spent considerable time praying in the chapel of St. Nicholas before the brethren arose for Matins; when the bell for Matins sounded, he quickly returned to his cell and appeared to have risen with the rest. After Matins he seems to have gone to bed. Such a routine was well known to his brethren and to some of the laymen in the city.[48]

On Wednesday morning, December 6, the feast of St. Nicholas, Thomas arose early as usual to celebrate the Mass of the feast in the chapel of St. Nicholas. During Mass, Thomas was suddenly struck (*commotus*) by something that profoundly affected and changed him (*mira mutatione*). "After this Mass he never wrote or dictated anything." In fact, he "hung up his instruments of writing" (an allusion to the Jews who hung up their instruments during the exile) "in the third part of the *Summa*, in the treatise on Penance." When Reginald realized that Thomas had altered entirely his routine of more than fifteen years, he asked him, "Father, why have you put aside such a great work which you began for the praise of God and the enlightenment of the world?" To which Thomas answered simply, "Reginald, I cannot." But Reginald, afraid that Thomas was mentally unbalanced from so much study, insisted that he continue his writing and return to his former routine, at least at a slower pace. But the more Reginald insisted, the more impatient Thomas became until he replied, "Reginald, I cannot, because all that I have written seems like straw to me." Reginald was mystified at this reply. But Thomas was serious; he could not go on. He was physically and mentally unable to do so. The only recourse he had was to prayer for himself, and acceptance of his inability to work.

Later in December or in January, Thomas expressed a desire to visit his sister, the Countess Theodora of San Severino.[49] In the company of Friar Reginald, Thomas "hastened there with great difficulty; but when he arrived and the countess came out to meet him, he could scarcely say a word." Thomas was like this, dazed, for the three days he remained at San Severino. According to Bartholomew, the countess was "very much alarmed," and asked Reginald, "What is wrong with Friar Thomas? He is completely out of his senses (*stupefactus*) and has scarcely spoken to me." Reginald answered, "He has been in this state since about the feast of St. Nicholas, and from that time onward he has written nothing."

Then again Reginald began to beseech Thomas to tell him why he refused to write and why he was so constantly dazed (*stupefactus*). After much urgent questioning and insisting, Thomas at last said to Reginald, "Promise me, by the living God Almighty and by your loyalty to our Order and by the love you bear me, that you will never reveal, as long as I live, what I shall tell you. All that I have written seems to me like straw compared to what has now been revealed to me."

According to Bartholomew, who was closer to the incident than Tocco, Gui, or Calo, and who heard it from John Giudice (who heard it from Reginald when he was on his deathbed), Thomas expressed the same reason for not writing to Reginald both at Naples and at San Severino: "I cannot; all that I have written seems like straw."[50] The only thing Tocco, Gui, and Calo add to this statement is that Thomas said, "The only thing I want now is that as God has put an end to my writing, He may quickly end my life also." After three days, Thomas and Reginald left San Severino for Naples, leaving the countess deeply disturbed (*multum desolata*).

The ancient biographers and witnesses at the canonization process do not give sufficient details of the extraordinary experience Thomas had on December 6. But from what little is recorded, it would seem that there were two aspects of the event: one physical and mental, the other mystical. The physical basis for the event could have been a stroke resulting in some brain damage or it could have been an acute breakdown of his physical and emotional powers due to overwork. While the possibility of a stroke resulting in brain damage through hemorrhage cannot be ruled out, it would seem rather that the physical basis for the experience of December 6 was a breakdown of his constitution after so many years of driving himself ceaselessly in the work he loved. In this case it would not have been a breakdown caused by mental disturbance, but it would have been a physical breakdown resulting in mental disturbance, anxiety, and a change in emotional values wherein the *Summa* and the Aristotelian commentaries no longer seemed important. Clearly after this experience there was impaired speech and a loss of manual dexterity and gait, which could have resulted from severe brain damage through hemorrhage.[51] In divine providence such a disturbance of mind and body are sometimes accompanied by a mystical experience, if not at the moment of affliction, then certainly within the period it lasts. In Thomas's case, the two aspects could have been simultaneous: everything he had done and worked for seemed "worthless," "trivial," and "like straw." In themselves these expressions do not necessarily indicate a mystical experience, for they can easily be the result of the physical condition itself. However, biographers and hagiographers see in them an expression of a mystical vision he experienced. The main point is that from December 6 onward Thomas could not return to the *Summa* or the commentaries on Aristotle even at a slower pace. He could neither teach nor write. All he could do was pray and go through the physical motions of life. In other words, there was clearly a physical basis for the extraordinary experience at Mass on December 6, 1273.

Once at Naples, according to John Coppa, a Neapolitan layman,[52] he and his brother, Friar Bonofilio, visited Thomas in his cell when he was ill and in bed. They "both saw a bright star come in at the window and remain for a while over Thomas's head; the star was about as large as the window through which it came." Then they saw it pass slowly out of the window. Bernard Gui places this incident between December 6 and the time Thomas left Naples for the Council of Lyons.[53] From this incident it is clear that the experience of December 6 was not entirely mystical; he was physically ill after it.

Shortly after the event just narrated, the order came that Thomas was to go to the Second Council of Lyons, called by Pope Gregory X. It was to begin on Monday, May 7, 1274, at Lyons, the temporary residence of the Pope in southern France. Since the main purpose of this fourteenth ecumenical council was the reconciliation of the Greeks with the Latin Church,

Thomas was asked to bring along a copy of his *Contra errores Graecorum,* which he had written at the request of Urban IV in the summer of 1263. Around the beginning of February, Thomas, Reginald, and an attendant named Friar James of Salerno set out for Lyons. At Teano, north of Capua on the Via Latina, they were joined by William, dean of Teano (who later became bishop of the place), and his nephew Roffredo (who later became dean). Leaving Teano, the company walked a few miles north toward Borgonuovo, where an incident occurred that could have resulted in the death of Thomas. Bartholomew of Capua notes the incident briefly: "Going down from Teano to Borgonuovo, Thomas accidentally struck his head against a tree that had fallen across the road, and was half stunned and hardly able to stand." It is not clear whether Thomas was traveling by donkey at this stage of the journey, as he was later to do, but the incident would be more significant if he were on a donkey and knocked off by the blow on the head and "hardly able to stand." The "tree" was undoubtedly a low branch extending over the road. This blow could have resulted in a clot on the top of the brain (subdural hematoma) that grew larger and larger every day; the fact that it was ingravescent is clear from the events of the next few weeks. In any case, Reginald and the rest rushed up to Thomas after the blow on the head, and asked whether he was injured. Thomas answered, "A little."[54]

Reginald, trying to provide a subtle diversion, reminded Thomas that he was on his way to the Council, where much good would be accomplished. Thomas replied, "Please God, that will be so." Then Reginald suggested that he and Friar Bonaventure would certainly be made cardinals, not knowing that Bonaventure had already been created a cardinal on June 3, 1273. Thomas answered, "I can serve the Order best as I am." But Reginald pressed on with the argument until Thomas cut him short and said, "Reginald, you may be quite sure that I shall go on exactly as I am." This story was reported to Bartholomew by Roffredo, "who was there and saw and heard everything."

It is not certain which route the travelers took after Borgonuovo. The bull of canonization seems to imply that they took the coastal route, the Via Appia; but some modern historians believe that Thomas took the inland route, the Via Latina, and revived childhood memories.[55] One argument used to suggest that Thomas and his companions took the inland route passing by Aquino, Roccasecca, and Monte Cassino is that Thomas must have written a letter to Bernard Ayglier, abbot of Monte Cassino,[56] while he was in the vicinity, perhaps in the Dominican priory in San Germano; but this argument is debatable. In any case, after a few hours' travel, Thomas became very exhausted and asked to stop at the castle of Maenza, where his niece Francesca lived, inland from the Via Appia near the Cistercian Abbey of Fossanova. Francesca was the wife of Annibaldo, Count of Ceccano, one of the patrons of the abbey; the abbot at that time was the old man Theobald, who belonged to the Ceccano family. It was already Lent.[57] Since Lent began on February 14 that year, it can be presumed that Thomas stopped at Maenza in the second half of February. Thomas remained at Maenza for "some days, because he became rather seriously ill." He could eat nothing and he completely lost his appetite. Reginald and the physician John di Guido tried desperately to induce Thomas to eat something solid. At one point Thomas thought he might be able to eat some fresh herrings, as he had in Paris. At that moment a fishmonger from Terracina passed by on the road with some sardines. Miraculously the fishmonger was found to have some fresh herrings, even though the man insisted that he had none, since they were not available in that part of the world. Thomas eventually ate the herrings, as did his niece Francesca, together with some Cistercians, Dominicans, and Franciscans who had come to visit Thomas.

It would seem, however, that Thomas was still able to celebrate Mass while at the castle of Maenza. Witnesses testified that he did so with extraordinary devotion and many tears. The Cistercians who had come to visit him remained "about four or five days." Among them were James of Ferentino, the prior, Peter of Montesangiovanni, John of Piedemonte, and Brother Fidelis of Ferentino. While Thomas was at Maenza, he got steadily worse so that he had to spend more time in bed. Toward the end of February, Thomas felt that his end was near and asked to be taken to the Cistercian Abbey of Fossanova. Thomas, in fact, had been invited by the prior, James of Ferentino, to come to the abbey. He was heard by many witnesses to say, "If the Lord is coming for me, I had better be found in a religious house than in a castle."[58] So he had himself carried by a donkey to the abbey, which was six miles away. The prior, the other monks, and his Dominican companions went with him. As he entered the cloister, he was heard to utter the words of Psalm 131:14: "This is my rest for ever and ever; here I will dwell, for I have chosen it." On the other hand, this verse of Psalm 131 may have been falsely attributed to Thomas by the Cistercians as justification for claiming the body of Thomas for almost a hundred years. Contrary to William of Tocco and the local tradition, Thomas was not given the abbot's cell in which to die, but rather a small room in the guesthouse. During the process of canonization, the new abbot, Nicholas, testified that Thomas lay ill in the monastery for "about a month." But this is a great exaggeration. Thomas arrived at the end of February, and by March 7 he was dead. Thomas lay ill in the guest room at Fossanova for not more than a week or two, at the most.

The monks of the monastery of St. Mary at Fossanova were extremely kind to Thomas in every way, and Thomas was a model of patience, gentleness, and humility, as all testified at the process of canonization. Thomas's condition continued to get worse, and on Sunday, three days before his death, Thomas made a general confession to Reginald and received the Eucharist. Abbot Theobald himself brought the Eucharist to him. Before receiving Communion, Thomas said in the presence of the "whole community of monks and many Dominicans and Friars Minor" many "beautiful things" concerning his firm belief in the real presence, and in particular this: "I have taught and written much on this most holy Body and on the other sacraments, according to my faith in Christ and in the holy Roman Church, to whose judgment I submit all my teaching."[59]

There is a persistent view, promulgated in part by William of Tocco,[60] that Thomas, knowing his end to be near, wished to leave a memorial of himself to the monks, who had asked for such a favor. According to Tocco, Thomas dictated "a brief commentary on the Canticle of Canticles." In all the early catalogues there is mention of a commentary *Super Cantica*. Whether this listing is the same as the "brief commentary" for the monks is not clear. In any case, there is no known commentary on the Canticles, short or long, that can be attributed to Thomas. The two versions in the printed collected works are spurious.[61] If a manuscript were to be found eventually that represents Thomas's deathbed commentary, it would have to be a very "brief" one in the form of a dictation or *reportatio*.

Thomas lingered on for three days after receiving viaticum. An aged priest and monk of Fossanova, named Peter of Montesangiovanni, testified that the Franciscan bishop of Terracina, Francis, was present with four or five Franciscans of his household, "many" Dominicans (presumably from the nearby priories of Anagni and Gaeta, and about a hundred monks and lay brothers of the monastery while Thomas lingered on.[62] On the day following his reception of viaticum, he was anointed, Thomas himself responding to all the prayers. Two days later, early Wednesday morning, March 7, Thomas passed peacefully from this life to his eternal reward. Considering that Thomas was only forty-nine years old and had written more than forty volumes in the service of others, we can paraphrase the words of Wisdom 4:13–14: He lived a long life in a short time, and because God loved him, He took him.

In the process of canonization many miracles were reported that occurred after the death of Thomas. Bartholomew of Capua recorded one that happened even before the body of Thomas was washed for burial, when the almost blind subprior of Fossanova received complete use of his eyes on contact with Thomas's body.[63] There is no need here to recount all those miracles, real or imagined, that are supposed to have occurred in connection with Thomas's body before and after he was buried. This was the chief concern of officials of the process of canonization, particularly the process at Fossanova. These miracles can be read in the process of canonization held both in Naples and in Fossanova, as well as in all the popular lives of Thomas.

William of Tocco recorded the formal entry of Thomas's death as follows:

> The aforesaid doctor died in the year of our Lord 1274, in the fourth year of the reign of Pope Gregory X, in the forty-ninth year of his life, during the second [imperial] indiction, on the seventh day of March in the morning.[64]

∘ But Bernard Gui, using an independent source, is equally emphatic in his statement that:

∘   He died in the Lord in the morning of the ninth (?) of March, at the beginning of the year 1274 of the Incarnation of the Lord, at the completion of his forty-ninth year and in the beginning of his fiftieth.[65]

Thus, according to Tocco, Thomas was in his "forty-ninth year" when he died, i.e., he had celebrated his forty-eighth birthday, but not yet his forty-ninth. This means that Thomas was forty-eight years old when he died, having been born in 1225/6. On the other hand, according to Bernard Gui, Thomas was "beginning" his fiftieth year, having celebrated his forty-ninth birthday, but not yet his fiftieth; on this reckoning Thomas was born in 1224/5, and died at the age of forty-nine. Not only is Gui more certain in his statement of Thomas's age than Tocco, but his entire chronology—which we have used—seems more probable.

No credence whatever can be given to the popular rumor that Thomas was poisoned to death by order of King Charles I of Naples. One story has it that the king asked Thomas the day before he departed for the Council of Lyons: "Friar Thomas, if the Pope inquires about me, what will you say?" Thomas replied: "I'll simply tell him the truth." The king is supposed to have thought over this reply and found it not to his liking. So he sent his personal physician together with some trustworthy companions to catch up with Thomas on the journey; two days later the physician administered the fatal poison that sent Thomas to heaven.[66] Another rumor had it that King Charles was afraid that Thomas might be elected Pope, and so he had the poison administered. Even Dante recorded this legend in his *Divine Comedy* (*Purgatorio* XX, 67–69):

> Charles [of Anjou] came to Italy, and
> He made a victim of Conradin; and then
> He sent Thomas to heaven.

Although this fourteenth-century rumor completely lacks foundation, it indicates that neither we nor they know the real cause of Thomas's death. This is usually the case with recorded natural deaths in the Middle Ages. However, I would suggest that Thomas's death might well have been caused by a hemorrhaged blood clot (subdural hematoma) brought on by the blow on the head from the overhanging tree, already mentioned. While such a diagnosis cannot be proved or disproved seven hundred years after the event, it remains a possibility.

The solemn Requiem Mass for Thomas was held at the monastery of Fossanova shortly after his death, perhaps, as was common, on the third day, i.e., on Friday, March 9, according to the rite used in Benedictine monasteries.[67] Lay people, relatives, and friends of the Aquino family attended in great numbers, together with Bishop Francis and his Franciscan companions, and a few Dominicans who had come from Anagni and Gaeta. It is surprising, however, that none of the Dominican authorities from Naples or Rome attended the funeral. A contemporary Dominican author points out that not only were there no Dominican authorities at the funeral, but there was not even a vicar to represent the authorities.[68] It would seem that Reginald of Piperno preached the sermon or made a short statement, in which he declared from personal experience the sanctity and purity of Thomas's whole life. At one point in his testimony Reginald said: "Before God I declare that I have always found him like a little child in purity; and I am sure that he never gave willing consent to a mortal sin."[69] By the fifteenth century, Thomas's angelic purity was so widely proclaimed that he acquired the scholastic title of "Angelic Doctor."

Many women, including the Countess Francesca from Maenza, came to Fossanova for the funeral, but none of them were allowed to enter the cloister where the funeral rites were celebrated. However, as a special concession to Francesca, the bier was brought to the monastery gates so that she could see her uncle's body for the last time. This was the occasion for loud demonstrations of grief from the women present and emotional excitement among all. We are even told that the donkey which brought Thomas to Fossanova broke its tether in the stables, ran up to the bier, and fell dead in its tracks![70] The body was then returned to the monastery church and interred in front of the high altar; miracles continued to be reported.

Although Thomas had come to the end of his last journey, his body had not. Shortly after the burial, the monks "began to worry that the corpse might be stolen [by the Dominicans], so they secretly transferred the body from this sepulcher to a chapel, called the chapel of St. Stephen, within the same monastery." According to the sworn testimony of the same witness, Peter of Montesangiovanni, about seven months later Friar Thomas appeared in a dream to prior James of Ferentino and said, "Return me to the original place," which meant that the prior's guilty conscience bothered him even in sleep. The coffin was exhumed, opened, a sweet odor filled the entire cloister, and the body was found to be incorrupt, despite the dampness of the ground and the bulk of Thomas's body. The prior then sang the Mass of a confessor (*Os justi*) in the presence of the whole community; he obviously felt that a Requiem Mass would be inappropriate.[71] This must have taken place around September 1274.

After the death of Pope Gregory X on January 10, 1276, it was rumored that Peter of Tarentaise, a Dominican master of Paris, might be elected Pope—as he was in the following June. The Cistercian monks feared that if he were elected, he would order Thomas's body to be returned to the Dominicans. Therefore, according to Bartholomew of Capua, the Cistercian monks "selected three representatives and one night they exhumed the corpse of Friar Thomas from its resting place; they cut off the head and placed it in a hiding place in a corner of the chapel which lies behind the choir—which the present witness has seen several times."[72] The monks at Fossanova reasoned that if the body had to be given to the Dominicans, they would have at least the head. Foster, however, denies that the corpse was decapitated at this time, since there is no mention of a missing head in a later exhumation.[73] Another exhumation seems to have taken place in 1288, when the Countess Theodora asked for the right hand, from which a thumb had already been removed by Reginald of Piperno before the funeral in 1274.

In 1303 another Dominican was elected Pope with the name of Benedict XI, and the Cistercians, again fearing the loss of their holy relic, transferred the corpse to a third location. Foster suggests that it might have been at this time that the head of

Thomas was removed. However, around this same time, certainly before the first canonization process began in 1319, the monks of Fossanova seem to have boiled the flesh off the corpse, so that they could keep the bones "in a small place." William of Tocco testified under oath at the first canonization inquiry that he had seen the bones in a small casket which was kept in the sacristy of the monastery of Fossanova.[74]

Finally in 1369, after much maneuvering by both Dominicans and Cistercians, Pope Urban V ordered that what remained of the body was to be given to the Order of Preachers. That same year, Urban V ordered the monks of Fossanova to give the head of Thomas to the bishop of Lucca, who then presented it to the Dominican master general Elias Raymond. Raymond Hugues, a witness who viewed the bones at this time, noted that they were "of reddish color, looking as if by boiling or some other change effected by heat, they had been violently detached from the flesh."[75] On Saturday, January 28, 1369, the relics were transferred to the old Dominican priory in Toulouse;[76] this priory was endangered by the French Revolution, but early in the Revolution Thomas's remains had been transferred to the church of St. Sernin in Toulouse for safekeeping. From 1369 until 1921 January 28 was observed in the Dominican Order as a second feast of St. Thomas, the main one being March 7, the day of his death. In the modern ecclesiastical calendar, the sole feast of St. Thomas is observed on January 28, since it falls outside of Lent. Today there is a new Dominican Priory in Toulouse dedicated to St. Thomas Aquinas; this priory claims as its foundation date 1216, the date of the original foundation. However, the relics of Friar *
Thomas are still preserved in the parish church of St. Sernin where they were transported for safekeeping. Thus, Thomas's last journey from Naples came to an end in Toulouse, where the Dominican Order began.

Controversies, Condemnation, and Canonization

(1274–1323)

The bizarre tactics employed by the Cistercians of Fossanova to keep the body of Thomas for themselves ended in 1369, ninety-five years after his death, when Pope Urban V ordered that the body and head be given to the Dominicans. By this time, Thomas's teachings had been heatedly controverted, by some condemned, and by others "canonized."

On Wednesday, May 2, 1274, the rector and procurators of the University of Paris together "with all the masters at present teaching in the faculty of arts" sent a touching letter to the Dominican chapter meeting in Lyons that year on Pentecost, May 20. In that letter[77] the masters expressed their grief on the death of Friar Thomas: "For news has come to us which floods us with grief and amazement, bewilders our understanding, transfixes our very vitals, and well-nigh breaks our hearts." They noted that once before they had written to the general chapter of the Order meeting in Florence and "begged that this man be restored to us—begged, alas, in vain." The masters in arts then stated their principal reason for writing, which was to have the body of Thomas buried in Paris, "the noblest of all university cities." If they could not have Thomas recalled in life, then perhaps they could have him in death. For them, only Paris had the right "to guard the bones of him whose youth was nourished, fostered, and educated here at Paris, which then received from him in return the inexpressible benefit of his teaching." Perhaps realizing the futility of this request, they expressed a second reason for writing to the capitular fathers. The second reason for writing was threefold: they asked the fathers to send them (a) "some writings of a philosophical nature, begun by [Thomas] at Paris, left unfinished at his departure, but completed, we have reason to believe, in the place to which he was transferred," (b) three translations which "he himself promised would be sent to us," namely, the commentary of Simplicius on *De caelo et mundo*, the exposition of Plato's *Timaeus* by Proclus, and a work entitled *De aquarum conductibus et ingeniis erigendis*, which seems to have been the *Pneumatica* of Hero of Alexandria, and (c) "any new writings of his own on logic, such as, when he was about to leave us, we took the liberty of asking him to write." It would seem, then, that among the writings Thomas left unfinished when he departed from Paris and completed in Naples must be placed his *Sententia super Metaphysicam*. The three translations mentioned were made by William of Moerbeke; they seem to have been in Thomas's possession by the time he left Paris in April 1272. The letter is not specific about the "new writings of his own on logic," which the masters asked him to write. Walz and others suggest that the treatise *De fallaciis* belongs to this group. However, a stronger case can be urged to show that *De fallaciis* is an early work, composed in 1244–45 during Thomas's confinement at Roccasecca. Foster flatly states that "there are no such works" (i.e., on logic) written by Thomas during the last period of his life.[78]

The reaction of the capitular fathers meeting in Lyons is unknown, for the acts of that chapter make no mention of Thomas whatever, neither his death nor the communication from the masters at Paris. Certainly the body of Thomas could not be sent to Paris, for it was in the hands of the Cistercians at Fossanova, who refused to give up the body of "so great a saint." Quite possibly the capitular fathers agreed to send the three translations requested by the masters and some of the philosophical works written by Thomas, whatever they were. The concern of the Parisian masters in arts confirms our belief that Thomas wrote the commentaries on Aristotle for their sake, and not for the sake of himself or of his Dominican students. However, it might be considered strange that none of Thomas's philosophical commentaries appear on the Parisian stationer's list of 1286.[79]

Unfortunately Thomas's writings could not stem the growth of Averroism among the masters in arts at Paris and the growing concern of Augustinist theologians, for whom the use of pagan philosophers, notably Aristotle and Averroes, was a dangerous innovation. The condemnation by Stephen Tempier, bishop of Paris, of thirteen explicitly Averroist theses on December 10, 1270, seems to have had little effect. By early January 1277, rumors of doctrinal unrest at Paris reached the papal court at Viterbo. On September 9, 1276, the aging Peter of Spain (of Lisbon), author of, among other things, the widely used *Summulae logicales*, was elected Pope at Viterbo and consecrated there on October 20, taking the name of John XXI. On January 18, 1277, John XXI wrote to Stephen Tempier, bishop of Paris since October 7, 1268, ordering him to ascertain by whom and where the errors in question had been taught or written, and to send him the information as soon as possible.[80] John, clearly, was concerned about such errors that were "prejudicial to the faith." Tempier's reply to this letter is now lost, but many historians tend to the opinion that "it is almost incredible that the Bishop of Paris could have left unanswered a letter from the pope."[81] In any case, between receipt of the Pope's letter and early March, Tempier and his theologians compiled a list of 219 propositions that should, in their view, be censured. This heterogeneous and disorderly compilation was produced in slightly more than a month, for on Sunday, March 7, 1277, on the third anniversary of Thomas's death, the list of 219 propositions prejudicial to the faith was promulgated.[82] From the patently disordered character of the list, it is obvious that many theologians had a hand in its compilation. It would seem that Tempier asked a number of theologians to compile their own lists and submit them "as soon as possible." The various compilations were then united to form the composite list of 219 propositions to be condemned. All the Averroist theses condemned in 1270 were repeated in the list of 1277. But a number of non-Averroist propositions, including those of Thomas, were also listed. Much has been written on this Parisian condemnation of 1277 that need not be repeated here. But it certainly had a far greater impact on the history of ideas than the earlier condemnation of 1270.

Normally, censured propositions are listed in some recognizable order. Mandonnet organized the propositions of 1277 under several headings: the nature of philosophy, the knowability of God, the divine nature, God's knowledge of particulars, His omnipotence, the production of the world, the nature of intelligences, celestial bodies and their influence on the world, the eternity of the world, necessity and contingence, the nature of man and his intellect, man's free will, and sundry propositions about theology and theologians.[83] Normally such censured propositions were excerpted verbatim from written works, but it has been notoriously difficult, if not impossible, except in a few instances, to locate the sources of the 219 propositions of 1277. However, Pope John XXI did say that he wanted to know not only the persons promulgating the errors, but also "the passages in which such errors are uttered or written." Perhaps some of the propositions were errors "uttered" by the arts masters in class, i.e., in *reportationes,* and not actually written by them in published works. Stephen Tempier ordered that all "rolls, books, and quaterni" containing such errors be sent to him or the chancellor within fifteen days under pain of excommunication. But despite this, some "sources" for the propositions have been discovered, or rescued from oblivion.

The condemnation of 1277 was clearly directed against the Averroists, among whom were Siger of Brabant and Boethius of Dacia, whose names are not mentioned in the condemnation, but only in the scribal rubric. The central epistemological tenet of these Averroists is noted in the prologue: "They say that those [propositions] are true according to philosophy, but not according to the Catholic faith, as if they were two contradictory truths, and as if contrary to the truth of Sacred Scripture there is truth in the damned gentiles," the philosophers. But even this blatant theory of the "double truth" is not found in the known writings of either Siger of Brabant or Boethius of Dacia.[84]

It is not clear why Tempier took upon himself the task of condemning 219 errors culled from the statements of Averroists and others, instead of submitting them to the Holy See as requested by John XXI. Nevertheless he took it upon himself to publish the list and excommunicate their authors without recourse to the Pope. John XXI, however, does not seem to have resented the highhanded action taken by Tempier, for in a second letter addressed to Tempier almost a month later on April 29, 1277, he seems to have condoned the action taken and notes that these errors are promulgated not only by philosophers, but also by theologians "who presume to dogmatize errors contrary to the purity of the true and catholic faith."[85] This seems to be an indication that John had in mind not only the philosophers Siger of Brabant and Boethius of Dacia, but also the theologian Thomas d'Aquino, some of whose ideas are to be found in the condemnation of March 7, 1277.

That some of Thomas's views were included in the Parisian condemnation has always been acknowledged by his contemporaries and by modern historians. But, as Gilson laconically observes, "the list of Thomistic propositions involved in the condemnation is longer, or shorter, according as it is compiled by a Franciscan or by a Dominican."[86] Mandonnet counts sixteen, even though almost none are found verbatim in Thomas's works; certain ideas, however, can be found in his writings, though considerably qualified. The following list of sixteen "Thomistic" propositions are given in their original order:

27. That God could not make souls to be numerically many. (Mandonnet's list, no. 115)

34. That the first cause cannot make several worlds. (27)

69. That separate substances do not change in their operation, because their appetition is one. (52)

77. That if there were a separate substance moving nothing, it would not be included in the universe. (50)

81. That, since intelligences have no matter, God cannot make several intelligences of the same species. (43)

96. That God cannot multiply individuals in a species without matter. (42)

97. That individuals of the same species differ by the sole position of matter. (116)

124. That it is not fitting to posit some intellects as more noble than others, because, since this diversity originates in their bodies, it would necessarily originate in their intelligences, and thus more noble and less noble souls would necessarily belong in diverse species, like the Intelligences. —Error, because thus the soul of Christ would not be more noble than the soul of Judas. (147)

129. That while passion and particular cognition (*scientia*) are actually present, the will cannot act against them. (169)

163. That the will firmly pursues what is firmly believed by reason, and that it cannot abstain from what reason prescribes; this necessity, however, is not coercion, but the nature of the will. (163)

173. That the cognition of contraries is the sole cause why the rational soul can will opposites, and that the power *simpliciter* cannot will opposites except *per accidens* and by reason of another one. (162)

187. That the fact we understand better or less well comes from the passive intellect, which he says is a sensitive power. — Error, because this is to posit one single intellect in all men or equality in all souls. (146)

191. That forms receive division owing only to matter. (110)

204. That separate substances are somewhere by reason of their operation. (55)

218. That an Intelligence, or Angel, or a separated soul is no-where. (53)
219. That separate substances are nowhere as to their substance. (54)

One of the underlying principles of this list is Thomas's firm conviction that first matter is pure potentiality having no act of its own whatever, neither formal nor existential, and that matter is the radical principle of individuation and multiplication in a species. For Thomas, the first act, no matter how small it is, constitutes a suppositum, a *hoc aliquid,* and every subsequent act must necessarily be accidental, i.e., an accident supported by substance. One of the immediate consequences of this prin-ciple, namely, the unicity of substantial form in every com-posite, is, strangely enough, omitted from this list.

To remedy this lacuna, Robert Kilwardby, the Dominican archbishop of Canterbury since October 11, 1272, proscribed a list of thirty propositions in logic, grammar, and natural philos-ophy in a document dated March 18, 1277, at Oxford, just eleven days after the Paris condemnation. Among the sixteen propositions in natural philosophy, there were three that directly pertained to the unicity of substantial forms in material com-posites.[87] The three Oxford theses listed as erroneous by Kil-wardby were:

6. That the vegetative, sensitive, and intellective [souls] exist simultaneously in time in the embryo.
7. That when the intellective soul is introduced, the sensitive and vegetative [souls] are corrupted.
12. That the vegetative, sensitive, and intellective [souls] con-stitute one simple form.

For Thomas Aquinas the simultaneous presence of many sub-stantial forms in a single composite is a metaphysical impos-sibility, since the very first actualization of first matter con-stitutes the substance and the essence of creatures. For the Dominican Robert Kilwardby and the Franciscan John Pecham, the view of Thomas was heretical, for the body of Christ in the tomb, separated from the soul, would not be divine, as faith teaches. For them a *forma corporeitatis,* a corporeal form

that constitutes "this body," had to be postulated antecedent
to other forms in order to ensure the identity of Christ's body on
the cross and in the tomb. Thomas faced this objection many
times in his works; for him even the dead body of Christ was
always united to the Divine Person hypostatically, and therefore
the "same body." When John Pecham succeeded Kilwardby as
archbishop of Canterbury on January 28, 1279, he reiterated
Kilwardby's views and re-emphasized the condemnation of
Thomas's philosophical view because of its theological consequences. In the fifty years following Thomas's death, the crucial
issue was not the real distinction between essence (*quod est*)
and existence (*esse*), as might have been expected, but the
unicity of substantial form.[88]

Shortly after Kilwardby's condemnation of thirty philosophical theses, Peter of Conflans, Dominican archbishop of Corinth, sent a strong letter to Kilwardby and chided him for calling
propositions in grammar, logic, and natural philosophy "heretical." Peter's letter is now lost, but we have a detailed reply to it
by Kilwardby.[89] D. A. Callus suggests that Peter's letter was
sent to Kilwardby on behalf of the Dominican curia, since all
bishops and archbishops were outside the jurisdiction of the
Order.[90] Kilwardby answered that he did not intend to declare
the propositions heretical, but only to prevent their being taught
at Oxford, because "some of them are philosophically at variance
with truth, since some are close to intolerable error, and others
patently iniquitous, being repugnant to the Catholic faith."[91]
To Kilwardby the new view proposed by Thomas was "fantastic,"
"false and impossible," and "repugnant to the Catholic faith." It
would seem that Peter himself maintained the pure potentiality
of primary matter and the unicity of substantial form, since
Kilwardby tried to reply to these basic propositions in his
letter.[92]

Although Thomas had many pupils who heard him in class,
he had few immediate followers who understood his teaching
and promulgated it. The earliest Thomists who defended his
doctrine in the period between 1274 and 1350 were, for the
most part, self-taught. It now seems certain that Thomas's earliest
editors were his secretaries at Naples. Some, like Friar Peter
d'Andria, transcribed Thomas's "illegible hand" into readable

script; others, like Reginald of Piperno, collected various disputed questions into three groups, and arranged the quodlibet questions in the order we have them today; still others "completed" the *Summa* by excerpting large sections from the *Scriptum* and reorganizing them in the framework of a *Supplement* more or less as Thomas had projected it before he died. There can be no doubt that Reginald of Piperno, who had an almost complete collection of Thomas's works, drew up the first catalogue that was submitted by Bartholomew of Capua in the canonization process forty-four years after the death of Thomas. These secretaries, working no doubt under the direction of Reginald, classified all the shorter works under the heading of *opuscula;* later editors distinguished between the "philosophical" and "theological" *opuscula.* Certain known works of Thomas, such as the office for Corpus Christi and some others, were not included in the primitive list because Reginald did not have a copy of them in his library. However, none of Thomas's secretaries could qualify as a Thomist. They were diligent workers who had a profound love of Thomas, but they were not philosophers or theologians. They could easily compile concordances, as they did the *Tabula Ethicorum* and *Supplement,* but they could not enter the speculative arena in defense of Thomas's teaching.

The two condemnations at Paris and Oxford in 1277, precipitous, clumsy, and partisan as they were, spelled victory for the Augustinists for the next fifty years. The main thrust of the Parisian condemnation was to preserve the omnipotence of God. One typical proposition condemned was the statement "God cannot move the heavens in a straight line, for then there would be a vacuum" (prop. 49). The authors of the condemnation maintained that God could do both, move the heavens in a straight line *and* create a vacuum! While God does not act this way in His "ordained power," He could do so by His "absolute power." Although the Parisian condemnation carried only diocesan authority, many scholastics outside of Paris took it as a norm of orthodoxy. Because of this condemnation, later theologians hinged many of their arguments on "the absolute power of God" (*potentia Dei absoluta*) as opposed to His "ordained power" (*potentia ordinata*). Fourteenth-century theologians were ob sessed by this distinction, particularly in their discussions of justification as an *acceptatio divina,* the divine acceptance of an individual.

Toward the end of 1279, William de la Mare, who succeeded John Pecham in the Franciscan chair at Paris, compiled a "correctory" of Thomas based on the differences between Thomas, Augustine, and Bonaventure. He excerpted 117 propositions from the *Summa theologiae,* disputed questions, quodlibets, and the commentary (*Scriptum*) on the first book of the *Sentences* as contrary to the truth and Franciscan teaching. This "correctory" was officially adopted by the general chapter of the Franciscans held at Strasbourg on May 17, 1282. This chapter stated that the minister general was to see to it that provincials "not permit the multiplication of the *Summa* of Thomas except for reasonably intelligent lectors, and then only together with the *Correctorium* of Friar William de la Mare written not in the margin, but in a separate text." The chapter further stated that "these corrections should not be transcribed by any secular person," but only by members of the Franciscan Order.[93] Among the Dominicans in the generation after Thomas, the *Correctorium* of William de la Mare was known as a "corruption" (*corruptorium*) of Thomas's teaching, and their own replies to it were known as the "correction of the corruption" (*Correctoria corruptorii*).

By 1284, five young Dominican masters had written replies to William's *Correctorium,* and also numerous treatises on the unicity of substantial form in material composites. The English Dominicans from William Hothum onward not only had their own tradition of Thomas's works, but also a forceful defense of his teaching. The replies to William de la Mare's correctory are distinguished by the opening word of the text. Thus one of the earliest replies was Richard Knapwell's *Correctorium "Quare,"* written in 1282–83, its title being derived from the opening words, "Quare detraxisti" etc. At the same time the English Dominican Robert Orford wrote his *Correctorium "Sciendum,"* and the outstanding English Thomist William Macclesfield wrote his *Correctorium "Quaestione."* In Italy, Rambert of Bologna wrote a reply entitled *Apologeticum veritatis.* All of these writings had the same end in view, namely, the defense of Thomas's teaching against the concerted effort of Franciscans to preserve and promulgate their own Bonaventurian doctrine against the innovations of Friar Thomas d'Aquino.

One of the tragic figures in this controversy was the English Thomist Richard Knapwell, a master of theology at Oxford, who incepted there in 1284.[94] From his own admission we know that he was trained in the so-called Augustinist tradition, and maintained the doctrine of plurality of forms, as Kilwardby himself had done.[95] After much study extending over a period of time, Richard became convinced of the rightness of Thomas's teaching on the nature of matter and form, and defended it vigorously in his *Correctorium "Quare"* against the Franciscan charges. As early as 1284, Knapwell's teaching came to the attention of John Pecham, who, as archbishop of Canterbury, renewed Kilwardby's condemnation in a letter of October 29, 1284. Disregarding this warning, Knapwell determined a disputed question in favor of the unicity of form. Pecham and his assistants compiled a list of "errors" from this disputed question, and Knapwell was summoned to appear in person before the archbishop on April 18, 1286, to defend himself or make retraction. For some reason Knapwell refused to appear, and in this refusal he had the support of his own provincial, William Hothum. When it became evident that Knapwell was not going to appear to defend his case or recant, Pecham convoked a solemn assembly and on April 30, 1286, condemned eight theses of Knapwell's as heretical; thereupon he imposed excommunication on him and on all who aided or counseled him. Among those present at this assembly was William Hothum, who protested the condemnation, and openly invoked the privilege of exemption. Insisting that the archbishop had exceeded his jurisdiction, Hothum lodged an appeal with the Pope.[96] Knapwell went to Rome to plead his case personally, but when he arrived he learned that Honorius IV had died on April 3, 1287. The Pope who eventually heard his case in 1288 was the Franciscan Jerome of Ascoli, who took the name of Nicholas IV. Nicholas did no more than impose perpetual silence on him. Unable to teach or write, Knapwell retired to Bologna, where he is said to have become insane and died a "wretched death" in 1288.[97]

After the condemnation of 1277, it became clear to many Dominicans that Thomas was not simply a member of the Roman

Province, but a member of the whole Order. The first evidence of this attitude appears in the general chapter of Milan in 1278, when the chapter appointed Raymond Mevouillon and John Vigoroux, both lectors at Montpellier, to go to England with full powers as visitators of the chapter to inquire diligently after those "who *in scandalum ordinis* showed disrespect for the writings of the venerable father Friar Thomas d'Aquino." These visitators had full power to punish, exile from the province, and even deprive from any office those found guilty.[98] Although the visitators to England could do nothing about Archbishop Kilwardby, they could take measures to prevent his attitude from prevailing in the English Province. However, on April 4, 1278, before the chapter of Milan convened, Kilwardby had been appointed cardinal bishop of Porto and Santa Rufina with residence in the Roman curia. His transfer made the work of the visitators easier.

In the same vein, the Dominican general chapter of Paris in 1279 stated that no attack on Thomas or his writings could be tolerated in the Order, and that provincials, priors, vicars, and visitators are not to forego punishing those who do so.[99] In 1286 the capitular fathers at Paris ordered that each and every Friar was to promote the teaching of the venerable master Friar Thomas d'Aquino, or at least to hold it as a defensible position; whoever acts contrary to this, even though he thinks differently from Thomas, is to be suspended *ipso facto*, be he master, bachelor, lector, or friar, absolution being reserved to the master general or a general chapter.

The general chapters said nothing further about the doctrine of Thomas until Durandus of Saint-Pourçain strongly opposed the teachings of Thomas in his commentary on the *Sentences* at Paris in 1307–8.[100] In 1309 the general chapter of Saragossa strictly enjoined on all lectors and sublectors that they teach and determine questions according to the doctrine and works of the venerable doctor Friar Thomas d'Aquino.[101] However, Durandus was finally promoted to the mastership at Paris, having revised his commentary on the *Sentences* to please authorities in the Order, and he lectured as master during the academic year 1312–13. During Lent 1313 Durandus was called to the papal curia at Avignon to be Master of the Sacred Palace. We do not know what prompted this move, but the call came from Pope Clement V, who had established permanent residence at Avignon and created there a papal "university" of the curia, the directorship of which was henceforth given to a Dominican as Master of the Sacred Palace. The general chapter meeting at Metz during Pentecost in 1313 stated that "since the doctrine of Friar Thomas d'Aquino is considered more sane and more common than any other, and since the Dominican Order is obliged in a special way to follow it, no one should dare teach, determine, or respond differently from what is commonly thought to be his teaching." Moreover no one was to be sent to the studium in Paris unless he had studied the doctrine of Friar Thomas for at least three years.[102]

In July 1314, a commission of Dominican theologians censured a long list of propositions taken from Durandus's commentary on the *Sentences*, and in the following year the chapter of Bologna stated that if anyone teaches contrary to the common doctrine of Thomas or contrary to the common teachings of the Church regarding the articles of faith, sound morality, or the sacraments of the Church, or proposes objections to them without resolving them, he is to be deprived of his teaching office entirely.[103] But by August 1317, Durandus was outside the jurisdiction of the Order, having been made bishop of Limoux (and later of Puy); in his third and final commentary on the *Sentences* he expressed his personal opinions contrary to the teaching of Thomas, free from control of the Order. By the time Thomas was canonized in 1323, almost all Dominicans had made the teaching of Thomas their own and considered it a privilege, as well as an obligation, to study and defend it.

Quite distinct from and independent of the doctrinal controversies that flourished in academic circles, there grew up around San Domenico and Fossanova a cult of Thomas, a popular devotion attesting to his holiness. This local cult, it would seem, had little or nothing to do with Thomas's doctrine, although it was respected—at a distance. What appealed to the people was his obvious sanctity confirmed by miracles: his profound personal devotion to God and neighbor, his childlike simplicity and humility, as well as his purity, poverty, and obedience. Throughout his life, Thomas's apostolic zeal was directed toward the intellectual needs of others and the Church; in death he continued to serve the needs of others through his example and miracles. One of the earliest devotions was to his angelic purity; from this devotion there arose the Confraternity of the Angelic Warfare, whose members wore a light cord around the waist, reminiscent of the cord Thomas was supposed to have been girded with by the angels after the attempted seduction.

After Thomas's burial at Fossanova, Reginald of Piperno returned to Naples and talked frequently and eloquently on the virtues of his master. Both William of Tocco and Tolomeo of Lucca were in the community at that time, and it seems that William in particular developed a deep devotion to Thomas. Before Reginald died at Anagni, somewhere around 1290, he made his last confession to Friar John of Giudice, and related many incidents, which were later presented by Bartholomew of Capua at the first canonization inquiry at Naples.[104] Both Reginald and John of Giudice were sources for much of William's information in his life of Thomas.

In 1294 the Roman Province of the Order, to which Thomas had belonged, was divided by the creation of a new province for the Kingdom of Sicily, the *provincia Regni*, which included Naples and its environs. The first provincial was Nicholas Brunacci, who had been one of Thomas's companions on the second journey to Paris in the winter of 1268-69. Walz is undoubtedly correct when he attributes the origins of Thomas's canonization process to the division of 1294.[105]

John XXII was elected Pope in 1316, and from the very beginning he was interested in the canonization of Thomas, so much so that Mandonnet believed that the initiative was taken by him.[106] It is certain that the Pope warmly favored the petition as soon as it was presented to him. The provincial chapter of the Sicilian Province met at Gaeta in September 1317. This chapter appointed William of Tocco to be the promoter of the cause of Thomas's canonization. He and a younger Friar, Robert of Benevento, were commissioned to collect materials concerning the birth, life, death, and miracles of Thomas to be submitted to the Holy See.[107] But even prior to this official act of the provincial chapter, William had been collecting such material, for in November 1316, William visited San Severino to gather information from the vast familial legends. No doubt William compiled the first draft of his biography of Thomas at this time. After his appointment as promoter of the cause, he again visited Marisco and other places, gathering information as quickly as he could. Meanwhile Tocco obtained letters petitioning for the canonization from Queen Mary of Sicily, Charles II's widow, and many other notables of Naples to be submitted to the Pope. Tocco must have been in his seventies when, armed with these documents and his *Life of Thomas* (*Hystoria Thomae de Aquino*), he and his young companion Robert of Benevento journeyed to Avignon, reaching the papal city around July or August of 1318.

At Avignon, William met Bernard Gui, who was then procurator of the Order at the curia and whose task was to act as an intermediary between the Order and the Holy See. He also met the greatest Church historian of his day, Tolomeo of Lucca, "who was now over eighty and a bishop."[108] At this time Bernard sketched his own *Life* of Thomas, based on Tocco's materials; the final version of Bernard's *Life* contained substantial additions, drawn from the official inquiry and from other sources, without, however, all the formalized rhetoric and pietistic asides so abundant in William's version.

Pope John XXII received the petition enthusiastically, and submitted William's materials to a commission of non-Dominican theologians, who carefully studied the documents, including the first draft of William's *Hystoria* of Thomas, throughout August and gave a favorable reply to the Pope. Thereupon John XXII officially opened the inquiry in his letter of September 13, 1318.[109] At the same time he appointed Humbert of Nontauro, archbishop of Naples, Angelo Tignosi, bishop of Viterbo, and Pandulf Savelli, papal notary, to conduct the inquiry into the sanctity of Friar Thomas. Pandulf, however, was absent, and his place was taken by two notaries.

The first inquiry was opened at the archbishop's palace in Naples on Saturday, July 21, 1319, and lasted until Tuesday, September 18, of that year. To assist the papal representatives, the official examiners commissioned Peter John of Rocco-Rarani of the diocese of Sabina, who was a public notary by apostolic and imperial authority, and Francis of Laureto of the diocese of Penna, who was a public notary by apostolic and regal authority; their task was "to draft an exact report in writing of the proceedings of the inquiry."[110] All the official documents pertaining to the inquiry were read on Saturday, and the interrogation of witnesses began on the following Monday. During the eight weeks that followed, forty-two witnesses were heard under oath and their testimony written down; sixteen were Cistercians of Fossanova, eleven were Dominicans, twelve were laymen, and three were of the secular clergy. Of these, only twelve had known Thomas personally: five Cistercians, five Dominicans, and two laymen.[111] When all witnesses had been heard, the official *Acta* of the proceedings were signed and sealed by the presidents and given to two minor clerics, Matthew of Viterbo, chaplain of the archbishop of Naples, and Peter of Viterbo, canon and delegate of the bishop of Viterbo, for immediate delivery to the Pope at Avignon. William of Tocco also traveled to Avignon on what was to be his last journey.

Two years went by, during which William composed the final version of his *Hystoria* of Thomas, 1320–21. Finally Pope John and his advisers decided that there were still many witnesses whose testimony had not been heard. Therefore he ordered a second inquiry to be made at Fossanova to list all the miracles that had happened. Accordingly William, already a very old man (*antiquus religiosus*), returned to Italy to prepare for the second inquiry, which was exclusively concerned with miracles. Shortly after this preliminary preparation, William of Tocco seems to have died, for his place was taken by John Regina of Naples, who as master in theology at Paris had disputed the question "Whether one can licitly teach the doctrine of Friar Thomas at Paris in all its conclusions" and determined it in the affirmative.[112]

The second papal inquiry took place at Fossanova in the chapter room of the Cistercians November 10–20, 1321. Altogether 112 witnesses were called; they were mainly lay people, many of whom did not even know their own age and could neither read nor write. Their brief testimonies were taken down by the appointed notaries in the presence of Peter Ferrin, bishop of Anagni (in whose diocese the body of Thomas lay), and Andrew, bishop of Terracina; Pandulf Savelli, although appointed by the Pope, was again not present. As this brief inquiry turned out, all of the miracles narrated took place after Thomas's death.

The "devil's advocate," whose task it is to oppose canonization, pointed out the obvious fact that Thomas had worked few, if any, miracles during his lifetime. Only three incidents could be found: the miraculous cure of Reginald at Molara (above p. 297), the cure of an unknown woman "afflicted by a flow of blood," who touched the *cappa* of Thomas after he preached at St. Peter's in Rome (according to Tocco and Peter Calo) or at Santa Maria Maggiore (according to the witness Leonard of Gaeta),[113] and the miracle of the herrings at Maenza (above p. 325). Interesting though these three "miracles" were, they were not sufficiently convincing to the devil's advocate as a sign of sanctity. According to John Gerson, chancellor of the University of Paris in the late fourteenth century, Pope John XXII overruled the devil's advocate, and stated that Thomas "worked as many miracles [in his lifetime] as questions he had determined" (*Tot miracula fecit, quot quaestiones determinavit*).[114] Gerson pointed out that Augustine, Gregory, Jerome, and many others did not work miracles during their lifetime, but have always been considered saints in heaven.

As "good hope" could be entertained concerning the canonization of Thomas, the Dominican general chapter at Rouen in 1320 ordained that each provincial should send to the Dominican curia as many florins as there were priories in the province to help defray expenses.[115]

By early 1323 it was already clear that Thomas would be canonized, and that the ceremony would take place in July. The papal solemnities for the occasion were scheduled from Saturday, July 16 (or Thursday, July 14), until Thursday, July 21, 1323. Monday, July 18, was set aside for the official canonization of Friar Thomas d'Aquino.[116] Thomas's canonization consisted of three parts: preliminary sermons praising the life of Thomas and recommending his canonization, the reading of the bull of canonization and the solemn Mass of the saint, and three days of Masses and sermons in his honor.

On Saturday, July 16, Pope John XXII preached the first sermon in a solemn consistory of cardinals and bishops. He began by praising the Dominican idea of poverty in which Friars have nothing of their own, although they have something in common just as the Apostles had. This point was in reference to the current theological controversy concerning Franciscan poverty. John went on to say that after the Apostles and early doctors of the Church, Thomas illuminated the truth more than anyone else. He praised his perpetual virginity and the sanctity that was confirmed "by not less than 300 miracles." John concluded that Thomas deserves to be in the catalogue of the saints.

This sermon was followed by another given by the Dominican Friar Peter Canterii, who on this occasion represented John of Naples, who was ill. If William of Tocco had been still alive, he would no doubt have preached this second sermon. The sermon concluded by requesting, on the part of the whole Dominican Order, the canonization of Friar Thomas. There followed a sermon by King Robert of Naples ("King of Sicily and Jerusalem"), at the end of which the king knelt and begged the canonization of Thomas. He was followed in turn by Eudes Sala, patriarch of Alexandria, Ingerran Stella, archbishop of Capua, John Stratford, bishop of Winchester, Gaillard de Saumate, archbishop of Arles, and by a Franciscan, John de Tixandrie, bishop of Lodève, whose commendation of Thomas was reportedly the greatest heard that day. In all, eight sermons were preached in this solemn public consistory; all speakers praised Thomas's sanctity and petitioned for his canonization. One of the chroniclers of this event, Friar Bentius, states that he was present in the company of the Pope from beginning to end.[117]

Both the anonymous chronicler and Friar Bentius are explicit about the main event, which took place on Monday, July 18, in the church of Notre-Dame des Doms in Avignon. The Holy Father presided. After the hymn "Veni creator Spiritus" was sung in the church crowded with patriarchs, cardinals, bishops, the King and Queen of Naples, many noblemen of Naples, and representatives of all religious Orders, the papal bull *Redemptionem misit* was read proclaiming Thomas to be a saint of the Holy Roman Church.[118] Then the hymn "Te Deum" was sung by all, after which Pope John XXII himself celebrated Mass in honor of St. Thomas "In medio ecclesiae," with the Gospel

"Vos estis sal terrae," as for the feast of St. Dominic. The Pope again preached, this time on the text "For thou art great and dost wonderful things" (Ps. 85:10).

Then King Robert of Naples proclaimed that the whole city of Avignon should celebrate the day "as though it were Christmas." Friar Bentius wrote in his chronicle that it would take too long to write down everything that happened that day; he says that he could not even remember everything, much less write about it.

On Tuesday the archbishop of Capua celebrated the solemn Mass of the saint in the Dominican church in the presence of the king and a number of cardinals. On Wednesday Jacques de Concots, Dominican archbishop of Aix-en-Provence, celebrated Mass there, and on Thursday, Henry, bishop of Metz, celebrated the solemn Mass of St. Thomas, on which day Thomas of San Severino, Count of Marisco and nephew of St. Thomas, financed the festivities for the whole city. Friar Bentius concluded his account by saying that "the reality of the solemnities lies beyond my words."[119]

Thus forty-nine years after his death, Thomas was declared a saint in the Holy Roman Church by Pope John XXII, a model to all not only in sanctity, but also in doctrine. It is clear that Pope John XXII wanted Thomas to be recognized not only for his sanctity and purity, but also for his wisdom, learning, and scholarship. As an anticlimactic measure, Étienne Bourret, bishop of Paris, revoked the sentence of excommunication and condemnation attached to the Parisian condemnation of 1277 from those propositions "insofar as they touch or seem to touch the doctrine of the aforesaid Blessed Thomas."[120] This public declaration of Thomas's orthodoxy was issued on February 14, 1325, almost forty-eight years after the original condemnation. This was a formality, having little or nothing to do with the real world; only Parisian canonists needed have worried about it. In England, the archbishop of Canterbury did not even bother to revoke Kilwardby's condemnation that was confirmed by John Pecham.

The canonization of Thomas was an event never to be forgotten by those who were in Avignon in the summer of 1323. It was a memorable occasion, not only for them, but for the whole Christian world. His light still shines in the chronicles of history and in the minds of those who read and understand his works in their historical and doctrinal context—but Thomas is not confined to the chambers of history; he is accessible to all generations who know how to read.

SUMMARY CHRONOLOGY

1220, Nov. 22	coronation of Emperor Frederick II
1224/25	birth of Thomas at Roccasecca
1230/31 to 1239	O.S.B. oblate at Monte Cassino
1239, spring-summer	home at Roccasecca
1239, Nov. 14, to April 1244	student at University of Naples
1243, Dec. 24	death of father, Landulfo
1244, late April	joined Dominicans at Naples
1244, early May	abduction on journey, attempted seduction at Montesangiovanni, taken to Roccasecca and mother
1244, May, to summer 1245	detained at home by mother
1245, July 17	deposition of Frederick II
1245, July or August	allowed to return to Order
1245, fall, to 1248	Paris for novitiate and study
1248, summer, to fall 1252	Cologne with Albert the Great
1250, Dec. 13	death of Frederick II
1250/51	ordained priest at Cologne
1252, fall, to spring 1256	*Sententiarius* at Paris
1256, between March 3 and June 17	inception as master in theology
1256 to 1259	regent master in theology at Paris
1259, June	Valenciennes, *ratio studiorum,* O.P
1259, July to Nov.	Paris, writing *Summa contra gentiles*
1259, end	left Paris for Naples
1260 to fall 1261	Naples, continuing *Summa contra gentiles*

1261, Sept., to Sept. 1265	Orvieto as lector
1262, Oct. or Nov.	arrival of Urban IV at Orvieto
1263, summer	resignation of Humbert of Romans, O.P.
1264, June	election of John of Vercelli, O.P.
1264, before Aug. 11	liturgy of Corpus Christi
1264, fall	completion of *Summa contra gentiles*
1264, Oct. 2	death of Urban IV at Perugia
1265, Sept. 8	assigned to open studium, Rome
1266	begins *Summa theologiae*
° 1267, summer	assigned to Viterbo, Clement IV
° 1268, Nov.	left Viterbo for Paris
1269, Jan., to 1272	second Parisian regency
1270, Dec. 10	condemnation of Averroism, 13 propositions
1272, after April 25	left Paris for Florence, Naples
1272, Sept.	regent of theology at Naples
1273, Dec. 6	breakdown, cessation of writing
1274, Feb.	set out for Council of Lyons
1274, mid-Feb.	injured head at Borgonuovo
1274, after Feb. 14	pause at Maenza, steadily worse
1274, end Feb.	brought to Fossanova by donkey
1274, March 7	death, Wednesday morning at Fossanova
1274, March 9	funeral at Fossanova, buried in front of high altar
1274, after March 9	transfer of body to second grave
1274, Sept.	body returned to original grave
1275, between Jan. and June	exhumation of body and decapitation
1277, March 7	condemnation of 219 propositions at Paris
1277, March 18	condemnation of propositions at Oxford
1294, summer	creation of *provincia Regni* (Naples)
1303, fall	body removed to third location at Fossanova; flesh boiled off before 1319
1317, Sept.	appointment of William of Tocco as promoter of Thomas's canonization
1319, July 21 to Sept. 18	first canonization inquiry, Naples
1321, Nov. 10 to 20	second canonization inquiry, Fossanova

1323, July 18	canonization of Thomas by John XXII at Avignon (cel. July 16–21)
1325, Feb. 14	revocation of Paris condemnation as to Thomas's teaching
1369, Jan. 28	transfer of relics to Toulouse

A BRIEF CATALOGUE OF AUTHENTIC WORKS

Although much has already been said in previous chapters concerning the authentic writings of Thomas d'Aquino, not every work was mentioned. Therefore a complete, separate listing of the titles and essential information is desirable. The most authoritative study in English of Thomas's works is that of I. T. Eschmann, O.P., "A Catalogue of St. Thomas's Works: Bibliographical Notes," in E. Gilson, *The Christian Philosophy of St. Thomas Aquinas* (New York: Random House 1956), 381–439. The "brief catalogue" given here in no way supplants the "Catalogue" of Eschmann. Rather it presupposes it. Eschmann's catalogue represents the best of Thomistic scholarship up to 1955, utilizing not only the latest European discoveries, but also his own profound insights after more than thirty-five years of study. Our brief catalogue proposes to give only the essential information, without entering into the weight of various arguments presented by scholars in this field.

There never has been for Thomas's writings a system of classification and enumeration universally accepted by Thomist scholars. The problem of enumeration, perhaps, will never be settled, for it is difficult to know whether Thomas's disputed "questions" should be numbered separately or as one work; the same situation is true of the quodlibets and the cycle of Lenten sermons that he preached in Naples in 1273. Consequently whereas Eschmann lists 98 works of Thomas in one enumeration, we list 102 in another.

Classification of Thomas's writings provided problems from the very beginning. The catalogue of Bartholomew of Capua, derived most probably from the list drawn up by Reginald of Piperno, divided the works of Thomas into three groups:

1. *Opuscula,* i.e., short works on various subjects, on various occasions, for various people, whose exemplars happened not to be at the Parisian stationer's.

2. *Parisian exemplars,* i.e., major works, the exemplars of which happened to be at the Parisian stationer's shop at the time of the catalogue.

3. *Reportationes,* i.e., works written down by a secretary or friend while Thomas was giving lectures or preaching, and hence not an *ordinatio* written and edited by Thomas himself, even though the work may have been corrected by Thomas afterward, as in the case of the *Lectura* on St. John's Gospel.

The catalogue in Prague MS 29 A XVII 1 divides the works into theological, philosophical, and *reportationes;* the *opuscula* are thus distributed between the theological and philosophical classifications. On the other hand, the catalogue of Prague MS 29 A XVII 2 lists the works as divided into commentaries (including the two *summae,* disputations, and all commentaries, whether they be biblical, Lombardian, Boethian, Dionysian, or Aristotelian), *opuscula,* and *reportationes.* This latter classification, which is followed by Nicholas Trevet, is the more common among later bibliographers. However, this threefold division of Thomas's works is most unsatisfactory. Eschmann considered the catchall classification of *"opuscula"* the most objectionable, particularly if these works are subdivided into philosophical and theological. Personally, I find the classification *"reportationes"* to be the most useless for bibliographical purposes, even though it is most important to know which works of Thomas were reported while he was teaching or preaching. As a category, however, it is accidental to the nature of bibliographical classification. Therefore a more specific classification would be desirable.

For the sake of some uniformity, we will follow the classification given by Eschmann, which was also followed in the *New Catholic Encyclopedia,* 1967 (art. "Thomas Aquinas, St."):

Theological Syntheses
Academic Disputations

Expositions of Holy Scripture
Expositions on Aristotle
Other Expositions
Polemical Writings
Treatises on Special Subjects
Expert Opinions
Letters
Liturgical Pieces and Sermons
Works of Uncertain Authenticity

As Eschmann pointed out, there may be some confusion between "Treatises on Special Subjects" and "Letters," because the letter form has often been eliminated by the original editor, and the work made to look like a treatise. That is true also of the Lenten cycle of sermons, all of which have been edited to look like scholastic treatises. Therefore Eschmann's classification is not urged here as an ideal, but as a convenient tool.

There have been ten more or less complete publications of Thomas's *Opera Omnia,* besides the Leonine edition still in progress. The two most accessible editions prior to the Leonine are:

Parma *Opera Omnia* (Parma: Fiaccadori 1852–73) in twenty-five folio volumes; reprinted New York: Musurgia 1948–50. This edition contains the invaluable *Tabula Aurea* of Peter of Bergamo (1473) in v. 25.

Vivès *Opera Omnia* (Paris: Vivès 1871–82) in thirty-four quarto volumes. The *Tabula Aurea* is contained in vv. 33–34.

The definitive text of Thomas's writings is being published by the Leonine Commission, established by Pope Leo XIII in 1880. The complete works when finished will fill fifty folio volumes. Meanwhile most of Thomas's writings have been published at various times by the Casa Marietti, Torino-Rome, in a convenient manual size; for the most part, the text in the Marietti edition is simply a reprint of an earlier published text, and does not pretend to be "critical."

In our brief catalogue we will list the Leonine edition where possible, the "vulgate" text of Parma, Vivès, and Marietti, and the English translation wherever one exists. In the absence of a Leonine text, we will note the most critical edition available.

As an aid to understanding the chronology of Thomas's works, the following dates in his academic career should be kept in mind:

1252–56	Bachelor of the *Sentences* at Paris
1256 (Sept.)– 1259 (July)	Regent master in theology at Paris
1259–1268 (Nov.)	Sojourn in Italy: Naples (1259–61); Orvieto (1261–65); Rome (1265–67); Viterbo (1267–68)
1269 (Jan.)– 1272 (April)	Second Parisian regency
1272 (Sept.)– 1273 (Dec.)	Regent master at Naples

A more detailed chronology of his life will be found on pp. 351–353.

THEOLOGICAL SYNTHESES

1. **Scriptum super libros Sententiarum.** Four books (Paris 1252–56). Autograph of Bk. III in Vatican MS Vat. lat. 9851, fol. 11ra–99vb (III, dist. 4, q. 2, a. 2 arg. 5 to dist. 34, q. 2, a. 2, sol. 2 ad 2), ed. Moos III, 170–1150. Extant MSS: 78 (Bk. I); 105 (Bk. II); autograph + 100 (Bk. III); 167 (Bk. IV); and almost 100 fragments of all books. See above, pp. 67–80.

Strictly speaking, this is not a "commentary" on Peter Lombard's *Sentences*, but rather "writings" (*scripta*), or elaborations of the text in the form of questions and discussions of relevant themes arising from the text. Ordinarily in the Middle Ages Peter Lombard's *Sentences* in four books was the official text on which bachelors in theology lectured from one to four years prior to inception as master. According to William of Tocco, Thomas composed his *Scriptum* while he was *baccalaureus Sententiarum* (1252–56). That does not mean, however, that the written work is a report of his day-to-day presentation in the lecture hall. Rather, it is a carefully elaborated and edited version of questions discussed in the classroom, polished after the event. Tocco also states that Thomas was still writing his *Scriptum* "at the beginning of his career as master," i.e., after his inception as master in the spring of 1256.

According to Tolomeo of Lucca, Thomas wrote a second version of Book I while teaching in Rome (1266–68), but abandoned the project when he conceived the idea of a *Summa theologiae*. Tolomeo also claims to have seen this version once at Lucca, "but then someone took it away and I never saw it again." It is generally agreed today that the second version of Book I is lost. However, the article on divine attributes (I *Sent.*, 2, 3) is an authentic *quaestio disputata* inserted perhaps by Thomas himself at this time; and I *Sentences*, prol. 3, 2, "Vel dicendum . . . ," also seems to be a later though authorized interpolation.

EDITIONS: Parma 6–8; Vivès 7–11; Mandonnet (Bks. I–II), 2 v. (Paris 1929); Moos (Bks. III–IV, dist. 22), 2 v. (Paris 1933, 1947); the text by Moos is to a certain extent corrected by MSS. Leonine version in progress. A critical text of this work is a major desideratum in Thomistic studies.

No English translation.

2. *Summa contra gentiles.* Four books (Paris, Naples, and Orvieto 1259–64). Entitled in some MSS as *Liber de veritate catholicae fidei contra errores infidelium*, but mentioned in all early catalogues as *Liber* or *Summa contra gentiles*. Autograph of Bk. I, c. 13, to Bk. III, c. 120, in Vatican MS Vat. lat. 9850, fol. 2ra–89vb. Extant MSS: autogr. + 184 complete and 20 fragments. See above pp. 130–34; 144–45.

According to Peter Marsilio's *Chronicle*, completed at Barcelona in 1313, St. Raymond of Peñafort, onetime master general of the Dominican Order (1238–40), asked Thomas d'Aquino "to write a work against the errors of the infidels" for Dominican missionaries preaching against Moslems, Jews, and heretical Christians in Spain (Aragon) and North Africa. The result was this *Summa* in four books, "which is thought to have no equal in its field." The testimony of Antonio of Brescia given at Naples in 1319 indicates that the work was begun in Paris. The common view today is that Thomas began writing at Paris toward the end of his third year of teaching as master (1258–59), but it is not certain how much of the treatise Thomas completed at Paris. Mandonnet, Chenu, and A. Dondaine maintain that Thomas completed the text up to III, c. 45, because some of the MSS end there. A. Gauthier and Walz-Novarina maintain that Thomas wrote only as far as I, c. 53, in Paris, the rest being written in Naples (1259–61) and Orvieto (1261–65), and completed in 1264 under Urban IV. In II, cc. 21, 88, 89, Thomas quotes Aristotle's *De generatione animalium* in the new Greek-Latin translation of Moerbeke completed shortly before December 23, 1260. Therefore the earliest possible date for the writing of Book II is 1261. It seems that IV, c. 69, was completed after his treatise *Contra errores Graecorum* (n. 63), since Thomas summarizes the same arguments concerning the consecration of unleavened bread in this *Summa* that he had used in the *Contra errores Graecorum* in the summer of 1263.

Dom Peter Marc (1896–1967) has argued that this *Summa* was written during Thomas's second Parisian regency (1269–72) and therefore was contemporary with the second part of the *Summa theologiae*. All evidence pointing to Paris is interpreted as referring to Thomas's second, rather than his first, Parisian regency; and the fact that Ramón Martin did not quote it in his *Capistro Iudaeorum* of 1267 is considered proof of later composition than generally thought. However, not only is Marc's dating contrary to all known facts, but the arguments employed by Marc are far from convincing.

EDITIONS: Leonine ed. 13–15 (Rome 1918–30); Leon. manual ed. Rome 1934; *Liber de veritate catholicae fidei contra errores infidelium*, vv. 2–3 (Torino: Marietti 1961), fully annotated with introd. by P. Marc, v. 1, 1967.

English trans.: *On the Truth of the Catholic Faith*, by Pegis, Anderson, Bourke, O'Neil (New York: Doubleday 1955–57), ⚬   5 v.

3. **Summa theologiae.** Three parts; second divided into two (Rome, ⚬   Viterbo, Paris, Naples 1266–73). Extant MSS: 246 (Ia pars); 220

(I–II); 280 (II–II); 213 (IIIa pars); 42 (Suppl.); and more than 235 fragments of various parts. See above, pp. 216–30; 256–63; 307–19.

This is Thomas's major work, the crown of his genius, begun for beginners in theology while he was teaching young Dominican students in the Roman studium at Santa Sabina (1265–67). The idea of composing a *summa* of theology for "beginners" may have occurred to Thomas as early as 1265; but he did not begin work on the *Summa* until 1266, when he discarded his plan to rework his commentary on the *Sentences*. The *prima pars* was completed at Viterbo in 1268, before Thomas was sent to Paris for a second time. Part I, q. 79, a. 4, was completed after November 22, 1267, for he utilized Themistius's paraphrase of Aristotle's *De anima*, translated at this date by William of Moerbeke. Therefore the whole *prima pars* seems to have been written between 1266 and the spring of 1268. However, Thomas seems to have begun Part I–II in Viterbo in 1268, i.e., before he was ordered to return to Paris, but we do not know how much he wrote before leaving Viterbo.

The whole *secunda pars* (except for the few questions written at Viterbo) was written during Thomas's second Parisian regency (1269–72). The first part of the second part (I–II) was completed toward the end of 1270; Thomas's last reference to *Metaphysics* Lambda as "Book XI" is in I–II, q. 111, a. 5, while the first reference to Lambda as "Book XII" is in II–II, q. 1, a. 8, obj. 1. Although we do not know the exact date when Moerbeke translated Book Kappa, thus rendering Book Lambda as XII, evidence seems to point to the end of 1270 or the beginning of 1271. Thus the *prima secundae* seems to have been completed at the turn of the year 1270, with the *secunda secundae* begun immediately after the beginning of 1271. The *secunda secundae*, the longest of all the parts of the *Summa*, was completed by the spring of 1272, when the first few questions of the *tertia pars* were written.

Apart from the first few questions, the whole of the *tertia pars* was written in Naples from September 1272 to December 1273. After December 6, 1273, Thomas could no longer write anything. The *Summa theologiae* breaks off with question 60, article 4, in the sacrament of Penance. The *Supplement,* intended to complete the *Summa,* is "put together with scissors and paste from pieces cut out of Aquinas's writings on the *Sentences* (especially Bk. 4)." This compilation was, no doubt, the work of Thomas's earliest editors working under the direction of Reginald of Piperno after Thomas's death on March 7, 1274.

Although the *Summa theologiae* was begun for "beginners in theology" (Prol.), it seems that only the *prima pars* fits this description; the rest shows Thomas at his best, groping for new solutions to new and old problems, armed with the best resources of his age.

EDITIONS: Leonine Part I (vv. 4–5, Rome 1888/89); Part I–II (vv. 6–7, 1891/92); Part II–II (vv. 8–10, 1895/97/99); Part III (v. 11, 1903); Supplement (v. 12, 1906). The haste of the Leonine editors to publish the *Summa* resulted in poor critical quality, except for the last five volumes. Only a few of the extant MSS were examined, and the early volumes are basically a reproduction of the Piana edition of 1570, the *editio princeps* of the complete work. —Marietti ed., Torino 1948, 4 v. (Leonine text without apparatus). —Ed. *Biblioteca de Autores Cristianos,* 5 v., Madrid 1952 (Leonine text without apparatus). —Ottawa, 5 v., 1941 (Piana text of 1570 with some Leonine variants; excellent notes and references throughout by I. T. Eschmann).

English trans.: English Dominicans (22 v.), London: Burns, Oates and Washbourne 1912–36; repr. 3 v., New York: Benziger 1947–48; bilingual ed. 60 v., New York: McGraw-Hill 1964– (in progress).

ACADEMIC DISPUTATIONS

4. *De veritate.* QQ. 1–29 (Paris 1256–59). Extant MSS: 95 (63 contain the complete text and 32 contain substantial fragments). See above, pp. 123–24.

These questions were disputed in Paris during Thomas's first Parisian regency and distributed over the course of three years. Thus questions 1–7 (in 67 articles) were disputed during the first year (1256–57); questions 8–20 (in 99 articles) were disputed during the second year (1257–58); and questions 21–29 (in 63 articles), during the third year (1258–59). The tendency today, following A. Dondaine, is to think of each "question" as the basic unit of a disputation, rather than the "article." From this it follows that Thomas disputed 29 times throughout the three years, rather than 229 times, as Mandonnet and Synave believed.

EDITIONS: Leonine ed. v. 22 in three parts (Rome: Leon. Comm. 1970–74); Parma v. 9; Vivès v. 15; Marietti 1953 and various dates, *Quaestiones Disputatae*, v. 1.

English trans.: *On Truth*, 3 v., trans. Mulligan-McGlynn-Schmidt (Chicago: Regnery 1952–54).

5. *De potentia.* QQ. 1–10 (Rome 1265–66). Extant MSS: 61, and 9 fragments. See above, pp. 198–212.

These questions were disputed at Rome (Subiaco MS 211, fol. 175r), most probably during Thomas's first year of teaching in the Roman studium at Santa Sabina. Mandonnet thought that these questions were disputed at Anagni and Orvieto (1259–63), but this view is no longer tenable.

EDITIONS: Leon. ed. v. 21, in preparation; Parma v. 8; Vivès v. 13; Marietti 1953, and various dates, *Quaestiones Disputatae*, v. 2.

English trans.: *On the Power of God*, trans. English Dominican Fathers (L. Shapcote), 3 v. (London: Burns, Oates and Washbourne 1932/34); idem, three books in one (Westminster, Md.: Newman 1952).

6. *De malo,* QQ. 1–16 (Rome 1266–67). Extant MSS: 70 complete and 13 fragments. See above, pp. 212–13.

There is no clear agreement among scholars as to the date of these disputations. Mandonnet argued that they were disputed in Italy between 1263–68, largely completed before the first part of the *Summa* (1267–68), and entirely completed before the second (1269–70). Walz argues that they were disputed at Paris in 1269–72. Lottin argues that it was written after the first part and before the second part of the *Summa*, and that both *De malo* and I–II are posterior to *Quodlibet 1* (Lent 1269). In Lottin's view, *De malo* was disputed in Paris before Thomas began writing I–II of the *Summa*. Gauthier argues more convincingly that *De malo* was begun after March 1266 in Rome, and that question 16 was completed in Viterbo after November 22, 1267, and before 1269, when Thomas was writing I–II; he concluded that *De malo* must have been disputed in Rome during the academic year 1266–67.

De malo, q. 6 (*De libero arbitrio*) and q. 16 (*De daemonibus*), are clearly extra-serial disputations inserted into *De malo*, where they do not belong (see below, n. 11). They were undoubtedly inserted by the earliest editors of Thomas's works, for they are found in their present position in *all* extant MSS.

EDITIONS: Parma v. 8; Vivès v. 13; Marietti, *Quaestiones Disputatae*, v. 2.

°   No English translation.

7. ***De spiritualibus creaturis.*** AA. 1–11 (Italy 1267–68). Extant MSS: 64. See above, pp. 213–14.

Article 3 of this work was completed after March 1266, when Moerbeke completed translating the commentary of Simplicius on the *Categories;* and article 10 was completed after November 1267, when Moerbeke completed Themistius's commentary on *De anima*. Grabmann suggests that this question may have been disputed between 1266 and 1268 at the court of Clement IV in Viterbo. We have suggested that it may have been disputed at
°   Viterbo between 1267–68, perhaps at the papal curia.

EDITIONS: Parma v. 8; Vivès v. 13; Marietti, *Quaestiones Disputatae*, v. 2; critical edition by L. Keeler (Rome: Gregorianum 1946).

English trans.: *On Spiritual Creatures*, trans. M. C. Fitzpatrick and J. J. Wellmuth (Milwaukee: Marquette 1951).

8. ***De anima.*** AA. 1–21 (Paris, February–April 1269). Extant MSS: 81 complete, and 13 fragments. See above, pp. 250–54.

There is no agreement on the date and place of this disputation. Mandonnet dated it between 1269–70 at Paris; Walz places it in Rome in 1266 prior to *De spiritualibus creaturis*. Two reliable

MSS give Paris as the place of the disputation (Klosterneuburg, Stifsbibl. 274, and Anger 418). Glorieux and J. H. Robb argue that it must have been held in Paris early in 1269; we have argued that the disputation must have taken place in Paris shortly after Thomas arrived in January 1269 for his second regency. It is certain that this disputation was held after the *prima pars* of the *Summa.* The entire question deals with problems then being disputed in the schools of Paris.

EDITIONS: Parma v. 8; Vivès v. 13; Marietti, *Quaestiones Disputatae,* v. 2; critical ed. of the non-Parisian tradition by J. H. Robb, *Quaestiones de anima* (Toronto: PIMS 1968).

English trans.: *The Soul,* trans. by J. P. Rowan (St. Louis 1949).

9. *De virtutibus in communi* (13 articles); *De caritate* (13 articles); *De correctione fraterna* (2 articles); *De spe* (4 articles); and *De virtutibus cardinalibus* (4 articles) (Paris 1269–72). Extant MSS: 52 complete, and 8 fragments. See above, p. 254.

All the early catalogues explicitly state that these questions were disputed in Paris during Thomas's second regency. They parallel questions in the second part of the *Summa theologiae* on which he was working at the time.

EDITIONS: Parma v. 8; Vivès v. 13; Marietti, *Quaest. Disp.* v. 2.

English trans.: *On the Virtues in General,* trans. J. P. Reid (Providence, R.I. 1951); *On Charity,* trans. L. H. Kendzierski (Milwaukee: Marquette 1960).

10. *De unione verbi incarnati.* AA. 1–5 (Paris, early April 1272). Extant MSS: 53. See above, pp. 307–13.

Mandonnet placed this disputed question at Viterbo in 1268, while Pelster and Walz consider it to have been disputed in Naples in 1272–73. We have argued that this question was determined at Paris in the early spring of 1272, while Thomas was writing III, q. 2, of the *Summa,* and before III, q. 17, aa. 1–2, which seems to have been written in Naples in late summer or early fall of 1272.

EDITIONS: Parma v. 8; Vivès v. 13; Mandonnet, *Quaest. Disp.* (Paris: Lethielleux 1925) v. 3; Marietti, *Quaest. Disp.* v. 2. No English translation.

11. Extra-serial disputations, i.e., disputations held individually, distinct from any given series, but inserted into larger works by the early editors of the writings of Thomas or by Thomas himself.

De libero arbitrio, inserted into *De malo* as question 6 (see above, n. 6). This question seems to have been disputed in Paris in 1270.

De daemonibus, inserted in *De malo* as question 16 (see above, n. 6). This was disputed after November 22, 1267, for in article 12 ad 1 Thomas quotes the paraphrase of Themistius on *De anima,* translated by Moerbeke at Viterbo at that date, but before the introduction of Kappa into the *Metaphysics* (a. 2, obj. 1).

De sensibus Sacrae Scripturae, appended to *Quodlibet 7* as question 6, articles 14–16. We have argued that this question was one of the four questions disputed at Thomas's inception in theology in the spring of 1256 (see above, pp. 105–7).

De opere manuali, appended to *Quodlibet 7* as question 7, articles 17–18. We have argued that this was the all-important "question three" disputed on the second day of inception in the spring of 1256 (see above, pp. 108–10).

De pueris in religionem admittendis, appended to *Quodlibet 4* as question 12, articles 23–24. This quodlibet was held in Paris, most likely during Lent 1271. Vatican MS Vat. lat. 779, fol. 20 v, clearly states that "these two articles were disputed by Friar Thomas against Gérard [of Abbeville] at the beginning of Lent." They constitute a disputation held at Paris against *Quodlibet 11* of Gérard of Abbeville, the last of which is a *quaestio de oblatis.* Thomas disputed this question before he wrote his *Contra doctrinam retrahentium a religione* against Gérard in the summer of 1271 (n. 54).

De attributis divinis, inserted in I *Sent.,* 2, 3, was probably disputed in Rome at Santa Sabina, when he was regent master between 1265–67.

De immortalitate animae, found in Vatican MS Vat. lat. 781,

fol. 47r–48r, unpublished, seems to be an authentic work of
Thomas according to Fries, A. Dondaine, and Eschmann.

Utrum anima coniuncta cognoscat seipsam per essentiam,
found in Oxford MS Bodl. Laud. Misc. 480, also seems to be
authentic according to Pelster, A. Dondaine, and Eschmann.

12–24. **Quaestiones de quodlibet I–XII** (Paris 1256–59; 1269–72).
Extant MSS: 137 complete, and 39 fragments. See above, pp.
126–27; 255–56.

The early catalogues of Thomas's works list only eleven quodlibets; the twelfth, discovered after 1300 and added to the original eleven, is actually a *reportatio* or notes in view of a determination. These quodlibets fall into two groups, the earliest of
which is the grouping 7–11 in a never varying series, and 1–6,
which often vary in the MSS. At Paris, quodlibets were held
only during Advent and Lent; consequently they are often
called Christmas or Easter quodlibets. The group 7–11 belongs
to Thomas's first Parisian regency.

1256, Christmas	Quodl. 7
1257, Easter	missing
1257, Christmas	Quodl. 8
1258, Easter	Quodl. 9
1258, Christmas	Quodl. 10
1259, Easter	Quodl. 11

The group 1–6, 12, belongs to Thomas's second Parisian regency:

1269, Easter	Quodl. 1
1269, Christmas	Quodl. 2
1270, Easter	Quodl. 3
1270, Christmas	Quodl. 12
1271, Easter	Quodl. 4
1271, Christmas	Quodl. 5
1272, Easter	Quodl. 6

However, as Gauthier and Eschmann point out, in *Quodlibet 6*,
held in Lent 1272, there are two quotations from *Metaphysics*
Lambda (a. 19) that refer to Book XI. Therefore the dating of
the second group is not entirely settled.

EDITIONS: Parma v. 9; Vivès v. 15; Mandonnet (Paris 1926); Marietti, *Quaest. Quodlibetales,* 1949 (with new enumeration).
No English translation.

EXPOSITIONS OF HOLY SCRIPTURE

25. **Expositio in Job "ad litteram"** (Orvieto 1261–64). Extant MSS: 59. See above, p. 153.

Tolomeo of Lucca places this exposition on Job under the pontificate of Urban IV, when, he says, Thomas "expounded the book of Job." The current text is a highly elaborated edition of lectures given in the Dominican Priory of San Domenico in Orvieto. It is contemporary with the *Summa contra gentiles,* Bks. II–III, in the sense that the commentary on Job and the *Summa contra gentiles* III, 64–113, deal with the problem of divine providence, and in the sense that both Job and the *Summa* utilize Moerbeke's new translation of Aristotle's work on animals. In the commentary on Job, Thomas expressly used the new translation eight times (c. 27, line 36; c. 40 [six times]; and c. 41, line 204). Moerbeke's translation of *De partibus animalium* was completed in Thebes on December 23, 1260; the other parts of Aristotle's work on animals were translated immediately before or immediately after this date. Thomas, therefore, could not have written this commentary on Job before 1261.

EDITIONS: Leon. ed. v. 26 (Rome 1965); Parma v. 14; Vivès v. 18.
No English translation.

26. **Postilla super Psalmos.** Ps. 1–54 (Naples 1272–73). Extant MSS: 5 complete, and 2 fragments. See above, pp. 302–4.

This work is a *reportatio* made by Reginald of Piperno while Thomas was lecturing in Naples. Bartholomew of Capua describes it as "on four nocturns of the Psalter," but Nicholas Trevet and most of the other early bibliographers who mention it list it as a postil "On three nocturns of the Psalter." Psalms 1–51, found in all published editions, comprise the nocturns for the ancient Office of Matins for Sunday, Monday, and Tuesday; Psalms 52–54, comprising the first three Psalms for Wednesday, was discovered by Uccelli in Naples (Regio Archivio 25) and published by him in Rome in 1880. The text of the Psalms commented upon is the Gallican Psalter of the Vulgate Bible, although Thomas used as well the Roman Psalter and the translation from the Hebrew also made by St. Jerome. The lectures on the Psalms were terminated abruptly on December 5, 1273.

EDITIONS: Parma v. 14; Vivès v. 18; Uccelli (Rome 1880).
No English translation.

27. *Super Cantica Canticorum.* See above, pp. 326–27.

All the early catalogues of Thomas's writings list a *Super Cantica,* and William of Tocco claims that Thomas dictated "a brief commentary on the Canticle of Canticles" on his death-bed at Fossanova. To date no commentary, long or "brief," has been found. The two commentaries printed in the Vulgate editions (Parma v. 14, 354–86, 387–426; Vivès v. 18, 557–607, 608–67) are spurious: the first commentary belongs to Hymo of Auxerre, the second to Giles of Rome.

28. *Postilla super Isaiam.* Autograph of c. 34:1 to c. 50:1 is preserved ❋ in Vatican MS Vat. lat. 9850, fol. 105ra–114vb. Extant MSS: autogr. + 19 complete, and 1 fragment. See above, pp. 120–21.

After the death of Thomas, Friar Jacobinus of Asti transcribed Thomas's *littera illegibilis* into legible script (see above, p. 300), and the full text belongs to the MS tradition. There seem to be two distinct parts: chapters 1–11 in the form and style of a university master, and chapters 12 to the end in the form and style of a literal gloss with no theological developments or discussion. There is no agreement on the dating of this commentary. Some, like Mandonnet, think it belongs early in Thomas's first Parisian regency (1256–57; or Walz, 1257–59), while others, like Glorieux, date it late in the second Parisian regency (1269–72). Eschmann seems to suggest that Thomas did not comment on Isaiah at either time in Paris, but makes too much out of the fact that there is an autograph; he argues that at both times in Paris Thomas had secretaries and would not have written it with his own hand. However, we have rejected this as a chronological principle. No doubt the two parts of the commentary are to be dated separately.

EDITIONS: Leon. ed. v. 28 in preparation; Parma v. 14, 427–576; Vivès v. 18, 688–821; v. 19, 1–65; Uccelli, 114ff.

No English translation.

29. *Postilla super Jeremiam.* Incomplete, breaking off at end of c. 42. Extant MSS: 5. See above, p. 45.

In the sixteenth century, Sixtus of Siena denied its authenticity because of its "sterility of doctrine." Following Eschmann, we have suggested that this work may have been a product of Thomas's years at Cologne under Albert as *cursor biblicus,* but that is only a possibility. This commentary could also be the result of his teaching in a Dominican priory as lector.

EDITIONS: Parma v. 14, 557–667; Vivès v. 19, 66–198.

No English translation.

30. *Postilla super Threnos.* Extant MSS: 2. See above, p. 45.

The problem of this commentary on the Lamentations of Jeremiah is the same as for the preceding. It seems to be a cursory reading of the text, devoid of theological discussion or development. We have suggested, following Eschmann, that this work may have been one of the texts that Thomas read "publicly" at Cologne as a *cursor biblicus* under Albert, but, again, there is no proof. It could also be the result of his teaching in a Dominican priory as lector.

EDITIONS: Parma v. 14, 668–85; Vivès v. 19, 199–225.

No English translation.

31. *Glossa continua super Evangelia (Catena aurea).* Gloss on all four Gospels taken from the writings of the Greek and Latin Fathers (Orvieto, Rome 1262/63–67). Extant MSS: *Super Matthaeum* (89 complete, and 17 fragments); *Super Marcum* (73

complete, and 7 fragments); *Super Lucam* (82 complete, and 11 fragments); *Super Johannem* (88 complete, and 5 fragments). See above, pp. 171–73.

Thomas's gloss on the four Evangelists was commissioned by Pope Urban IV at Orvieto in the early years of their friendship, i.e., late 1262 or early 1263. The gloss on Matthew was finished and dedicated to Urban in 1263; this date is fixed by Parma MS Bibl. Palat. 1, written in 1263. The glosses on the other three Evangelists were dedicated to Cardinal Annibaldo d'Annibaldi, Thomas's close friend and former pupil at Paris, after the death of Urban in 1264. For this continuous gloss, especially from the gloss on Mark onward, Thomas procured the service of an unknown Greek scholar to translate certain passages from the Greek. The *Catena aurea* was completed by the time Thomas left Rome for Viterbo in 1267.

EDITIONS: Parma v. 11–12; Vivès v. 16–17; Marietti 1953, 2 v.

English trans.: *Catena Aurea* (Oxford 1841–45), 4 v.

32. *Lectura super Matthaeum. Reportatio* (Paris 1256–59). Extant MSS: 4 complete, and 1 fragment. See above, pp. 121–22.

This *lectura* is almost certainly of Parisian origin, but it is not altogether clear whether it was delivered in Thomas's first or second Parisian regency; it is commonly thought, however, to belong to the first (1256–59). Mandonnet argued that it was taught over a period of two years, because it is twice the length of the lectures on Isaiah, but this argument is based on an unproved assumption. The *reportatio* was written down by Friar Peter d'Andria (perhaps, but not certainly, for the first fourteen chapters) and by Ligier de Besançon (perhaps chapters 15 to the end, chapter 28).

The two earliest catalogues list it as "defective" and "incomplete," referring, no doubt, to two lacunae in the three Italian MSS known, and found in all printed editions. The first is from Matthew 5:11 to 6:8, the other is 6:14–19. In other words, in the Marietti edition, numbers 444–582 (lect. 13–17) and numbers

603–10 (lect. 19) are spurious. In the printed edition of 1527 and in all subsequent editions, the lacunae were filled from the commentary of Friar Peter de Scala, O.P. (d. 1295). The authentic text is found in Basel, University Library MS B. V. 12, as H.-V. Shooner has shown.

EDITIONS: Parma v. 10, 1–278; Vivès v. 19, 226–668; Marietti 1951 and various dates.

No English translation.

33. **Lectura super Johannem. Reportatio** (Paris 1269–72). Extant MSS: 33 complete, and 13 fragments. See above, pp. 246–47.

According to Tolomeo of Lucca, Thomas himself wrote the commentary on the first five chapters (*expositio*), while Reginald of Piperno reported the rest. All the early catalogues note that Thomas himself "corrected" Reginald's *reportatio*. This "correction" and "revision," no doubt, was the result of the desire of Adenulf of Anagni, a secular student, to pay for a fair copy of the entire lecture series. There can be no doubt that these lectures were given by Thomas during his second Parisian regency (1269–72); C. Spicq has argued in favor of the academic year 1270–71.

EDITIONS: Leon. ed. v. 31 in preparation; Parma v. 10, 279–645; Vivès v. 19, 669ff.; v. 20, 1–376; Marietti 1952 and various dates.

No English translation.

34. **Expositio et lectura super Epistolas Pauli Apostoli.** Part *reportatio* by Reginald, part edited by Thomas himself. Extant MSS: 30 complete, and 7 containing only the commentary on the Letter to the Hebrews. See above, pp. 247–49; 305.

Mandonnet and many others hold that Thomas commented twice on St. Paul, once in Italy between 1259–65, and again in Naples in 1272–73, but that the second time he commented only as far as 1 Corinthians 10, this latter being an *expositio*. Since it is certain that Thomas lectured on some of Paul's letters in Paris, Glorieux places the *expositio* at Paris between

1270–72, rather than at Naples, on the grounds that this part is a work written and edited by Thomas himself and that he would not have had time to edit it at Naples before he stopped abruptly on December 6, 1273. However, the state of the "vulgate" text is more complex.

The "vulgate" text is composed of five heterogeneous pieces: (a) the edited text written or dictated by Thomas (*expositio*), covering Romans to 1 Corinthians 7:9; (b) an inserted text from the *Postilla* of Peter of Tarentaise through the version of Nicholas of Goran, covering 1 Corinthians 7:10 to the end of chapter 10; (c) a *reportatio* by Reginald of Piperno from an early *lectura* (possibly originally on the whole of St. Paul, given in the Italian period), covering 1 Corinthians 11 to Hebrews; (d) a carefully written commentary on Hebrews "up to chapter 11" (Bernard Gui); (e) the rest of Hebrews to the end, 13:25. The commentary on Hebrews is not only mentioned separately by Bernard Gui, but it also circulated separately (7 extant MSS).

The only point we have argued is that Thomas did not lecture on Paul at Naples, but rather at Paris during his second regency.

EDITIONS: Parma v. 13; Vivès vv. 20–21; Marietti 1953 and various dates, 2 v.

English trans.: *Commentary on St. Paul's Epistle to the Galatians,* trans. F. R. Larcher (Albany, N.Y.: Magi Books 1966); *Commentary on St. Paul's Epistle to the Ephesians,* trans. M. L. Lamb (Albany, N.Y.: Magi Books 1966).

35. **Commendatio Sacrae Scripturae.** Two *principia* (Paris, April or May 1256). Extant MSS: 2. See above, pp. 96–105.

These two *sermones* were discovered by Uccelli in Florence, Bibl. Cent. MS Conv. Soppr. G. 4. 36 (Santa Maria Novella), and immediately recognized as *principia,* i.e., inaugural lectures. The first *Commendatio S. Scripturae* is based on the text "Rigans montes de superioribus," etc. (Ps. 103:13), and was presented by Thomas on the second day of his inception as master in theology in the spring of 1256 (Tocco, *Hystoria,* c. 16). The second *sermo* complements the first and is more traditional as a *commendatio.* It is a division of all the books of Scripture, based on the text of Baruch 4:1, "Hic est liber mandatorum," etc. Mandonnet, assuming that Thomas was a *cursor biblicus* at Paris for two years before reading the *Sentences,* claimed that the second *sermo* was Thomas's *principium* when he began cursory reading of the Bible in 1252. However, we have argued that Thomas was never *cursor biblicus* at Paris, and that the *sermo secundus* was delivered by Thomas on the first *dies legibilis* following inception, i.e., at his *resumptio,* "in which lecture he brought to completion his incomplete inaugural lecture given *in aula.*"

EDITIONS: Parma v. 1, xxvi–xxx; Marietti, *Opuscula theologica* I, 435–43; Mandonnet IV, 481–90.

No English translation; partial trans. Bourke, 61–62.

EXPOSITIONS ON ARISTOTLE

36. **Sententia super Peri hermenias.** Incomplete, terminating in II, 14, 19b26 (II, lect. 14) (Paris 1270–71). Extant MSS: 21 complete, and 2 fragments.

From the dedicatory letter (*Epistola nuncupatoria*) it would seem that Thomas commented on Aristotle's *Peri hermenias* at the request of William Berthaut, provost of Louvain from 1270 or certainly 1271 on. Even though the commentary is incomplete, the letter was written *after* the commentary ("expositionem adhibere curavi"). The Aristotelian text used was the Greek-Latin version that came into existence with the commentary of Ammonius, completed by Moerbeke at Viterbo in September 1268. Thomas may have begun his exposition at Viterbo and continued it in Paris, leaving it incomplete for some unknown reason. Some MSS claim that death prevented Thomas from completing the work, but that does not seem likely. In I, 1, lect. 3, n. 5, Thomas refers to *Metaphysics* Lambda as Book XI, suggesting a date prior to the beginning of 1271. The only sources he used, besides Aristotle himself, were Ammonius and Boethius in his longer commentary on the *De interpretatione* (*ed. secunda*). The commentary of Thomas is most important for his view on the truth and falsity of future contingent propositions (I, lect. 13–15). An exemplar of this commentary was available from the

Parisian stationer's in 1304. Thomas's commentary was "completed," or "continued," by various Dominicans, among them Gratiadei of Esculo (d. 1341), Robert de Vulgarbia (?), and Thomas de Vio (Cajetan). The best modern study of Thomas's commentary is by J. Isaac, *Le 'Peri Hermeneias' en occident* (Paris: Vrin 1953).

EDITIONS: Leon. ed. v. 1 (Rome 1882); Marietti 1955 and various dates (Leonine text with few notes).

English trans.: *Aristotle on Interpretation: Commentary by St. Thomas and Cajetan,* trans. J. T. Oesterle (Milwaukee: Marquette 1962).

37. *Sententia super Posteriora Analytica.* Two books (Paris 1269–72). Extant MSS: 55 complete, and 4 fragments.

The basic text on which Thomas commented seems to be the vulgate version of James of Venice (mid-twelfth century), but he also had at his disposal the new version by William of Moerbeke, as Minio-Paluello pointed out in 1952. The date of the new version is not known, nor is the date of Thomas's commentary certain. Mandonnet placed it at Viterbo "around 1268 or thereafter," prior to his commentary on the *Peri hermenias.* Grabmann and Walz tend to date it at Paris, 1269–72. This Aristotelian work on scientific methodology deeply influenced all of Thomas's systematic writings.

EDITIONS: Leon. ed. v. 1 (Rome 1882); Marietti 1955 and subsequent dates (Leonine text with few notes).

English trans.: Thomas Aquinas, *Commentary on the Posterior Analytics of Aristotle,* trans. F. R. Larcher (Albany, N.Y.: Magi Books 1970).

38. *Sententia super Physicam.* Eight books (Paris 1269–70). Extant MSS: 64 complete, and 10 fragments.

Thomas changed from the *Physica veteris translationis* (James of Venice) to the *Moerbekana* (whose date is unknown) during the composition of the work. Mandonnet dated Thomas's commentary at Rome in 1265, before the *prima pars* of the *Summa.*

However, it is most unlikely that this commentary was written
before the *prima pars* (see above, n. 3). Throughout, *Metaphysics* Lambda is quoted as Book XI, therefore prior to the beginning
of 1271. The principal source throughout is the commentary of
Averroes, with whom Thomas frequently disagrees.

EDITIONS: Leon. ed. v. 2 (Rome 1884), but the Latin text
of Aristotle in this edition is unreliable; Marietti 1954 (Leonine
text without variants or notes).

English trans.: *Commentary on Aristotle's Physics*, trans. R. J.
Blackwell et al. (New Haven: Yale 1963).

39. *Sentential de caelo et mundo.* Incomplete, terminating in III, 3,
302b9 (III, lect. 8) (Naples 1272–73). Extant MSS: 38 complete,
and 5 fragments. See above, p. 316.

The Aristotelian text on which this commentary is based is the
new Greek-Latin version by Moerbeke, who also translated the
important commentary of Simplicius, completed on June 15,
1271. Robert Grosseteste translated the Greek text up to III, 1,
299a11; Moerbeke revised this and translated III–IV with the
commentary of Simplicius. For reasons never clarified, Eschmann
states that Thomas's commentary is not an "unfinished work," as
commonly held, but "complete" as far as it goes, for Thomas
"knew no more Aristotelian text of *De caelo* than which he
explained" ("Catalogue," n. 31). However, (1) Moerbeke translated Bks. III–IV directly from the Greek, and Thomas commented on III, 1–3, of this version; (2) in the commentary itself, Thomas indicates that he knew the existence of the part
not commented on by him, e.g., at III, lect. 2, n. 1: "in quarto
libro ibi 'De gravi autem et levi'" (= IV, 1); and at III, lect.
3, n. 2: "Partim autem inferius in hoc eodem libro" (= III, 5);
(3) in other works, e.g., *Summa* I, Thomas knew and referred to
all four books in the versions of Gérard of Cremona (d. 1187)
and Michael Scot (c. 1235), both made from the Arabic. It
would seem that Thomas terminated this commentary in 302b9
when he ceased all writing on December 6, 1273. Thomas's
basic source throughout is the commentary of Simplicius. Thomas
was much more familiar with Simplicius in this work than he

was when writing *Metaphysics* Lambda, where Thomas makes certain errors concerning Ptolemy and other astronomers.

EDITIONS: Leon. ed. v. 3 (Rome 1886); Marietti 1952 (Leonine text with cross references).

No English translation.

40. **Sententia super libros De generatione et corruptione.** Incomplete, terminating in I, 5, 322a33 (I, lect. 17) (Naples 1272–73). Extant MSS: 4. See above, p. 316.

This commentary was written after his exposition of the *Physics* and *De caelo:* "as we have made clear (*manifestavimus*) in VIII *Physic.* and in I *De caelo*" (*De gen.*, I, lect. 7, n. 1). It was certainly composed at Naples, where William of Tocco saw him writing this commentary, which he believed to have been Thomas's "last work in philosophy." It was not known to the Parisian stationer's even as late as 1304; consequently there is no Parisian manuscript tradition, and only four extant MSS. Throughout, Thomas is concerned with the *sententia Aristotelis*, and he seems to utilize only Aristotle and Averroes: "ut dicit Averroes in expositione huius loci" (I, lect. 15, n. 2).

EDITIONS: Leon. ed. v. 3 (Rome 1886); Marietti 1952 (manual; Leonine text).

No English translation.

41. **Sententia super Meteora.** Incomplete, terminating in II, 8, 369a9 (Paris or Naples 1269–73). Extant MSS: 11 complete, and 3 fragments. See above, p. 316.

According to the Leonine edition of this text, Thomas's commentary ends in II, 5, 363a20 (II, lect. 10). However, A. Dondaine has definitively shown that Thomas commented on chapters 7 and 8, ending with 369a9 (three more *lectiones*); the additional commentary is found in 6 MSS (A. Dondaine, AFP 36 [1966] 81–152). Apparently Thomas's commentary on chapter 6 is completely lost. The basic text is that of Moerbeke, who translated Books I–III anew from the Greek. Thomas's commentary was "completed" by at least three Parisian masters in arts before Peter of Auvergne's "continuation."

EDITIONS: Leon. ed. v. 3 (Rome 1886); Marietti 1952 (Leonine text with cross references).

English trans.: I, lect. 8–10, by L. Thorndike, *Latin Treatises on Comets* (Chicago Univ. Press 1950), 77–86.

o 42. **Sententia super De anima.** Three books (Paris 1269–70). Extant MSS: 67 complete, and 12 fragments. See above, pp. 216; 232–33, note 63.

According to the earliest catalogues, the commentary on Book I is a *reportatio* by Reginald of Piperno, while that on Books II–III is an *expositio*. Although the same version of the text is used throughout, namely, that of Moerbeke made at Viterbo in 1268, it is difficult to account for the *reportatio* of Book I. In II, lect. 7, n. 695, the words "which we have diligently treated else-
o where" seem to refer to *De unitate intellectus contra Averroistas*, written in 1270 (see below, n. 55). Eschmann thought that the commentary was written before the II–II of the *Summa*, thus placing at least Books II–III between 1270–71. However, *Metaphysics* Lambda is always cited as XI, as Gauthier pointed out.
o Therefore it would seem that this commentary was written before the beginning of 1271.

EDITIONS: Parma v. 20, 1–144; Vivès v. 24, 1–195; Marietti (ed. Pirotta) 1925, and subsequent dates.

English trans.: *Aristotle's De Anima with the Commentary of St. Thomas Aquinas*, trans. K. Foster and S. Humphries (New Haven: Yale 1951).

43. **Sententia de sensu et sensato.** Extant MSS: 41 complete, and 3 fragments.

This commentary on one of the *parva naturalia* is based on the Greek-Latin version of Moerbeke, and was known to the Parisian stationer's in 1304. It seems to have circulated independently from its companion piece *De memoria et reminiscentia*. Usually it is dated close to Thomas's commentary on *De anima*. Thomas is clearly familiar with Moerbeke's translation of Alexander of Aphrodisias's commentary on *De sensu*, the date of which is unknown.

EDITIONS: Parma v. 20, 145–96; Vivès v. 24, 197–267; Marietti (ed. A. M. Pirotta) 1928 and subsequent dates.

No English translation.

44. *Sententia de memoria et reminiscentia.* Extant MSS: 48 complete, and 1 fragment.

This commentary on one of the *parva naturalia* is associated with the previous work (n. 43) and dated near it and the commentary on *De anima.* It is not certain whether it was included in the stationer's list of 1304 under the title of *De sensu,* "10 pecias." It is based on the Moerbeke version of the text.

EDITIONS: Parma v. 20, 197–214; Vivès v. 24, 269–92; Marietti (ed. A. M. Pirotta) 1928 and subsequent dates.

No English translation.

45. *Sententia super Metaphysicam.* Twelve books (Paris, Naples [?] 1269–72). Extant MSS: 74 complete, and 19 fragments.

This commentary is extremely difficult to date because of its length at a time when the Moerbeke version of the *Metaphysics* came into existence, and the number of secretaries employed in the Naples MS Bibl. Naz. VIII. F. 16. It would seem that Thomas did not compose this commentary in the order of the Aristotelian books. The version of the text was not that of Moerbeke throughout. Generally the commentary on Books II–III, where *Metaphysics* Lambda is constantly referred to as XII, seems to be later than Book V, lect. 7, to Book VII, lect. 16, where Lambda is referred to as XI. On this basis, Books I and IV would also be early, while from Book VII, lect. 17, to the end of Book XII, Lambda is always referred to as XII. All that we can be certain of at this stage is that the commentary on *Metaphysics* XII is earlier than the commentary on *De caelo* (above, n. 39).

EDITIONS: Leon. ed. v. 46 in preparation; Parma v. 20; Vivès vv. 24–25; Marietti (Cathala and Spiazzi) 1950.

English trans.: *Commentary on the Metaphysics of Aristotle,* trans. J. P. Rowan, 2 v. (Chicago: Regnery 1964).

46. **Sententia libri Ethicorum.** Ten books (Paris 1271). Extant MSS: 86 complete or almost complete, and 1 fragment. See above, p. 283.

Older historians—and some contemporary writers—place the commentary in Rome or "in the environs of Rome" in 1265-67, or generally "around 1266," at least in first draft. However, Gauthier has shown that the commentary on the *Ethics* was contemporary with the II-II of the *Summa:* thus *Ethicorum* I, lect. 6, corresponds with II-II, qq. 80-81; *Ethicorum* IV, lect. 8-9, a little before II-II, q. 129; and *Ethicorum* VII, lect. 10, corresponds to II-II, q. 155. Consequently the commentary on the *Ethics* was written in 1271 and, possibly, the early part of 1272. Gauthier has also shown that Thomas became aware of the existence of *Metaphysics* Kappa (XI) between the writing of *Ethicorum* I, lect. 1, n. 1 (ed. Pirotta), and *Ethicorum* I, lect. 6, n. 79. This interval corresponds to the time between the end of I-II and the beginning of II-II (see above, n. 3). Thus Thomas's awareness of *Metaphysics* Kappa seems to have begun early in 1271.

The Latin text Thomas commented upon was a revision of the Grosseteste translation (1246-47). It used to be thought that Moerbeke made this revision, but it has been adequately demonstrated that the revision did not come from Moerbeke's hand; for one thing, if it had, the text Thomas had would not have been so corrupt. Gauthier suggests that the revision Thomas had came into existence around 1270.

EDITIONS: Leon. ed. v. 47 (Rome 1969); Parma v. 20; Vivès vv. 25-26; Marietti 1949.

English trans.: *Commentary on the Nicomachean Ethics*, C. I. Litzinger, 2 v. (Chicago: Regnery 1964).

47. **Sententia libri Politicorum.** Incomplete, terminating in III, 6, 1280a6 (III, lect. 6) (probably Paris 1269-72). Extant MSS: 27 complete, and 2 fragments.

The Aristotelian text upon which this commentary is based is Moerbeke's revision of Books I and II (made by an anonymous earlier translator), and Moerbeke's translation of Books III-VIII, completed around 1260. Thomas commented only as far as III, 6, 1280a6, namely "on the first, second, and part of the third with the supplement of master Peter of Auvergne on all the rest" (Cat. Bibl. Pont. 1317). The Parisian stationer's, however, disregarded Thomas's commentary on the first six chapters of Book III, and substituted Peter of Auvergne's commentary from the beginning of Book III to Book VIII. Therefore some MSS carry both commentaries on III, 1–6, while others substitute the commentary of Peter from the very beginning of Book III.

It is impossible to determine the date of Thomas's commentary: Mandonnet placed it in the "vicinity of 1268"; Grabmann suggests "the vicinity of 1272"; while Walz and Eschmann date it 1269–72 during Thomas's second Parisian regency.

Although Thomas rarely quoted parts of the *Politics* not commented upon by him, one should note that there are four such passages in the authentic part of *De regno* (n. 62), not noted by the Leonine editors: *Pol.* V, 12 (I, 10, n. 82); *Pol.* VI, 4 (II, 7, n. 141); *Pol.* V, 3 (II, 7, n. 138); and *Pol.* VI, 4 (II, 7, n. 141). Therefore Thomas was aware of the full translation made by Moerbeke as early as 1265, when he wrote *De regno*.

EDITIONS: Leon. ed. v. 48 (Rome 1971); Marietti 1951. No English translation.

OTHER EXPOSITIONS

48. ***Expositio super librum Boethii De trinitate.*** Incomplete, terminating in chapter 2 (q. 6, a. 4) (Paris 1258–59). Autograph, Vatican MS Vat. lat. 9850, fol. 90ra–103vb, from question 3, article 2, to the end. Extant MSS: Autogr. + 19. See above, pp. 134–38.

The actual exposition of Boethius's *De trinitate* is very brief, the main burden of the exposition being a discussion of several questions arising from the text. Thomas was the only scholastic of the thirteenth century to comment on this text, which had been widely commented upon in the twelfth century. Chenu discovered that Annibaldo d'Annibaldi implicitly quotes from Thomas's work (q. 2, a. 2 ad 7) in his commentary on the

Sentences (I, q. 1, a. 1 ad 2), when he was a bachelor under
⊙ Thomas (perhaps 1258–60).

EDITIONS: Definitive text, B. Decker, *Expositio* . . . (Leiden:
Brill 1955); Marietti 1954, *Opuscula Theol.*, II, 313–89.

English trans.: *The Trinity and the Unicity of the Intellect*,
trans. Sister R. E. Brennan (St. Louis: Herder 1946); *On Search-
ing into God* (q. 2), trans. V. White (Oxford: Blackfriars 1947);
Divisions and Methods of the Sciences (qq. 5–6), trans. A. A.
Maurer (Toronto: PIMS 1953).

49. *Expositio in librum Boethii De hebdomadibus.* Incomplete, terminating in n. 46 (lect. 5) (Paris 1256–59). Extant MSS: 32. See
   above, pp. 137–38.

This exposition of the third Boethian tractate in theology, unusual for the thirteenth century, is generally dated in conjunction
with the previous item (n. 48) as being written during the
first Parisian regency, 1256–59. Occasion unknown.

EDITIONS: Parma v. 17, 349–96; Vivès v. 28, 468–81; Marietti, *Opuscula Theol.*, II, 391–408.

No English translation.

50. *Expositio super Dionysium De divinis nominibus* (Rome 1265–
   67). Extant MSS: 26 complete, and 1 fragment. See above, pp.
   174–75; 197.

This is Thomas's first large-scale venture into Greek theology.
Mandonnet suggested that it was written "after 1260," while
Walz places it in 1261. It was certainly written before Moerbeke
completed his translation of Proclus's *Elementatio theologica* at
Viterbo, on May 18, 1268. Without compelling reasons, we have
suggested that these lectures may have been given to Dominican
students at Santa Sabina in Rome, 1265–67.

EDITIONS: Parma v. 15, 259–405; Vivès v. 29, 374–580; Marietti 1950.

No English translation.

51. ***Expositio super librum De causis*** (Paris 1271–72) Extant MSS: 55 complete, and 7 fragments.

The *Liber de causis* was often considered an authentic Aristotelian text (*In Boeth. De trin.*, q. 6, a. 1, obj. 2); more often, however, it was quoted without author. Once Moerbeke had translated Proclus's *Elementatio theologica* (completed at Viterbo on May 18, 1268), the origin of *De causis* was immediately recognized as "excerpts" from Proclus, "particularly as everything contained in this book [*De causis*] is contained in the other much more fully and elaborately" (Prol.). Throughout, *Metaphysics* Lambda is quoted as Book XII; therefore Thomas's *Expositio* was written after the beginning of 1271. Saffrey argues that it must have been written "in the first half of 1272." An exemplar of this work was in the hands of the Parisian stationer's in 1304, and listed as *Sententia De causis*, 7 pecias.

EDITIONS: Critical text established by H.-D. Saffrey (Fribourg: Soc. Phil. 1954).

No English translation.

POLEMICAL WRITINGS

52. ***Contra impugnantes Dei cultum et religionem*** (Paris, September–October 1256). Extant MSS: 54 complete, and 26 printed editions. See above, pp. 88–91.

This detailed refutation of the *De periculis novissimorum temporum* by William of Saint-Armour (fifth and final version completed by August 1256) was written after Thomas's inception as master (spring 1256) and before word reached him of the condemnation of William's work on October 5, 1256. Tolomeo of Lucca explicitly noted that it was written "infra autem magisterium," meaning perhaps before Thomas began the academic year or perhaps before his acceptance into the *consortium magistrorum*. Thomas's polemical work exercised no influence on the condemnation of *De periculis*, nor was Thomas at the papal curia with Albert and Bonaventure to defend the mendicant cause. Thomas seems to have completed his *Contra impugnantes* at Paris before learning of the condemnation of October 5.

EDITIONS: Leon. ed. v. 41 A (Rome 1970); Parma v. 15; Vivès v. 29; Marietti 1954, *Opuscula Theol.*, II, 5–110.

English trans.: *An Apology for the Religious Orders*, trans. J. Procter (London 1902; Westminster, Md.: Newman 1950).

53. ***De perfectione spiritualis vitae*** (Paris, late 1269–early 1270). Extant MSS: 114 complete, and 4 fragments. See above, pp. 266–68.

The first twenty-three chapters are directed against Gérard d'Abbeville's *Contra adversarium perfectionis christianae*, published in the summer of 1269; chapters 24 to 30 are an answer to additional objections raised by Gérard. Although the first twenty-three chapters are a reply, Thomas tried to write an objective treatise on the nature of the spiritual life and the life of perfection; however, the last seven chapters are a return to polemical writing.

EDITIONS: Leon. ed. v. 41 B (Rome 1969); Parma v. 15; Vivès v. 29; Marietti 1954, *Opuscula Theol.*, II, 115–53.

English trans.: in three unpublished M.A. dissertations, by G. J. Guenther, C. G. Kloster, and J. X. Schmitt (Saint Louis Univ. 1942–44).

54. ***Contra doctrinam retrahentium a religione*** (commonly called ***Contra retrahentes***) (Paris, summer 1271). Extant MSS: 25 complete, and 26 printed editions. See above pp. 268–70.

This work is a reply to Gérard d'Abbeville and the Geraldini, who would prevent boys from entering religious life. In some MSS it is directed against "the pestiferous doctrine" of Gérard and his followers. According to the Leonine editors, this treatise was written between Lent 1271 (Q. disp. *De ingressu puerorum in religione*) and Advent 1271 (*Quodl.* 5 and II–II, q. 189).

EDITIONS: Leon. ed. v. 41 C (Rome 1969); Marietti 1954, *Opuscula Theol.*, II, 159–90.

English trans.: *An Apology for the Religious Orders*, trans. J. Procter (London 1902; Westminster, Md.: Newman 1950).

55. *De unitate intellectus contra Averroistas* (Paris 1270). Extant
   MSS: 56. See above, pp. 277–79.

This treatise is a reply to an unknown work by Siger of Brabant, on the nature of the intellect, which Siger held to be one
for all mankind. This fact and date are established by Oxford
MS, Corpus Christi College 225: "Thomas wrote this [work]
against master Siger of Brabant and many other regents in philosophy at Paris in the year of our Lord 1270." However, the particular treatise against which this treatise is directed is not yet
known; it was written before the condemnation of Averroism on
December 10, 1270.
   EDITIONS: Reliable text established by L. W. Keeler (Rome:
Gregorianum 1936); Parma v. 16, 208–24; Vivès v. 27, 311–35;
Marietti 1954, *Opuscula Phil.*, 63–90 (Keeler text without apparatus).
   English trans.: *The Trinity and the Unicity of the Intellect*
(based on text in Parma ed.), trans. R. E. Brenan (St. Louis
Univ. 1946).

56. *De aeternitate mundi contra murmurantes* (Paris, spring 1270).
   Extant MSS: 89 complete. See above, pp. 286–88.

This work is a reply to one of the questions disputed by John
Pecham at his inauguration in the spring of 1270. Pecham's text
has been published by I. Brady in *Comm. Studies* (Toronto:
PIMS 1974). The point of Thomas's argument is that one cannot
prove by reason that the world had a beginning, as this fact is
known only by faith.
   EDITIONS: Parma v. 16, 318–20; Vivès v. 27, 450–53; Marietti
1954, *Opuscula Phil.*, 105–8.
   No English translation.

TREATISES ON SPECIAL SUBJECTS

57. *De fallaciis ad quosdam nobiles artistas* (Roccasecca 1244–45).
Extant MSS: 65 complete. See above, pp. 34–35.

This youthful explanation of fourteen kinds of fallacious reasoning seems to be based on the *Fallaciae maiores* of Peter of Spain, rather than on the actual text of Aristotle's *Sophistici elenchi*. Scholars are divided on the date of this treatise; some, such as Grabmann and Walz, date it late in the career of Thomas, putting it in the years 1268–72; Mandonnet originally denied its authenticity, because it is not listed in the "official catalogue" presented by Bartholomew of Capua (1319), but he later admitted that it could have been written in 1244–45. Michelitsch unreservedly dates it 1244. Our own conviction is that it was written for former classmates in arts at the University of Naples, while Thomas was in confinement at Roccasecca in 1244–45.

EDITIONS: Parma v. 16, 377–87; Vivès v. 27, 533–48; Perrier (*Opuscula*, Paris 1949), 430–61; Marietti 1954, *Opuscula Phil.*, 225–40.
No English translation.

58. *De ente et essentia ad fratres et socios suos* (Paris 1252–56). Extant MSS: 189 complete. See above, pp. 78–79.

This is one of the earliest treatises written by Thomas. Tolomeo of Lucca notes that Thomas wrote it before he became master in theology ("infra magisterium"), i.e., before March 1256. Clearly it was written for the sake of his *confrères* at Saint-Jacques. Thomas's principal source is Avicenna.

EDITIONS: Roland-Gosselin on the basis of 8 Parisian MSS (Le Saulchoir 1926; Paris 1948); L. Baur on the basis of the "vulgate" text and 11 Italian and German MSS (Münster 1926); C. Boyer corrected the Piana ed. on the basis of Roland-Gosselin and Baur, when they agreed: Marietti 1954, *Opuscula Phil.*,

5–18 (repr. of Boyer); Perrier on 2 Parisian MSS (*Opuscula,* Paris 1949), mainly on Bibl. Nat. lat. 14546.

English trans.: two translations before that of A. A. Maurer (Toronto: PIMS, 2nd ed. 1968, based mainly on text by L. Baur); J. Bobick, *Aquinas on Being and Essence* (Notre Dame 1965).

59. **De principiis naturae ad fratrem Sylvestrum** (Paris 1252–56). Extant MSS: 82 complete. See above, p. 79.

No doubt this work was written at the request of an otherwise unknown Friar Sylvester at Saint-Jacques during Thomas's years as *baccalarius Sententiarum* (1252–56). Tolomeo explicitly states that it was written before Thomas became master ("infra magisterium"). It deals with the principles of change, namely, matter, form, and privation, as well as with the four causes of change in nature; the doctrine is much more explicit than is found in Aristotle's *Physics* I–II.

EDITIONS: Parma v. 16, 338–42; Vivès v. 27, 480–86; Marietti 1954, *Opuscula Phil.,* 121–28; J. J. Pauson (critically established text), Fribourg-Louvain 1950.

English trans.: R. I. Henle and V. I. Bourke, Latin text and Eng. trans. (St. Louis Univ. 1947); R. Kocourek (St. Paul: North Central 1948).

60. **Compendium theologiae ad fratrem Reginaldum socium suum.** Incomplete, terminating in second part, *De spe,* c. 10 (Paris or Naples 1269–73). Extant MSS: 82, of which 38 contain only the first part (*De fide*), and 3 only the second part (*De spe*); and 13 fragments. See above, pp. 317–18.

Divided into three parts—faith, hope, and charity—this treatise ends abruptly within c. 10 of the second part. *De fide* covers briefly the whole of Catholic doctrine, the sacraments alone excepted, in 246 chapters. Bologna, Archiginnasio MS a 209 (end of thirteenth century) ends with the note: "Friar Thomas d'Aquino wrote thus far, but alas, prevented by death, he left it incomplete." Despite this statement, many scholars date the *Compendium* early: Lottin places *Compendium* c. 202 prior to *Summa theologiae,* I–II, q. 81, and *De malo,* q. 4, a. 1; Chenu considers it contemporary with the *Summa contra gentiles.* Both of these conjectures are based on doctrinal comparisons.

○   EDITIONS: Parma v. 16, 1–85; Vivès v. 27, 1–127; Marietti 1954, *Opuscula Theol.,* I, 13–138.

English trans.: L. Lynch, trans. (New York 1947); C. Vollert, *Compendium of Theology* (St. Louis Univ. 1947).

61. *De substantiis separatis* (or *De angelis*) *ad fratrem Reginaldum socium suum.* Incomplete, ending in c. 20 (Paris or Naples 1271–73). Extant MSS: 29. See above, p. 318.

This important work on the nature of separate substances, which some, including Thomas, call angels, was written after May 18, 1268, since Thomas twice quotes Proclus's *Elementatio theologica,* and after the beginning of 1271, since Thomas refers four times to *Metaphysics* Lambda as XII. Some MSS claim that Thomas was unable to finish because of death; more precisely, the *terminus ante quem* would be December 6, 1273.

EDITIONS: Leon. ed. v. 40 D (Rome 1968); Parma v. 16, 183–207; Vivès v. 27, 273–310; Marietti 1954, *Opuscula Phil.,* 21–58; critically established text based on 12 MSS: F. J. Lescoe (West Hartford, Conn. 1962).

English trans.: *Treatise on Separate Substances,* trans. F. J. Lescoe (West Hartford, Conn. 1959).

62. *De regno* (or *De regimine principum*) *ad regem Cypri.* Incomplete, ending in II, c. 4 (= first 21 chapters); "completed" by Tolomeo of Lucca in four books (Rome 1265–67). Extant MSS: 86. See above, pp. 189–95.

This treatise on governance by temporal rulers was to have been a gift to Hugh II of Lusignan, King of Cyprus (d. December 1267.) The fact that Thomas wrote some treatise called *De regno* is clear from all the early catalogues, and the termination of the work in II, 4, "ut animi hominum recreentur," is established from the extant MSS. However, Eschmann claimed that the extant twenty-one chapters have been contaminated by Tolomeo of Lucca, who strongly defended Guelf, or papalist, claims. We

have argued that the text is authentic up to II, 4, and that it
does not contradict other passages in Thomas's writings. °

EDITIONS: Parma v. 16, 225–91; Vivès v. 27, 336–412; Marietti °
1954, *Opuscula Phil.*, 257–358 (all four books); Perrier, *Opuscula*
(Paris: Lethielleux 1947), 223–67.

English trans.: *On Kingship*, trans. G. B. Phelan and I. T.
Eschmann (Toronto: PIMS 1949).

EXPERT OPINIONS

63. ***Contra errores Graecorum, ad Urbanum IV Pontificem Maxi-
mum.*** Two parts (Orvieto, summer 1263). Extant MSS: 57. See
above, pp. 168–71.

Early in 1263, Urban IV asked the expert opinion of Thomas
on a *Libellus de processione Spiritus Sancti et de fide trinitatis
contra errores Graecorum*, compiled by Nicholas of Durazzo,
bishop of Cotrone in Calabria, southern Italy, which purported
to prove that the Greek Fathers of the Church taught the Roman
doctrine of *filioque*. Thomas was very cautious about the authorities alleged, and "ill at ease" with the *Libellus*. However, in
time the *Libellus* was forgotten, and Thomas's work was considered an arsenal of arguments against the Greeks. The treatise
was finished before Thomas composed *Contra gentiles* IV, c. 69,
on the consecration of unleavened bread (n. 2).

EDITIONS: Leon. ed. v. 40 A, together with the *Libellus de fide
trinitatis* (Rome 1967); Parma v. 15, 239–58; Vivès v. 29, 344–
73; Marietti 1954, *Opuscula Theol.*, I, 315–46, together with
Libellus (Uccelli), 347–412.

No English translation.

64. ***Responsio ad fr. Joannem Vercellensem de articulis 108 ex
opere Petri de Tarentasia*** (Rome 1265–66). Extant MSS: 4.

This work is not mentioned in any of the early catalogues,
but its authenticity is established by 4 MSS and the content of
Thomas's replies. An unknown critic, or detractor, excerpted 108
propositions from Peter of Tarentaise's commentary on the *Sen-*

tences, I–II, as B. Smeraldo has shown. These propositions were submitted to Thomas by master general John of Vercelli (1264–83) for his expert opinion. In general, Thomas exonerates Peter and blames his "detractor" for suspecting the worse. Peter became archbishop of Lyons, 1272, cardinal of Ostia, 1273, and Pope Innocent V, 1276.

EDITIONS: Parma v. 16, 152–62; Vivès v. 27, 230–47; Marietti *Opuscula Theol.*, I, 223–40; the textual corrections proposed by R. J. Martin ("Notes critiques au subject de l'Opuscule IX," *Mélanges Auguste Pelzer*, Louvain 1947, 303–23) should be taken into consideration.

No English translation.

65. *Responsio ad fr. Joannem Vercellensem de articulis 42 (43)*
(Paris, April 2, 1971). Extant MSS: 34. See above, pp. 290–91.

On April 1, 1271, Thomas received a list of forty-three questions from the master general, John of Vercelli, for his expert opinion; the same questionnaire was sent to Albert the Great in Cologne and Robert Kilwardby in England. In his reply, Thomas combined his response to questions 8 and 9, perhaps by an oversight, thus bringing his list to forty-two instead of forty-three questions. This list from the master general combines the previous lists sent by Friar Bassiano of Lodi, the lector at Venice, and by his students to Thomas for judgment (nn. 75–76).

EDITIONS: Parma v. 16, 163–68; Vivès v. 27, 248–55; Marietti 1954, *Opuscula Theol.*, I, 211–18. The reply of Kilwardby was edited by Chenu, *Mélanges Mandonnet* (Paris 1930), I, 191–222; the reply of Albert was edited by Weisheipl, *Mediaeval Studies* 22 (1960), 316–54.

No English translation.

66. *De forma absolutionis sacramentalis ad generalem magistrum Ordinis* (Paris, "feast of St. Peter's chair," February 22, probably 1269). Extant MSS: 43 complete, and 2 fragments.

The *Libellus* sent by the master general, John of Vercelli, insisted that the indicative form of sacramental absolution, "I absolve you," should not be used, but rather that the deprecatory form, "May God absolve you," should be used instead. Thomas argued in favor of the indicative form as more expressive of the power given by Christ to the Apostles and the Church, and he insisted that it would be presumptuous to deny the validity of the indicative formula then used in the Latin Church.

EDITIONS: Leon. ed. v. 40 C (Rome 1969); P. Castagnoli, *L'opuscole 'De forma absolutionis' di San Tommaso d'Aquino*, 2nd ed. (Piacenza: Collegio Alberoni 1933); Marietti 1954, *Opuscula Theol.*, I, 173–80 (Castagnoli text without apparatus).

No English translation.

67. *De secreto* (Paris 1269). Extant MSS: 43.

This is a report of a committee of seven masters established by the general chapter at Paris in 1269, to deal with the authorship of a commentary on the *Sentences* claimed by two Dominicans, Joannina de Colonia, an Italian, and Joannes de Colonia, a German. The purpose of the six questions submitted to the committee by the general chapter was to determine whether a superior or judge could command that a subject reveal a secret, whether this secret be under the seal of confession or whether the brother had written a letter to his confessor outside of confession, but under the oath of secrecy. All the members of this commission except Thomas replied that the superior had no authority to force such a subject to reveal the secret. Thomas, in a minority report, claimed that the superior could command the subject to reveal the secret. His basic principle was that if a secular judge could demand an answer under oath, so could the religious superior. Today's sympathies would be with the majority report that no one can be forced to incriminate himself under oath.

From this it is clear that *De secreto* is simply a committee report and not a treatise or a letter written by Thomas. However, the text was included among the *opuscula* as early as the late thirteenth century in Paris MS Bibl. Nat. lat. 14546.

EDITIONS: Mandonnet v. 4, 497–501 (from the Paris MS); Marietti 1954, *Opuscula Theol.*, I, 447–48 (Mandonnet text).

No English translation, but see Bourke, 143–46.

LETTERS

68. **De propositionibus modalibus** (probably Roccasecca, 1244–45).
Extant MSS: at least 32. See above, pp. 34–35.

This short statement in 114 lines is undoubtedly excerpted from a letter written by Thomas to one or more of his classmates at the University of Naples, while he was confined at Roccasecca. Even I. M. Bocheński, who edited the work on the basis of 4 MSS, and whose judgment was originally severe, maintained its authenticity but dated it early in the life of Thomas.

   EDITIONS: Bocheński, *Angelicum* 17 (1940), 180–221; Marietti 1954, *Opuscula Phil.*, 243–44.

No English translation.

69. **De articulis fidei et Ecclesiae sacramentis ad archiepiscopum Panormitanum** (Palermo). Two brief parts: *De articulis fidei*, and *De ecclesiae sacramentis* (Orvieto 1261–65). Extant MSS: 277.

The popularity of this remarkable summary of the articles of faith and the heresies against each one is attested to by the great number of extant MSS. The archbishop of Palermo, probably Leonardo "de Comitibus," asked Thomas to write a short work that could be memorized, dealing with the articles of faith "from the Creed of the Fathers," i.e., the Apostles' Creed, and all the basic errors concerning them; the archbishop apparently asked for the same presentation for all the sacraments of the Church. The six articles pertaining to the divinity of Christ and the six pertaining to His humanity are set forth, and all the errors concerning the twelve articles are briefly named and refuted. Although the sacraments of the Church are included in the fourth article of the Creed, they are discussed separately in part two, because the archbishop explicitly asked for a special discussion of the sacraments and the heresies concerning them. Thomas's knowledge of the various heresies in the history of the Church is most remarkable. This list of errors and various heresies should be compared with that in *Super I–II Decretalem* (n. 71).

Mandonnet affirmed that this letter was written in 1261–62; Walz dates it as anywhere between 1260 and 1268.

EDITIONS: Parma v. 16, 115–22; Vivès v. 27, 171–82; Marietti °
1954, *Opuscula Theol.*, I, 141–51.

English trans.: (2nd part) *Catechetical Instructions of St. Thomas*, trans. J. B. Collins (New York: Wagner 1939; 1953).

70. **Responsio ad Bernardum [Ayglier] Abbatem Casinensem** (perhaps on way to Lyons, 1274). Extant MS: 1.

The text of this letter is written in the margin of Montecassino MS 82, containing the *Moralia* of Gregory the Great. It was discovered and made public in 1875 by Dom Luigi Tosti, who was under the impression that the text was an autograph of Thomas's *littera illegibilis;* however, this view is no longer held by anyone. The letter concerns a difficult point in Gregory, dealing with predestination.

EDITIONS: A. Dondaine, "La lettre de Saint Thomas à l'Abbé °
du Mont-Cassin," *Comm. Studies* (Toronto: PIMS 1974); Mandonnet, *Opuscula*, v. 3, 249–51 (one sentence and one considerable passage is lacking at the end); Marietti 1954, *Opuscula Theol.*, I, 249–50 (repr. of Mandonnet).

No English translation.

71. **Expositio super primam et secundam Decretalem ad Archidiaconum Tudertinum** (Todi). (Most likely addressed to Giffredus d'Anagni, socius to the provost of Saint-Omer, Adenulf d'Anagni, and archdeacon of Todi in the 1260s.) Extant MSS: 28.

The *decretales* in question are the first, *Firmiter*, and the second, *Damnamus*, formulated at the fourth Council of the Lateran in 1215, and incorporated in the *decretales* of Gregory IX as part of medieval Canon Law. The first chapter, *Firmiter*, is a profession of faith in God, who is one and triune; the second is a condemnation of Joachim of Fiore's rejection of Peter Lombard's doctrine on the Trinity. Thomas's work is a commentary on both chapters from a theological point of view. This work should be studied in connection with *De articulis fidei* (n. 69).

EDITIONS: Leon. ed. v. 40 E (Rome 1968); Marietti 1954, *Opuscula Theol.*, I, 417–26.

No English translation.

72. ***De rationibus fidei contra Saracenos, Graecos et Armenos ad Cantorem Antiochiae*** (Orvieto 1264). Extant MSS: 71 complete, 6 almost complete, and 4 fragments. See above, pp. 175–76.

This reply to an unknown cantor of Antioch addresses itself to five objections posed by Mohammedans, Greeks, and Armenians. Thomas cautions the cantor not to attempt to prove the truths of faith by pure reason, and he refers three times "elsewhere" to a work "which treats the same subject more fully." These references are undoubtedly to the *Summa contra gentiles,* IV, which was completed at Orvieto in 1264 (n. 2). Walz gives the dating 1261–64, and suggests that the cantor of Antioch wrote to Thomas at the suggestion of his bishop, a Dominican named Christian Elias (?).

EDITIONS: Leon. ed. v. 40 B (Rome 1969); Parma v. 16, 86–96; Vivès v. 27, 128–43; Marietti 1954, *Opuscula Theol.*, I, 417–26.

No English translation.

73. ***De motu cordis ad Magistrum Philippum de Castrocaeli*** (Paris 1270–71). Extant MSS: 119.

According to the catalogue of Bartholomew of Capua, this letter and another on the mixture of elements (n. 74) were both addressed to a certain "master Philip of Castrocaeli," who is otherwise unknown. Mandonnet suggested that master Philip may have been a physician, professor first at Bologna and later at Naples; but no evidence is given. The purpose of this letter is to show that the motion of the blood and heart is produced by "nature" and not by "soul" or any outside force. Both Mandonnet and Walz give the date as Naples 1273; Eschmann suggests Paris 1270–71. This is one of the treatises preserved by Godfrey of

Fontaines (Paris MS Bibl. Nat. lat. 14546) as a topic of special
current interest.

EDITIONS: Perrier, *Opuscula*, I, 63–69 (basic text: Paris Bibl.
Nat. lat. 14546); Parma v. 16, 358–60; Vivès v. 27, 507–11; Marietti 1954, *Opuscula Phil.*, 165–68.

No English translation.

74. ***De mixtione elementorum ad Magistrum Philippum de Castrocaeli*** (probably Paris 1270–71). Extant MSS: 110.

In the catalogue of Bartholomew of Capua, this letter and the
one called *De motu cordis* (n. 73) were both addressed to
"master Philip of Castrocaeli." The purpose of this letter is to
show that elements remain in compounds virtually, not formally,
and that the new form of the compound operates through powers
that remain. This brief extract was added to the anonymous
"continuation" of Thomas's commentary on *De generatione et
corruptione* as part of n. 7 in I, lect. 24 (cf. Leonine ed., III,
Appendix I, pp. xix–xx: "Circa secundum autem diversi . . .")
with many variants from the "vulgate" text.

EDITIONS: Perrier, *Opuscula*, I, 19–22 (Paris Bibl. Nat. lat.
14546); Parma v. 16, 353–54; Vivès v. 27, 502–3; Marietti 1954,
Opuscula Phil., 155–56.

No English translation.

75. ***Responsio ad lectorem Venetum de articulis XXX*** (Paris, before
April 1, 1271). Extant MSS: 5. Text A (cf. n. 76).

The recipient of this letter was Friar Bassiano of Lodi, lector
at the Dominican Priory of SS. Giovanni e Paolo in Venice. This
is the first in a series of letters on special questions, most of them
insignificant, that eventually involved the master general, John
of Vercelli, and the replies of three masters in theology (see n.
65). According to the study of J. Destrez, Friar Bassiano sent a
list of thirty questions in March 1271, to which Thomas replied
(text A); this letter is found in only 5 MSS, of which Destrez
knew 4. Shortly after, some of the students at Venice sent
Thomas an additional series of six questions ("articuli iterum
remissi"). Later the lector sent another list of thirty-six articles,

which included three items from the students' list. Thomas replied to this longer list, which Destrez calls text *B* (n. 76), before April, when the list of forty-three questions was sent by John of Vercelli (n. 65).

○   EDITIONS: text established by Destrez from 4 MSS in *Mélanges Mandonnet* (Paris: Vrin 1930), 174a–86a; Marietti 1954, *Opuscula Theol.*, I, 193–97.

No English translation.

76. Responsio ad lectorem Venetum de articulis XXXVI (Paris, before April 1, 1271). Extant MSS: 34. Text B (cf. n. 75).

This is the longer and more polished reply to Friar Bassiano's list of thirty-six questions, most of which are identical with the earlier list and also found in the reply to John of Vercelli (n. 65). None of the queries or replies has anything to do with Latin Averroism, of great concern to the Parisian scholars at that time, or with neo-Augustinism, supported by many Parisian Franciscans, Dominicans, and seculars.

○   EDITIONS: Vivès v. 27, 256–63; Marietti 1954, *Opuscula Theol.*, I, 199–208 (from the text established by Destrez, loc. cit., 174b–89b). The "articuli iterum remissi a quibusdam scolaribus," extracted from text *B*, are in Vivès v. 32, 832–33 (after Uccelli).

No English translation.

77. Responsio ad lectorem Bisuntinum [Besançon] de articulis VI. Extant MSS: 53.

Friar Gerald of Besançon, lector of the Dominican Priory there, sent Thomas six questions asking whether certain peculiar ideas could be preached from the pulpit, viz., whether the star that appeared to the Magi was in the form of a cross, whether the cross had a human figure on it, whether it had the figure of a crucifix, whether the small hands of the infant Jesus created the stars, whether the Virgin Mary thought of Simeon's prophecy, that a sword would pierce her heart, seven times a day until the resurrection of Christ, and whether circumstances affecting the category of a light sin must be confessed in the sacrament of

Penance. In general, Thomas advised that such things should not be preached from the pulpit.

EDITIONS: Parma v. 16, 175–76; Vivès v. 27, 264–65; Marietti 1954, *Opuscula Theol.*, I, 243–44.

No English translation.

78. ***De emptione et venditione ad tempus.*** Addressed to Friar James of Viterbo, lector of Florence (Orvieto c. 1262). Extant MSS: 17.

This work is not listed in any of the catalogues before 1400, but its authenticity is accepted by all modern scholars. This brief letter concerning buying and selling on credit must be seen in the light of Thomas's doctrine on usury and the rapidly developing commercial life of thirteenth-century Florence. James of Viterbo, lector in the Dominican Priory of Santa Maria Novella, was appointed procurator general of the Dominican Order in 1265 and later archbishop of Taranto, 1270–73. Friar James mentions that he is seeking the opinion of the "Archbishop Elect of Capua," as well as that of Thomas, in this difficult case of conscience. Marino of Eboli, one of Thomas's former students, was archbishop-elect of Capua from January 13, 1252, until May 28, 1266, when he was re-elected. Thomas states at the beginning of his reply that he had consulted Cardinal Hugh of Saint-Cher on the matter; Hugh died at Orvieto, where Thomas was living, on March 19, 1263. Hugh seems to have come to Orvieto when the papal curia arrived in October 1262; therefore, Thomas's reply must have been written between October 1262 and March 1263.

EDITIONS: critically established text by A. O'Rahilly in *Irish Ecclesiastical Record* 31 (1928), 162–64; Marietti 1954, *Opuscula Theol.*, I, 185–86 (O'Rahilly text).

English trans.: O'Rahilly, "On Buying and Selling on Credit," loc. cit., 164–65.

79. ***Epistola exhortatoria de modo studendi ad fratrem Joannem.***
Probably authentic. Extant MSS: at least 9.

This work is not listed in any of the earliest catalogues; the earliest mention of it is in a letter of Bl. Venturino of Bergamo (d. 1346) to Friar Eginolf of Ehenheim. This brief letter of

thirty-five to forty lines lists sixteen rules to be followed for fruitful study. Although its authenticity has been tentatively accepted by all scholars since Quétif-Echard (*Scriptores Ord.
Praed.*, Paris 1719, I, 622), historical grounds are weak, as Grabmann pointed out. Mandonnet called it a "slightly doubtful
work."

EDITIONS: Parma v. 17, 338; Vivès v. 28, 467; Marietti 1954,
Opuscula Theol., I, 451.

English trans.: "The Letter of Thomas Aquinas to Brother
John *De modo studendi*," by V. White, *Life of the Spirit* (Oxford: Blackfriars, Dec. 1944), Suppl. 161–80.

○ 80. *De regimine Judaeorum ad Ducissam Brabantiae* (Paris 1270–
71). Extant MSS: 83.

This short reply to eight questions concerning the treatment of
Jews in the Duchy of Brabant is addressed to Marguerite of
France, daughter of Louis IX. She married John I of Brabant
in February 1270, and died in 1271. Therefore Thomas's reply
must be dated 1270–71. Seven out of the eight queries deal with
financial relationships with Jews, while the eighth deals with the
legality (Council of Lateran, 1215) of a distinctive garb to be
worn by Jews in Christendom.

EDITIONS: Perrier, *Opuscula*, I, 213–19 (basic text: Paris Bibl.
Nat. lat. 14546, i.e., notebooks of Geoffrey of Fontaines); Parma
v. 16, 292–94; Vivès v. 27, 413–16; Marietti 1954, *Opuscula Phil.*,
249–52.

No English translation.

○ 81. *De sortibus ad Dominum Jacobum de Burgo* (?) (Paris, "summer vacation," c. 1271). Extant MSS: 51.

Apparently the recipient of this letter, "Lord James," had
asked for clarification of the whole question of lots and deciding
by lot. Thomas divides his reply into five parts: the kind of thing
about which lots are cast, the purpose of casting lots, the various
ways of doing so, the source of their efficacy, and the morality of
having recourse to lots. Although both the recipient and the date
of this letter are unknown, Eschmann points out the parallelism

between this letter and *Summa* II–II 95, 3–8 (written in 1271), and *Quodlibet* 12, 35 (disputed in Advent 1270).

EDITIONS: Parma v. 16, 310–16; Vivès v. 27, 439–48; Marietti 1954, *Opuscula Theol.*, I, 159–67.

No English translation.

82. *De occultis operationibus naturae, ad quendam militem ultra-montanum.* Extant MSS: 82.

According to the catalogue of Bartholomew of Capua, the recipient of this letter is the same as the one for the following letter (n. 83), but we do not even know his name. Mandonnet suggested that this letter was written in Paris, 1269–72, in which case the ultramontane knight would have been an Italian. The problem concerns certain activities, in natural bodies, that seem to have no natural origin, such as magnets attracting iron. For Thomas all such actions are natural, either by an intrinsic principle, which is the substantial form, or by powers instilled by the heavenly bodies; in either case the activity is natural. Mandonnet arbitrarily assigned the date as 1269–72, when Thomas was in Paris for the second time.

EDITIONS: Perrier, *Opuscula*, I, 203–10 (based on Paris MS Bibl. Nat. lat. 14546); Parma v. 16, 355–57; Vivès v. 27, 504–7; Marietti 1954, *Opuscula Phil.*, 159–62.

English trans.: *The Letter of St. Thomas Aquinas De occultis operibus naturae ad quendam militem ultramontanum*, trans. J. B. McAllister (Washington, D.C.: Cath. Univ. 1939).

83. *De iudiciis astrorum, ad quendam militem ultramontanum.* Extant MSS: 85.

Both Tolomeo of Lucca and Bernard Gui claim that this work was addressed to Reginald of Piperno, but this claim is most improbable, as Eschmann pointed out. Bartholomew of Capua explicitly states that this letter and the previous one (n. 82) were addressed to the same ultramontane knight. Thomas's brief reply discusses the morality of consulting astrologers in one's affairs. He distinguished between those things that depend on the stars directly, such as the weather, bodily dispositions, agriculture, and the like, and activities that depend upon free will, which in no way depends on the stars. Therefore it would be a "grave sin" to consult the stars in these matters for the devil can make use of such superstition for his own purposes.

    EDITIONS: Parma v. 16, 317; Vivès v. 27, 449; Marietti 1954, *Opuscula Theol.*, I, 155.

No English translation.

LITURGICAL PIECES AND SERMONS

84. *Officium de festo Corporis Christi, ad mandatum Urbani Papae IV* (Orvieto, July–August 1264). See above, pp. 176–84.

We have argued that the original Roman liturgy for the feast of Corpus Christi, promulgated by Urban IV on August 11, 1264, by the bull *Transiturus,* was the work of Thomas d'Aquino in the sense that he revised earlier liturgies and wrote new hymns and prayers for the occasion. Although Tolomeo of Lucca is the earliest witness to this fact, grounds for denying his veracity are not sufficient. The original text of the Mass ("Cibavit eos") and the office ("Sacerdos in aeternum") have not yet been reconstructed. The text found in the modern Breviary and in the "vulgate" editions is the fifteenth-century version first published by Antonio Pizzamano in his edition of the *opuscula* in 1497. The procrastination of the Dominican Order to admit the feast into its *Ordinarium* in 1265 has been alleged as proof against Thomas's authorship.

    EDITIONS: Parma v. 15, 233–38; Vivès v. 29, 335–43; Marietti 1954, *Opuscula Theol.*, II, 275–81.

85. *Orationes: Adoro te, Gratias tibi ago, Omnipotens sempiterne Deus,* etc.

The Vivès edition lists twelve prayers traditionally attributed to Thomas, some of which are still published in the Roman Missal and Breviary. Dom A. Wilmart has studied the MS tradition of the "Adoro te devote" and makes a good case in favor of Thomas's authorship. F. J. E. Raby has shown that the hymn

"Adoro te devote" must have been written before 1280–94, when Jacopone da Todi wrote one of his poems on the same subject (*Speculum* 20 [1945], 236–38), but this fact does not attest Thomas's authorship. Eschmann points out that there is no MS evidence of Thomas's authorship during the first fifty years, at least, after Thomas's death. Therefore, while tradition strongly accepts Thomas's authorship, historical documentation is still lacking.

EDITIONS: Parma v. 24, 241–44; Vivès v. 32, 819–23; Marietti 1954, *Opuscula Theol.*, II, 285–89; older form of "Adoro devote," ed. Wilmart, *Auteurs spirituels* (Paris 1932), 393; text of "Concede mihi" and an early English translation, "A Prayer Attributed to St. Thomas Aquinas," A. I. Doyle, *Dominican Studies* 1 (1948), 229–38.

86. *Collationes super Credo in Deum* (Lenten sermons; Naples 1273). Extant MSS: 141 complete; 28 others contain a revised form by Henry of Hassia.

These sermons on the Apostles' Creed were preached in the vernacular during Lent 1273 at San Domenico, Naples. The Latin version of these sermons was quickly turned into a scholastic commentary on the Creed, shortly after Thomas's death. It would seem that each of the twelve articles of faith was originally a single sermon. See *De articulis fidei*, n. 69.

EDITIONS: Parma v. 16, 135–51; Vivès v. 27, 203–29; Marietti 1954, *Opuscula Theol.*, II, 193–217.

English trans.: In *The Three Greatest Prayers*, by L. Shapcote (London: Burns, Oates and Washbourne 1937).

87. *Collationes super Pater Noster* (Lenten sermons; Naples 1273). Extant MSS: 85.

These sermons on the "Our Father" were made to look like scholastic treatises divided on the basis of an introduction, salutation to the Father, and seven petitions.

EDITIONS: Parma v. 16, 123–52; Vivès v. 27, 183–98; Marietti 1954, *Opuscula Theol.*, II, 221–35.

English trans.: In *The Three Greatest Prayers,* by L. Shapcote (London: Burns, Oates and Washbourne 1937).

88. *Collationes super Ave Maria* (probably Lenten sermons; Naples 1273). Extant MSS: 84.

It is not certain whether these sermons on the Angelic Salutation were preached in Naples or earlier in Rome. It has always been of interest to Dominican preachers and theologians, especially during the Renaissance, who were forbidden to maintain the Immaculate Conception of the Virgin Mary, because it was considered contrary to the commonly accepted teaching of Thomas. In one passage, however, Thomas seems to say that the Blessed Virgin "incurred neither original nor mortal nor venial sin": "[nec originale] nec mortale nec veniale peccatum incurrit" (not emended in Marietti, n. 1120). Eschmann and Rossi insist that this passage, with emendation, "resists the most thoroughgoing paleographical examination." However, another passage (Marietti, n. 1116) states that "the Blessed Virgin was conceived, but not born, in original sin." See G. F. Rossi, *Divus Thomas* (Piacenza) 57 (1954), 442–66.

EDITIONS: Rossi, *Divus Thomas* (Piacenza) 34 (1931), 465–76; Marietti 1954, *Opuscula Theol.,* II, 239–41.

English trans.: In *The Three Greatest Prayers,* by L. Shapcote (London: Burns, Oates and Washbourne 1937); J. B. Collins, *Catechetical Instructions of St. Thomas Aquinas* (New York 1953); L. Every, *Dominicana* 39 (1954), 31ff.

89. *Collationes de decem praeceptis.* Frequently entitled *De duobus praeceptis caritatis et decem legis praeceptis* in late MSS and catalogues (Lenten sermons; Naples 1273). Extant MSS: 79 complete, and 13 fragments.

Although Tolomeo of Lucca and Bernard Gui fail to mention this work, it is listed in the catalogues of Bartholomew of Capua, Nicholas Trevet, and the two Prague catalogues among the *reportata* "recollected" by Peter d'Andria; that is, the points in the vernacular sermon were jotted down and later written out in Latin "after Thomas had preached." Like the other sermons in this Lenten cycle (nn. 86–88), the *Collationes de decem praeceptis* was originally a *reportatio*, later organized to look like a scholastic treatise, which it is not.

EDITIONS: Parma v. 16, 97–114; Vivès v. 27, 144–70; Marietti 1954, *Opuscula Theol.*, II, 245–71.

English trans.: *The Commandments of God*, trans. L. Shapcote (London 1937).

90. **Sermons.** Research on Thomas's sermons has not progressed far enough to assert which sermons published under his name are authentic. These sermons cannot be determined from the catalogues, but only from the MSS, a work now undertaken by Bertrand Guyot, O.P., for the Leonine Commission.

The editors of the Piana edition (1570–71), v. 16, and those of subsequent editions, published a large number of sermons taken from Vatican MS Vat. lat. 3804, all of which are spurious. In the Paris edition of 1660, 210 spurious sermons were attributed to Thomas. Of the 49 sermons published in the Vivès edition (v. 32, 663–815), only 9 can be considered authentic. In Eschmann's "Catalogue" (nn. 80–89), 15 sermons and 3 *exordia* are listed as authentic. However, Eschmann lists as "sermons" 2 *principia* that are here listed as inaugural lectures (see above, n. 35) presented in connection with Thomas's inception in theology.

WORKS OF UNCERTAIN AUTHENTICITY

91–97. *De instantibus; De natura verbi intellectus; De principio individuationis; De natura generis; De natura accidentium; De natura materiae; De quatuor oppositis.*

The authenticity of these seven philosophical *opuscula* has been debated with considerable vigor for more than half a century, not counting the misgivings Capreolus and Cajetan expressed about some of them. They are considered a related group because they are omitted in one block of catalogues (Bartholomew of Capua, Nicholas Trevet, the two Prague catalogues) and mentioned in another tradition (Tolomeo of Lucca, Bernard Gui, and the *Tabula* of Stams). Mandonnet, who considered the catalogue of Bartholomew to be an "official list," rejected the authenticity of all of them, while Grabmann, Rossi, and many others, rejecting the priority of Bartholomew's catalogue, defend their authenticity. Eschmann rightly considered that their authenticity cannot be established or rejected until more is known about the origin of the two MS traditions represented by the two sets of catalogues.

EDITIONS: Parma v. 15; Vivès vv. 27–28; Marietti 1954, *Opuscula Phil.* Cf. index.

98. ***De demonstratione.*** This work also was rejected by Mandonnet on the basis of Bartholomew's catalogue, but accepted by Grabmann and Rossi on the basis of Vatican MS Vat. lat. 807.

EDITIONS: Parma v. 16, 375–76; Vivès v. 27, 531–32; Perrier, *Opuscula*, I, 465; Marietti 1954, *Opuscula Phil.*, 221–22.
No English translation.

99. ***De differentia verbi divini et humani.*** Extant MSS: 31.

This is no more than an extract of Thomas's *lectura* on John (n. 33), lect. 1, which circulated independently of the *lectura*.

100. ***De sensu respectu singularium.*** Extant MSS: 7.

This is an extract from Thomas's commentary on Aristotle's *De anima,* Bk. II, lect. 12, which circulated independently of the full commentary (n. 42).

101. ***De natura luminis.*** Extant MSS: 7.

This work also is an extract from Thomas's commentary on Aristotle's *De anima,* II, lect. 14, which circulated independently. This and the two previous items (nn. 100–1) are authentic in the sense that the text is an extract from an authentic work, but they are not authentic in the sense that Thomas wrote them as separate works.

With this catalogue we bring to an end this anniversary volume on the life, thought, and works of Friar Thomas d'Aquino. While there is much we have discovered about him and his writings through historical and doctrinal analysis, there is still much that escapes our present knowledge. Only further research into the manuscript tradition and solidly established texts can bring us to a fuller knowledge of his life and work. Apart from the two works on logic that Thomas composed at Roccasecca, Thomas spent twenty-one years in the apostolate of the pen—1252 to 1273. Although Thomas "always had four secretaries with him" to help in the composition and distribution of his works, he "always had recourse to prayer" when the work was difficult (Madrid, Bibl. Nac. MS 8979). Thomas lived a long life in a short time, and because God loved him, He took him on March 7, 1274, at the age of forty-nine.

PRIMARY SOURCES

References in notes are as brief as possible. To facilitate this, the basic sources must be kept in mind.

Fontes Vitae Sancti Thomae Aquinatis, Toulouse, originally published as supplements to *Revue Thomiste,* 1911–34:
1) Peter Calo, *Vita S. Thomae Aquinatis,* 17–55.
2) William of Tocco, *Hystoria beati Thomae,* 65–145.
3) Bernard Gui, *Legenda S. Thomae,* 168–222; *De miraculis,* 222–56.
   These three lives, edited by Dominicus Prümmer, O.P.
4) *Processus canonizationis Neapoli,* 267–407, ed. M.-H. Laurent, O.P.
5) *Processus canonizationis Fossae Novae,* 411–510, ed. M.-H. Laurent, O.P.
6) *De canonizatione,* 511–32, ed. M.-H. Laurent, O.P.
7) *Documenta* (Fasc. VI of *Fontes*), ed. M.-H. Laurent, O.P. (Saint-Maximin: *Revue Thomiste* 1937), 531–677.

Tolomeo of Lucca, *Historia Ecclesiastica,* lib. 22, c. 17–lib. 23, c. 16, in L. A. Muratori, *Rerum Italicarum Scriptores,* XI. Milan 1724.

Gerard de Frachet, *Vitae Fratrum,* ed. B. M. Reichert, O.P., in *Monumenta Ordinis Praedicatorum Historica* (=MOPH) I. Rome 1897.

Thomas of Cantimpré, *Bonum universale de apibus.* Douai 1605.

S. *Thomae Aquinatis Vitae Fontes Praecipuae,* ed. A. Ferrua, O.P. Alba: Ed. Domenicane 1968. Contains only Tocco's *Hystoria,* Gui's *Legenda,* Naples *Processus,* and selections from Tolomeo of Lucca, Gérard de Frachet, and Thomas of Cantimpré.

Acta Capitulorum Generalium Ord. Praed. (1220–1303), ed. B. M. Reichert, O.P., MOPH III. Rome 1898; *Acta* (1304–78), MOPH IV. Rome 1899.

Acta Capitulorum Provincialium Provinciae Romanae (1243–1344), ed. T. Kaeppeli, O.P., MOPH XX. Rome 1947.

Chartularium Universitatis Parisiensis, ed. H. Denifle, O.P., and E. Chatelain. I, Paris 1889; II, Paris 1891. (=*Chart. U. P.*)

Monumenta Conventus Sanjacobei Lutetiae Parisiorum, in *Analecta S.O.P.,* I (1893) and IV (1896). (=*Monumenta conv. SJ*)

SELECT SECONDARY STUDIES

Bourke, Vernon J., *Aquinas' Search for Wisdom.* Milwaukee: Bruce 1965. (=Bourke)

Callus, Daniel A., *The Condemnation of St. Thomas at Oxford.* Oxford: Aquinas Papers, n. 5, 1946.

Castagnoli, Pietro, "Regesta Thomistica. Saggio di cronologia delle vita e scritti di S. Tommaso." *Divus Thomas* (Piac.) 30 (1927), 704–24; 31 (1928), 110–25, 249–68; 32 (1929), 57–66, 444–58. (="Regesta")

Chenu, M.-D., *Introduction à l'étude de s. Thomas d'Aquin* (Univ. of Montréal, publ. de l'Institut d'études médiévales, 11), Montréal and Paris 1950. Engl. tr. *Toward Understanding St. Thomas,* A.-M. Landry and D. Hughes. Chicago: Regnery 1964.

Chesterton, Gilbert Keith, *St. Thomas Aquinas.* London: Hodder & Stoughton 1933.

Coffey, Reginald M., *The Man from Rocca Sicca.* Milwaukee: Bruce 1944.

D'Arcy, Martin C., *Thomas Aquinas.* Boston: Little, Brown 1930.

De Groot, J. V., *Het Leven van den H. Thomas van Aquino.* Utrecht: Van Rossum 1907.

Destrez, I., *Études critiques sur les oeuvres de saint Thomas d'Aquin, d'après la tradition manuscrite.* Paris: Vrin 1933.

Dondaine, Antoine, *Les secrétaires de s. Thomas.* Rome: Comm. Leonine, 2 v., 1956. (=*Secrétaires*)

Douie, Decima L., *The Conflict Between the Seculars and the Mendicants at the University of Paris in the Thirteenth Century.* Oxford: Aquinas Papers, n. 23, 1954.

Eschmann, Ignatius T., "A Catalogue of St. Thomas's Works: Bibliographical Notes," in E. Gilson, *The Christian Philosophy of St. Thomas Aquinas.* New York: Random House, 1956. (="Catalogue")

Foster, Kenelm, *The Life of Saint Thomas Aquinas. Biographical Documents*. Trans. and ed. with introd. London: Longmans, Green 1959. (=Foster)

Glorieux, Palémon, *Répertoire des Maîtres en Théologie de Paris au XIIIᵉ siècle*. 2 v. Paris: Vrin 1933. (=Répertoire)

——, "Essai sur les commentaires scripturaires de saint Thomas et leur chronologie," *Rech. d'Théol. an. et méd.* 17 (1950), 237–66.

Grabmann, Martin, *Die Werke des hl. Thomas von Aquin*, 3rd ed. Münster: Aschendorff 1949. (=Die Werke)

——, *Guglielmo di Moerbeke, O.P., il traduttore delle opere di Aristotele*. Rome: Gregorianum 1946. (=Guglielmo)

——, *Einführung in die Summa theologiae des hl. Thomas von Aquin*. Freiburg i. Br.: Herder 1928. Engl. tr. *Introduction to the Theological Summa of St. Thomas*, John S. Zybura. St. Louis: Herder 1930.

——, *Thomas von Aquin: Personlichkeit und Gedankenwelt*, 2nd ed. Munich: Kösel 1946. Engl. tr. from 1st ed. (Munich 1926) *Thomas Aquinas, His Personality and Thought*. London: Longmans, Green 1928.

——, *The Interior Life of St. Thomas Aquinas*. Tr. N. Ashenbrener. Milwaukee: Bruce 1951.

Mandonnet, Pierre, *Des Écrits authentiques de s. Thomas d'Aquin*, 2nd ed. rev. and corr. Fribourg: S. Paul 1910. (=Écrits)

——, *Siger de Brabant et l'Averroïsme latin au XIIIᵉ siècle*, 2nd ed. IIe Partie: Textes inédits, Louvain 1908. Ie Partie: Étude critique, Louvain 1911. (=Siger)

——, "Date et naissance de saint Thomas d'Aquin," *Revue Thomiste* 22 (1914), 652–64.

——, "Chronologie des questions disputées de saint Thomas d'Aquin," *Revue Thomiste*, n.s., 1 (1918), 266–87, 340–71.

——, "Chronologie sommaire de la vie et des écrits de saint Thomas," *Revue des sc. phil. et théol.* 9 (1920), 142–52. (="Chronologie sommaire")

——, "La canonisation de saint Thomas d'Aquin," *Mélanges Thomiste*, I. Paris: Vrin 1923, 1–48.

——, "Thomas d'Aquin lecteur à la curie Romaine: Chronologie de séjour (1259–1268)," *Xenia Thomistica*. Rome 1925, III, 9–40. (="Lecteur")

——, "Thomas d'Aquin, novice prêcheur (1244–1246)," *Revue Thomiste* 7 (1924), 243–67, 370–90, 529–47; 8 (1925), 3–34, 222–49, 396–416, 489–533. (="Novice Prêcheur")

——, "Chronologie des écrits scripturaires de saint Thomas d'Aquin," *Revue Thomiste* 11 (1928), 27–46, 116–55, 211–45; 12 (1929), 53–69, 132–45, 489–519. (="Écrits scripturaires")

Maritain, Jacques, *Le Docteur Angélique.* Paris: Desclée 1930. Engl. tr. *St. Thomas, Angel of the Schools,* J. F. Scalon. London: Sheed & Ward 1946.

Maritain, Raïssa, *St. Thomas Aquinas, The Angel of the Schools,* tr. J. Kernan. New York: Sheed & Ward 1935.

Mélanges Thomiste, 2 v. Kain (Belgium): Le Saulchoir 1923.

Petitot, Hyacinthe, *The Life and Spirit of Thomas Aquinas,* tr. Cyprian Burke. Chicago: Priory Press 1966.

Pieper, Josef, *Guide to Thomas Aquinas,* tr. R. and C. Winston. New York: Pantheon 1962.

St. Thomas Aquinas 1274–1974: Commemorative Studies. 2 v., ed. A. A. Maurer. Toronto: Pont. Inst. of Mediaeval Studies 1974. (=*Comm. Studies*)

Sertillanges, Antonin, *St. Thomas Aquinas and His Work,* tr. Godfrey Anstruther. London: Burns, Oates and Washbourne 1932.

Vann, Gerald, *St. Thomas Aquinas.* New York: Benziger 1947.

Vansteenkiste, C. M. J., "Tommaso d'Aquino," *Bibliotheca Sanctorum,* XII (Rome 1969), 544–63.

Wallace, W. A.; J. A. Weisheipl, "Thomas Aquinas, saint," *The New Catholic Encyclopedia* (1966), 14, 102–15.

Walz, Angelus, *San Tommaso d'Aquino,* Rome 1945. Engl. tr. *Saint Thomas Aquinas: A Biographical Study,* Sebastian Bullough. Westminster, Md.: Newman 1951. (=*Walz*)

——, *Saint Thomas d'Aquin.* Adopt. Française par Paul Novarina. Louvain: Publ. Univ. 1962. (=*Walz-Novarina*)

——, "Chronotaxis vitae et operum s. Thomae de Aquino," *Angelicum* 16 (1939), 463–73.

——, *Luoghi di San Tommaso.* Rome: Herder 1961.

Xenia Thomistica. 3 v., ed. Sadoc Szabó. Rome: Vatican Press 1925.

Chapter I

1. Gui, *Legenda*, c. 39: "inchoante tunc dominicae incarnationis anno MCCLXXIIII, vitae autem suae anno XLIX terminante et anno quinquagesimo inchoante." *Fontes* 205.

2. *Hist. Eccl.*, lib. 23, c. 10, Muratori, *Rerum Ital. Script.* XI, col. 1170: "obiit autem quinquagesimo vitae suae anno, alii dicunt XLIV, habens in Magisterio annos XX." Although Muratori gives the reading as "forty-four" instead of "forty-eight," the correct reading is the latter, according to the correction provided by B. de Rubeis in his *Dissertationes criticae* I, c. 8, and by P. Mandonnet, "Date de naissance de S. Thomas d'Aquin," *Revue Thomiste* 22 (1914), 652, fn. 1.

3. *Proc. canoniz. Neapoli*, c. 19: "videbatur sibi quod fuerit quinquagenarius vel sexagenarius." *Fontes* 291.

4. *Proc. canoniz. Neapoli*, c. 15: "erat, ut sibi videbatur, annorum quinquaginta vel circa." *Fontes* 287.

5. *Proc. canoniz. Neapoli*, c. 83: "in quatrogesimo octavo anno finisse dicitur communiter dies suos." *Fontes* 384.

6. "Anno 1220 die 16 Aprilis nascitur divus Thomas in castro Roccasicca, patre Landulfo Comite Aquinate, matre Theodora Theatis Comitis filia." B. De Rubeis, *Diss. crit.*, I, c. 1, ed. Leonina, *Opera S. Thomae*, I, lv.

7. *Hystoria*, c. 65: "quadragesimum nonum annum suae vitae perficiens, quinquagesimum inchoaret aeternae gloriae jubileum," *Fontes* 138.

8. "Vitae autem suae anno XLIX terminante et anno quinquagesimo inchoante." Gui, *Legenda*, c. 39. *Fontes* 205.

9. P. Mandonnet, op. cit., 652, fn. 1.

10. See Walz, 2.

11. T. Leccisotti, "Il Dottore Angelico a Montecassino," *Revista Filos. neo-Schol.* 32 (1940), 533, fn. 2; see document in *Fontes,* Doc. IX, 541.

12. *Hystoria,* c. 1. *Fontes* 66.

13. See Ernst Kantorowicz, *Kaiser Friedrich der Zweite,* Berlin: Biondi 1931, v. 2, index.

14. Cf. F. Pelster, "La familia di S. Tommaso," *Civiltà Cattolica* 74 (1923), 404.

15. Doc. II–III. *Fontes* 532–35.

16. See Foster, 162.

17. Doc. V. *Fontes* 536–37.

18. Doc. X. *Fontes* 541.

19. F. Scandone, "La Vita, la Famiglia e la Patria di S. Tommaso," in *San Tommaso d'Aquino, O.P., Miscellanea Storico-Artistica* (Rome 1924), 1–110.

20. Dante, *De vulgari eloquentia,* I, c. 12.

21. Tolomeo, *Hist. Eccl.,* lib. 22, c. 20, col. 1151.

22. Mandonnet, "Novice Prêcheur," 523.

23. Tocco, *Hystoria,* c. 44. *Fontes* 118.

24. Tolomeo, *Hist. Eccl.,* lib. 22, c. 21, ed. cit., col. 1152.

25. Ibid., c. 42

26. Tocco, *Hystoria,* c. 63. *Fontes* 137.

27. Doc. X. *Fontes* 541.

28. *Proc. canoniz. Neapoli,* c. 62. *Fontes* 350–51.

29. Tocco, *Hystoria,* c. 37. *Fontes* 111.

30. See *Canoniz. S. Thomae, Fontes* 518.

31. Tocco, *Hystoria,* c. 2. *Fontes* 67.

32. Scandone, op. cit., 67–69; cf. Foster 161; Bourke 3.

33. Tocco, *Hystoria,* c. 3; Gui, *Legenda,* c. 2; Calo, *Vita,* c. 2; *Proc. canoniz. Neapoli,* n. 90.

34. Tocco, *Hystoria,* c. 2. *Fontes* 67.

35. Gui, *Legenda,* c. 3. *Fontes* 169.

36. *Proc. canoniz. Neapoli,* n. 76. *Fontes* 371.

37. B. De Rubeis, *Diss. crit.,* I, c. 1, ed. cit., 55b.

38. Tolomeo, *Hist. Eccl.,* lib. 22, c. 20: "ibidem in sua pueritia in logicalibus et naturalibus optime profecit."

39. Doc. IV. *Fontes* 535–36.; Mandonnet, "Date de naissance," *Revue Thomiste* 22 (1914), 663.

40. Tocco, *Hystoria,* c. 5. *Fontes* 70, fn. 1; B. De Rubeis, *Diss. crit.,* I, c. 4; Bourke 20–21.

41. Here we have further confirmation of the year of Thomas's birth. We can now limit it to the months between July 23, 1224, and March 7, 1225. From this it would seem that Thomas was born in the last few months of 1224 or the first two months of 1225, as argued above.
42. Tocco, *Hystoria*, c. 4. *Fontes* 70.
43. Tocco, *Hystoria*, c. 5. *Fontes* 70.
44. Doc. VII. *Fontes* 539.
45. Op. cit., 133.
46. See C. H. Haskins, *Studies in the History of Mediaeval Science* (Cambridge: Harvard 1924), 250.
47. Walz, 20.
48. Ibid., 20, fn. 7.
49. Rashdall, *Universities of Europe in the Middle Ages*, ed. F. M. Powicke and A. B. Emden (Oxford 1936), II, 24, fn. 1; see Origlia, *Istoria dello Studio di Napoli* (Naples 1753), I, 102.
50. Cf. E. Kantorowicz, op. cit., 267–68.
51. *Chart. U. P.* I, 78–80, n. 20.
52. See Haskins, op. cit., 242–71.
53. See J. A. Weisheipl, "The Curriculum of the Faculty of Arts at Oxford in the early Fourteenth Century," *Mediaeval Studies* 26 (1964), 143–85.
54. Calo, *Vita*, c. 4. *Fontes* 20.
55. Gui, *Legenda*, c. 3. *Fontes* 169–70; Foster 26.
56. Tocco, *Hystoria*, c. 5. *Fontes* 70. Calo, *Vita*, c. 4. *Fontes* 20.
57. Gui, *Legenda*, c. 4. *Fontes* 170.
58. Denifle, *Die Entstehung der Universitäten des Mittelalters* (Berlin 1885).
59. Baeumker, *Petrus von Hibernia, der Jugendlehrer des Thomas von Aquin und seine Disputation vor König Manfred*, in Sitz. d. Bay. Akad. d. Wissenschaften, Munich 1920.
60. M. Grabmann, "Magister Petrus von Hibernia, der Jugendlehrer des hl. Thomas von Aquin; seine Disputation vor König Manfred und seine Aristoteleskommentare," *Mittelalterliches Geistesleben* (Munich 1926), I, 249–65; A. Pelzer, "Un cours inédit d'Albert le Grand sur la Moral à Nicomaque, recueilli et rédigé par saint Thomas d'Aquin," *Revue néo-scolastique* 23 (1922), 356.
61. See C. H. Haskins, "Science at the Court of the Emperor Frederick II," *American Historical Review* 27 (1922), 669–94, revised in *Studies in the History of Mediaeval Science*, ed. cit., 242–71; M. Grabmann, "Kaiser Friedrich II und sein Verhältnis zur aris-

totelischen und arabischen Philosophie," *Mittelalterliches Geistesleben*, II, 103–37.

62. M. B. Crowe, "Peter of Ireland, Teacher of St. Thomas Aquinas," *Studies* (1956), 443–56; "Peter of Ireland's Approach to Metaphysics," *Miscellanea Mediaevalia* (Berlin 1963), II, 154–60.
63. Bourke, 21–22.
64. Cf. Bourke, 31–32.
65. *Catalogus Generalis Ordinis Praedicatorum* (Vatican 1967), 39.
66. Jordan of Saxony, *Libellus de principiis*, n. 6. MOPH 16, 28.
67. Ibid., n. 7.
68. *Acta Canonizationis*, n. 35. MOPH 16, 153.
69. Ibid., n. 35; Jordan, *Libellus*, n. 10, 31.
70. Anon., *Vita Beati Dominici* (before 1260), ed. *Analecta Ord. Praed.*, 4 (1899), 299b.
71. W. Hinnebusch, *History of the Dominican Order*, I (Staten Island, N.Y.: Alba House 1965), 20.
72. Ibid., 20.
73. Ibid., 19.
74. Ibid., 20–38.
75. Jordan, *Libellus*, nn. 39–43. MOPH 16, 45–46.
76. M.-H. Laurent, *Monumenta Historica S. P. Dominici*. MOPH 15, n. 60.
77. Humbert of Romans, *Legenda*, n. 40. MOPH 15, 400.
78. C. Eubel, *Hierarchia Catholica Medii Aevi*, 2nd ed. (Munich 1913), I, 207.
79. Jordan, *Libellus*, ed. cit., n. 40.
80. Ibid., n. 51, 49–50.
81. Nicholas Trevet, *Annales sex regum Angliae*, 1135–1307, ed. T. Hog (London: English Hist. Soc. 1845), 209.
82. Humbert of Romans, *De vita regulari*, Prol., n. 12, in *Opera*, ed. J. J. Berthier (Rome 1889), I, 41.
83. Cf. Hinnebusch, op. cit., 279–338.
84. Ibid., 279.
85. *Constitutiones Antiquae*, Dist. II, cap. 23, ed. H. Denifle in *Archiv. f. Lit.-u. Kirchengeschichte*, I (Berlin 1885), 221. Cf. revised constitutions of Raymond of Peñafort, Dist. II, cap. 1, ed. R. Creytens, "Les Constitutiones des Frères Prêcheurs dans la Rédaction de s. Raymond de Peñafort (1241)," in *Archivum FFr. Praed.* 18 (1948), 48.
86. *Sum. theol.* II–II, q. 188, a. 6.
87. Gui, *Legenda*, c. 5. *Fontes* 170.

88. Ibid.; Tolomeo, *Hist. Eccl.*, lib. 22, c. 20. For a rejection of these claims see Foster, 59–60, fn. 11.
89. H. D. Scheeben, "Die Konstitution des Predigerordens unter Jordan von Sachsen," *Quellen u. Forschungen z. Gesch. d. Dominikanerordens in Deutschland*, 38 (1941), 57, n. 14, 2.
90. Tolomeo, *Hist. Eccl.*, lib. 22, c. 22; Tocco, *Hystoria*, c. 8. *Fontes* 173.
91. Cf. Mandonnet, "Thomas d'Aquin, novice prêcheur," *Revue Thomiste*, 29 (1924), 251–55.
92. Tolomeo, *Hist. Eccl.*, lib. 22, c. 20.
93. Mandonnet, "Novice Prêcheur," 256–57; 370–90.
94. Gui, *Legenda*, c. 5. *Fontes* 171. Foster, 60, fn. 12.
95. Tocco, *Hystoria*, c. 7. *Fontes* 72.
96. Gerard de Frachet, *Vitae Fratrum*, ed. Reichert. MOPH 1, 201.
97. Gui, *Legenda*, c. 5. *Fontes* 171.
98. Tolomeo, *Hist. Eccl.*, lib. 22, c. 20, trans. Foster, op. cit., 129.
99. Thomas of Cantimpré, *Bonum universale de apibus* (Douai 1605), 81.
100. Mandonnet, "Novice Prêcheur," 387–90. Doc. 9. *Fontes* 541.
101. Dante, *Inferno* 13; cf. Foster, 61, fn. 15.
102. Tocco, *Hystoria*, c. 10. *Fontes* 74–76.
103. *Proc. canoniz. Neapoli*, n. 58. *Fontes* 345. Cf. Foster, 63, fn. 20; 349.
104. *Historisches Jahrbuch* 29 (1908), 774–84.
105. Walz, 28.
106. Gui, *Legenda*, c. 7. *Fontes* 175.
107. Mandonnet, "Novice Prêcheur," 235–36.
108. Gui, *Legenda*, c. 6. *Fontes* 172.
109. Gui, *Legenda* c. 8. *Fontes* 175. This agrees with Tocco (c. 11) and Peter Calo (c. 8).
110. *Proc. canoniz. Neapoli*, n. 76. *Fontes* 372.
111. *Vitae Fratrum*, c. 17, n. 3, ed. cit., 201.
112. Gui, *Legenda*, c. 8. *Fontes* 175.
113. Tocco, *Hystoria*, c. 9. *Fontes* 74.
114. Walz, 38.
115. Grabmann, *Die Werke*, 348–52.
116. Mandonnet, "Novice Prêcheur," 406–9.
117. Bocheński, "Sancti Thomae Aquinatis De Modalibus Opusculum et Doctrina," *Angelicum* 17 (1940), 180–218.
118. Gui, *Legenda*, c. 9; cf. Tocco, *Hystoria*, c. 11, and Tolomeo, *Hist. Eccl.*, lib. 22, c. 21.

119. *Vitae Fratrum,* ed. cit., 201; *Proc. canoniz. Neapoli,* n. 76. *Fontes* 372.
120. Gui, *Legenda,* c. 9. *Fontes* 176.
121. Tolomeo, *Hist. Eccl.,* lib. 23, c. 21; Tocco, *Hystoria,* c. 12. *Fontes* 77.
122. Gauthier, *Sententia libri Ethicorum, Opera Omnia,* Leon. ed. 47 (Rome 1969), 236*; *Tabula libri Ethicorum, Opera Omnia,* Leon. ed. 48 (Rome 1971), Appendix xv–xvii.
123. *Regula monachorum,* c. 8 (PL 83, 877–78). Cf. Gratian, *Decretum,* dist. 37, in *Corpus Iuris Canonici,* Pars Prior: Decretum Gratiani, ed. A. Friedberg (Leipzig 1924), col. 135–40. G. G. Meersseman, "In libris gentilium non studeant. L'étude des classiques interdite aux clercs au moyen âge?" *Italia Medioevale e Umanistica,* I (1958), 1–13.
124. *Const. Antiq.,* dist. II, cap. 28, ed. cit., *Archiv,* I, 222.
125. Bourke, 39.
126. Cf. J. A Weisheipl, "Albertus Magnus and the Oxford Platonists," *Proc. of the Am. Cath. Phil. Assoc.,* 1958, 124.
127. Jordan, *Epistola,* 20.
128. Albert, *De natura locorum,* tr. III, c. 2, ed. Borgnet IX, 571.
129. Albert, *Physica* I, tr. I, c. 1.
130. Walz-Novarina, 66.
131. Albert, *Metaphysica* I, tr. 1, c. 1, ed. Borgnet VI, 2b. Cf. J. A. Weisheipl, "Albertus Magnus and the Oxford Platonists," loc. cit., 129.
132. Albert, *De animalibus* XXVI, ed. Stadler, II, 1598: "nec aliquis in eo potest deprehendere quod ego ipse sentiam in philosophia naturali."
133. Albert, *Metaphysica* XIII, tr. 2, c. 4: "In qua non dixi aliquid secundum opinionem meam propriam, sed omnia dicta sunt secundum positiones Peripateticorum; et qui hoc voluerit probare, diligenter legat libros eorum, et non me, sed illos laudet vel reprehendat."
134. "Et hoc dico propter quosdam inertes, qui solatium suae inertiae quaerentes, nihil quaerunt in scriptis nisi quod reprehendant." Ed. Borgnet, VIII, 803.
135. *In Epist. B. Dionysii Areopagitae, Ep.* 7, n. 2, B, ed. Borgnet, XIV, 910.
136. See G. G. Meersseman, *Geschichte der Albertismus,* 2 v. (Paris 1933; Rome 1935).
137. Tocco, *Hystoria,* c. 12. *Fontes* 77.
138. Tocco, *Hystoria,* c. 12. *Fontes* 78.

139. Tocco, *Hystoria*, c. 12. *Fontes* 79.
140. Scheeben, "Albert der Grosse und Thomas von Aquino in Köln," *Divus Thomas* (Fr.), 9 (1931), 32ff.
141. Tocco, *Hystoria*, c. 12. *Fontes* 79.
142. See Walz-Novarina, 70–71.
143. Bourke, 48.
144. Thomas of Cantimpré, *Bonum universale de apibus*, ed. cit., I, 20; Tolomeo, *Hist. Eccl.*, lib. 23, c. 21.
145. Bull of Canonization, n. 1. *Fontes* 520.
146. Tocco, *Hystoria*, c. 14. *Fontes* 80.
147. P. Glorieux, "Techniques et Méthodes en usage à la Faculté de Théologie de Paris, au XIIIᵉ siècle," AHDLMA 32 (1968), 114.
148. Tocco, *Hystoria*, c. 14. *Fontes* 81.

Chapter II

1. Gui, *Legenda*, c. 12. *Fontes* 179. See below, chapter 3, pp. 106–7.
2. *Acta canoniz. Bologna*, test. Fr. John of Navarre, n. 26. MOPH 16, 143–44.
3. Hinnebusch, *History of the Dominican Order*, ed. cit., I, 51.
4. *Monumenta conv. SJ*, I (1893), 66, esp. fn. 2.
5. *Const. Antiq.*, ed. Denifle, loc. cit., dist. II, c. 1, t. 2; cf. *Monumenta conv. SJ*, I, 66.
6. Hinnebusch, op. cit., 58.
7. M.-H. Vicaire, *Saint Dominic and His Times* (London: Darton, Longman & Todd 1964), 260 and 507, fn. 9.
8. *Chart. U. P.*, I, 101–2, n. 44.
9. Hinnebusch, op. cit., 73, fn. 112.
10. The view that master John of St. Albans was an Englishman is supported not only by the *Monumenta* of Saint-Jacques, loc. cit., 67b., but also by Eugene Bernard, *Les Dominicains dans l'Université de Paris* (Paris: De Soye 1883), 2, and by Du boulay, *Hist. Univ. Paris* (Paris 1666), III, 92. See alternative biography in Glorieux, *Répertoire*, I, 274, n. 114.
11. *Monumenta conv. SJ*, 67b.
12. Vicaire, op. cit., 260.
13. Jordan of Saxony, *Libellus de principiis*, n. 53. MOPH 16, 50.
14. The *Monumenta* erroneously gives the date as August 6, 1217; see 68a.
15. *Chart. U. P.*, I, 100, n. 43.
16. See Hinnebusch, op. cit., 63.
17. Jordan of Saxony, *Libellus*, n. 59, ed. cit., 53.
18. *Acta canoniz. S. Dominici*, n. 26. MOPH 16, 144.

19. Jordan, *Libellus*, n. 57, 52.
20. Ibid., n. 3, 26.
21. Ibid., n. 56, 51.
22. Ibid., nn. 56–57, 51–52.
23. Gerard de Frachet, *Vitae Fratrum*, ed. cit., 24.
24. Vicaire, op. cit., 268–70.
25. Ibid., 270–71.
26. For a description of Reginald's vestition, see the account given in Frachet, *Vitae Fratrum*, I, 5, p. 26.
27. *Monumenta conv. SJ*, 32. F. Ehrle places this at the end of November, "S. Domenico, le Origini del Primo Studio Generale del suo Ordine a Parigi e la Somma Theologica del Primo Maestro, Rolando da Cremona," *Miscellanea Dominicana* (Rome 1923), 86.
28. Jordan, *Libellus*, n. 66, 56.
29. Ibid., n. 74, 60.
30. Hinnebusch, op. cit., 63.
31. *Monumenta conv. SJ*, 136, 140, 422–23.
32. Hinnebusch, op. cit., 256.
33. Letter of Honorius III "Ex litteram tenore" of September 15, 1223, in *Monumenta conv. SJ*, 427b.
34. *Monumenta conv. SJ*, 133, fn. 1. See Vicaire, op. cit., 260–61.
35. *Chart. U. P.*, I, 137, n. 79.
36. Cf. Glorieux, *Répertoire*, I, 274, n. 114.
37. "Studia nostra, praesertim generalia, sunt publica." *Const. FFr. S.O.P.*, n. 641, ed. Gillet (Rome 1932), 234; *Const. FFr. S.O.P.*, nn. 217–18, ed. Theissling (Rome 1925), 62–63; also nn. 871–72, p. 162; *Constitutiones, Declarationes, et Ordinationes Capitulorum Generalium S.O.P.*, Vincentio Fontana, ed. Jandel (Rome 1862), n. *28, p. 206; nn. *24–*25, p. 450.
38. *Monumenta conv. SJ*, 69; for other recruits see ibid. This Geoffroy de Blévex is listed by Glorieux as the third Dominican master in the chair of France (1235–42) under the name of Godefroid of Bléneau; see *Répertoire*, I, 59–61, n. 5.
39. A. Walz, *Compendium Historiae Ordinis Praedicatorum* (Rome 1948), 30. The statement in *Brevis hist. conv. Parisiensis*, in Martène, *Veter. Script. et Monument.*, VI, 552, must be an exaggeration: "Under him [Jordan of Saxony] so many masters in theology, doctors in law, bachelors and masters in arts and an innumerable number of others entered the Order of Preachers at Paris!" See *Monumenta conv. SJ*, 427.
40. See *Monumenta conv. SJ*, 423–25.

41. Ibid., 511b.
42. Paris MS Mazarine lat. 795 contains Books I, II, and IV (incomplete), while MS Bergamo Bibl. Civica 6.129 contains Book III. The pioneering study of this *Summa* was undertaken by F. Ehrle (op. cit.) and continued by later scholars, notably by E. Filthaut.
43. Glorieux, *Répertoire*, I, 42, n. 1.
44. See *Acta Sanctorum*, Feb. III (Venice 1736), 151–59; *Bibliotheca Sanctorum*, III, 320.
45. Glorieux, *Répertoire*, I, 291, n. 126.
46. The *Monumenta* of Saint-Jacques gives 1225 as the year, which is correct, for the Parisian calendar year began on March 25.
47. See Glorieux, *Répertoire*, I, 43–51, n. 2.
48. Nicholas Trevet, *Annales sex regum angliae*, ed. T. Hog (London: English Hist. Soc. 1845).
49. *Chart. U. P.*, I, 65, n. 5.
50. Cf. *Chart. U. P.*, I, 85, n. 27.
51. *Chart. U. P.*, I, nn. 37, 76.
52. J. Moorman, *A History of the Franciscan Order from Its Origins to the Year 1517* (Oxford: Clarendon 1968), 132.
53. V. Doucet, *Alexandri de Hales Summa Theologica*, ed. Quaracchi, IV, cli-clii.
54. Here we follow the more accurate dates of J. Moorman, op. cit., 131–33, rather than that of P. Glorieux, *Répertoire*.
55. E. Gilson, *The Philosophy of Saint Bonaventure*, trans. I. Trethowan and F. J. Sheed (London 1938), 45.
56. See Glorieux, *Répertoire*.
57. See *Chart. U. P.*, II, 692, n. 1188, item 9.
58. Ibid., I, 79, n. 20.
59. *Contra quattuor labyrinthos Franciae*, ed. P. Glorieux, AHDLMA 19 (1952), 187–335.
60. Bacon, *Opus Minus* (1267), ed. J. S. Brewer, *Opera quaedam hactenus inedita* (London: R. S. 15), 329; also *Chart. U. P.*, I, 473, n. 419.
61. W. Principe, *The Theology of the Hypostatic Union in the Early Thirteenth Century*, II (Toronto: PIMS 1967), 14.
62. Incidentally there is a note in Bernard Gui's *De quattuor in quibus* to the effect that Thomas particularly wanted to see Fishacre's commentary: "Qui super Sententias profundissime scripsit, cuius scripta S. Thomas desiderabat habere." ed. T. Kaeppeli. MOPH 20, 36.
63. See H. Denifle, "Quel livre servait de base a l'enseignement des Maîtres en Théologie dans l'Université de Paris," *Revue Thomiste* 2 (1894), 149–61.

64. Peter Calo, *Vita*, c. 11. *Fontes* 30.
65. Gui, *Legenda*, c. 11. *Fontes* 11.
66. See J. A. Weisheipl, "The Evolution of Scientific Method," in *The Logic of Science*, ed. V. E. Smith (New York: St. John's Univ. 1964), 59–86, esp. 74–81.
67. *De doctrina christiana*, I, c. 2, n. 2 (PL 34, 19); *Sentences* I, dist. 1, c. 1, n. 1.
68. *Glossa in Quatuor Libros Sententiarum Petri Lombardi*, ed. Quaracchi 1951, I, *Introitus*, n. 8, p. 4.
69. Glorieux, "L'Enseignement au Moyen Age: Techniques et Méthodes en usage à la Faculté de Théologie de Paris, au XIIIᵉ siècle," AHDLMA 43 (1968) 65–186, esp. 137–41. Glorieux's vast knowledge and analysis of the materials at hand have succeeded in replacing Charles Thurot's *De l'organisation de l'enseignement dans l'université de Paris au Moyen Âge*, published in 1859. However, Glorieux's work relies in great measure on two collections of university statutes: *Chart. U. P.*, II, 691–97, n. 1188, collected 1335–66, and II, 697–704, n. 1189, collected 1385–87. As invaluable as these two collections are in themselves for understanding common procedure in the early and mid-fourteenth century, they cannot be used globally to determine the procedure of individual masters in the thirteenth century, since many of the individual statutes were not enacted until a later date. For instance, we do not know whether Thomas was obliged to present an *introitus* or *principium* for each book of the *Sentences*, simply because we do not know when this custom began or when it was enacted into law. It would seem that the practice of giving a *principium* was in existence by 1253 (*Chart. U. P.*, I, 242, n. 219). Until each statute can be traced back to its origins, there will always be the danger of trying to fit the man to the mold.
70. These two *sermones* were found in Florence MS Conventi soppressi (S. Maria Novella), G. 4. 36, fol. 268v–271v. This MS belonged at one time to Remigii de'Girolami, a faithful disciple of St. Thomas.
71. Tocco, *Hystoria*, c. 14. *Fontes* 81. Gui, *Legenda*, c. 11. *Fontes* 178. Tolomeo, *Hist. Eccl.* lib. 22, c. 21, col. 1152.
72. See J. A. Weisheipl, "The Meaning of *Sacra doctrina* in *Sum. theol.* I, 1," *The Thomist* 36 (1974).
73. *Sum. theol.* I, q. 13, a. 11 ad 1. See A. A. Maurer, C.S.B., "St. Thomas on the Sacred Name 'Tetragrammaton,'" *Mediaeval Studies* 34 (1972), 275–86.

74. Peter Lombard, *Sent.* II, dist. 24, c. 9 (Quaracchi 1916), I, 424, n. 206. Cf. Alexander of Hales, *Sum. Theol.*, P. II, q. 107, n. 6; Bonaventure, *Comm. in II Sent.*, dist. 24, P. II, a. 3, q. 1; and Albert the Great, *In II Sent.*, dist. 24, F. a. 9, also 1 sed contra; *Sum. de Creat.*, tr. IV, q. 69, a. 3, pla. 3, q. 2; also idem q. 3.

75. Deman, "Le Péché de Sensualité," *Mélanges Mandonnet* (Bibl. Thomiste 13, Paris 1930), I, 266–67.

76. "Ideoque tentatio, quae est ex carne, non fit sine peccato," *De sacramentis*, P. 7, c. 9 (PL 176, 290). Peter Lombard, *Sent.*, ed. cit., n. 173.

77. Notice the change from *In II Sent.*, dist. 21, A. a. 4; dist. 24, F. A. 8; *Sum. de Creat.*, tr. IV, q. 69, a. 3, pla. 3, q. 2 to the later doctrine found in *Sum. theol.*, P. II, tr. 15, q. 92, memb. 1 and memb. 4.

78. *Sum. theol.* I–II, q. 74, a. 3 ad 3, as compared to *In II Sent.*, dist. 24, q. 3, a. 2; throughout the *QQ. Disp. de malo*, the first movements in each category of grave matter in the seven deadly sins are venially sinful antecedent to awareness or consent. Cf. O. Lottin, "La Doctrine Morale des Mouvements Premiers de l'Appétit Sensitif aux XIIe et XIIIe Siècles," AHDLMA 6 (1931), 49–173; T. Deman, op. cit., 265–83.

79. Medieval theologians, including Thomas, carefully distinguished physiological and biochemical changes in the body (*primo primi motus*) from the true formal structure of the emotion instigated by the internal cogitative power of man; these initial emotions were called *secundo primi motus*. After the time of Alphonsus Liguori (d. 1787), theologians disregarded physiological changes normally accompanying emotions, and called the initial emotion proper the *primo primi motus*. A comparative schema will clarify the difference:

	Medieval theol. after William of Auxerre	*Contemporary theol.* following S. Alphonsus
Bodily change	motus primo primus	
Antecedent emotion	motus secundo primus	= motus primo primus
Semi-deliberate	motus secundus imperf.	= motus secundo primus
Fully deliberate	motus secundus perf.	= motus deliberatus, seu motus secundus

This change of terminology caused considerable confusion in the study of the writings of Thomas and other medieval theologians who taught that what Alphonsus called *primo primi motus* were in truth venially sinful; they are what theologians today call "temptations of the flesh." The teaching of Thomas on this point as compared to Alphonsus Liguori is too complex to explain here. I have discussed this matter in full elsewhere.

80. *Chart. U. P.*, I, 220–21, n. 194.

81. II *Sent.*, dist. 44, dub. 3, ed. Quaracchi II, 1016.

82. E. A. Synan, "Brother Thomas, the Master, and the Masters," *Comm. Studies* (Toronto: PIMS 1974).

83. See M. Grabmann, "Hilfmittel des Thomasstudiums aus alter Zeit: Abbreviationes, Concorantiae, Tabulae," *Mittelalterliches Geistesleben* (Munich 1936), II, 424–89, esp. 452–81. P. Mandonnet, "Premiers travaux de polémique thomiste. Deuxième partie— Les Concordantiae," *Revue des sc. phil. et théol.* 7 (1913), 244– 62; F. Stegmüller, *Repertorium Comm. in Sent. Petri Lombardi* (Würzburg 1947), II, n. 867–77.1, pp. 405–7.

84. Grabmann, ibid., 453; Mandonnet, ibid., 247–48.

85. Grabmann, ibid., 455.

86. *Opera Omnia* (Parma 1864), 17, 404a–12b.

87. *Concordantiae dictorum et conclusionum D. Thomae de Aquino*, in *Tabula Aurea* of Peter of Bergamo (Rome 1517), fol. 1ra–36vb; this third part of the *Tabula Aurea* is not usually printed with the better-known index of terms.

88. *Chart. U. P.*, II, 692, n. 1188, item 5.

89. Ibid., item 18, pp. 692–93.

90. Gui, *Legenda*, c. 10. *Fontes* 177.

91. Tolomeo, *Hist. Eccl.*, lib. 22, c. 21, col. 1152.

92. Trevet, *Annales*, ed. T. Hog (London 1845), 289.

93. T. Kaeppeli, *Scriptores Ord. Praed. Medii Aevi* (Rome: S. Sabina 1970), I, n. 317.

94. Details of this controversy have been studied by many scholars since the pioneer work of F. X. Seppelt (1902) and Max Bierbaum (1920). A full bibliography can be found in Y. M.-J. Congar, "Aspects ecclésiologiques de la querelle entre mendiants et séculiers dans la second moitié XIIIᵉ siècle et le début du XIVᵉ," AHDLMA 28 (1961), 35–151, esp. fn. 19–21. To these may be added John Moorman, op. cit., 127–31, and D. L. Douie, *The Conflict Between the Seculars and the Mendicants at the University of Paris in the Thirteenth Century* (London: Aquinas Papers, n. 23, Blackfriars 1954).

95. *Chart. U. P.*, I, 226–27, n. 200.
96. *Bonum Universale de Apibus*, II, c. 10, n. 21ff.
97. *Chart. U. P.*, I, 252–58, n. 230.
98. Bacon, *Opera quaedam hactenus inedita*, ed. Brewer (London 1859), 428.
99. *Chart. U. P.*, I, 310, n. 273.
100. "Les universités au XIIIᵉ siècle," *Revue Historique*, 1931/1, 217–38; 1931/2, 1–15.
101. *Chart. U. P.*, I, 226, n. 200.
102. Ibid., I, 284, n. 247.
103. Ibid., I, 253, n. 230.
104. *Acta Cap. Gen.*, I, 65–66 nota. MOPH 3 (Rome 1898).
105. *Chart. U. P.*, I, 242–43, n. 219.
106. Ibid., I, 247–48, n. 222.
107. Ibid., I, 252–58, n. 230.
108. Salimbene, *Chronica*, MGH, Script. 32, 1254; J. G. Bougerol, *Introduction à l'Étude de saint Bonaventure* (Paris: Desclée 1961), 241.
109. See Protocol of the Commission at Anagni, ed. H. Denifle, *Archiv f. Litt. u. Kirchengesch. d. M.-A.*, I (1885), 99–142.
110. Published under the name of Nicole Oresme by Martène and Durand, *Veterum Scriptorum et Monumentorum* (Paris 1733), 9, col. 1271–1446. The MS of Saint-Victor, from which this text is published, is equally uncertain about its author: "Liber Bonaventurae secundum aliquos, secundum alios magistri Nicolai Oresme."
111. *Chart. U. P.*, I, 272–75, n. 243; 292–97, n. 256. Cf. esp. notes in Denifle, *Das Evangelium aeternum und die Commission zu Anagni*, loc. cit., 70–88.
112. *Chart. U. P.*, I, 267–70, n. 240.
113. Ibid., I, 276–77, n. 244.
114. Ibid., I, 279–85, n. 247.
115. Ibid., I, 286–87, n. 249.
116. See Y. M.-J. Congar, op. cit., 45.
117. P. Glorieux, "Le 'Contra Impugnantes' de s. Thomas: ses sources, son plan," *Mélanges Mandonnet* (Paris 1930), I, 75.
118. *Chart. U. P.*, I, 308–9, n. 272.
119. Ibid., I, 309–13, n. 273.
120. Ibid., I, 297–98, nn. 257–58.
121. Ibid., I, 307, n. 270.
122. Ibid., I, 283, n. 247.

123. "Volumen illud immutatus fuit quinquies successive." *Resp.* VI, 360; *Opera Omnia,* 109. Cf. Leon. ed., 41, A 10, fn. 5 and 6.

124. Apparently it was the fifth and final version that found a place in the printed *Opera Omnia* of William of Saint-Amour (Constance 1632), 17–72, from which M. Bierbaum drew his excerpts, *Bettelorden und Weltgeistlichkeit an der Universität Paris, 1255–1272, Franzisk. Studien,* Beiheft 2 (Münster 1920), 1–36. Cf. Congar, op. cit., 45.

125. *Chart. U. P.,* I, n. 288, notes on p. 333.

126. *Opera* V, 116–98.

127. Ed. M. Bierbaum, op. cit., 37–168.

128. *Opera Omnia,* ed. Leon., 41 A.

129. *Chart. U. P.,* I, 337–38, n. 291.

130. "Catalogue," 407.

131. Tocco, *Hystoria,* c. 19. *Fontes* 91–93.

132. *Opera Omnia,* ed. Leon., 41 A, preface § 7. 12.

133. Tolomeo, *Hist. Eccl.,* lib. 22, c. 21, col. 1152

Chapter III

1. *Chart. U. P.,* I, 311–12, n. 273.

2. *Acta,* MOPH 3, 82–83. The *Chronicle of the Masters General* states, "From this time on cardinals and prelates used to say with a certain sigh of relief: Beware of the litanies of the Friars Preachers, for they work miracles"–the specific reference being to the propitious death of Pope Innocent IV, December 7, 1254. Ibid., 83, fn. 1.

3. *Chart. U. P.,* I, 321, n. 280.

4. Ibid., I, 317–19, n. 279.

5. Tocco, *Hystoria,* c. 16. *Fontes* 84–85.

6. *Chart. U. P.,* I, 219, n. 191.

7. Tocco, *Hystoria,* c. 16. *Fontes* 84. Gui, *Legenda,* c. 12. *Fontes* 179: "Expleto cursu bachallarii in legendo Sententias Parisius gratiose." Calo, *Vita,* n. 10. *Fontes* 28: "post decursum studii fructuose completum."

8. Tocco, *Hystoria,* c. 14. *Fontes* 81: "scripsit in bachallaria et in principio sui magisterii."

9. *Chart. U. P.,* I, 307, n. 270.

10. Cf. ibid., fn. 1.

11. *Chart. U. P.,* I, 306, n. 269.

12. Walz, 69; cf. *Chart. U. P.,* I, 284, n. 247.

13. Callo, *Vita,* n. 10. *Fontes* 28. Tocco, *Hystoria,* c. 16. *Fontes* 85.

Gui, *Legenda*, c. 12. *Fontes* 179. Gerard de Frachet, *Vitae Fratrum*, pt. 4, c. 24. MOPH I, 216.

14. Foster, 69, fn. 33.
15. Cf. *Fontes* 85, fn. 1.
16. *Chart. U. P.*, I, 75–76, n. 16.
17. Ibid., 137, n. 79.
18. Cf. ibid., 283, n. 247.
19. Ibid., I, 283–84.
20. Ibid., II, 693–94, n. 1188, note 5; cf. Glorieux, "L'Enseignement au Moyen Âge," loc. cit., 141–47.
21. *Opuscula Theologica*, ed. R. A. Verardo (Torino: Marietti 1954), I, 441–43; Engl. trans. without biblical quotations, Bourke, 61–62.
22. G. Abate, "Intorno al cronologia di S. Tommaso d'Aquino," *Misc. Franc.* 50 (1950), 231–47; Bourke, 60–61, fn. 24.
23. *Chart. U. P.*, II, 693, n. 1188.
24. See *Opuscula Theologica*, ed. R. A. Verardo, ed. cit., I, 433–34 for current view.
25. Denifle, *Chart. U. P.*, II, 694, fn. 5: "in qua lectione perficiat suum in aula incompletum principium."
26. Bourke, 78–80; Walz-Novarina, 223; Eschmann, "Catalogue," 389.
27. Bourke, 79.
28. Chenu, *Introduction*, 242.
29. Walz-Novarina, 223.
30. Castagnoli, "Regesta," 31 (1928), 253–56.
31. *Bulletin Thomiste*, I (1924), 41–42.
32. See Walz-Novarina, 92, fn. 9; Chenu, *La théologie comme science au 13e siècle*, 3rd ed. (Paris 1957), 99–100.
33. Denifle, "Quel livre servait de base à l'enseignement des Mâitres en Théologie dans l'Université de Paris," *Revue Thomiste* 2 (1894), 161.
34. Cf. *Sum. theol.* I, q. 1, a. 8 ad 2.
35. Walz, 111, and 213, fn. 128.
36. Tocco, *Hystoria*, c. 27. *Fontes* 100.
37. Ibid.: "Qui rarissime habuerat primum motum." For the technical meaning of this term, see above, chap. 2.
38. Cf. A. Dondaine, *Secrétaires*, 198–99. Bourke, 82–83, 103 text and note 33; Walz-Novarina, 105.
39. Statute 18, *Chart. U. P.*, II, 693, n. 118; Glorieux, "L'Enseignement au Moyen Âge," 100–3.
40. *Chart. U. P.*, I, 331–33, n. 288.
41. Ibid., I, 333–35, n. 289.

42. Ibid., I, 335–37, n. 290.
43. Ibid., I, 338–40, n. 293.
44. Ibid., I, 342–46, n. 296.
45. Ibid., I, 354–56, n. 309.
46. Ibid., I, 359–61, n. 312.
47. Ibid., I, 362, n. 314.
48. Bougerol, op. cit., 241.
49. *Chart. U. P.*, I, 354–67, n. 317.
50. Ibid., I, 366.
51. Bourke, 63–66.
52. Cf. Glorieux, "L'Enseignement au Moyen Âge," 108–11.
53. Mandonnet, *Écrits*, 31.
54. Edited by Mandonnet from Bibl. Nat. MS lat. 3112, fol. 58–59, *Écrits*, 29–31; *Proc. canoniz. Neapoli*, c. 85. *Fontes* 386–89; originally published by S. Baluzius in his *Vitas Paparum Avenionensium*, III, [6]–[9]. Cf. Mandonnet, *Écrits*, 28.
55. Eschmann, "Catalogue," 393.
56. Mandonnet bases his argument for alternating between New and Old Testaments on statute 11 of the codification "not before the year 1335" ("Écrits scripturaires," 11 (1928), 40, fn. 1; *Chart. U. P.*, II, 692, n. 1188). But this statute applies only to *cursores;* the whole context of this statute leaves no other interpretation. The whole text reads as follows: "Item nota, quod admissi ad lecturam Biblie debent solum legere duos libros, et tales sicut voluerint eligere, scilicet unum de veteri Testamento, et alium de novo, etc." Denifle's explanatory note leaves no room for doubt. Therefore, this statute cannot be used to prove that masters had to alternate between the New and Old Testaments in their teaching of the sacred page.
57. Gui, *Legenda*, c. 16; Foster, 38.
58. Tocco, *Hystoria*, c. 31. *Fontes* 105–6. Gui, *Legenda*, c. 16. *Fontes* 184–85. Calo, *Vita*, c. 17. *Fontes* 37.
59. *Proc. canoniz. Neapoli*, n. 59. *Fontes* 346. Foster, 98.
60. *Codices Manuscripti Operum Thomae de Aquino*, ed. H. F. Dondaine and H. V. Shooner (Rome: Commissio Leonina 1967), I, 3–4. Grabmann, *Die Werke*, 429–33.
61. Dondaine, *Secrétaires*, 200–1.
62. Tocco, *Hystoria*, c. 28 (*Fontes* 102), c. 29 (*Fontes* 104), c. 30 (*Fontes* 104).
63. Castagnoli, strangely enough, dismisses the incident recorded by William of Tocco concerning the visit of the two Apostles to aid

in the composition of a commentary on Isaiah. He says that there is no question of Thomas's *dictating* this passage to Reginald, for we have the actual autograph ("Regesta," loc. cit., 63–64). But this argument has no force, since the incident of dictation could refer either to a passage not in the autograph or to a dictation of the *littera illegibilis* of the autograph.

64. Nicholas Trevet, *Annales*, ed. cit., 290; Grabmann, *Die Werke*, 263–64; F. Stegmüller, *Repertorium Biblicum*, n. 8048f. (1955), 338–39.

65. Walz-Novarina, 96.

66. Gui, *Legenda*, c. 34. *Fontes* 200–1. Tocco, *Hystoria*, c. 42. *Fontes* 115. *Proc. canoniz. Neapoli*, n. 66. (*Fontes* 356), n. 78 (*Fontes* 376).

67. Mercati, *Appunti su Niceto ed Aniano traduttore di S. Giov. Chrisostomo* (Vatican: Studi et Testi 5, 1901), n. 12, p. 142.

68. Cf. C. Baur, *S. Jean Chrysostome et ses oeuvres dans l'histoire littéraire* (Louvain-Paris 1907), 62, fn. 2; 74.

69. "Le catalogue officiel," in Mandonnet, *Écrits*, 31, n. 69; Nicholas Trevet, *Annales*, ed. cit., 290.

70. Guindon, "La Lectura super Matthaeum," *Revue de l'Université de Ottawa*, Section spéciale, 25 (1955), 213–19.

71. Shooner, "La 'Lectura in Matthaeum' de s. Thomas," *Angelicum* 33 (1956), 121–42.

72. MS Vat. Urb. lat. 25, to which Bartholomew of Spina had access, has a scribal note in chap. 5: "At this point the major part of the fifth chapter is missing and a third part of the sixth, namely to the words 'Sic orabitis, etc.' as in the original." However, Shooner noted that the rest of the Basel MS is not identical with the printed text and may be the version of the second scribe writing simultaneously with the first. If that is the case, then one cannot say that only one scribe took down chapters 1–14 (Peter d'Andria), while another took down chapters 15–18 (Ligier de Besançon). In this case, the statement of Walz-Novarina (96) would have to be modified. In that case the *Lectura super Matthaeum* would be a *reportatio* with two scribes involved.

73. Mandonnet, *Écrits*, 30, item 28. *Fontes* 388.

74. Dondaine, *Secrétaires*, 209–16.

75. Humbert of Romans, *Vita Regulari, Instructiones de Officiis Ordinis*, c. 2, ed. J. Berthier (Rome 1889), II, 260.

76. Mandonnet, "Les disputes quodlibétique de s. Thomas d'Aquin," Introduction to *S. Thomae Aquinatis Questiones quodlibetales* (Paris: Lethielleux 1926), 8 pp.; "Saint Thomas d'Aquin créateur

de la dispute quodlibétique," *Rev. des sc. phil. et théol.* 25 (1926), 477–505; 26 (1927), 5–38.

77. Eschmann, "Cataloque," nn. 5–16, pp. 392–93.

78. *Chart. U. P.*, II, 107–8, n. 642.

79. Ibid., I, 390–92, n. 342.

80. Ibid., I, fn. 5, 392.

81. Ibid., I, 391.

82. Cf. P. Glorieux, *Répertoire,* I, 113–17, nn. 18–19.

83. Peter Marc, *Introductio* to *Liber de Veritate Catholicae Fidei contra errores infidelium* (Torino: Marietti 1967), 72–73 and 613.

84. *Proc. canoniz. Neapoli,* n. 66. *Fontes* 355.

85. Walz, 84; Bourke, 123–24; Eschmann, "Catalogue," 385–86; Grabmann, *Die Werke,* 290–94, etc.

86. Here is not the place to review the massive work of Dom Marc and his attempt to date the *Summa contra gentiles* contemporary with the *Summa theologiae.* This must still be done. Since Marc's chronology for the *Summa theologiae* differs from our own, it might be well to note it: I, begun in February 1269; I–II, begun toward the end of February 1270; II–II, begun around the twentieth of March 1271; and III, begun in December 1272. (Cf. 407.) For how Marc's work affects the chronology of all the other works of Thomas, see sect. B of article V, pp. 406–24. We must remember that during his second Parisian regency, Thomas not only carried out his duties as full-time professor, but also wrote the entire *secunda pars,* commented on Aristotle, defended the rights of mendicants against the attacks of Gérard d' Abbeville, and responded to numerous requests for his expert opinion. It is physically impossible to fit the *Summa contra gentiles* into such a heavy program.

87. For a study of this MS, see *Codices Manuscripti Operum Thomae de Aquino,* ed. H. F. Dondaine and H. V. Shooner, I (Rome 1967), 3–4 with bibliography; *Opera Omnia,* Leon. ed., 13–14, by Peter Paul Mackay; A. Dondaine, *Secrétaires,* 92–95.

88. Chenu, *Introduction,* 251, fn. 1.

89. A. Dondaine, *Secrétaires,* 92, fn. 25.

90. Walz-Novarina, 223, following A. Gauthier, *Contra Gentiles,* liv. 1er (Paris: Lethielleux 1961), 20–59.

91. Tolomeo, *Hist. Eccl.,* lib. 22, c. 24, col. 1153.

92. Eschmann, "Catalogue," n. 2, p. 380.

93. *Chart. U. P.,* II, 108, n. 642.

94. L.-B. Geiger, "Abstraction et séparation d'après saint Thomas," *Rev. des sc. phil. et théol.* 31 (1947), 3–40. There is also an ex-

cellent translation into English with an informative introduction by A. A. Maurer, *Divisions and Methods of the Sciences* (Toronto: PIMS 1953). P. Wyser's text of qq. 5–6 has been corrected and published in full by Bruno Decker, *Expositio super librum Boethii De trinitate* (Leyden: Brill 1955).

95. Eschmann and Chenu date this commentary 1260–61. See Eschmann, "Catalogue," n. 40, p. 406. M-D. Chenu, *La Théologie comme science au XIIIe siècle*. 2nd ed. Pro manuscripto. Le Sauchoir 1943, 81.

96. Gui, *Legenda*, c. 28. *Fontes* 194: Also Tocco, *Hystoria*, c. 47. *Fontes* 121: Calo, *Vita*, c. 24. *Fontes* 44.

97. Gui, *Legenda*, c. 32. *Fontes* 198.

98. Ibid. *Fontes* 199: Foster, 51.

99. Castagnoli, "Regesta," 65.

100. *Chart. U. P.*, I, 385–86. Cf. *Acta Capitulorum Generalium*, MOPH 3, 94, fn. 1; the text of the commission's work, pp. 99–100, differs slightly from the text in the *Chartularium*.

Chapter IV

1. Tolomeo, *Hist. Eccl.*, lib. 22, c. 22.

2. Ibid., c. 24.

3. Mandonnet, "Lecteur," III, 9–11.

4. See Bourke, 107–8; Walz-Novarina, 115–16.

5. *Chart. U. P.*, I, 505, n. 447, fn. 5.

6. Walz, 87; Walz-Novarina, 117.

7. Dondaine, *Secrétaires*, 186.

8. Doc. 30. *Fontes* 582.

9. Mandonnet, "Lecteur," 11; idem, "Chronologie sommaire," 114, 147–48; also Walz, 88; Walz-Novarina, 116; Castagnoli, "Regesta," 446; Bourke, 108.

10. *Proc. canoniz. Neapoli*, n. 47. *Fontes* 326.

11. Tolomeo, *Hist. Eccl.*, lib. 22, c. 24.

12. Eschmann, "Catalogue," 386; Marc, *Introductio*, 4, fn. 1.

13. Cf. Tocco, *Hystoria*, cc. 27 and 63. *Fontes* 101, 136. Testimony of Leonardo de Gaieta, *Proc. canoniz. Neapoli*, n. 75. *Fontes* 369.

14. Cf. Walz, 88, fn. 6.

15. Doc. 30. *Fontes* 582.

16. Ibid.

17. Hinnebusch, op. cit., 185, fn. 127; cf. 218.

18. Mandonnet, "Lecteur," 26.

19. Doc. 30. *Fontes* 582: "Assignamus fr. Thomam de Aquino pro *lectore* in conventu Urbeventano in remissionem suorum peccatorum."
20. *Acta Cap. Gen.*, I, MOPH 3, 138.
21. Grabmann, *Guglielmo*, 43.
22. Abh. d. Bay. Akad. d. Wiss., philos.-philolog. u. hist. Klasse, 27/1–2 (Munich 1912).
23. "Ist das 'philosophische Universalgenie' bei Magister Heinrich dem Poeten Thomas von Aquin?" *Historisches Jahrbuch* 38 (1917), 315–20.
24. Cf. Walz, "Alberto Magno," *Bibliotheca Sanctorum* (Rome 1961–69), I, 703.
25. Cf. *Physica*, II, tr. 1, c. 1.
26. Albert, *Sum. theol.*, P. II, q. 77, membr. 3, ed. Borgnet, 33, 100.
27. Gervasio Vacce, "Giovanni Campano," *Enciclopedia Italiana*, 8, 594.
28. Grabmann, *Guglielmo*, 85.
29. Bourke, 110.
30. *The Universities of Europe in the Middle Ages*, new ed. F. M. Powicke and A. B. Emden (Oxford 1936), I, 360.
31. *Siger*, 39.
32. Tolomeo, *Hist. Eccl.*, lib. 22, c. 24.
33. Ed. by G. Meerssemann, *Laurentii Pignon Catalogi et Chronica. Accedunt Catalogi Stamsensis et Upsalensis Script. Ord. Praed.* (Rome 1936), 62.
34. Cf. Grabmann, *Guglielmo*, 65–68.
35. Ibid., 52–54.
36. Tocco, *Hystoria*, c. 17. *Fontes* 88.
37. *Sententia libri Ethicorum*, ed. Leon., 42 (Rome 1969), introd. 232*–33*.
38. It is true that in 1920 Mandonnet considered the following works to have been composed in Italy between 1265 and 1268, and composed more or less in the following order: the *Physics*, the *Metaphysics*, the *De anima*, the *De sensu et sensibili*, the *De memoria*, the *Ethics*, the *Politics*, and the *Posterior analytics*. "Chronologie sommaire," 150. As research and scholarship progressed the commentaries on Aristotle have more and more been recognized as late compositions. Today not one can be firmly dated before the second Parisian regency.
39. Walz, "L'Aquinate a Orvieto," *Angelicum* 35 (1958), 176.
40. Tolomeo, *Hist. Eccl.*, lib. 22, c. 24.
41. For our information we rely mainly on the researches of H. Deni-

fle, *Die Entstehung der Universitäten des Mittelalters* (Berlin 1885), and of Raymond Creytens, "Le Studium Romanae Curiae et le Maître du Sacré Palais," AFP 12 (1942), 5–83.

42. On the origin and growth of this fourteenth-century legend, see R. Loenertz, "Saint Dominique écrivain, maître en théologie, professeur à Rome et Maître du Sacré Palais," AFP 12 (1942), 84–97.

43. Cf. V. M. Fontana, *Syllabus magistrorum sacri palatii apostolici* (Rome 1663), 61ff.

44. *Decretales* V, tit. 5: De magistris, cc. 1–4, ed. Friedberg II, 768–70.

45. W. Stubbs, *Memoriale fratris Walteri de Coventris* (London 1873), II, 198.

46. *Chart. U. P.*, I, 90–93, n. 32.

47. Full text in Denifle, *Die Entstehung*, 302–3, fn. 323 plus fn. 326, and Creytens, op. cit., 16.

48. Rashdall, *The Universities*, ed. cit., II, 28. However, it was always the teacher of theology who held primacy of office.

49. Creytens, op. cit., 20.

50. Cf. Creytens, op. cit., 20–21.

51. *In III Decretalium lib. Commentaria* (Venice 1581), fol. 13r.

52. From the fourteenth century and especially the fifteenth century onward, the status of a "college" (*collegium*) must be recognized. Generally it meant a *studium generale* which had the right to promote students to degrees (*ad gradum magisterii*), but was not a "university" even in the sense of Oxford or Cambridge. By 1421 the Dominican *studium generale curiae*, i.e., the general studium of the order that was directly under the control of the general chapter, and located in the city where the papal curia happened to be, was such a "college." Cf. *Acta Cap. Gen.* (Metz 1421), MOPH 8, 170–71. A "college" in this sense is not the same as a residence hall for poor scholars (Merton, Balliol), nor an integral teaching part of the university (Saint-Jacques, Sorbonne), nor a college of physicians or lawyers (*Collegium medicorum, Collegium legistarum*), i.e., associations.

53. Creytens, op. cit., 30–31, 66–74.

54. Creytens, op. cit., 69.

55. *Acta Cap. Gen.*, MOPH 3, 34–35.

56. E. Esteban, *Analecta Augustiniana* (Rome 1907–16), 2, 227; Creytens, op. cit., 37. Creytens (p. 50) finds a hint of this in the Dominican general chapter of Bologna, 1267, quoted above, namely that "the provincial of the Roman province should see to

it that the priory where the curia resides should be provided with suitable friars for the needs of the curia, particularly the prior and the lector" (MOPH 3, 138). This may or, more probably, may not be the case, but it does not affect our argument concerning the studium; nor does it officially refer to the lector of the priory as *lector curiae Romanae.*

57. *Analecta Aug.,* 3, 375.
58. *Analecta Aug.,* 2, 372, 385, 387; Creytens, op. cit., 39ff.
59. MOPH 20, 72.
60. Creytens, op. cit., 55.
61. For the resolution of this situation, see Creytens, op. cit., 42–44.
62. General Chapter of Bologna in 1306: *Analecta Aug.,* 3, 54.
63. Denifle, *Die Entstehung,* 310–17; Creytens, op. cit., 82.
64. E. Berger, *Les registres d'Innocent IV,* 3, n. 5547; Creytens, op. cit., 61–62.
65. *Sententia libri Ethicorum,* ed. Leon., 47 (Rome 1969), 259*–68*.
66. Alexander of Hales, *Summa theologica,* IV, Prolegomena (Quaracchi 1948), xc.
67. G. Geenen, "En marge du Concile de Chalcédone: Les textes du Quatrième Concile dans les oeuvres de saint Thomas," *Angelicum* 29 (1952), 43–59; I. Baches, *Die Christologie des hl. Thomas v. Aquin und die griechischen Kirchenväter* (Paderborn 1931).
68. Cf. Thomas Aquinas, *Contra errores Graecorum,* prologue, Leon. ed., 40 (Rome 1967), A 71, 46–61.
69. Geenen, op. cit., 50.
70. A. Dondaine, "Nicolas de Cotrone et les sources du *Contra errores Graecorum* de s. Thomas," *Divus Thomas* (Fr.) 29 (1950), 313–40.
71. Ibid., 316–17, following Glorieux, claims that Thomas must have seen the *Libellus* by 1256–57, when he wrote his *Contra impugnantes Dei cultum et religionem,* for in this work he quotes a passage from Pseudo-Cyril (*Contra impugnantes,* c. 3, § 7, Leon. ed., 41 [Rome 1970], A 68, 459–69) that could only have come from the *Libellus* § 98, 49–58 (Leon. ed., 40 A, p. 146). Dondaine further argues that the Emperor for whom the *Libellus* was written must have been Theodore II Lascaris (1254–58). While the quotation seems convincing enough, the evidence is too weak to support such a drastic conclusion. Thomas and Nicholas may have used a common source, thus excusing Nicholas from culpability in the matter of falsification. It is strange that Thomas used no other quotation from the *Libellus* before

1263, while in his *QQ. de potentia* and in the *Catena* on Matthew he does utilize other quotations taken from the *Libellus*.

72. H. Dondaine, preface, *Opera Omnia*, ed. Leon., 40 (Rome 1167), A 8, § 4.
73. Eschmann, "Catalogue," 415.
74. Ibid., 397.
75. Nicholas Trevet, *Annales*, ed. cit., 288.
76. *Commentary on the Four Gospels by S. Thomas Aquinas*. Vol. I, pt. 1, 2nd ed. (Oxford & London 1864). Preface iii-iv.
77. *Epistola dedicatoria, Opera Omnia* (Paris: Vivès 1876) 16, 499.
78. "St. Thomas et les Pères," DTC, XV/1, 743.
79. Walz, 96; Grabmann, "Die Schrift *De rationibus fidei contra Saracenos, Graecos et Armenos ad cantorem Antiochenum*," *Scholastik* 17 (1942), 187–216.
80. Foster, 142, fn. 17.
81. The first work mentioned by Tolomeo as commissioned by Urban was the *Catena aurea* previously discussed. Tolomeo makes no mention of *Contra errores Graecorum*.
82. Tolomeo, *Hist. Eccl.*, lib. 22, c. 24, col. 1154.
83. Tocco, *Hystoria*, c. 17. *Fontes* 88.
84. Eschmann, "Catalogue," n. 76, 424; for a fuller bibliography of the question before 1949, see Grabmann, *Die Werke*, 365–72.
85. F. Callaey, "Origine e Sviluppo della Festa del 'Corpus Domini,'" *Eucaristia*, ed. A. Piolanti (Rome: Desclée 1957), 907–32.
86. P. Browe, ed., *Textus antiqui de festo Corporis Christi*, in *Opuscula et Textus*, ser. Lit. (Münster: Aschendorff 1934), 4, 21–23.
87. C. Lambot, "L'Ufficio del S.m. Sacramento," *Eucaristia*, 827.
88. Browe, op. cit., 23–26.
89. Ibid., 26–27.
90. *Oxford Dictionary of the Christian Church*, ed. F. L. Cross (London: OUP 1958), 183b–84a; B. Pesci, "Il Miracolo di Bolsena," *Eucaristia*, 1025–33.
91. "Transiturus de mundo," *Bullarium Romanum*, III, P. I (Rome 1740), 414b–16b. Here the date of promulgation is missing, but easily found elsewhere. A. Potthast, *Reg. Pont. Roman.* (Berlin 1875), n. 18998, II, 1538. The full text is found in *Corpus iuris canonici*, ed. E. Friedberg (Leipzig 1879–81), II, col. 1174–77.
92. C. Lambot, op. cit., 828. The full text is in Browe, op. cit., 27–33.
93. C. Lambot, "La Bulle d'Urbain IV à Ève de Saint-Martin sur l'Institution de la Fête-Dieu," *Scriptorium* 2 (1948), 69–77. Browe, op. cit., 34–35.

94. Opusculum 59 in the Roman edition of Thomas's works; 52 in the Parma edition.
95. Cf. G. Morin, "L'Office cistercien pour la Fête-Dieu comparé avec celui de saint Thomas d'Aquin," *Revue Bénédictine* 27 (1910), 236–46.
96. *Clementinarum lib. III*, tit. 16, cap. un., *Corpus iuris canonici*, ed. cit., II, col. 1174–77.
97. MOPH 4, 109.
98. MOPH 4, 138; this ordinance was repeated verbatim in the following year at Barcelona, MOPH 4, 144.
99. Walz, 109.

Chapter V

1. Walz, 106; Walz-Novarina, 134–35.
2. Doc. 19. *Fontes* 568.
3. Ibid., 567–68.
4. MOPH 20, 32.
5. Cf. Bibliography in *Opuscula Philosophica*, ed. R. M. Spiazzi (Torino: Marietti 1954), 254–55.
6. See Alfred O'Rahilly, "Notes on St. Thomas: IV. *De regimine principum,*" *Irish Ecclesiastical Record* 31 (1928), 396–410; "V. Tholomeo of Lucca, the Continuator of the *De regimine principum,*" ibid., 606–14. The day before Fr. Eschmann died on April 11, 1968, I had a long talk with him at the hospital and I asked him whether he thought the *De regno* to be authentic. He shook his head thoughtfully and said, "No, I don't think so."
7. Grabmann, *Die Werke*, 330–36.
8. *Écrits*, 104.
9. *Hist. Eccl.*, lib. 23, c. 13.
10. *Écrits*, 99.
11. Grabmann, *Die Werke*, 331.
12. O'Rahilly, op. cit., 405.
13. The early part of the text, i.e., the "authentic" part, was translated by G. Phelan and I. T. Eschmann, *St. Thomas on Kingship to the King of Cyprus* (Toronto: PIMS 1949); the full Latin text including the addition by Tolomeo is published in *Opuscula Philosophica*, ed. cit., 257–358.
14. Grabmann, *Die Werke*, 353.
15. Eschmann, "Catalogue," 414.
16. Eschmann, "St. Thomas Aquinas on the Two Powers," *Mediaeval Studies* 20 (1958), 177–205.
17. O'Rahilly, op. cit., 398.

18. Thomas, *In II Sent.*, dist. 44, expos. textus, trans. Phelan and Eschmann, 107.

19. *De regno* I, 14, § 110–111, trans. cit., 62–63.

20. Eschmann, "Two Powers," 189.

21. Ibid., 198–204.

22. In the authentic portion of *De regno*, Thomas explicitly cites Aristotle's *Politics* V, 12; VII, 7; V, 3; VI, 4. Hence he had already read Moerbeke's translation when he wrote *De regno*, and not just the *translatio imperfecta*, which he knew when he was commenting on Matthew (1256–59), and composing *Summa contra gentiles* (1259–64), *De potentia* (1256–67), and *Expositio in Job* (1261–63). Since the reference in *De potentia* is only to Book I, it is difficult to know which translation Thomas had in mind. The date of Moerbeke's translation of the *Politics* is not known, but it is generally considered to be around 1260. (Praef. *Sententia libri Politicorum*, ed. Leon. (Rome 1971), 48, § 3, A 8.) Thus it is possible that *De regno* and *De potentia* are contemporary, and that Thomas had read Moerbeke's translation by 1265.

23. MOPH 20, 32.

24. MOPH 20, 36.

25. MOPH 3, 153.

26. Naples, Regio Archivio 25, quoted by Mandonnet, *Écrits*, 41.

27. Trevet, *Annales*, ed. cit., 287–88.

28. Mandonnet, "Chronologie sommaire," 148.

29. Grabmann, *Die Werke*, 306.

30. Dondaine, *Secrétaires*, 209–16.

31. This work (PL 42, 1213–22) was generally attributed to Augustine by all of Thomas's contemporaries; it is actually the work of Gennadius, as one tradition of MSS testifies. (See C. H. Turner, "The *Liber Ecclesiasticorum Dogmatum* Attributed to Gennadius," *Journal of Theological Studies* 7 [1906], 78–99.) It would seem that Thomas always referred to this work without author. In the *Summa contra gentiles*, *Summa theologiae*, and in all the disputed questions, Thomas cites it without author, even at the very end of *Summa theologiae* III, e.g., 79, 3; 80, 10, and ad 5. (Cf. *Indices*, ed. Leon. [Rome 1948], 16, p. 204.) Only in three passages of the printed editions are there attributions to Augustine or Gennadius: *In III Sent.*, dist. 2, a. 1, a. 3, sol. 2, where the name of Gennadius is an interpolation; the University Exemplar, Pamplona MS Cabildo 51, fol. 12va, mentions no author. The critical text of *De veritate*, q. 28, a. 2, obj. 8,

states "secundum Augustinum," but no mention of *Liber Eccl. Dogmat.* The only problem is in *Quodlibet 12,* 10, where the reply reads: "Augustinus hanc quaestionem non determinat, sed indeterminatam relinquit in lib. *De eccl. dogmat.* Sed ille liber non est Augustini, sed Gennadii" (ed. Vivès 15, 600a; ed. Marietti, p. 228b, n. 235). Obviously the phrase "But that book is not by Augustine, but by Gennadius" is a marginal gloss that has crept into the text. However, it would seem that the first part attributes the work to Augustine! Either the printed text is corrupt or *Quodlibet 12* must be dated earlier.

32. Mandonnet, "Chronologie des questions disputées," *Revue Thomiste* 23 (1918), 284–85, 342, 346, 354.

33. O. Lottin, "La date de la question disputée 'De malo,'" *Revue d'hist. eccl.* 24 (1928) 373–88.

34. Gauthier, "La date du Commentaire de saint Thomas sur l'Éthique à Nicomaque," RTAM 18 (1951), 66–105.

35. Clm. 3287, and Lisbon, Bibl. Nac. 262. Cf. Grabmann, *Die Werke,* 304–5.

36. Eschmann, "Catalogue," 390–91.

37. Tolomeo, *Hist. Eccl.,* lib. 22, c. 24.

38. Bourke, 139; "The Nicomachean Ethics and Thomas Aquinas," *Commemorative Studies* (Toronto: PIMS 1974).

39. "Saint Thomas et l'Éthique à Nicomaque," Appendix *Opera Omnia,* ed. Leon., 48 (Rome 1971), v-xxv.

40. Trevet, *Annales,* ed. cit., 289.

41. Mandonnet, *Écrits,* 31.

42. Grabmann, *Die Werke,* 93, 97–98; Gauthier, Appendix *Opera Omnia,* loc. cit., xxiv, fn. 1.

43. Gauthier, ibid., xxiv.

44. *Hist. Eccl.,* lib. 23, c. 15, 1172–73.

45. *Legenda,* c. 53. *Fontes* 217.

46. Hayen, "S. Thomas a-t-il édité deux fois son Commentaire sur le livre des Sentences?" RTAM 9 (1937), 219–36.

47. A. Dondaine, *Bulletin Thomiste* 6 (1940–41), 100–8; Grabmann, *Die Werke,* 288–89.

48. Eschmann, "Catalogue," 387.

49. Tolomeo, *Hist. Eccl.,* lib. 22, c. 39, 1162.

50. *De locis theologicis,* 12, c. 2, n. 4 (Rome 1900), III, 13.

51. "Catalogue," 387.

52. Ibid., 388.

53. Cf. J. A. Weisheipl, "The Meaning of 'Sacra Doctrina' in *Sum. theol.,* I, q. 1," *The Thomist* 38 (1974).

54. M.-D. Chenu, "La théologie comme science au XIIIᵉ siècle," AHDLMA 2 (1927), 69.

55. G. F. Van Ackeren, *Sacra Doctrina* (Rome 1952).

56. *De verit.*, q. 10, a. 12; *Sum. contra gentiles* II, cc. 10–11.

57. This argument can be simply expressed by the medieval axiom: "The work of nature is the work of intelligence." (*Opus naturae est opus intelligentiae.*) The origin of this axiom is not known, but it is deeply rooted in the teaching of Plato, Aristotle, and the Moslem philosophers; it makes sense to Platonists, Aristotelians, Jews, Moslems, and Christians alike. Cf. J. M. Ramirez, O.P., *De hominis beatitudine*, I (Madrid 1942), 240–44.

58. Grabmann, *Guglielmo*, 135–40; Eschmann, "Catalogue," 387.

59. *Acta Cap. Gen.*, I, MOPH 3, 138.

60. Walz-Novarina, 135.

61. *Proc. canoniz. Neapoli*, n. 47. *Fontes* 226.

62. Gui, *Legenda*, c. 34. *Fontes* 201. Tolomeo, *Hist. Eccl.*, lib. 22, c. 39.

63. Thomas, *In III De anima*, lect. 12, n. 785. This seems to be an implicit recognition of the non-Aristotelian authorship of *Liber de causis*, which Thomas realized after May 18, 1268, when William of Moerbeke translated the *Elementatio theologica* of Proclus at Viterbo. For Albert the Great, the *Liber de causis* is a natural complement to *Metaphysics* Lambda: "Indeed when this book [*De causis*] is joined to the 11th book [i.e., Lambda] of first philosophy, the task is completed" (*De causis* II, tr. V, c. 24). Albert argues that in Mu and Nu, Aristotle discusses the opinions of others, while in *De causis* he proposes the plain truth about separated substances. "Consequently that book must be attached to first philosophy, so as to reap its final perfection" (ibid., II, tr. I, c. 1, ed. Borgnet, 10, 434a). If Thomas, too, considered *De causis* to be Aristotle's completion of Lambda, then his discovery of the authorship of this work would make him say "the complement of that science [of metaphysics] has not yet come down to us," etc. In this case, Thomas's commentary on Aristotle's *De anima* must postdate May 1268.

64. Grabmann, *Guglielmo*, 147–48.

65. Cf. P. Thillet, *Studi Med.* (Paris 1963), 29–36.

66. Ibid., 31.

67. Grabmann, *Guglielmo*, 160–62; Thillet, op. cit., 30.

68. Thillet, ibid., 31–32.

69. Gui, *Legenda*, c. 28. *Fontes* 194.

70. Gui, *Legenda*, c. 25. *Fontes* 191.
71. Gui, *Legenda*, c. 25. *Fontes* 192; Foster, 45.
72. Bierbaum op. cit., 208–19.
73. Y. M.-J. Congar, "Aspects ecclésiologiques de la querelle entre Mendiants et Séculiers," AHDLMA 28 (1961), 46–48.
74. Walz-Novarina, 149.
75. C. H. Scheeben, "Albert der Grosse: Zur Chronologie seines Lebens," *Quellen u. Forschungen zur Geschichte des Dominikanerordens in Deutschland* 27 (1931), 90–92.
76. *Siger*, I, 88; "Lecteur," 31–38.
77. Necrology in Mandonnet, "Lecteur," 39.
78. Ibid., 29.
79. Eschmann, "Catalogue," 427; Mandonnet, "Lecteur," 30, fn. 2. Ed. Vivès, 32, 692ff.
80. Mandonnet, ibid., 31.
81. Castagnoli, "Regesta," 454–57.

Chapter VI

1. Gui, *Legenda*, c. 35. *Fontes* 201; Foster, 53.
2. Glorieux, *Répertoire*, schema insert I, 228–29.
3. Dondaine, *Secrétaires*.
4. Ibid., 203, fn. 58.
5. Tocco, *Hystoria*, c. 17. *Fontes* 89: Gui, *Legenda*, c. 32. *Fontes* 199.
6. *Proc. canoniz. Neapoli*, n. 58. *Fontes* 345.
7. Gui, *Legenda*, c. 32. *Fontes* 199; Foster, 51.
8. Gui, ibid., Foster, 51 and fn. 77.
9. Dondaine, *Secrétaires*, 204.
10. Cf. P. Marc, *Liber de veritate catholicae fidei*, Introd. I (Torino: Marietti 1967), 377.
11. Gauthier, "La date du Commentaire de saint Thomas sur l'Éthique à Nicomaque," RTAM 18 (1951), 103, fn. 91.
12. Lottin, *Psychologie et morale*, I (1942), 252–62.
13. Ramírez, *De hominis beatitudine*, III (Madrid 1947), 192.
14. Glorieux, *Répertoire*, tables between 228–29.
15. Mandonnet, *Écrits*, 31.
16. *Hist. Eccl.*, lib. 23, c. 15.
17. M. Grabmann, "Adenulf von Anagni, Propst von Saint-Omer († 1290)," *Traditio* 5 (1947), 269–83; *Die Werke*, 265–66.
18. Gui, *Legenda*, c. 16. *Fontes* 184; Foster, 38.
19. Tocco, *Hystoria*, c. 17. *Fontes* 88.

20. Glorieux, "Essai sur les commentaires scripturaires de saint Thomas et leur chronologie," RTAM 17 (1950) 254–58.
21. Eschmann, "Catalogue," 395–96.
22. See discussion in introd. to St. Thomas Aquinas, *Quaestiones de anima*, ed. James H. Robb (Toronto: PIMS 1968), 34–37.
23. Glorieux, "Les questions disputées de saint Thomas et leur suite chronologique," RTAM 4 (1932), 26–27.
24. In his commentary on the *Sentences* Thomas attributed the well-known *De spiritu et anima* (PL 40, 779–932) to Augustine, as did all of his contemporaries. The four citations of this work in the first part of the *Summa* (the only part in which quotations of this work are to be found) attributes it to no author, but uses the passive voice "it is said in the book *De spiritu et anima.*" However, in his questions *De spiritualibus creaturis*, disputed at Viterbo (1268–69) and contemporary with the first part of the *Summa*, Thomas says: "That book is not by Augustine, nor is it very authoritative" (*De spirit. creat.*, a. 3 ad 6). Thomas rejected Augustine's authorship for a second time in *De anima*, a. 9 ad 1. Finally, in that same work he says: "That book *De spiritu et anima* is not by Augustine, but is said to have been [written] by a certain Cistercian; nor should one worry much about what is contained therein" (a. 12 ad 1). The work, in fact, is by Alcher of Clairvaux, a twelfth-century Cistercian.
25. Lottin, "La date de la question disputée 'De malo'," RHE 24 (1928), 373–88. Lottin has also argued that *De malo*, qq. 6 and 16, were originally separate disputations. Question 6 on free choice is one of the best and most profound discussions of the complex question of human freedom. It seems to have been discussed in Paris during Thomas's second regency prior to *Sum. theol.* I–II, qq. 9–10. Question 16 on demons is also an extraserial disputation, discussed separately from the series *De malo*. However, the earliest manuscripts of *De malo* all contain question 6 and question 16 in their present position.
26. *Chart. U. P.*, I, 108, n. 642; and I, 646, n. 350.
27. Eschmann, "Catalogue," 391–93.
28. Mandonnet, *Siger*, I, 98–103; F. J. Roensch, *The Early Thomistic School* (Dubuque: Priory Press 1964), 10, 22, fn. 35; cf. A. Callebaut, "Jean Pecham O.F.M. et l'Augustinisme," AFH 18 (1925), 441–72; Mandonnet, *Bulletin Thomiste* 3 (1926), 104–7.
29. *Proc. canoniz. Neapoli*, n. 77. *Fontes* 374.
30. F. Ehrle, "John Peckham über den Kampf des Augustinismus

und Aristotelismus in der zweiten Hälfte des 13. Jhs.," *Zeitschrift f. kath. Theologie* 13 (1889), 184–85; C. T. Martin, *Registrum epistolarum fr. Iohannis Peckham* (London 1885), III, 900; *Chart. U. P.*, I, 634, n. 523.

31. Trevet, *Annales*, ed. cit., 299–300.

32. Letter to Olivier, Bishop of Lincoln, June 1, 1285: Ehrle, op. cit., 186; *Chart. U. P.*, I, loc. cit.

33. See also G. K. Schleyer, *Anfänge des Gallikanismus in 13. Jahrhundert: Der Widerstand des Französischen Klerus gegen die Priviligierung der Bettelordnen* (Berlin 1937); D. L. Douie, *The Conflict Between the Seculars and the Mendicants at the University of Paris in the 13th Century* (London: Blackfriars 1954).

34. For the chronology of the different works produced during the second phase of the conflict, see Glorieux, "Les Polémiques *Contra Geraldinos:* Les pièces du dossier," RTAM 6 (1934), 5–41; idem, "*Contra Geraldinos:* L'enchaînement des polémiques" RTAM 7 (1935), 129–55; Y. M.-J. Congar, "Aspects ecclésiologiques," AHDLMA 28 (1961), 35–151, esp. 46–48.

35. In the Middle Ages solemn profession was considered permanent and irrevocable, i.e., it was thought that not even the Holy See could dispense one from such vows. At the same time there were no "temporary vows," such as religious profess today in religious communities; what was called a *professio simplex* was not a vow, but a promise. In practice today, the Holy See dispenses from all vows and even from the priesthood.

36. These same points are discussed by Thomas in a more succinct manner in *Summa theologiae* II–II, qq. 183–84. This part of the *Summa* was written in the winter of 1271–72 after all the main treatises had been written. Not only the issues, but also the arguments are derived from actual controversy.

37. *Opera Omnia*, ed. Leon., 41 (Rome 1969), C 5–C 8 § 2.

38. For Thomas, the "age of reason" usually comes with puberty; it is the age of *moral discretion*, the age when the child becomes "capable of deceit" (*doli capaces*), i.e., capable of mortal sin, virtue, and vows (II–II, q. 88, a. 9; q. 189, a. 5, etc.). Thomas nowhere mentions the age of *speculative discretion*, which is necessary to receive first Communion at the canonical age of seven. Thus, while most boys reach the age of moral discretion around the age of fourteen (and the age of twelve for girls) they *can* take religious or matrimonial vows, but the positive law of the Church and religious Orders require a later age.

39. See E. Gilson, *Dante the Philosopher*, trans. D. Moore (London: Sheed & Ward 1952), esp. 257–81.

40. *Chart. U. P.*, I, 451, n. 409.

41. *Chart. U. P.*, I, 486–87, n. 432.

42. *Chart. U. P.*, I, 499–500, n. 441.

43. *Martini continuatio Brabantina*, MGH Script. 22, 263.

44. Ehrle, op. cit., 175.

45. Cf. T. Kaeppeli, *Scriptores Ordinis Praed. Medii Aevi*, I (Rome: S. Sabina 1970), 246.

46. *Chart. U. P.*, I, 543, n. 473.

47. Albert, *De quindecim problematibus*, ed. Mandonnet, *Siger*, II, 30.

48. F. Van Steenberghen, "Le 'De quindecim problematibus' d'Albert le Grand," *Mélanges Auguste Pelzer* (Louvain 1947), 415–39.

49. Albert, *De quindecim problematibus*, ed. cit., 51.

50. Mandonnet, *Écrits*, 30.

51. Grabmann, *Die Werke*, 326.

52. Cf. B. H. Zedler, Thomas Aquinas *On the Unity of the Intellect Against the Averroists*, trans. and introd. (Milwaukee: Marquette 1968), 8–9.

53. Siger, *Quaestiones de anima intellectiva*, q. 3, ed. Mandonnet, *Siger*, II, 152.

54. Ibid.

55. *Chart. U. P.*, I, 277–79, n. 246.

56. *Psychologie et morale*, I (Louvain 1942), 252–62.

57. Pelster, "Die Übersetzungen der aristotelischen Metaphysik in den Werkes des hl. Thomas v. Aquin," *Gregorianum* 17 (1936), 393.

58. Cf. D. A. Callus, "Les Sources de saint Thomas," *Aristote et Saint Thomas d'Aquin* (Journées d'étude internationales, Louvain 1957), 105–9.

59. Eschmann, "Catalogue," 401.

60. Gauthier, "La date du Commentaire de saint Thomas sur l'Éthique à Nicomaque," RTAM 18 (1950), 66–105; Appendix, *Opera Omnia*, ed. Leon. (Rome: S. Sabina 1971).

61. H.-D. Saffrey, *Sancti Thomae de Aquino Super librum de causis Expositio* (Fribourg: Textus Philosophici Friburgenses 4/5 1954), Introd., 33–36.

62. Cf. Eschmann, "Catalogue," 404.

63. I. Brady, "John Pecham and the Background to the *De aeternitate mundi* of St. Thomas Aquinas," *Comm. Studies* (Toronto: PIMS 1974).

64. Tocco, *Hystoria*, c. 26. *Fontes* 99–100. Cf. D. L. Douie, *Archbishop Pecham* (Oxford 1952), 13–46.

65. Ehrle, op. cit., 186.

66. E. Gilson, *History*, ed. cit., 350–60.

67. See letter of Pecham to the Roman curia, January 1, 1285, and letter to the bishop of Lincoln, June 1, 1285, in Ehrle, op. cit., 180–86.

68. Letter of Pecham to the chancellor and masters of Oxford, December 7, 1284, in Ehrle, op. cit., 178.

° 69. See D. A. Callus, "The Origins of the Problem of the Unicity of Form," *The Thomist* 24 (1961), 120–49; *The Condemnation of St. Thomas at Oxford* (Oxford: Aquinas Soc. of London, n. 5, 1946).

° 70. See J. A. Weisheipl, "The *Problemata Determinata XLIII* ascribed to Albertus Magnus (1271)," *Mediaeval Studies* 22 (1960), 303–54; for the background to these questions, see J. Destrez, "La Lettre de saint Thomas d'Aquin dite Lettre au Lecteur de Venise d'après la tradition manuscrite," *Mélanges Mandonnet* (Paris 1930), I, 117–26.

71. I have compared the responses concerning the first five queries in "The Celestial Movers in Medieval Physics," *The Thomist* 24 (1961), 286–326.

72. See Glorieux, *Répertoire*, I, 129, n. 28.

Chapter VII

1. Mandonnet, *Siger*, I, 196–213.

2. *Chart. U. P.*, I, 502–3, n. 445; see ibid., I, 138, n. 79.

3. Glorieux, *Répertoire*, I, 129, n. 28.

4. See O. Lottin, "St. Thomas à la faculté des arts de Paris aux approches de 1277," RTAM 16 (1949), 292–313. Gauthier, "Trois commentaires 'averroïstes' sur l'Éthique à Nicomaque," AHDLMA 16 (1947–48), 187–336; W. Dunphy, "The *Quinque Viae* and Some Parisian Professors of Philosophy," *Comm. Studies* (Toronto: PIMS 1974).

5. Walz, 139–40.

6. Walz, 140.

7. MOPH 20, 39.

8. *Chart. U. P.*, I, 501–2, n. 443.

9. MOPH 3, 325.
10. Walz, 142.
11. *Proc. canoniz. Neapoli,* n. 60. *Fontes* 247–48.
12. Tolomeo, *Hist. Eccl.,* lib. 23, c. 10; Foster, 135–36.
13. Walz, 143.
14. Walz, 146–47.
15. Doc. 25. *Fontes* 575.
16. Doc. 26. *Fontes* 576–78.
17. Walz, 154.
18. Doc. 27. *Fontes* 578–79.
19. Doc. 28. *Fontes* 579–80.
20. Walz, 146.
21. See explicit in J. Destrez, *Études critiques sur les oeuvres,* I, 162; Bourke, 187.
22. Dondaine, *Secrétaires,* 202.
23. *Proc. canoniz. Neapoli,* n. 77. *Fontes* 373.
24. Tocco, *Hystoria,* c. 29. Fontes 103. This incident is also recorded by Bernard Gui, *Legenda,* c. 26 (*Fontes* 192–93) and by Peter Calo, *Vita,* c. 16 (*Fontes* 35–36), who both undoubtedly depend upon Tocco for their source.
25. Tocco, *Hystoria,* c. 43. *Fontes* 117. Gui, *Legenda,* c. 25. *Fontes* 192. Tocco gives as his source Friar Raymond Etienne, a Dominican from the Province of Toulouse and later archbishop of Ephesus, who heard it from Marino of Eboli, archbishop of Capua.
26. Bernard Gui gratuitously and erroneously added that the work on which Thomas was then engaged was the *Summa contra gentiles.* Tocco, *Hystoria,* c. 43. *Fontes* 117: Gui, *Legenda,* c. 25. *Fontes* 192. Foster, 45, cf. 73, fn. 60.
27. *Proc. canoniz. Neapoli,* n. 43. *Fontes* 320. Tocco *Hystoria,* c. 43. *Fontes* 117.
28. Gui, *Legenda,* c. 53. *Fontes* 219.
29. P. Batiffol, *History of the Roman Breviary,* trans. A. M. Y. Baylay (London: Longmans 1912), 77.
30. See W. R. Bonniwell, *A History of the Dominican Liturgy* (New York: Wagner 1944), 130–45, esp. 136.
31. Batiffol, op. cit., 157–64.
32. Quoted by Glorieux, "Essai sur les commentaires scripturaires," RTAM 17 (1950), 250.
33. Cf. *Sum. theol.,* Ottawa ed., III, q. 2, a. 6, fn. b 20.
34. Tocco, *Hystoria,* c. 34. *Fontes* 108.
35. Doc. 31. *Fontes* 585; Foster, 154.

36. Callus, "Les Sources," 130–31.

37. Eschmann, "Catalogue," 402.

38. *Proc. canoniz. Neapoli,* n. 58. *Fontes* 345.

39. A. Dondaine and L. J. Bataillon, "Le Commentaire de saint Thomas sur les Météores," AFP 36 (1966), 81–152.

40. Ibid., 127–33.

41. Grabmann, *Die Werke,* 315; Eschmann, "Catalogue," 411–12.

42. *Opera Omnia,* ed. Leon., 40 (Rome 1968), D 7, § 3.

43. *Proc. canoniz. Neapoli,* n. 87 (*Fontes* 391); n. 70 (*Fontes* 362); n. 93 (*Fontes* 399); n. 88 (*Fontes* 393).

44. Tocco, *Hystoria,* c. 48. *Fontes* 122.

45. *Proc canoniz. Neapoli,* n. 89. *Fontes* 393–94.

46. *Proc. canoniz. Neapoli,* n. 77. *Fontes* 372–73.

47. *Proc. canoniz. Neapoli,* n. 77. *Fontes* 373–74.

48. Ibid.

49. Bartholomew of Capua, *Proc. canoniz. Neapoli,* n. 29. *Fontes* 377. Tocco, *Hystoria,* c. 47. *Fontes* 120. Gui, *Legenda,* c. 27. *Fontes* 193–94. Calo, *Vita,* c. 24. *Fontes* 43–44.

50. *Proc. canoniz. Neapoli,* n. 79. *Fontes* 377. Cf. Foster, 124, fn. 73–74

51. See Edmund Colledge, "The Legend of St. Thomas Aquinas," *Comm. Studies* (Toronto: PIMS 1974).

52. *Proc. canoniz. Neapoli,* n. 87. *Fontes* 391–92.

53. Gui, *Legenda,* cc. 36–37. *Fontes* 202. Foster, 53–54.

54. *Proc. canoniz. Neapoli,* n. 78. *Fontes* 375.

55. See Walz, 161–62; Bourke, 209.

56. The definitive edition of this letter has been published by A. Dondaine, "La lettre de saint Thomas à l'ábbe du Montecassin," *Comm. Studies* (Toronto: PIMS 1974).

57. *Proc. canoniz. Neapoli,* n. 50. *Fontes* 334.

58. *Proc. canoniz. Neapoli,* n. 8. *Fontes* 277.

59. *Proc. canoniz. Neapoli,* n. 49. *Fontes* 332.

60. Tocco, *Hystoria,* c. 57. *Fontes* 131.

61. See Grabmann, *Die Werke,* 354–57; Eschmann, "Catalogue," 395; Glorieux, "Essai sur les commentaires scripturaires," 249.

62. *Proc. canoniz. Neapoli,* n. 51. *Fontes* 335–36.

63. Ibid.

64. Tocco, *Hystoria,* c. 65. *Fontes* 138.

65. Gui, *Legenda,* c. 39. *Fontes* 205. The assertion that the date was March 9 would seem to be a scribal error rather than a personal one.

66. Doc. 56. *Fontes* 670–71.

67. Cf. note by Laurent in *Proc. canoniz. Neapoli, Fontes* 335, fn. (a).

68. C. D. Boulogne, *Saint Thomas D'Aquin: Essai Biographique* (Paris 1968), 193.

69. Gui, *Legenda*, c. 41. *Fontes* 206.

70. Gui, *Legenda*, c. 40. *Fontes* 206. Tocco, *Hystoria*, c. 62. *Fontes* 135. Calo, *Vita*, c. 31. *Fontes* 50.

71. *Proc. canoniz. Neapoli*, n. 8. *Fontes* 278.

72. *Proc. canoniz. Neapoli*, n. 80. *Fontes* 380.

73. Foster, 80–81.

74. *Proc. canoniz. Neapoli*, n. 65. *Fontes* 354–55. See Foster, 81; Bourke, 215–16.

75. C. Douais, *Les reliques de saint Thomas d'Aquin* (Paris 1903), 84. Cf. Mandonnet, "Canonization," 17–18, fn. 2.

76. *Historia translationum, ActaSS*, March, I, 723–31.

77. English translation in Foster, 153–55.

78. Foster, 157, fn. 9.

79. *Chart. U. P.*, I, 644, n. 530.

80. *Chart. U. P.*, I, 541, n. 471.

81. Gilson, *History*, 504.

82. *Chart. U. P.*, I, 543–55, n. 473.

83. Mandonnet, *Siger*, II, 175–91.

84. A. A. Maurer, "Boethius of Dacia and the Double Truth," *Mediaeval Studies* 17 (1955), 233–39.

85. A. Callebaut, "Jean Pecham, O.F.M. et l'Augustinisme," AFH 18 (1925), 441–72; text ed., 459–60.

86. Gilson, *History*, 728, fn. 52.

87. *Chart. U. P.*, I, 558–59, n. 474; See D. A. Callus, *The Condemnation of St. Thomas at Oxford* (Oxford: Aquinas Papers, n. 5, 1946).

88. See the comprehensive work of Frederick J. Roensch. *The Unicity of Substantial Form and Its Implications in the Early Thomistic School* (Dubuque: Priory Press 1964).

89. F. Ehrle, "Der Augustinismus und der Aristotelismus in der Scholastik gegen Ende des 13. Jahrhunderts," *Archiv f. Litt.-u. Kirchengeschichte des Mittelalters* 5 (1889), 614–32; A. Birkenmajer, "Der Brief Robert Kilwardbys an Petrus von Conflans," *Vermischte Untersuchungen zur Gesch. d. M-A. Phil.*, BGPMA 20 (1922), 36–69; cf. Laurent Doc. 39 (*Fontes* 617, fn. 1).

90. Callus, "Condemnation," 13.

91. Ehrle, "Der Augustinismus," 614.

92. Roensch, op. cit., 174–77.

93. "Definitiones capituali generalis Argentinae," AFH 26 (1933), 139.
94. A. B. Emden, *Biographical Register of the Univ. of Oxford*, II, 1058; D. L. Douie, *Archbishop Pecham* (Oxford 1952), 280–301; Roensch, op. cit., 34–40.
95. *Correctorium "Quare,"* ed. P. Glorieux (Paris: Bibl. Thom. 11, 1927), 206.
96. Roensch, op. cit., 38; see fn. 103.
97. Ibid., 67, fn. 104.
98. MOPH 3, 199
99. MOPH 3, 204.
100. Glorieux, *Répertoire* I, 214–20, n. 70.
101. MOPH 4, 38.
102. MOPH 4, 64–65.
103. MOPH 4, 81.
104. See *Proc. canoniz. Neapoli*, n. 79. *Fontes* 376–78.
105. Walz, "Historia Canonizationis S. Thomae de Aquino," *Xenia Thomistica* III, 121. But nothing was done officially until 1317.
106. Mandonnet, "La canonization," *Mélanges Thomistes* (Kain: Le Saulchoir 1923), 1–48.
107. Mandonnet, ibid. 19–20.
108. Foster, 7.
109. *Proc. canoniz. Neapoli*, n. 3. *Fontes* 269–71.
110. *Proc. canoniz. Neapoli*, n. 1. *Fontes* 267, Foster, 82.
111. Mandonnet, "La canonisation," 31.
112. See text and study by C. Jellouschek, *Xenia Thomistica* III, 73–104.
113. See Tocco, *Hystoria*, c. 53; Gui, *Legenda*, c. 29; Calo, *Vita*, c. 24; *Proc. canoniz. Neapoli*, n. 75.
114. J. Gerson, *Opera* (Antwerp 1706), II, 712, quoted by Mandonnet, "La canonisation," 39.
115. MOPH 3, 123.
116. In the two extant documents there is a discrepancy as to when the papal ceremonies began, whether on July 14 or July 16. The anonymous chronicler states without hesitation or uncertainty that the series of sermons began on "Thursday before the feast of St. Alexius, which was the second Ides of July," i.e., on Thursday, July 14. In the account of Friar Bentius, the ceremonies began "on the day preceding the feast of St. Alexius," i.e., on Saturday, the sixteenth of July, since the feast of St. Alexius was celebrated in the Middle Ages on July 17 (see *De canonizatione, Fontes* 513). There is no possible way of determining the exact date with the information we have at present. However, there are a

number of instances in the Middle Ages when preliminary matters were attended to on a Saturday, while the real task began on the following Monday, e.g., the canonization process at Naples, discussed above. Furthermore, if the anonymous chronicler is right, then nothing was scheduled for July 15–16, which seems most unlikely.

117. *Fontes* 516.
118. *Fontes* 519–30.
119. *Fontes* 518.
120. *Chart. U. P.*, II, 280–81, n. 838; *Fontes* 666–69.

References are to page number and line. *Corrigenda* and *addenda* to notes are found under the page on which the note is cited.

3.16-23   We know with certainty that Thomas died on the morning of March 7, the nones of March, 1274. The principal source for this date is Friar William of Tocco, the official promoter of the cause of Thomas's canonization appointed in 1317 by the Provincial Chapter of the Sicilian Province of Dominicans; he explicitly states that "he died in the year 1274, in the fourth year of Pope Gregory X, in the forty-ninth year of his life, during the second [imperial] indiction, on the seventh day of March in the morning." Taken literally, this means that Thomas was only forty-eight years old, and therefore born in 1226. Bernard Gui, however, the Dominican Procurator General at the papal curia in Avignon who wrote a few years later, expanded or perhaps corrected William when he said that Thomas died "at the end of the forty-ninth and beginning of the fiftieth year of his life."[1] This would make Thomas forty-nine years old and almost fifty when he died, thus placing the date of his birth early in 1225 or late in 1224. The papal historian and bishop Tolomeo of Lucca (c. 1236–1327), writing around the same time, hesitated between the two statements when he noted that Thomas "died in the fiftieth year of his life, while others say forty-eight."[2] The usual date given for his birth is 1224/25.

10.9   *eliminate:* or 1231

15.25/413 fn.52.   *add:* See biographical item on Michael Scot
             by L. Minio-Paluello, *Dictionary of Scientific Bio-*
             graphy (New York 1974), 9:361a–365b, and C. H.
             Haskins, *Studies in the History of Mediaeval*
             Science (Cambridge: Harvard 1924), esp. chap.
             12–13.

22.20/414 fn.78   *add:* For Alexander Stavensby, see A. B.
             Emden, A *Biographical Register of the University*
             of Oxford (OUP 1959), 3:2217b.

24.12/414 fn.85.   *add:* ed. A. H. Thomas, *De oudste Constitu-*
             ties van de Dominicanen (Louvain 1965), p. 358
             lines 2–3.

25.19   *contemplare: contemplari*

27.32   For Friar Thomas Agni da Lentini (d. 1277) see
             Quétif-Echard, *Scriptores O.P.*, 1:358a–360b.

29.16   *feroci: feroces*

39.5   For the relationship between Thomas and Albert,
             see J.A. Weisheipl, *Thomas d'Aquino and Albert*
             His Teacher, Gilson Lecture 2 (Toronto: PIMS
             1980).

39.27/416 fn.126.   *add:* See my "Life and Works of St. Albert
             the Great," *Albertus Magnus and the Sciences*, ed.
             J.A. Weisheipl (Toronto: PIMS 1980), esp. pp.
             15–19. In that study I suggest that Albert was
             sent to Paris in 1241 shortly after John of Wildes-
             hausen was elected Master General of the Order at
             Paris on May 20, 1241.

40.29   Guéric: Guérric

42–44   On Albert's Aristotelianism, see J.A. Weisheipl,
             "Albert's Disclaimers in the Aristotelian Para-
             phrases," *Proceedings of the Patristic, Mediaeval*
             and Renaissance Conference (Villanova), 5
             (1980) forthcoming.

42.38   them: him

43.30   See for example St. Albert, *In II Sent.* dist.13,a.2

ad 5: "Unde sciendum quod Augustino in his quae sunt de fide et moribus plusquam philosophis credendum est, si dissentiunt. Sed si de medicina loqueretur, plus ego crederem Galeno, vel Hippocrati; et si de naturis rerum loquatur, credo Aristoteli plus vel alii experto in rerum naturis." (Borgnet 27:247a)

44.7/416 fn.136. *add*: See Jean-Daniel Cavigioli, "Les écrits d'Heymericus de Campo sur les oeuvres d'Aristote," *Freiburger Zeitschrift für Philosophie und Theologie*, 28 (1981), 293–371.

45.16–39 Clearly Thomas's *Super Isaiam* is a work of a *cursor biblicus* apparently done at Cologne under Albert; see my review of the Leonine text of *Opera Omnia*, 28, for *The Thomist*, 43 (1979), 331–37.

47.21 Albert's text of *De unitate intellectus* is published in the Cologne edition of his works, 17/1 (Münster 1975), 1–30. See the statement of Albert concerning this in the *Summa theologiae* ascribed to him: "Haec omnia aliquando collegi in curia existens ad praeceptum domini Alexandri papae [1254–61], et factus fuit inde libellus, quem multi habent, et intitulatus est 'contra errores Averrois'. Et hic etiam posita sunt, ut perfectior sit scientia Summae theologiae." (ed. Borgnet 33:100b).

60.30 Blévex: Bléneau

64.11 Sainte-Germain: Saint-Germain

67.13–14 bequest: intercession

64.34 forty: fifty || thirty: ten

66.6 Guéric of Saint-Quentin 1233–42: Quérric of Saint-Quentin 1233–45

74.15/421 fn.77. *add:* Here we are assuming the authenticity of the *Summa theologiae* (also known as *Summa de mirabili scientia dei*) often ascribed to Albert. But see A. Hufnagel, "Zur Echtheitsfrage der Summa theologiae Alberts des Grossen," *Theol.*

Quartalschrift (Tübingen), 146 (1966), 8–39, and attempts of Siedler and Simon to authenticate it, *Opera Omnia* (ed. Colon. 34/1, 1978), Prol. § 1, v–xv.

79.34–35   shortly before: between 1252 and

80.3/422 fn.94.   See also M.-M. Dufeil, *Guillaume de Saint-Amour et la Polémique Universitaire Parisienne, 1250–1259* (Paris: Picard 1972).

81.14/423 fn.100   1931/1: 1930/1

81.33   Saint-Armour: Saint-Amour

84.29/423 fn.109.   *insert after line 1:* "Das Evangelium aeternum und die Commission zu Anagni,"

91.26–39   *substitute:*
This is confirmed by the statement of Tolomeo of Lucca who states that *Contra impugnantes* was written "against William of Saint-Amour *infra autem magisterium,*" that is, after he had become a master.[133] Since most scholars agree today that *Contra impugnantes* was written in the period of September–October (or November) 1256, and since, as we have suggested, Thomas received the *licentia docendi* and incepted in theology sometime in April 1256, it was indeed written when Thomas was already a master.

121.1–6   *comment:* Considering the preface of the Leonine editors of Thomas's commentary *Super Isaiam* (Leon. ed. v.28), it is now certain that the whole of this work was produced by Thomas as a *cursor biblicus* at Cologne; see my review of this volume in *The Thomist,* 43 (1979), 331–337.

121–123   It now seems likely that the *Super Matthaeum* of Thomas was not written or delivered at Paris during his first regency, since it seems to show traces of his own work on the *Catena aurea,* written at Orvieto, and the text of Aristotle's *Politics.* Moreover if the story of Thomas and the students overlooking the city of Paris is true,

Thomas might have hoped for a complete copy (*perfectum*) of pseudo-Chrysostom's *Opus imperfectum;* both this and Chrysostom's authentic homilies were at St-Jacques at the time of Hugh of Saint-Cher, who used them extensively.

126.39/427 fn.75. *add:* On the nature of Quodlibet disputations in theology at Paris in the thirteenth century, see John F. Wippel, "The Quodlibetal Question as a distinctive literary genre," *Les genres littéraires dans les sources théologiques et philosophiques médiévales* (Louvain-la Neuve 1982). It would seem that these disputations were also in two parts: the *disputatio* proper and the *determinatio* on a subsequent day. See also L.E. Boyle, "The Quodlibets of St. Thomas and Pastoral Care," *The Thomist*, 38 (1974), 232–256; repr. in *Patoral Care, Clerical Education and Canon Law, 1200–1400* (London: Variorum Reprints 1981), II.

127.5   "de quodlibet" : "de quolibet"

128.6–10   Note that the earlier list, which Denifle puts around 1286, since it carries no date (Chart. U.P., I, 644–49, n.530), contains all the major *quaestiones disputatae*, but only 14 *pecias* of Quodlibets. Destrez, dating this list between 1275–80, argued that these quodlibets refer to only the second series (Quodl.1–6) and not the first.

130.12   James II : James I

134.17–18   *substitute:* lines of chapter 2; it consists of a scholastic analysis of the Prooemium, chapter 1, and the opening lines of chapter 2 together with six

137.4/429 fn.95. *add:* Since *In Boeth. De trin.* must have been written after Book I of the *Sentences* (1252) and before Annibaldo's own commentary (before 1260), it might have been written anytime between 1253–58.

137.5–16   *delete*

143.23	twenty-five : fifteen
144.8	Viterbo : Orvieto
144.9–10	*delete* : (omitting . . . live)
144.12	Viterbo : Paris for the second time.
151.35	were : might have been
154.11	Viterbo : possibly Viterbo
166.18	Theodokos : Theotokos
166.21	Christodokos : Christotokos
172.34	Matthaeum" : *add:* (meaning the *opus imperfectum* of pseudo-Chrysostom)
179.8	1952 : 1252
181.15	*Sacris solemnis* : *Sacris solemniis*
182.24–25	the dying Christ of Calvary : the Christ who died (*Christus passus*) on Calvary
184.33	died : resigned

189.26/434 fn.7.   *add:* See L.P. Fitzgerald, "St. Thomas Aquinas and the Two Powers," *Angelicum*, 56 (1979), 515–556; Leonard E. Boyle, "The *De Regno* and the Two Powers," *Essays in Honour of Anton Charles Pegis*, ed. J.R. O'Donnell (Toronto : PIMS 1974), 237–247; Jeremy Catto, "Ideas and Experience in the Political Thought of Aquinas," *Past and Present*, 71 (May 1976), pp.3–21.

195.15/435 fn.23.   *add:* Leonard E. Boyle has suggested that the studium established at Santa Sabina would better be called a "studium personale." See "The Setting of the *Summa theologiae* of Saint Thomas", Gilson Lecture 5 (Toronto: PIMS 1982), pp.9–10.

195.31	studium only for : studium at least for
203.14–16	*delete:* The truth of the matter . . . teaching. *Comment:* On this see J.A. Weisheipl, "The Date and Context of Thomas's *De aeternitate mundi*," *Graceful Reason*: Essays in Honour of Joseph Owens, ed. Lloyd Gerson (Toronto: PIMS 1983) forthcoming.

205.14–33   *Note:* This is the position of the Mutakallimūn presented and refuted by Moses Maimonides, *Guide of the Perplexed,* I, 71–76, and frequently taken up by St. Thomas, see *Sum. contra gent.,* III, c.69, and parallel places

209.29   ovum: add: (literally "female blood")

210.13–14   the will, however . . . chooses it : the will, however, freely chooses the particular end known by the intellect.

210.30   perfection : actualization

212.26   in Viterbo : before going to Paris

212.32   1267 or more probably : 1266 or more probably

213.31   probably : possibly

216.218   *comment:* On all of this see H.-F. Dondaine, "Alia Lectura Fratris Thome? (Super I Sent.)," *Mediaeval Studies,* 42 (1980), 308–336; and esp. Leonard E. Boyle, " 'Alia Lectura Fratris Thome'," *Mediaeval Studies,* 45 (1983), 418–428; see also the older study by B. Lamaigre, "Perfection de Dieu et multiplicité des attributs divins," *Revue de Sciences phil. et théol.,* 50 (1966), 198–236.

217.5   someone took it away : I was transferred. *Note:* See the critical text of Tolomeo in A. Dondaine, "Les 'Opuscula fratris Thomae' chez Potémee de Lucques," *Archivum Fratrum Praedicatorum,* 31 (1961), 142–203 at 155: "sed inde subtractus nusquam ulterius vidi." Bernard Gui, however, clearly read *subtractum* and thought the book was stolen.

221.2   *between lines 2 and 3 read:*
           1) For all Christians:

221.2   *between lines 11 and 12 read:*
           2) For particular Christians:
              A. as to graces freely given *(gratiae gratis datae):*
                 1. for knowledge, viz. prophecy, rapture (qq.171–175)

      2. for speech, viz. gift of tongues (qq.176–177)

      3. for miracles (qq.178)

    B. as to forms of life, viz. contemplative, active, or mixed (qq.179–182)

    C. as to states of life, viz. for all, bishops, religious (qq.183–189).

221.34   Viterbo : Italy

225.18–22   *substitute:*

It is the very nature of sacred doctrine to possess arguments, metaphorical language, and many senses. Hence sacred doctrine is not to be identified with the habit of faith, the habit of constructed theology, the written word of Scripture, or with preaching.

226.11–19   *substitute:*

In analyzing the first query, Thomas explains that there are two kinds of self-evident truths: (i) those that are self-evident "in themselves *(in se)*, but not to us *(non quoad nos)*," and (ii) those that are self evident both "in themselves *(in se)* and to us *(quoad nos)*." That a proposition be self-evident in itself and to us, we must perceive the predicate as belonging necessarily and immediately to the subject. We do perceive such a belonging in all definitions (known to us), all first principles of human reason once we know the meaning of the terms (as "the whole is greater than any part," or "two and three are five"), and sense perception of what *de facto* exists *(per se nota sensibus)*. But there are other propositions in which the predicate may in truth belong to the subject, such as "God exists," but this is not self-evident to us *(quoad nos)*. If we were to see God "face to face" (1 Cor 13:12) as we see this printed page, then it would be self-evident to us that His existence is identical with His nature. That is, it would be immediately evident to us that He exists necessarily. Until that blessed day, however, His existence is not self-evident to us, and therefore it must be demonstrated.

226.38 existence.: *add:* Invariably Thomas discussed the argument only in the context of whether His existence is self-evident *(an sit per se nota).*

229.36/437 fn.57. *add:* See J.A. Weisheipl, "The Axiom 'Opus naturae est opus intelligentiae' and its Origins," *Albertus Magnus-Doctor Universalis 1280/1980,* ed. G. Meyer & A. Zimmerman (Walberberger Studien, 6), Mainz: Grünewald 1980, 441–463.

230.21 Orvieto : Viterbo, if indeed he was so assigned.

230.25 was written : might have been written

230-239 *comment:* On this whole matter of whether Thomas was in fact assigned to Viterbo, 1267–68, see René A. Gauthier, "Quelques questions à propos du commentaire de S. Thomas sur le *De anima,*" *Angelicum,* 51 (1974), 419–472. There is no clear proof that Thomas was so assigned. Even Mandonnet did no more than infer this from the legislation of the general chapter of Bologna in 1267 that "the prior provincial of the Roman province should diligently see to it that the priory, where the [papal] curia happens to be *(fuerit),* has suitable friars for the needs of the curia, especially the prior and the lector." Gauthier's case is entirely hypothetical: if Thomas had been assigned to Viterbo and known William of Moerbeke personally, he *would have had* a better Latin text of *De anima* than he had to comment upon. But we do not know when Moerbeke made his translation or revision, and we are not yet certain when Thomas wrote his commentary, even assuming that his exposition of Book I of *De anima* is consecutive with Books II–III—that is the point to be demonstrated. We are certain that William completed his translation of Themistius's commentary on the *De anima* of Aristotle at Viterbo on November 11, 1267; see colophon in edition of Themistius by G. Verbeke (Louvain, 1957), lviii. Thomas, however, did not always wait for Moerbeke's revisions, nor did he always prefer them slavishly, as seems clear from his *Senentia super Metaphysicam*.

231.5   five : four

235.13/437 fn.65. *substitute:* Alexandre d'Aphrodise, *De Fato ad Imperatores: version de Guillaume de Moerbeke,* éd.crit. avec introd. par Pierre Thillet (Paris: Vrin 1963), 29–36; see also the latest and most accurate listing of translations by L. Minio-Paluello, entry "Moerbeke, William of," *Dictionary of Scientific Biography* (New York 1974), 9:434–440.

235.21   translaton: translation

235.22/437 fn.66 *add:* R.A. Gauthier, art.cit. *Angelicum,* 51 (1974), 419–472.

    " fn.67. *add:* M. Clagett, *Archimedes in the Middle Ages.* II: *The translations from the Greek by William of Moerbeke* (Philadelphia: Am. Philos. Soc. 1976). These works of Archimedes were translated continuously from February to December 10, 1269; see ibid. p.6. Although it is commonly thought that MS Ottob. lat. 1850 in the Vatican Library is Moerbeke's autograph copy (ibid. pp.3, 28–53), this is not altogether certain.

237.23   presumptions : presumptious

247.2   *add note:* See AAS, 50 (1958), 150–153; also *Divino afflante Spiritu* (Sept.30, 1943), AAS, 35 (1943), 297–325, trans. in *The Catholic Mind,* 42 (1944), 257–283; see also James A. Weisheipl, "An Introduction to the Commentary on the Gospel of Saint John," St. Thomas Aquinas, *Commentary on the Gospel of St. John,* Part I (Albany, N.Y.: Magi Books, 1980), 3–19.

254.24/439 fn.25.   *delete:* "Lottin has also agreed . . . present position." *as duplication from body of the book*

255.3   *delete:* (Viterbo)

256.28 ff.   On the nature of the *secunda pars* see Leonard E. Boyle, O.P., "The Setting of the *Summa theologiae* of Saint Thomas" (Gilson Series, 5) 7 March 1982 (Toronto: PIMS 1982.

261.8   *Note subdivisions given in addendum above for p.221.*

262.7   authority: status

262.11   *delete line:* fection . . . implications of

266.19   *delete:* the young

269.28   *Latria* is the technical theological term designating an act of worship (religion) directed solely to God, i.e. an act of "adoration". It is distinct from the more general act of piety (*pietas*), which when directed to one of the saints, is technically called *dulia* or "veneration."

272.36 ff.   *comment:* For the most recent life of Siger of Brabant, see Fernand Van Steenberghen, *Maître Siger de Brabant* (Louvain: Philosophes médiévaux, 21, 1977)

273.27/441 fn.41.   *add:* Van Steenberghen, ibid. pp. 71–79.

285.14   steam: stream

286.17 ff.   *comment:* On the whole question of Thomas's *De aeternitate mundi*, see my reconsideration, "The Date and Context of Thomas's *De aeternitate mundi,*" *Graceful Reason,* Essays Presented to Joseph Owens, ed. Lloyd Gerson (Toronto: PIMS 1983). Briefly, my point is that this work was directed not so much against any one master or any particular work, but against a common view of the *communitas Parisiensis*, and that it should be dated in the spring of 1271, after Thomas commented on Book VIII of Aristotle's *Physics*.

287.30–32   *substitute:*
           But to this day no one has been able to identify

the point of the argument or the actual incident involving Thomas's intervention on behalf of the Fourth Lateran Council (1215).

290.9/442 fn.69. *add:* J.A. Weisheipl, "Albertus Magnus and Universal Hylomorphism: Avicebron," *Albert the Great;* Commemorative Essays, ed. F.J. Kovach and R.W. Shahan (Norman: Univ. of Oklahoma 1980), 239–260.

290.31/ " fn.70. For Kilwardby's replies to the same questionnaire see H.-F. Dondaine, "Le 'De 43 Questionibus' de Robert Kilwardby," AFP 47 (1977), 5–50.

296.35/443 fn.11. *add:* By that date (1272) Tolomeo of Lucca was around thirty-six years old. See A. Dondaine, "Les 'Opuscula fratris Thomae' chez Ptolémee de Lucques," AFP 31 (1961), 142–203, esp. 157–169.

296.39–297.1 *delete sentence* "On arriving . . . June 1, 1272."

297.33 This letter of Thomas addressed to Bernard Ayglier, abbot of Monte Cassino, is usually dated during Lent of 1273; see Antoine Dondaine, "La lettre de saint Thomas a l'abbé du Montcassin," *Thomas Aquinas 1274–1974: Commemorative Studies* (Toronto: PIMS 1974), 1:87–108.

303.17 noctural: nocturnal

314.18–20 It would seem that Robert Grosseteste, the first teacher of the Oxford Franciscans (1229/30–1235), was the first to argue that God would have become man even if Adam had not sinned; see James McEvoy, *The Philosophy of Robert Grosseteste* (Oxford: Clarendon 1982).

315.16 the dying Christ: the Christ who died (*Christus passus*) on Calvary

315.20 the dying Christ: the Christ who died

315.21 dying: dead

315.34 See Dom Anscar Vonier, *A Key to the Doctrine of the Eucharist* (Westminister: Newman 1948); this is the best presentation in English of Thomas's teaching on the Eucharist as both sacrament and sacrifice.

317.1/444 fn.37.   add: For a contrary view see J.A. Weisheipl, "The Commentary of St. Thomas on the *De caelo* of Aristotle," *Sapientia* (Buenos Aires), 29 (1974), 11–34.

317.5   For Sutton's continuation see *De generatione et corruptione continuatio per Thomam de Sutona,* ed. Francis E. Kelley (München: Bayerische Akademie der Wissenschaften, Bd 6, 1976).

317.32 ff.   On the difficulties of dating the *Compendium theologiae* see preface, *Opera Omnia,* ed. Leon. 42, p. 8.

444 fn.42.   add: J.A. Weisheipl, "Thomas's Evaluation of Plato and Aristotle," *The New Scholasticism* 48 (1974), 100–124.

319.8   on two: on the two

319.13   it: they

328.1   *delete:* using an independent source

" .3   ninth (?): Nones

331.28–30   However . . . for safekeeping: On October 21, 1974, the relics of St. Thomas were transferred from St. Sernin to the restored church of the Jacobins during the festivities in Toulouse commemorating the seventh centenary of the death of St. Thomas.

334.12/445 fn.82.   add: For the background of the Parisian condemnation of 1277 see John F. Wippel, "The Condemnations of 1270 and 1277 at Paris," *Journal of Medieval and Renaissance Studies* 7 (1977), 169–201; idem, *The Metaphysical Thought of Godfrey of Fontaines* (Washington: Catholic University 1981), *passim;* L. Hödl, "Neue Nachrichten über die Pariser Verurteilung der thomasischen Formlehre," *Scholastik* 39 (1964), 178–196; for an examination of the condemned articles see Roland Hissette, *Enquête sur les 219 articles condamnés à Paris le 7 Mars 1277* (Louvain 1977).

336.19 (n.124.2)   this diversity originates: this diversity cannot originate

337.14   Some light is shed by John Wippel on why this typically Thomistic thesis is strangely missing, op.cit. Godfrey 318–19, and notes.

338.19/445 fn.89.   *add:* Franz Ehrle, *Gesammelte Aufsätze zur Englischen Scholastik*, ed. F. Pelster (Rome: Storia e Letteratura 1970).

340.3   For the original context of this distinction see Gedeon Gál, "Petrus de Trabibus on the Abosolute and Ordained Power of God," *Studies Honoring Ignatius Charles Brady, Friar Minor,* ed. R.S. Almagno and C.L. Harkins (St. Bonaventure: Franciscan Inst. 1976), 283–292.

340.36   "Quaestione.": *add:* Behind these Oxford Dominicans stood the towering figure of Thomas Sutton (Anglicus), who was the most original thinker among the English Dominicans of his day. At Paris Jean Quidort wrote his *Correctorium "Circa"* around 1282–84; see edition by J.P. Muller, *Studia Anselmiana* 12–13 (Rome 1941); Thomas Kaeppeli, *Scriptores Ord. Praed. Medii Aevi* (Rome 1975), 3:517–524.

343.24   Puy; Le Puy ‖ *insert:* finally as bishop of Meaux

Summary Chronology: *delete* assignment to Viterbo, summer 1267, and Viterbo as point of departure for Paris, Nov. 1268.

A BRIEF CATALOGUE

358.9   Rome (1265–67): Rome (1265–68)

358.10   *delete:* Viterbo (1267–68)

359.7   (1266–68): (1265–68)

359.10   someone took it away: I was transferred elsewhere

359.10–12   It is . . . lost. However: This "second version" is to be found in whole or in part in the margin of Oxford, Lincoln College MS 95; see L.E. Boyle,

" 'Alia Lectura Fratris Thome'," *Mediaeval Studies,* 45 (1983), 418–28.

360.35	*add:* rept. Notre Dame University Press 1975.
360.37 (= last).	*delete:* Viterbo
361.6	(1265–67): (1265–68)
361.11	*delete:* at Viterbo
361.17	in Viterbo: in Italy
361.19	*delete:* before leaving Viterbo.
361.21	at Viterbo: in Italy
361.38 (= last).	60: 90
362.27	(in progress): –1973.
364.15	No English translation: English trans.: *Disputed Questions on Evil,* trans. John and Jean Oesterle (South Bend: Notre Dame Univ. Press 1983).
364.25	*add:* if indeed Thomas resided there before going to Paris for his second regency.
367.1	*delete:* unpublished
367.2	*add:* Edited on basis of three MSS, Leonard A. Kennedy, "A New Disputed Question of St. Thomas Aquinas on the Immortality of the Soul," AHDLMA 45 (1978), 205–223.
367.4	*after 480 insert:* fol.193r–195r.
367.5	*add:* ed. L.A. Kennedy, "The Soul's Knowledge of Itself. An Unpublished Work Attributed to St. Thomas Aquinas," *Vivarium* 15 (1977), 34–45.
367.6	12–24 . . . de quodlibet: 12–23 . . . de quolibet
368.26	No English translation: English trans. in preparation by Martin Yaffe and Anthony Damico.
369.23–370.8	*replace item 28 completely:*

28 **Exposito super Isaiam ad litteram** (Cologne 1249–52). Autogr. Is.34:1–50:1 in Vatican MS Vat.lat. 9850, fol.105ra–11vb. Extant MSS: autogr. +16 complete, and 2 frag.

After the death of Thomas the autograph of this work and many others was left to Reginald of

Piperno and the Dominican Library at Naples, where it remained until 1354. Sometime between 1290 and 1303 Friar Jacobino of Asti, "of the Province of Lombardy, then studying in the General Studium at Naples, transliterated [the autograph] into legible script (*ad litteram legibilem*) together with a fuller rendering of the authorities (*auctoritatum*) . . . for the benefit of Friars of our Order, and so that copies could be made of the aforesaid writings" (Bologna, Bibl. Univ. MS 1655, fol.70va). The transcription of Jacobino established the manuscript tradition.

As to date of composition, there is no unanimity. Some scholars, like Mandonnet and Walz, make it an early Parisian work (1256–57), others, like Glorieux, place it in the second Parisian regency (1269–72), while Eschmann divided the text into two roughly equal parts: the magisterial early chapters (1–11) and the cursory later chapters (12–66), which included the autograph fragment (34–50:1). The magisterial first part, containing frequent and abundant theological developments, Echmann considered typical of a Parisian master, but the cursory later chapters which included the autograph must have been written when Thomas had no secretaries, probably in Italy. Now the Leonine editors, assuming the integral unity of the text, date the autograph after the *reportatio* of Albert's lectures on pseudo-Dionysius (before 1248) and before the autograph of *Scriptum super III Sententiarum* (c.1254–55); they have shown that *Super Isaiam* is the work of a *cursor biblicus*, and therefore to be dated in Paris 1252–53. But, if as we have argued, Thomas was *cursor biblicus* under Albert at Cologne and not at Paris, the *Postilla super Isaiam* was composed and presented at Cologne before going to Paris in 1252. It is Thomas's first theological work, but it is the performance of a *cursor*, heavily dependent on Hugh of Saint-Cher and other common sources. See my review of the Leonine volume in *The Thomist*, 43 (1979), 331–337.

EDITIONS: Leon.ed. v.28 (Rome 1974); Parma v.14,427–576; Vivès v.18,688–821; v.19,1–65; Uccelli (Rome 1880), 3–254.

No English translation.

370.16   *add:* One should note, however, the colophon in one of the MSS formerly at Cheltenham in the Library of Sir Thomas Phillips 551, dated 1455, which has: "Usque huc Fratris Thome scriptum Jeremie translatum a fratre <Petro> de Andria de littera Thome in litteram legibilem" (quoted, Leonine editors 28:10°b). Peter of Andria was one of Thomas's secretaries during the second Parisian regency and at Naples, where he reported the *Collationes in decem praeceptis.*

372.5   *add:* See H.-V. Shooner, "Notes sur les manuscrite des commentaires bibliques de s. Thomas (à propos du "Repertorium biblicum" de F. Stegmüller)," *Bulletin Thomiste* 10 (1957–59), 99–112; also "La Date de la 'Lectura super Matthaeum' de s. Thomas," ibid. pp. 153–157.

372.24   No English translation: English trans.: *Commentary on the Gospel of St. John*, Part I, trans. J.A. Weisheipl and R.R. Larcher (Albany, N.Y.: Magi Books 1980); Part II (in preparation).

373.25   *add: Commentary on St. Paul's First Letter to the Thessalonians and the Letter to the Philippians*, trans. F.R. Larcher and Michael Duffy (Albany, N.Y.: Magi Books 1969).

375.2   *add:* Thomas Sutton (fl.1280–1300),

375.6   *add:* See P. Osmund Lewry, "Two Continuators of Aquinas: Robertus de Vulgarbia and Thomas Sutton on the Perihermeneias of Aristotle," *Mediaeval Studies*, 43 (1981), 58–130.

375.29   (Paris 1269–70): (Paris 1270–71)

376.2–4   Throughout . . . 1271: Throughout, *Metaphysics* Lambda is quoted both as Book XI and XII, indicating that Thomas was still working on the *Physics* when Moerbeke's translation of Kappa arrived in Paris toward the end of 1270 and the beginning of 1271.

377.2   *add:* See J.A. Weisheipl, "The Commentary of St. Thomas on the *De caelo* of Aristotle," *Sapientia,* 29 (1974), 11–34.

377.5   No English translation: English trans.: *Exposition of Aristotle's Treatise On the Heavens,* Books I–III, trans. R.F. Larcher and P.H. Conway (Columbus: College of St. Mary of the Springs, 1964). (Pro manuscripto)

377.19   *add:* Completed by Thomas Sutton (Oxford, Merton College MS 274, fol.92rb–121ra), ed. by F.E. Kelley, *Expositionis D. Thomae Aquinatis in libros . . . continuatio per Thomam de Sutona* (Munich: Bay. Akad. d. Wissenschaften, Bd. 6, 1976).

378.5   (Paris 1269–70): (Italy 1267–69)

378.14   seem to refer . . . n.55): seem to refer to *Summa contra gentiles,* II, c.56 ff. (see above, n.2).

378.19–20   Therefore . . . 1271: Gauthier has shown that Thomas's commentary on the *De anima* was composed in Italy before going to Paris for the second time in 1269; see R.A. Gauthier, "Quelque questions à propos du commentaire de S. Thomas sur le De anima," *Angelicum* 51 (1974) 419–72.

379.10   *add:* It would seem that for St. Thomas *De memoria* was the second book of *De sensu,* as Fr. Gauthier suspects.

379.13   No English translation: English trans. in progress by Edward M. Macierowski.

379.32   *add:* and subsequent dates

381.25   (Paris 1258–59): (Paris 1252–59)

381.26	103vb: 104vb
381.30	only scholastic: only major scholastic
382.2	*add:* Assuming B. Decker's principle (p.44) that the discussion of theological method and revelation is fuller in this work than in *Scriptum super I Sent.*, it would seem that the commentary could have been written any time after 1252 when Thomas had finished the prologue to the *Sentences*.
385.12	EDITIONS: *add:* Leonine ed. v.43 (Rome 1976), preface 245–87; text 291–314.
385.17	Brenan: Brennan
385.18	*add:* B. Zedler, *On the Unity of the Intellect Against the Averroists,* (Milwaukee: Marquette 1968).
385.19 ff.	*replace item 56 completely:*

56 **De aeternitate mundi** (Paris, spring 1271). Extant MSS: 89 complete.

Following Mandonnet many scholars considered this work to be a philosophical treatise within the Averroist crisis at Paris around 1270. But, as Chenu acknowledged, it is clearly a theological problem that is discussed, one that was occasioned by the reception of Aristotle's writings on the eternity of the world by Christian and Jewish believers in revelation as narrated in the Book of Genesis concerning creation in time. Following Moses Maimonides, Thomas always distinguished the fact of creation, knowable by philosophical reason, from "creation in time", knowable only by revelation (*Scriptum super II Sent.*, dist.1,q.1). Some modern scholars (Pelster, Bukowski) consider this treatise to be an early work, directed against St. Bonaventure; others (Brady) consider it to be a late Parisian work, directed perhaps against a determination by John Pecham early in 1270. Elsewhere I have argued that Thomas's *De aeternitate mundi* is not against any one person or determination, but against the common position of Parisian Masters (*communitas Parisiensis*), and composed after Thomas had commented on Aristotle's *Physics* 8, when he became personally convinced, contrary to Moses Maimonides (and his own earlier view), that Aristotle really thought that he had "demonstrated" the eternity of motion, time, and the world. Therefore this treatise is to be dated in spring 1271, at the earliest. See my study "The Date and Context of Thomas's *De aeternitate mundi*," *Graceful Reason* (Essays in Honour of Joseph Owens), ed. Lloyd Gerson (Toronto: PIMS 1983), forthcoming.

EDITIONS: Leonine ed. v.43 (Rome 1976), preface 33–81; text 85–89; Parma v.16, 318–20; Vivès v.27, 450–53; Marietti 1954, *Opuscula Philosophica*, 105–08.

English trans.: C. Vollert, *On the Eternity of the World* by Thomas Aquinas, Siger of Brabant, St. Bonaventure (Milwaukee: Marquette 1964), [19]–[25].

386.3	65: 66
386.17	EDITIONS: *add:* Leonine ed. v.43 (Rome 1976), preface 383–400; text 403–418;
386.22	189 complete: 181 complete.
386.25	"infra magisterium": "nondum existens magister"
386.29	EDITIONS: *add:* Leonine ed. v.43 (Rome 1976), preface 317–361; text 369–381;
387.17	EDITIONS: *add:* Leonine ed. v.43 (Rome 1976), preface 3–32; text 39–47;
388.3	*add:* Therefore J. Perrier and others would date the two parts of this work separately, early for *De fide* (1259–65), and late for the incomplete *De spe* (1272–73). Van Steenberghen, however, considers *De fide* to be contemporary with *De potentia* (1265–67).
388.4	EDITIONS: *add:* Leonine ed. v.42 (Rome 1979), preface 3–70; text 83–205;

389.2   *add:* See esp. L.P. Fitzgerald, "St. Thomas Aquinas and the Two Powers," *Angelicum,* 56 (1979), 515–556; Jeremy Catto, "Ideas and Experience in the Political Thought of Aquinas," *Past and Present,* 71 (1976), 3–21.

389.3   EDITIONS: *add:* Leonine ed. v.42 (Rome 1979), preface 419–444; text 449–471;

390.7   EDITIONS: *add:* Leonine ed. v.42 (Rome 1979), preface 263–273; text 279–294;

390.24   EDITIONS: *add:* Leonine ed. v.42 (Rome 1979), preface 299–320; text 327–335;

391.34   EDITIONS: *add:* Leonine ed. v.42 (Rome 1979), preface 475–83; text 487–88;

392.10   EDITIONS: *add:* Leonine ed. v.43 (Rome 1976), preface 385–400; text 421–22;

393.5   EDITIONS: *add:* Leonine ed. v.42 (Rome 1979), preface 211–241; text 245–257;

393.18   EDITIONS: *insert* Leonine ed. v.42 (Rome 1979), preface 399–409; text 413–15;

395.1   Bibl.Nat. lat. 14546: Bibl.Nat. lat. 16297

395.3   EDITIONS: *add:* Leonine ed. v.43 (Rome 1976), preface 95–122; text 127–130;

395.6   No English translation: English trans.: "Saint Thomas Aquinas on the Movement of the Heart", Vincent R. Larkin, *Journal of the History of Medicine,* 15 (1960), 22–30.

395.19   EDITIONS: *add:* Leonine ed. v.43 (Rome 1976), preface 135–151; text 155–157;

395.22   No English translation: English trans.: "Saint Thomas Aquinas: *On the combining of the Elements,*" trans. Vicent R. Larkin, *Isis,* 51 (1960), 67–72.

396.5   EDITIONS: *add:* Leonine ed. v.42 (Rome 1979), preface 299–320; text 321–324;

396.18   EDITIONS: *add:* Leonine ed. v.42 (Rome 1979), preface 299–320; text 339–346;

397.3   EDITIONS: *add:* Leonine ed. v.42 (Rome 1979), preface 349–352; text 355–56;

397.26   EDITIONS: *add:* Leonine ed. v.42 (Rome 1979), preface 383–390; text 393–94;

398.12 ff.   *replace item 80 completely:*

80   **Epistola ad comitissam Flandriae** <de regimine Judaeorum> (Paris 1271). Extant MSS: 83 complete.

This short reply to eight queries is usually taken to be a response to the Duchess of Brabant concerning the governance of Jews; and the Duchess is usually taken to be Alice of Bourgogne, wife of Henry III, Duke of Brabant (d. Feb.26, 1261). But in fact the letter was addressed to the more illustrious Marquerite of Constantinople, daughter of King Louis IX of France, who was Countess of Flanders from 1244 to February 1286. For more than four decades Marquerite was a generous benefactoress of the Dominican Order (and Franciscan), a fact Thomas noted in his opening words; the Countess and Thomas probably met at the General Chapter of the Dominican Order at Valencienns (June 1259), within her territory. Marguerite apparently put eight questions of conscience to Thomas and to at least one other Master in Theology in 1271. Since the first four and the last query deal with Jews in her kingdom (the last being about the distinctive garb required by the Council of Lateran 1215), this letter is often entitled *De regimine Judaeorum.* But most often it is mistakenly called *Responsio ad Ducissam Brabantiae,* as in the Leonine edition, as has been amply demonstrated by Father Leonard Boyle, O.P.

EDITIONS: Leonine ed. v.42 (Rome 1979), preface 361–71; text 375–78; Perrier, *Opuscula* I,213–19 (basically Paris, Bibl.Nat. lat. 14546);

Parma v.16,292–94; Vivès v.27,413–16; Marietti, *Opuscula Philosophica* (1954), 249–52.

English trans.: "On the Government of Jews in Aquinas," *Selected Political Writings*, ed. with introd. by A.P. d'Entrèves, trans. J.G. Dawson (Oxford: Blackwell 1948), pp.84–95.

398.27	Jacobum de Burgo (?): Jacobum de Tonenga (?)
399.3	EDITIONS: *add:* Leonine ed. v.43 (Rome 1976), preface 207–224; longer text 229–38; shorter text 239–41;
399.20	EDITIONS: *add:* Leonine ed. v.43 (Rome 1976), preface 163–178; text 183–186;
400.5	EDITIONS: *add:* Leonine ed. v.43 (Rome 1976), preface 189–179; text (= 20 lines) 201;
440.24	*add:* Pierre-Marie Gy, "L'Office du Corpus Christi et S. Thomas d' Aquin: état d'une rescherche," *Revue de Science philosophique et théologique*, 64 (1980), 491–507; idem, "Le texte original de la tertia pars de la *Somme Théologique* de S. Thomas d'Aquin dans l'apparat critique de l'édition Léonine: Le cas de l'eucharistie," *Rev. Sc. ph. th.*, 65 (1981), 608–616.
400.32	a good case: a weak case
403.23	*add:* L.-J. Bataillon, "Un sermon de S. Thomas d'Aquin sur la parable du festin," *Rev. Sc. ph. th.*, 58 (1974), 451–456; see forthcoming study and provisory text of sermons by Fr. Bataillon in same journal for summer 1983.